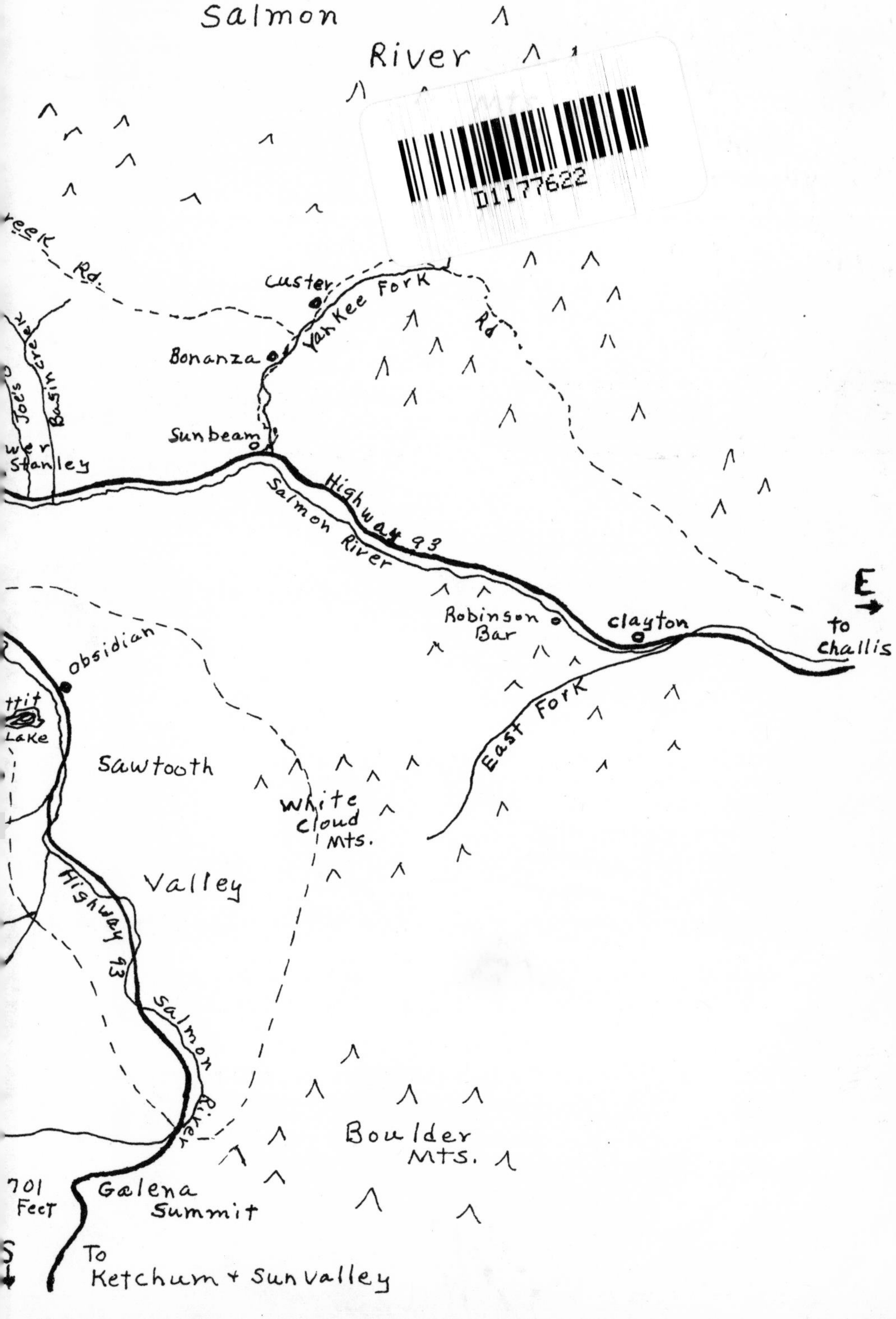

Salmon
River

Creek Rd.
Custer
Yankee Fork
Bonanza
Rd.
Sunbeam
Highway 93
Salmon River
Joe's Basin
wer Stanley

D1177622

obsidian
ttit Lake
Sawtooth
White Cloud Mts.
Valley
Highway 93
Salmon River

Robinson Bar
Clayton
East Fork

E
to Challis

Boulder Mts.

701 Feet
Galena Summit

S
To Ketchum + Sun Valley

Tommy Briscoe

Jim:
It was a pleasure working in the same building. To bad you have to leave "GOD'S country". Take Care
Ruthie ☺ (Cyprus mines)

JIM IT'S BEEN FUN
TAKE CARE & KEEP IN TOUCH
ByRON

Jolyn Lewis

Jim,
Its been a pleasure knowing you. When its a scorcher in Tucson, remember Idaho and Challis.
Faye

Jim, I really appreciate your cooperation
Frank

Jim,
Take care. Drink a few beers. Hope you feel + your head don't hurt.
Ken Thompson

To Jim Brady,   Sept. 1981

A token of our appreciation!

Jim —
we appreciate
your help.
Fred H.

**Stanley-Sawtooth
Country**

Jim,
your one of a kind.
It's been my pleasure
working with you.
God Bless
Cathy
Willis

Jim,
Good luck
in Houston.
Harlan

Stanley-Sawtooth Country

ESTHER YARBER

with assistance of

EDNA MCGOWN

The colorful story of a rugged, scenic part of Idaho
now included in the
Sawtooth National Recreation Area,
its people, and a way of life dictated
by their surroundings

1976
Printed by
Publishers Press
Salt Lake City, Utah
United States of America
Year of the Bicentennial

ACKNOWLEDGEMENT

We are indebted to Rupert Niece for giving of his time and helping us compile much of our information, especially in our mining chapter, to Altha Davis for her help with the "Gold Bowls" story, to Margaret Crouson for her version of "The Miner's Commandments" secured with the help of the Placer County Library staff, Auburn, California, to Ron Curio for his contribution, to Verna Wilton, Librarian, Challis Public Library, to the personnel at Custer County Courthouse, Blaine County Courthouse, and Pocatello Public Library, to Ferris Weddle for his notes, and to Fred Curio (Pocatello Photographer) for his excellent reproduction of certain old pictures loaned to us by different oldtimers. For the loan of these pictures and or/information, our special thanks to Esther Foley, Rosemary Paul Hoskins, Rupert and Bonda Niece, Sylvia Shaw, Nellie Vierra, Roberta Greene, Mrs. Sadie Merritt, Carrie Casto Williams, Ted and Phyllis Williams, Bud and Stella Merritt Critchfield, Myrta Merritt Thompson, Tom Chivers, Piero and Mabel Piva, Kathleen Markle, Irene Pfeiffer, Mildred Cothern Hendrick, Arch Savage, Florence Rowles, Clarence Kimpton, Harry and Martine Fleming, Madge Yacomello, Marie Williams Sullivan, William Schindler, Margaret Nichols, Marian Willis Jackson, Bryan Connyers, Dan and Violet Maag, Vernon Winters, Clyde Gillispie, Laura Lightfoot, Elizabeth Sliger, Jack Seagraves, Alta Horton Ellis, Martin Pollock, Ricky Pierce, and Dan Wooley. To these people and to all those hardy pioneers and settlers in the Stanley-Sawtooth Country . . . to them, we dedicate this book.

Edna McGown and Esther Yarber

Note: Edna McGown and I have shared in this writing from the start, she having assisted every way she could. Yet none of it would have ever reached print had it not been for the encouragement and support of our families and my husband, Lyman Yarber. Bless them one and all.

Esther Yarber

i

TABLE OF CONTENTS

Acknowledgement i
Introduction 1
In the Beginning 4
Lure of Gold 8
Stanley Basin Firsts 16
Seafoam Mining 19
Valley Creek Mine 30
Buckskin Mine 37
Stanley Basin Mining 39
Stanley Basin Dredging 52
Ways of Prospectors and Miner's Commandments 63
The Forest Service 68
Names of Geographic Features 73
Lakes, Streams and Fish 75
Early Promotions and Proposals 80
Birds and Game 83
Trappers and Trapping 89
Cattle Grazing 95
Ranging Sheep 102
Stanley — Two Towns, Fueds, Fights and Post Offices ..107
First School Days in the Stanley Basin 131
Stanley and Sawtooth Valley Schools 139
First Sawtooth Valley Schools 147
Homesteaders ... Prelude to: 149
David and Louise Clarke 152
Frank Gilbert Fisher 156
The Frank Wise Shaw Family 162
Dave Williams 169
Ranger William Horton 176
The C. M. Foleys 180
The Critchfield Family 190
Other Settlers and Squatters in the Region 195
The Benners 211

The Leslie S. "Tink" Niece Family .220
Herbert H. and Mary Marshall 232
William and Sadie Merritt 238
The George and Will Paul Families 247
John and Josephine Thompson 254
Charley Thompson 261
Other Stanley Families 264
"Trapper" Fisher 292
The Single Ones 300
Early Day Holidays 332
Bootlegging for an Honest Buck .340
Catching Up With the Times 346
Wild Stagecoach Ride 359
"Scrapbook" Stanley-Sawtooth Country 363
Bibliography 389
Crude Map of Approximate Locations of
Homestead Ranches 391
Key to Numbers on Map 392

LIST OF ILLUSTRATIONS

Locating Central Idaho's Stanley-Sawtooth Country . . . . End papers
Forest Service sign near headwaters of the Salmon River 5
Sawtooth Valley as seen from viewpoint on Galena Summit 7
Forest Service sign (historical) 9
Forest Service sign on Highway 93 12
Old mill at Vienna Mine 13
Remains of the one old cabin at site of Sawtooth City in 1970 14
Remains of cabin at Wagontown in late 1960s 21
Russell Vaughn dog team with mail and supplies for Seafoam Mine . . .22
Forest Service sign of old Wagontown site near Cape Horn 23
Power house and dwelling at Seafoam Mine area in late 1920s 24
Frank "Slim" Love with his tame coyote 25
Supplies pulled by hand from Stanley to Valley Creek Mine 32
Valley Creek Mine in 1930s: Mrs. F. Schindler watching
    Wm. Soule pan gold 34
The Fred Schindler family, Valley Creek Mine in the 1930s 36
A small bottle of gold dust 40
Deserted miner's cabin on Joe's Gulch 42
Remains of old stamp mill on Joe's Gulch 42
Pulley wheel at Jones' mill on Joe's Gulch 42
Forest Service road sign to old Sturkey Placers on Kelly Creek 45
Hydraulic placer mining at Sturkey Placers in early 1900s 46
Sturkey cabins built about 1887. Picture taken about 1940 47
Remains of Henry Sturkey cabins in 1974 48
Pipe-line to carry water from reservoir to placer diggings 48
Head gate on Kelly Creek reservoir in early 1930s 48
Remains of head gate in 1973 49
"All going out and nothing comin in" (drawing) 50
Members of the Henry Willis family and friends .55
Henry Willis home on Stanley Creek 55
Machinery used in dredging in Stanley Basin, 1930s 59
The Slim Davis family by "Doc" Day home in Stanley Basin 61
Jay Davis, only youngster in camp 61
"Gold" Prospector (drawing) 63
Example of U.S. Forest Service depictive signs 68
Valley Creek Ranger Station built in 1908-09 72
Valley Creek Ranger Station built in 1933 72
Big Redfish Lake 75
Day's catch of Salmon caught near Cape Horn in early 1900s 76

Snow scene in Challis National Forest 79
Picturesque scene in Stanley Basin 81
Dave and Carrie Williams hunting mountain goat in early 1920s 84
Bears were numerous during early days in the
    Stanley-Sawtooth country 86
Inside the L. S. Niece Store, Lower Stanley, 1916 87
"Dutch Charley" Rochling with "Faith", "Hope" and "Charity" 92
Bear caught in Trapper Fisher's trap, May 1924 93
Roundup time in the Stanley Basin during the 1920s 96
Cattle being trailed to Ketchum for shipment in early 1930s 97
Trailing cattle up Salmon River before U.S. Highway 93 98
Tom Chivers . . . Cattleman 99
Chivers cattle trailing down Highway 93 . . . fall of 1973 100
Cattle grazing in Stanley Basin 101
Sheep grazing in Sawtooth Valley area 104
Sheep wagon, once a familar sight in the Stanley-Sawtooth country . .106
Upper Stanley about 1902 109
Lower Stanley store and boarding house, 1910 110
Upper Stanley, 1916 111
Group of Citizens at Lower Stanley, 1917 112
Back of Niece store and the Leslie Niece residence, Upper Stanley . . .114
Upper Stanley about 1925 117
Upper Stanley, girls on Punch and Judy, 1923 118
Upper Stanley garage with owner, Frank "Juggy" Niece, 1930s 119
Upper Stanley Post Office, Alta Moore Postmistress, 1923 120
Sawtooth Valley Post Office, 1910-20 122
Lower Stanley in the 1940s 127
The John Thompson ranch home in upper end of Stanley Basin 132
Lower Stanley schoolhouse, students and teacher, 1915 140
Lower Stanley school girls ready for Easter party, 1918 141
School children at Upper Stanley, 1921 142
Upper Stanley school children 1928 146
Implement sometimes used to measure land (drawing) 151
Dave and Louise Clarke at home in Sawtooth Valley, about 1905 152
Mr. and Mrs. Frank Fisher with Bonda Niece in front
    Obsidian Post Office 158
Mr. and Mrs. Frank Shaw, early settlers in the Sawtooth Valley 163
Frank Shaw ranch home in winter 164
Majorie Shaw and her mother, Mrs. Frank Shaw, 1933 167
Frank Shaw ranch home in summer 168
Dave and Carrie Williams 172
Ranger Horton inside Pole Creek Ranger Station about 1910 177
The Carroll Foley "Mesa Del Monte" ranch in Sawtooth Valley 181
Old Achen cabin schoolhouse in Sawtooth Valley,
    students 183
Esther Foley in her Model-T, early 1920s 185
Carroll Foley on his way to cut wood 188
Critchfield family at ranch cabin about 1915 190
Andrew Critchfield with team and wagon, 1915 .192
Henry Middleton 196
Ed. Fleming's bull team ready for trip to Fisher mill in
    Sawtooth Valley 200

Thomas Williams 202
Sandy Brooks and his dog team 209
Mrs. Martha Benner, winter of 1912-13 211
Harve Stout delivering supplies, winter of 1912-13 213
Leslie S. and Ellen Niece, 1903 220
L.S. Niece Store, Lower Stanley, 1914 226
Niece family inside boarding house, 1914 226
Mrs. Lizzie Snyder Bohney and Mary "Mother" Marshall at
    Merritt ranch 236
Winter of 1911 at Merritt ranch home 239
Group of citizens on old road out of Lower Stanley, 1914 243
"Hobo Lantern" (drawing) 246
George Paul, early settler in the Stanley Basin 247
Molly Paul, wife of George Paul 248
Remains of old Paul stopping place in Stanley Basin 249
William Paul on homemade skiis with canvas housings,
    winter of 1912-13 251
Lillie Paul helping with haying on the Paul ranch 251
Members of Shaw family visit the John Thompsons about 1910 256
Sunday dinner at the Thompson ranch 258
Mrs. Josephine Thompson ready for a pack trip 259
Lottie Thompson and daughter, Dorothy, at Rose's cabin in
    Stanley Basin 263
Trail traveled by Daisy Cooper on her way to McGown place 265
"Calling the square dance" (drawing) 272
Ready for a hay-ride on the Thompson ranch 274
Hotel Stanley with owner, Affie Cothern, and daughters
    standing on porch 277
Group of citizens on porch of Hotel Stanley about 1930 278
"Doc" and Affie Cothern 280
Little Gridley Rowles playing with dog at Rose cabin in Stanley Basin .282
George Moore 283
Barney Lanier by his enclosed sleigh 284
Barney Lanier family at ranch in Stanley Basin 285
William "Bill" Wooley and his pet cougar 286
The Salmon River can be treacherous in the springtime 287
"Gee, Mom my hands are cold!" (drawing) 289
Yankee Fork gold dredge 290
Henry "Trapper" Fisher out on trapline in winter 292
"Trapper" Fisher fiddlin' a lively tune 296
Alvah P. Challis in his late years 301
Henry Sturkey 302
Rubble remaining in drain-off ditch at Sturkey Placers in
    Stanley Basin 303
Cabin in the pines (drawing) 306
Hauling in the winter's wood supply 310
Lemuel Lynch 314
Road sign to Joe's Gulch where much mining went on in the
    early days 316
William "Bill" Soule 317
Packed and ready for a prospecting trip 318
Gold rocker like ones used by early miners 319

Frank "Juggy" Niece 322
Sawtooth Mountains admired by people through the years 323
Remains of the Charles Franklin cabin in Stanley Basin............326
Henry Middleton with his Model-T and friend, Walt Lynch 328
John Weidman working at Sturkey Placer in 1940s 329
Building site of Sturkey Placer, used by John Weidman 330
T.R. "Trapper" Green with winter catch 331
Road up Salmon River in winter, about 1916......................335
Christmas program at Stanley school 337
Birthday party at old Cooper place in Stanley Basin, 1912 339
Arch Savage with his dog team used to haul supplies 341
The Carroll Foleys in Model-T, Galena grade (Hell's Own Pass) 347
First road up Salmon River in summer, about 1916 349
Forest Service telephone at Redfish Lake, 1920s 352
Clyde Torrey 357
Winter Wonderland 358
Wild Stage Coach Ride (drawing) 359
Fences ... the old and the new in Stanley Basin 364
Remains of old hay press in Stanley Basin 366
Frank Brockway 372
Who ... Who ... Whoo (drawing) 374
First Sunday School class, 1914 377
Group of residents, Lower Stanley, 1914 378
Work crew shoveling snow near Mormon Bend 379
"Dad" Cameron with his pack horse in Stanley Basin...............381
Drunken Buckaroo Ride (drawing) 382
Oldtime Medicines (drawing) 387

INTRODUCTION

To our knowledge, no history of scope or extent has ever before been written on the Stanley-Sawtooth country. And while this account may be far from complete, that which is contained within these pages is as nearly so as we were able to research records and other available sources. Many of the details and little stories pertinent to our subject were given to us by different oldtimers whom we feel are well qualified to supply such information. After all, they helped to make a part of *that* history and know first-hand what it was like to live in a land where it was extremely harsh and raw minus today's modern conveniences.

Once called a "Timeless Land and a Part of God's Cathedral," the Stanley Basin and Sawtooth Valley are a parcel and part of Idaho where nature insists on being met on its own terms. Here winter reigns supreme some seven and eight months out of a year, and unless one prepares himself, he can perish from lack of foresight. Indians and early trappers knew this, and because there was always the possibility of being isolated from the rest of the world by deep, drifting snows, they dared not linger beyond the golden days of October in this awesome and solemnly beautiful land.

At first, prospectors, too, were wary of the winters here, and only after rich gold strikes were made on the Yankee Fork, did they risk remaining in winter. It was they who laid the groundwork and opened the way for others to follow. Those who did were a hardy lot. They had to be in order to survive in temperatures of 40-50 degrees below zero. For the sakes of their health and well-being, they had to prepare by having plenty of firewood and food on hand, warm clothing, reading material, a few small projects of interest, much fortitude, and above all keep a sense of humor. Since many miles and many dangers lay between them and available supplies and/or help

1

available at Challis to the northeast, or at Ketchum over Galena Summit to the south, all who stayed prepared accordingly.

After the area was thrown open to homesteading, other settlers came. While most stayed and went on to improve on what they had chosen, others gave up and went elsewhere. Cattlemen and sheep men came, and the Forest Service took over the management of rangelands. Lode mining and gold dredging came into its own, and by the Twenties, both Stanley Basin and Sawtooth Valley had taken on the aspects of a thriving, prosperous region. Then the townsites of Lower and Upper Stanley were platted, located a mile apart near the mouth of Valley Creek ... and thereby trouble began among the residents. Which town would have the school? Which would have the post office? After much fighting and fueding between themselves, how it finally came to be resolved, we leave it for you, our reader, to judge.

In this writing we have endeavored to "tell it like it was" by presenting the facts and relating numerous little stories throughout this book ... some humorous and some tragic, but all depicting life as it was lived in the area while it was yet still young. How these people, walled in by four rugged mountain ranges, sustained themselves physically and mentally without doctors or hospital facilities, electricity, hard-surfaced roads, and 4-wheel drives is a story in itself. They had no church, yet most of them were deeply religious. Fish and game were theirs for the taking. Yet they did not abuse the privilege, using what they took for food and sometimes as a means to supplement their often meager incomes. They worked hard, and they played hard, making their own entertainment. All were considered as neighbors and friends and always treated as such regardless of the miles which often existed between them. Now and then some different, or odd character came to reside among them, but every man, woman, and child was accepted for the way he was and treated with a warm friendliness unequaled anywhere in the West.

These then were the pioneers, and although we have taken note in our writings of changes wrought down through the years, basically this is their story ... the miners and prospectors, homesteaders and ranchers, forest rangers and townspeople ... all who had a decided part in the building of the Stanley-Sawtooth country, thus making it possible for it to

2

become accessible for others to share its many facets of nature and scenic beauty. Here are mighty mountains to climb and to photograph, wildlife and wild flowers to see and enjoy, numerous campgrounds, resorts and guest ranches, lakes and streams to fish, plus many other things that make the Sawtooth National Recreation Area the vacation wonderland that it is.

IN THE BEGINNING

When God laid down the region known as the Stanley Basin and Sawtooth Valley, He walled it with four rugged mountain ranges - the Salmon River, the Boulders, White Clouds, and Sawtooths - and tucked it snug and serene in the heart of Central Idaho's high country. Here He made winters long and bitter cold, summers short and delightful, and thereby decreed that only the hardiest of people would put down roots in its soil.

For them, and those who would come to see, He mineralized the mountains, planted an abundance of wildlife, and spread carpets of luscious grasses, sage, and wild flowers across the Basin and Valley floors. For them, He studded the region with numerous jewel-like lakes, gurgling streams and hot springs, and from these He said, "Let there be born a river." And there was. Today we call it the main Salmon River, and sometimes "The River of no Return", so fast it flows, dropping through canyons and gorges on its way to join the Snake River west of Riggins, Idaho.

From atop Galena Mountain of the Boulder Range, the Salmon River can be seen, beginning with a trickle at the foot of the Sawtooth Mountains, gathering its first headwaters as it winds its way along the Valley floor. Its principle tributaries, from its start to Lower Stanley, are French Creek, Beaver Creek, Smiley Creek, Pole Creek, Williams Creek, Fisher Creek, Gold Creek, Fishhook Creek, and Valley Creek. This is the only and longest river confined wholly within one state anywhere in the Nation. With a length of 420 miles, it has a North, South, East, and Middle Fork, aside from the main Salmon River.

In way of defining how God went about his creation of the Stanley-Sawtooth Country, geologists tell us its history goes back to the Idaho Batholith intrusion in Cretaceous times,

4

Forest sign near the headwaters of Salmon River.

through thickening and depositing of sedimentary rocks on the bottom of a slowly sinking sea in Paleozoic times, with later intrusion of the Sawtooth Mountains. Even today tiny patches of glacial ice can still be found on the northern slopes of the higher peaks, particularily Thompson Peak in upper Goat Creek Valley.

Indians

However done, it was eons before this land felt the footsteps of man. At first these were made by wandering Indian tribes. Yet the Indians lingered not, for to them, like the Yankee Fork country a short ways downstream, this was the "land of deep snows", and only in summer would they come to hunt and fish.

In time there was one tribe who came to reside in and near the area. They were called the "Sheepeaters" because of their taste for the mountain sheep so plentiful in the region. According to the Redfish lake legend, these Indians were once a part of a tribe made up of outcasts from various other tribes, and who called themselves "Indians of the Clouds". With the coming of gold seekers in the Valley and the Basin, after the death of their leader, they fled to the surrounding mountain ranges. Whether the legend be true or not, the Sheepeater Indians were the ones blamed for the massacre of an encampment of Chinese miners on Loon Creek, just over the ridge, in the very early spring of 1879.

5

First Trappers

Although the Louisana Purchase was made in 1803, and fur companies established in the Great Northwest even before Lewis and Clark made their trek in 1805-06, no white man had ever set eyes on the Stanley-Sawtooth country before 1824. He came in the person of Alexander Ross, a Scot school teacher transplanted to Canada, and who, at the age of twenty-eight, relinquished his profession to fall in with John Jacob Astor's Pacific Fur Company in 1811.

From the start, Ross was curious to know what lay southwest of Pierre's Hole and Henry's Fork. Even so, it was thirteen years later before he was able to organize a party to make the expedition. In the spring of 1824, with a mixed party of Canadians and Indians, numbering fifty-five, he penetrated from what we know as Montana over Lost Trail Pass to the mouth of the Lemhi where the town of Salmon is now located. He named this junction of rivers "Canoe Point". Here, he cached over 1,000 beaver pelts to lighten their load, and went on to explore much of the Lost River drainage, working his way to the Boise and Weiser areas, and eventually to Big Wood River. Near its headwaters, he was drawn by the splendor of the Sawtooth and Boulder Mountains.

"What lies beyond?" he wrote in his journal, "On the Morrow we shall see." And see they did, from Galena Summit (elevation 8,701 ft.), which he called "Simpson Mountain" in honor of the governor of Manitoba, Canada . . . date: September 18, 1824. While he stood there with those of his party, enthralled by the wild, scenic beauty of the valley spread below, Ross calculated that by following the river (Salmon) downstream, they could surely connect back at Canoe Point by mid-October. This was important with winter near, coupled with the fact he had agreed to meet back with Old Pierre when the party had split on the Lost River that spring. Therefore, he knew he could not tarry long in the Valley and Basin, but felt he must explore this enchanting region at any cost.

The party found wild game plentiful on the Valley and Basin floors. Deer and elk herds were feeding everywhere. However, Ross was most impressed by the number of grizzly and black bears. He made notes in his journal of observing dozens on a four-acre plot where "they were rooting like a bunch of pigs. There were nine in one place, and we shot seven at one time." *Note: When he spoke of the bears rooting, he was referring to the*

6

camas lilly bulbs that grow abundantly in parts of the Stanley Basin, and which were relished as food by the animals and Indians.

October arrived turning the region into a riot of color. A decided chill filled the air. Many beaver had been added to the party's count, and it was time to go. Reluctantly, turning downstream, as they progressed through the steep-walled canyons (where Highway 93 now bends alongside the Salmon River toward Clayton) travel became slow and precarious. At one point, Ross even considered backtracking their route, but time was short and they went on. After the loss of several horses packed with beaver pelts down the shaley mountain side, they finally emerged where the Salmon bends northward (two miles south of where the town of Challis was located in 1878), weary in bone and body. Here they rested a day, then went on to meet Old Pierre, and back to winter quarters at Astoria, Oregon.

There Ross told of their exploration of the beautiful, wild river and the region where it gathers its headwaters. Ross was soon followed by other trappers, namely; Jed Smith, John Work, Peter Skene Ogden, Nathaniel Wyeth, Captain Bonneville, and Milton Sublette.

Sawtooth Valley as seen from viewpoint on Galena Summit.

LURE OF GOLD

First Prospectors- Stanley Party

After gold was discovered in California, the rush to the West was on. By spring of 1860, it had reached into the Nez Perce country of the Great Northwest when a party, led by Captain Edward D. Pierce, found gold in the streambed of Orofino Creek. Word went out, people came in, and prospectors moved on in search of more new fields. In their wake mining camps sprang up like mushrooms southward in the Clearwater, Salmon, Boise, Snake, and Weiser River areas. . . . Elk City, Dixie, Florence, Leesburg, Boise Basin camps, Warrens, Silver City, to name a few. Yet not until Idaho was made a Territory on March 3rd, 1863, did they attempt to prospect the Stanley-Sawtooth country.

On July 5th of that year, a party of twenty-three men by way of Warrens forced their way through the mountains, entering the Basin section by the route now known as the Lowman road, coming from the Boise Basin direction. They too, were awe-inspired by the sight of the majestic Sawtooths, and marveled at the way the many crystal streams tumbled from the canyons of the Salmon River Mountains across the Basin floor to make up the headwaters of Marsh Creek, flowing into the Middle Fork of the Salmon River. After passing over Blind Creek Summit, they marveled even more at the lush green growth afforded by Valley Creek and its tributaries all the way down to the main Salmon River, just before it bends through the canyon and narrows toward Sunbeam.

This party was not long in finding the gold they sought in the sands of the many streams in the Basin area. They promptly staked claims and worked awhile, but short supplies and the remoteness of the region, coupled with trouble with hostile Indians, deemed it foolish for them to remain.

8

Until now the Basin bore no name. Thus, upon abandoning their claims, in honor of Captain John Stanley, oldest member of the party, they christened the saucer-like bowl "Stanley Basin". When leaving the scene, several members of the group vowed to return someday.

Forest sign.

Idaho Territory

Although many new settlements were located in Idaho Territory during the Sixties, again more time passed before other prospectors ventured into the Stanley-Sawtooth region. In this period, soon after enactment of the bill creating Idaho Territory, Boise won over Lewiston for the site of the Territorial Capitol. "After all," political leaders argued, "We are but a skip and a jump from the Boise Basin mining camps, and that is where the largest concentration of people reside. Why, at this time over 10,000 live in Idaho City (first called West Bannack) alone."

Also, between 1863 and 1868, Territorial boundries were changed several times; whittled from 325,000 (one source claims 326,373) square miles, and its four original counties made into seven.... namely, Nez Perce, Idaho, Shoshone, Oneida, Alturas (the Salmon and Wood Rivers included in Alturas), Boise, and Owyhee Counties. In ensuing years these were divided into forty-four counties, and the square miles whittled to 83,557 — the State of Idaho at the present time.

First Mining in Sawtooth Region

And so it was, after the Stanley party deemed the Stanley-

9

Sawtooth country too remote from supply sources to stay on, gold was discovered during the early Seventies on the Yankee Fork of the Salmon River, a short distance downstream from the Basin rim. Nevertheless, migration to this district was slow until capital came in. But in 1878-79-80, as the mining camps of Bonanza City and Custer built up and a toll road was built from Challis into the district, people moved in by the hundreds.

Meanwhile, prospectors were now traveling through the Stanley-Sawtooth Country over the divide, to and from the Wood River area where rich deposits of silver-galena ore were soon found. With only a foot trail on which to travel, naturally they were unable to make the trip in one day. And, naturally too, while stopping to camp overnight in the Sawtooth Valley they took time to pan the streams for "color."

That is how it was with Levi Smiley and T.B. Mulkey in May of 1878. After finding "paydirt" in the sands of a stream now known as Smiley Creek, they followed it to its source and to a site above its headwaters in the Sawtooth range. Here they found a large outcropping of quartz, but exploration was cut short because of the Bannock Indian uprising that summer.

Knowing the Bannock, Shoshone and Sheepeater Indians often used the Sawtooth region as a summer camp, Smiley and Mulkey declined to return until that fall. Beginning in October, they staked claims on the Emma, Flagstaff, Ferguson, and Last Chance before winter closed in on them.

Back at Bonanza City on the Yankee Fork, they had no trouble enlisting the company of E.M. Wilson, J.B. Ritchey, C.G. Ferguson, J.F. Kinsley, J.W. Smith, George Pease, James O'Leary, and John Bower. Together, this group of men, with Smiley and Mulkey, in the summer of 1879, made several other strikes including the Silver King, Columbia, Nellie, Nellie Extension, and the Vienna . . . the latter being the most prominent and discovered by E.M. Wilson. News of these new strikes soon reached the surrounding mining camps, and the stampede to the Sawtooth Valley was on.

Extensive exploration of the area that summer revealed the Sawtooth mineral belt as being about two miles wide and ten miles long, and cut by Beaver and Lake Creeks. These actually form three natural divisions, or canyons . . . Smiley Canyon, Beaver Canyon, and Lake Canyon. The region being mostly very fine feldspathic granite with occasional dykes of por-

10

phyry, the ore was generally composed of quartz carrying sul-phurets and ruby silver with some gold.

Smiley and other prospectors, recognizing the fact that ore from all the mines in the Sawtooth district would require roasting or chlorination for successful amalgamation, soon set about attracting outside capital to the area. By October of that year several mining companies had been formed, and many of the mines purchased in what was by then called "The Sawtooth Mining District Number 134." Among these companies were The Pacific Iron Works, of San Francisco, who paid $30,000 for the Pilgrim Mine: The Columbia Beaver Company of New York, The Silver King Mining and Milling Company, and the Vienna Consolidated financed by a group from Wisconsin. The latter was managed by Chris J. Johnson whom records credit with much of the development of the Vienna group of mines.

By now the mining camp of Sawtooth City, located in Beaver Canyon, and Vienna, located in Smiley Canyon, had been established. Everyone was optimistic regarding the mining future of the Sawtooth Valley, and needless to say, opening of spring, 1880, brought many changes for the people who had defied the cruel winter to live there.

First Road Over Galena Summit

One of these changes included the construction of a toll wagon road going over Galena Summit to the Wood River country. Completed that summer, this was the first road ever built in that direction. To be sure, it was extremely narrow, steep-graded, and treacherous. Nevertheless, until mills could be built on the mining properties in the Sawtooth region, many wagonloads of ore were freighted over the grade to be processed at the Philadelphia Smelter at Ketchum. This road, useable only in summer months, was improved on from time to time, but not to any extent until the advent of the automobile some years later. *(Note under Roads and Highways elsewhere in this book.)*

Growth and Decline of Sawtooth Mining

By the summer of 1882, the mining camp of Vienna, at the foot of the Sawtooth range, on Smiley Creek, had grown to a population of 800 persons. Business buildings and cabins in and about the townsite numbered to the count of 200. There were three general merchandise stores, two meat markets, two livery and feed stables, six restaurants, two Chinese laundries,

11

and five saloons . . . one of which was owned and operated by the partners of Will Casto and Tim Cooper. One of the stores belonged to H. Lefevre Jr. and E.B. Shaw, and another, including a bank section on the premise, was run by Isador Morris, William Kruse ran a hotel in town, and E.O. Hall operated a nearby sawmill. That year the town was awarded a post office with William Caston appointed as postmaster.

On July 4th, 1882, the first issue of a five-column newspaper, called the *Vienna Reporter,* made its appearance. The paper was published by Stevens and Jones in a new building erected by local miners, free of charge with lumber donated by a Mr. Corbet, for that purpose. The new paper met with much enthusiam, and to insure its success, Vienna residents subscribed over $300 in cash paid before the second issue. The paper was destined to be short-lived, however, for by November that same year, it had consolidated with the *Ketchum Keystone Newspaper* in the Wood River area.

At Sawtooth City in Beaver Canyon, near the Pilgrim Mine (located by Matt Womack), population had increased to 600 persons by the summer of 1882. Here was located three restaurants, four saloons, two hotels . . . one of which featured

Forest sign on Highway 93.

12

"twenty-five good beds with real mattresses brought over Galena Summit," a laundry, blacksmith shop, livery stable, tailor shop, assay office, and a post office which was also awarded that year with George Belden as postmaster. Other businesses included two or three boarding houses, real estate and law firms, a carpenter shop, and even a homemade furniture store.

Laid out in several block squares along the banks of Beaver Creek, at one time the townsite presented a somewhat picturesque sight against the backdrop of the Boulder and Sawtooth Ranges.

Although of short duration, a kind of friendly fued developed between the two mining towns. *As the Wood River Times* put it, "a feeling not unlike that which exists between Bellevue and Hailey in the Wood River country at this time". For awhile, the fued even reached the point of running two stages between the camps — Fisher of Vienna ran one, and Pierson of Sawtooth City ran the other. During the winter of 1882-83 the fued ended and a more settled atmosphere prevailed that spring when extensive exploration of existing mines in both districts got underway.

Everyone was busy, and for the next two years the mining camps buzzed with activity, even during the winter months.

Old mill at Vienna Mine.

Several mills were built in both Beaver and Smiley Creek Canyons. One was an exact duplicate of the General Custer Mill on the Yankee Fork of the Salmon River, and built by the same man — a Captain Owens. Christened "The Vienna", and owned by the Vienna Consolidated Mining Company, the mill was equipped with two large revolving roasters, twenty stamps, and a two hundred horsepower Corliss engine fired by steam. Its reducing capacity was fifty tons of ore every twenty-four hour period, as also was the Columbia and Beaver Mills. The latter proved somewhat inefficient because of faulty foundations for its machinery until overhauled in 1885.

Peak developement of the mines in the Sawtooth Valley came in 1884-85. That winter the weather turned extremely bitter and cold. Temperatures dropped to 40 and 50 below zero and stayed there for days on end. Snow on snow, beginning early and lasting until late June that year, piled up building high. Supplies ran short and people suffered in both Vienna and Sawtooth City. The corduroy road between the two camps was closed well into July. Meanwhile, mines and mills in each of the districts worked off and on through the winter but bullion had to be stockpiled and shipment delayed until summer.

As a result, that fall many of the miners took their families and sought refuge in other localities. Some returned the following spring of 1886, but as it were, mining in the Sawtooth

One old cabin left standing at site of Sawtooth City . . . held up by trees. Picture taken 1970.

region began a slow decline. Some activity continued for awhile thereafter, with occasional revivals down through the years. Eventually slumps in the silver market caused closure of the mills, making ghost towns of Vienna and Sawtooth City. During the depression years a great many of the buildings were razed for the lumber contained in them. On those remaining, time, weather and vandals have taken heavy toll, and today only a few old foundations, rotted logs, and rubble mark the site of these once busy mining camps.

Some mining authorities claim the region was never fully developed, attributing failure to indifference and mismanagement on the part of the early day companies who worked the properties. Whether this be true or not, the Sawtooth mining district, like many areas now confined within the boundaries of the Sawtooth National Recreation Area, continues to be a potential source of mineral wealth.

STANLEY BASIN FIRSTS

Mining: Second Prospectors

Although the Stanley-Sawtooth Country had been generally avoided by prospectors until after the discovery of gold on the Yankee Fork of the Salmon River during the Seventies, news of the Stanley party's 1863 claims in the Stanley Basin, and the parties failure to remain there, were well remembered by others in the Boise Basin mining camps in the spring of 1864. That April twenty-five more prospectors gave it a try. Among this group were Dick "Norwegian Billy" Douglas, John Barracks, Don Grant, George Fairbanks, Duncan Ferguson, Thomas Conroy, and James Buckley, who was the locator of Buckley Bar. Yet, they too, found it impractical to remain in the area at that time.

For the next nine years other prospectors ventured that way, but only in the summer months. Finally, in 1873, A.P. Challis, who had numbered in the Stanley party ten years before, along with a partner, Henry Sturkey, located rich placer ground on Kelly Creek (then called Summit Gulch). Following prospecting from area to area, A.P. Challis had been in the California gold rush, and was forty years old (considered well past middle age in those days) when he at last drifted to Leesburg, high in the Salmon River Mountains above where the town of Salmon is now located. It was shortly after this that he came to settle on a small creek which bears his name in the vicinity of where he later helped to lay out the townsite of Challis — also named for him. *For more on his life refer to second section of this book.*

Bannock Indians

Before 1878, aside from the Kelly Creek placers, a few other worthwhile discoveries were made in the Stanley Basin, but none were worked to any extent because of hostile Indians in the area. This Indian hostility climaxed that spring as settlers

16

on the Camas Prairie (Idaho County) went about tilling the land to plant crops. As hundreds of acres of Camas lilly bulbs, one of the staple foods of most of the tribes, were turned under by the plow, or were rooted up and eaten by pigs which the settlers had brought in, the Indians rose up in arms.

Choosing "Buffalo Horn" as their leader, they waged a battle against the whites all along the Salmon River until subdued by General Howard of the regular army and several volunteer companies. This was the Bannock Indian War, lasting only through the summer. However, when most of the Indians went back to Fort Hall, near Pocatello, some escaped to become renegades, seeking sanctuary with the Sheepeater tribe in the Salmon River Mountains.

From this vantage, for some time, small bands of renegades, using hit and run tactics, went on to plunder and to murder more whites up and down the river. The Sheepeaters, being a shy people generally, but because of the renegades in their ranks, were blamed for much of the marauding for the rest of the year.

Sheepeater Indian War

One instance occurred when an encampment of Chinese placer miners were murdered and robbed that winter. Captain Reuben Bennard, promptly dispatched to the scene, reported that he could find no fresh Indian signs, but assuming the massacre to be the work of the Sheepeaters, found an old trail and set out in pursuit through heretofore unexplored, unmapped country, which even today is considered some of the most dangerous and roughest in all the Northwest. This fact, coupled with adverse weather conditions, swollen streams, and short supplies, made Bennard's assignment the most difficult in all his army career.

Historical accounts state that all the Chinese miners on Loon Creek were killed by the marauders in the early spring of 1879, but there are other versions of the story. One goes that a tough, rowdy group of white men, holed up on the Middle Fork of the Salmon River, masqueraded as Indians and committed the act. Later, while living off the dead men's gold, they laughed upon learning the Indians were being blamed for the deed. "That's the way we planned it," they said, "And that's why we allowed one to get away."

The "one" referred to was a Chinaman named Matuse, and it

is said that for him one of the tributaries of Mayfield Creek came to be called "China Creek." Seems he escaped with a few bags of gold that became very heavy while wading through the deep snow. As he neared Loon Creek Summit a storm came up. Seeking refuge under a rock overhang a short distance from the mouth of this small stream, he buried the gold there before going on. At Bonanza City, on the Yankee Fork, the next day, he told of his ordeal and escape and witnessing of the murders of his countrymen by "alee Endeens."

Another story goes: as a boy growing up in the Yankee Fork country, old oldtimer remembered in later years of hearing old miners and prospectors tell about how they "did in the Chinks on Loon Creek in the winter of '78 and '79, and then let the Sheepeaters take the blame for it." However, as the oldtimer recalled, "Every time anyone tried to pin them down on it where the law was concerned, they would change their story fast — and needless to say, they stuck together like glue. So actually, it was impossible to determine if they really committed the deed, or just enjoyed telling tall tales."

As to whether Captain Bennard was able to route the Sheepeater Indians, he finally did secure the surrender of approximately fifty Indians, including women and children. This was only after he and his men had suffered extreme hardships and untold frustrations in country most mountain men avoided in those days because of the exceptionally rugged terrain. John S. Ramey, acting as scout for "that greenhorn army," as he called the troops, said it was a miracle that any of them survived such a rugged wilderness experience. Even historians wrote, "To say the Sheepeater Campaign was a success would be incorrect."

In any case, while Bennard and his men rested at one point of this safari, they camped on the headwaters of Rapid River in the Seafoam area. It was here several of the packers and scouts found indications of rich lead-silver deposits and later told about their discoveries. Thus, in the summer of 1880 Ike Daly, Sam Foutez, Danskin, Burns, Elliot, and others (names not known) went to the locale to stake claims. This was the beginning of the Seafoam and Greyhound Mines.

SEAFOAM MINING

Note: Although separated from Stanley Basin proper by a steep mountain called "Vanity Summit," the Seafoam area is often referred to as a part of the Stanley region.

While the Stanley Basin sets high, rimmed by tall rugged mountains, over Vanity Summit the terrain becomes a series of heavy-timbered, rough mountains, one blending into the other. Gulches and benches are few, and even the creeks tend to drop into deep gorge-like canyons. To see this area one can only wonder at the fact prospectors were able to negotiate such country before any semblance of a road existed there.

Nevertheless, the first group of prospectors mentioned previously, were soon followed by a second group. Those included were J.W. Stoddard, J. Dowling, Manuel Fontsy, David Edgerton, Malcom McLane, and Alex McDonald. Both groups made worthwhile quartz discoveries. Other prospectors came, made more discoveries, and filed claims in Lemhi County even though the area was said to be located in the Yankee Fork mining district at that time.

So it went until the turn of the century. The majority of the prospectors kept up the assessment work on their claims, and mines changed hands many times before outside capital would undertake mining and milling in such a remote area. Finally, in the spring of 1904, the Snowstorm Mining and Milling Company, headed by William McKinley Flynn, was formed, and that September was able to erect a smelter on the Snowstorm property after packing machinery by mule train from the little settlement of Stanley.

About this same time, the Greyhound Mining and Milling Company was organized, and S.M. Smith was made manager. They, too, packed in machinery with which to build a 40-ton capacity smelter on their property located on Sulphur Creek.

Part of the claims here were placers discovered that spring by W.J. McConnell, Patrick Dowling, S.L. Tipton, Charles Hayes, and Mr. and Mrs. S.M. Smith. Location was on a small flat, or kind of bar, alongside the creek, and where the tiny community of Seafoam soon sprang into existence. Later this was known as the Greyhound mining camp, and another community established near the Seafoam Mine on Float Creek was called Seafoam.

Aside from the mills and usual mine buildings, both camps afforded large boarding houses, bunkhouses, cabins for married men, and offices for the management. Greyhound boasted a post office, awarded in 1906 with William Brown as postmaster, and kept it until 1910. No mail service was provided after that until 1927, when Seafoam was granted a post office naming Alma Ballinger as postmistress. This was terminated after a year, and mail for anyone living in the area has been relayed from the town of Stanley since.

In 1903 William Rideout and James Green built a supply station near where the ranger station is now located, on Capehorn Licks. This greatly benefited prospectors and miners going to and from the Seafoam area as the station not only provided a fine supply of merchandise, but also a hotel of sorts, a bath house, and stables.

The Blackhawk Mining Company incorporated in January, 1905, named major stockholders as:

W.M. Courtis, Detroit, Michigan
Col. Judson Spofford, Lewiston, Idaho
C.O. Stockslager, Boise, Idaho
James M. Stevens, Blackfoot, Idaho
A.J. Pierce, Pocatello, Idaho
C.V. Hansen, Mackay, Idaho
E. Williams, Challis, Idaho
Milton Brown, Challis, Idaho
John Mullen, Custer, Idaho
Collister P. Huston, Challis, Idaho

Ore from the Blackhawk mine group assayed at $113.80 per ton in gold and silver values, while the Snowstorm group assayed 76.3% lead, 6.4% zinc and contained properties of 16.7 ounces of silver and 2.9 ounces gold to the ton; thereby showing a decided difference in the composites of the geological aspect of the area and its mineral contents.

Regarding John Mullen of Custer, named above, John was an oldtime prospector and had been partners with J.O. Swift and W.H. Watt in the Swell Mine in the Seafoam district. Issues of the Challis *Silver Messenger* newspaper, 1893, carried the required number of notices of forfeiture against the two partners for having failed to provide their part of the assessment work on the mine for nine or so years. Failing to come forward in this connection, by law, Mullen became sole owner of the claim.

Another such instance involved the Ochre Lode claim located in 1887 by I.N. Daly, and situated between the Seafoam mine group and Josephus Lake. Daly deeded his brother, Joseph, and wife, Rebecca, a half interest. The Dalys sold the mine to Chris Morler and A.M. Wilson in 1900. Morler and Wilson hired Charles Crane to do the assessment work, and failing to pay the cost, lost the mine to Crane in 1901. Although the Mullen and Crane cases are but two examples, several mines in the Seafoam area changed hands this way, aside from ones sold outright.

At the foot of Vanity Mountain on the Stanley Basin side, at one time Mose Storher had built two log buildings where he operated a store and furnished lodging for packers going in and out of the Seafoam mining district. This was called "Wagontown" even after he moved from the site in 1895. At that time

Remaining cabin at Wagontown in the late 1960s.

21

he purchased the Arthur McGown Sr. store near where the tiny settlement of Stanley had been established in 1890. The Stanley location was a kind of half-way point on the pack train route, and had been built by the McGowns who, after the first mining boom had declined in the Yankee Fork district, had moved there from Bonanza City. This little settlement proved very convenient for the packers, especially those packing ore. They could unload here for pickup by wagons going to the smelter at Ketchum over Galena Summit, then reload with supplies kept at the store and needed back at the mines.

A rough wagon road was constructed over Vanity Summit by the Greyhound Mining Company in 1905. Charging toll until all the construction cost was defrayed, the road was in constant need of maintenance and was useable only in summer. This is still true today, even though the Forest Service, using modern equipment, work diligently and consistently at keeping the road open for truck and car travel. As the steep-sided mountain

Russell Vaughn with dog team hauling supplies and mail to the Seafoam Mine.

continues to erode away by winter snows and summer storms, to allow passage, blasting and culvert repair are necessary sometimes two and three times each season.

Going over Vanity Summit to the Seafoam area today, looking off to the right through the heavy timber, on a small flat in a sharp bend of Rapid River, one can see a number of old ruins at the foot of the mountain. At one time this was where a power plant, a sawmill, and the home of the mining superintendent stood . . . all property of the Greyhound Mining Company.

A wild, boisterous stream, Rapid River finds birth on the slope of Feltham Peak, and flowing northwestward, picks up waters of numerous little creeks on its journey to join the Middle Fork of the Salmon River in the Idaho Primitive Area. The majority of mines in the Seafoam district were located on Sulphur, Float, Josephus, and Seafoam Creeks. Although too many to mention all the mines in this locality, a few of the names were: Birdie Girl, Ella B, Bulldog, General Grant, White Dog, Lakeview, Niagara, Greenhorn, Mountain King, Tracy, Republican, Greyhound, and B.R.S. The Yellow Metal was owned and worked in 1901 by George McGowan and a man named Tremper. The Black Pig was owned by Dr. C.L. Kirtley of Challis, Idaho, and the Logan Lode was located by W.W. Logan and Charles Glascock. Aside from these, there were the Seafoam, Sheep Mountain, and others . . . both quartz and placer claims.

Before and after the road was built over Vanity Summit, for a number of years a small group of Pennsylvania business men, with great faith in the country, persisted in backing several of the Seafoam mines. Slowly and scientifically, six large veins were developed that eventually paid off in high values of lead-silver and gold. This was 1927, and by then the properties were a part of the Seafoam Mines Corporation, comprising 17 quartz claims and 6 millsites.

Nineteen twenty-seven and twenty-eight was the winter Rupert Niece and Bud Critchfield carried the mail and a few

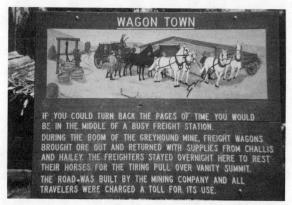

Forest sign at the site of old Wagontown near Cape Horn.

23

supplies into the area on snowshoes and with a dog team. Down through the years time has almost stood still during the winter months in much of this region beyond State Highway 21, demanding respect today as it did yesterday. But whether then or now, undertaking of such a contract constitutes a cold, laborious job. However, the two young men, at the time both being strong and healthy, took their assignment in stride, bivouacing overnight at old Wagontown at the foot of Vanity Summit. Barring a heavy snowstorm, they went over the summit the next day, made their deliveries, spent the night at the mines boarding house before their return trip back to the town of Stanley — a distance of 40 miles.

One interesting note concerning the people who elected to spend that winter in the Seafoam community appeared in a letter dated November 30, 1927, and read as follows:

"There are forty-one persons in this camp, including eleven women and children. Thanksgiving Day dinner at the Seafoam Mines Corporation dining room was attended by all employees and their families, except the power plant operator. Thirty-seven were present, and the dinner was followed by dancing, enjoyed by all until 1 A.M. Music was furnished by Womack and Judge. A fine storm of snow and wind that had been raging

Power house and dwelling at Seafoam Mine in the late 1920s.

24

for four days did not deter the attendance or mar the pleasure of the evening. Snow is now 40 inches deep on the level and six feet on Vanity Summit.

The fifty-ton fine grinding ball mill and all other machinery is running smoothly, power being supplied by the 230 H.P. hydro-electric power plant four miles distant. Mine work is going forward in two shifts, using air drills. Stopeing operations on high grade free-milling gold ore will start in December."

. . . .

Like the Stanley Basin and Sawtooth Valley, the Seafoam region has its intriguing aspects in connection with odd characters and events. One is the story of "The Mystery Man."

The Mystery Man

Seems a man named Frank Love appeared in the country about 1918 or 1919 with a pet coyote he had raised from a pup.

Frank "Slim" Love with his pet coyote.

Selecting a rather remote spot, he built himself a log cabin and settled down to run a pack train now and then in summer, and do a bit of trapping in the winter. On the main trail he erected a sign reading, "Frank Love, Pack Train."

Frank was a silent, peculiar man. He seldom went to town, and then only bought the barest of necessities. With the coyote as his only companion, he had very little to do with anyone. People in the area began to wonder about him . . . especially when various tools and food items began to come up missing from the different miner's cabins while they were at work in their mines.

Then one day someone changed his sign on the main trail from reading "Frank Love, Pack Train" to read "Frank Love, Pack Rat." To say Frank was upset upon discovering the changed sign would be putting it mildly. He grabbed his gun from where he kept it just inside his cabin door, stormed up and down the trail, and swore vengence on the person who dared to call him a "pack rat." He never found out who made the change, of course, and thereafter, became more withdrawn than before.

On August 20, 1942, Mel Shepard, a Forest Service employee, found Frank "Slim" Love dead beside the trail near his horse corral. He had evidently died of a heart attack since the halters for his horses were still slung over his arm. The coroner was called, but due to the condition of the body, it was decided to bury him where he had fallen. It was estimated that he had been dead about fifteen days. Registration papers found among his possessions showed that he had been born in Cleveland, Ohio in 1882. No living relatives could be located, although the Custer County Sheriff, Lee Clark, made every effort to do so.

Now and then some oldtimer who knew Frank "Slim" Love, after relating the story will ponder remarks like, "Old Slim was sure a mysterious fellow. Just wonder if he was hiding or looking?"

Seafoam's Lost Mine

In the Twenties, a mining engineer by the name of Eldredge, who was working in the Seafoam area, stopped to rest at the cabin of an old man. After introductions, the old man said, "Glad you stopped by. I have some ore from my mine over there. Maybe you can tell what it is. Blamed stuff is harder than diamonds, and I got a good 6-foot vein of it."

Examining the ore, Eldridge knew it contained a large percent silver, but, because of its hardness, asked the old man to allow him to take a few samples for assay. Reports defined it as a high grade nickel ore. Since at that time nickel had no special value, the ore was put aside and forgotten.

Then World War II came along and there was a great need for nickel, causing Eldredge to remember the old man's mine in the Seafoam district. He, himself, was in his seventies by now, and he knew the old man had been dead a good many years. Then as the government's needs for strategic metals grew more desperate, thinking he could go directly to the old man's location, he persuaded his daughter to accompany him to the locale. At the Seafoam Guard Station, they hired horses from the ranger there and set out for the site.

When they did reach the vicinity, however, everything appeared changed to Eldredge, and try as he might, he was unable to even locate the ruins of the old man's cabin or mine. Giving up after several days of fruitless searching, on the way back to the ranger station, they met Clarence Kimpton who was doing some prospecting in the area. After telling Kimpton his story, he ended by commenting that his age and health prevented him from searching any farther. Before parting, Eldredge drew a map of the approximate locale and gave it to Kimpton.

Naturally, Kimpton, too, spent some time trying to locate the lost mine, but he had no better luck than did Eldredge in his attempt to find the ruins where the mine should be. Probably to him, the terrain appeared more changed than the map had indicated. Yet as sure as the snow flies and the storms come in the Seafoam district, there is a "good solid 6-foot vein" of nickel ore just waiting to be relocated by someone sometime in the future.

The Seafoam Earthquake

A number of people still living today in and around the Stanley-Sawtooth country remember well the "big earthquake of 1944 in the Seafoam area." Marvin Larson is one. As a forest ranger there at the time, he was riding sheep range on Fontes Creek near Sheep Mountain, Tuesday, July 11th. Hearing rumblings and feeling a rather strong tremor, he never thought too much about it when it quieted. But the next day, at the guard station at 1:35 P.M. a heavy shock shook the buildings so badly that the occupants feared they would collapse any second.

Twenty minutes later another wave came, not quite as severe as the first one. Waves continued until 10 P.M. . . . 17 in all. By 5 A.M. the next morning, 5 more had been felt, the last one being as severe as the first one the day before.

Tremors continued on through Saturday the 15th . . . some as strong as the first one, and some not quite so strong. All day Sunday things remained comparatively quiet until 9:30 P.M., then another shock came. Six thirty A.M. brought another, and again at 5:35 P.M. and 5:45 P.M. The last waves were somewhat lighter, as though the shocks were dying away. All were accompanied by deep rumblings with a sound like distant thunder, and each time, just beforehand, the sun became strangely shadowed, as though veiled by a pall of smoke or steam.

During that uneasy week, several persons barely missed death by the unpredictable nature of the shock waves. For example: Fern Larson and Johnny Grubb were going down Rapid River, and had just climbed out of the canyon when they heard a deafening roar behind them. Returning, two days later, they found a whole section of the canyon wall and the trail below Lime Creek caved into the River.

Clarence Kimpton and young Buck Allen were on Soldier Creek the morning of July 12th. After breakfast, finding their three mules and bell mare gone, they tracked them to a point outside the creek canyon. All four animals were jumpy and nervous, and try as they might, the two men were unable to drive them back into the canyon. After much chasing about, the mules wheeled and headed in the direction of the Seafoam Ranger Station. After six miles in that direction, the mules wheeled again, heading toward the Middle Fork of the Salmon River. Buck Allen was after them when the first quake hit. Hearing a loud roar and crashing of rocks, he looked back along the trail below Sheepeater Springs where he had just passed under a high cliff overhang near the creek in time to see a whole cliff come crashing into the bottom of the canyon.

Meanwhile, Kimpton, after his part of the chase in the direction of Seafoam, had turned up Muskeg Creek and was on a high point of the trail at the time of the first quake. He, too, was able to witness huge rocks and boulders crashing below into the creek canyon.

Walt Armeson felt the shocks at Greyhound Lookout. At the time of the first one he was sitting on the ground. On the tremors that followed he was in the tower, and being above the terrain, was able to follow the line of the quake, noting Seafoam directly in line with the fault.

At the same time, a Mr. Clark, working along the fault line up Seafoam Creek, later said, "Rocks rose at least a foot off the ground, like someone had set off a series of blasts all the way up the hill. Somehow I managed to stumble and fall, seeking safety behind a large fir tree. Although the shock never lasted long, it seemed like I huddled there for hours watching the giant boulders and rocks crashing down the mountainside around me."

Fortunately, those in the area escaped unharmed while many sections along the different trails were badly damaged. When the tremors finally subsided, along Fontes Creek, rocks continued to fall for several days. In many places, several hundred yards long, two and three inch wide cracks were found in the earth's surface. Even Vanity Mountain was affected. One rock, weighing some five tons, crashed onto the road blocking it for several days before equipment could be moved in to move it away.

Thus the quakes ended. Those in the quake area at the time have not forgotten that week in July, 1944 and the feeling of uneasiness which accompanied the experience.

As for mining in the Seafoam district today, miners come and go as always, mostly during the summer months. In a way the area has enjoyed three good booms . . . first around the turn of the century, a second in the Twenties, and again in the Forties. Although an overall number of men employed by the various companies would be difficult to determine, due to seasonal turnovers, one report estimated 100 there in 1882. Another reported 50 working at the Greyhound Company in 1909, and Walter Hovey Hill & Hecla Mining Company were working 20 men in the summer of 1926.

Aside from mining and forest service activities in the Seafoam area, because of its semi-primitive terrain, many people find recreational values there too . . . fishing, hunting, and camping around Josephus Lake where a forest campground is located. It matters not that the roads are steep and narrow with only a few places wide enough for passing, for any time after the snows melt in the spring until snow flies again in the fall, one can meet numerous trail bikes, campers, trucks, and other vehicles going and coming in and out of the mountainous Seafoam region.

THE VALLEY CREEK MINE

The Valley Creek Mine, situated in the foothills on Valley Creek near its headwaters and in close proximity to the Buckskin Mine over the ridge, was first located by T.H. Woodward, Thomas Cassidy, H.F. Powell and J.T. Grant in August, 1884. Claims were the Crescent, Valley Creek, and Last Chance. Records fail to show what happened within the next sixteen years. It is known, however, that the claims were acquired by E.J. Micheal sometime before 1900. He changed the name of the Crescent to the Creston and the Last Chance to the Deep Lode, did some developement work, and sold all three claims to Judge Littleton Price of Hailey, Idaho in August, 1900, for the sum of $2,000. Both Cassidy and Woodward were deceased at this time.

After purchasing the properties, Judge Price failed to do the necessary assessment work, and the claims lapsed. He relocated all three on June 23rd, 1902, then applied for, and received a patent on them that same fall. At the time he recorded his relocation, he also located the Y.A.M., the Wizzard, the Captain Stanley, and the Barrier. These were not patented. Needing help and capital, the Judge then formed the "Stanley Gold Mining Company" with himself and J.B. Hastings and Wayne Darlington named as the main shareholders. In August of 1902, the company made a deal for the old 20-stamp quartz mill that was a duplicate of the General Custer Mill on Yankee Fork, built in 1882 at Vienna in the Sawtooth Valley, and had the mill disassembled and moved to the Valley Creek property. Here, the mill was rebuilt and renovated to begin work on the Valley Creek ores.

This required a crew of forty men, and when all was ready in the summer of 1903, mining and milling went ahead until the spring of 1905, but not without interruptions, said to be mostly due to disagreement among the company shareholders. What-

30

ever the trouble was, the property finally sold at sheriff's sale in the fall of 1905, and was purchased by the bank at Hailey. A group from Pittsburg, Pennsylvania, called the "Pittsburg Mining and Milling Company," seemed to have backed the bank's move inasmuchas a member of the group, D.P. Carpenter, was made manager of the mine and mill the following July (1906). At that time work was resumed with a full force and went smoothly well into September.

A report by Robert N. Bell, State Mine Inspector for that year, read as follows: *The Valley Creek property carries a large vein of $10 gold ore, but its association with a little lead makes it difficult to treat, and a satisfactory extraction of the values has not been made so far. It is anticipated that additional machinery can overcome this difficulty, and that the mine will be an important producer. The vein is large, and the value good.*

The mine and mill worked continuously for the next three years. Ore was mostly gold and silver averaging $7.00 to the ton. Described as quartz with lead carbonates, sulphides, and pyrites carrying gold and silver values, this ore required milling to consist of amalgamation, cyanide treatment and concentration. Cyanide tanks on the property were lined with 4" x 6" redwood timbers that provided a maximum of efficiency when in operation. The 20-stamp mill, being steam powered, used a great deal of wood in its furnaces. On the job, Ray Mahoney was the one who saw to this.

Although most of the work done on the Valley Creek mine was done in summer and fall, some was also done in winter. An item appearing in the December 15, 1903 issue of the *Silver Messenger Newspaper* printed at Challis, Idaho stated: *Ten men arrived from Hailey to work at the Valley Creek Mine for the winter. Wages are $3.50 per day, and since the nearest store is over 12 miles away and the snow is deep everywhere in the Stanley Basin country, they think they will be able to save every penny of their pay.*

This item was typical of several such reports from time to time through the years, and a rather accurate report of how the miners would be snow-bound once they arrived at the Valley Creek camp. The camp was composed of a boarding house, bunkhouse, a number of storage sheds, and several cabins for the benefit of mining personnel and miners who brought their families to be with them while they worked there. Wages continued at $3.50 for an eight hour shift with $5.25 paid for a twelve hour shift through 1909.

31

During this time, George Sewell was mill foreman. Some of the workmen were John Boyd, Ralph Baxter, William Lutz, Aaron Slouthower, Fred Calkins, and Leslie Niece. Niece, with his wife, three year old son, and infant daughter, occupied one of the log cabins across the stream from the mill in the winter of 1907.

Bill Merritt and John Thompson furnished meat for the boarding house. In the winter all supplies had to be brought in by hand sled from Stanley, fifteen miles away from the site. This necessitated most commodities to be purchased in bulk and brought into camp before the winter snows fell.

A load of supplies pulled by hand from Stanley to the Valley Creek Mine.

The Fort Pitt Mining and Milling Company came on the scene about 1907-08, apparently resulting from a merger with the Pittsburg company, or perhaps the eliminations of certain stockholders and entrance of others. In any case, the Fort Pitt Company owed the First National Bank at Shoshone, Idaho the sum of $2,600 which was paid by J.S. Darrah in April 1909. In turn, Darrah was to be reimbursed plus interest within 90 days by the Fort Pitt Company. However, the company failed to pay Darrah. When Darrah died, the debt was included in his estate, and Ben Darrah, as administrator, sued the Fort Pitt Company for $3,796 in November 1910.

In 1911, William Lutz also sued the company for back wages owed him from July, 1909 to October, 1910. Lack of money

32

and/or poor management prevented Lutz from being paid, and as it turned out, on August 18, 1911, he became owner of the Valley Creek Mine.

From that time until 1928 little was done at the Valley Creek property. That year L.B. Lyman bought the holdings for back taxes from Custer County. In March, two months later, he made a deed to M.A. Lyman. By now the machinery had become rusted and somewhat obsolete, so again nothing was done on the property aside from the assessment work. On January 6, 1933 M.A. Lyman sold out to William A. Soule, lock, stock, and barrel, for the sum of $85.00. Fred Schindler, a candy salesman for Sweet's Candy Company at Salt Lake City and in and out of the Stanley Basin for many years, became a partner with William (Bill) Soule in the property that same spring.

The two men, after a good offer, leased the mine and mill to the Western Gold Exploration Company. Frank H. Gunnell, general manager for this company, estimated ore reserves exposed in one of the mines at 450,000 tons that would run about $20 to the ton. This company built a new milling plant which, after completion in early 1942, was successfully treating 60 tons of ore daily in April that spring. At that time, an article published in *Western Mineral Magazine* said the management hoped to increase its production to full capacity of 100 ton per day. The article then went on to say the construction of the mill was started after development disclosed a substantial tonnage of milling grade ore, and that during the first 60 days of operation the mill had produced $11,505 worth of concentrates that resulted in an earning of $2,865.

The mines leased to Western Gold Exploration Company consisted of three main claims. These were referred to as "NO. 1, NO. 2, and NO. 3." Oldtimers who have worked on the property say one of the mines, located with a tunnel opening just above the old mill was called "The Glory Hole," and said it was thought to be the richest mine in the group. NO. 1 claim was a kind of open pit type mine where power shovels were used to mine the ore. The ore was trucked to the milling plant. In addition to the milling plant, the company's equipment included a caterpillar tractor, two power shovels, dump trucks, an air compressor, and a great deal of modern mining equipment that was used for both underground and surface mining.

Auxiliary equipment and buildings on the Valley Creek

property included a modern water system and storage reservoir, a portable welder, a steam power plant for heating and wood sawing, an assay office, a mining office, and a lumber mill. There were two camps: one with five buildings at NO. 1 property, and two buildings at NO. 2 property.

Sampling, according to the *Western Mineral Magazine* article, done by the Freeport Sulphur Company, gave reports on the different mine dumps and old tailings estimating values averaging from $8.00 to $8.75 per ton.

The new milling plant, designed and construction supervised by Frank Gunnell, used two processing methods for the recovery of the minerals . . . gravity concentration was one, and the other was counter decantation cyanide used mainly for silver and gold.

Bill Soule and Fred Schindler, owners of the Valley Creek mining property, were not only partners in the venture, but also the best of friends. Soule was the oldest of the two men and had come to the Stanley Basin country in the early 1900s.

Valley Creek Mine in the 1930 s. Mrs. Fred Schindler
watching William "Bill" Soule pan for gold.

Always in search of the pot of gold at the end of the rainbow, like most prospectors and miners, he believed wholeheartedly that it was just waiting for him in one of his placer diggings or mine tunnels where he staked a claim. Nonetheless, he was better than most in his various undertakings, and although a kind of jack-of-all-trades, while he lived in the Stanley Basin, he worked as an electrical engineer, did rather professional photography, was a homesteader among other vocations. In mining, aside from his partnership with Schindler, he also worked in partnership with other miners on other mine properties.

In time the Western Gold Exploration Company's lease on the Valley Creek mine properties expired and was not renewed, thought to be due to ever increasing production costs and many restrictions imposed on mining operations within the boundries of the National Forest by the government. When Bill Soule died in 1946, Fred Schindler took over the mine properties. Married to Lena Jacobsen from Salt Lake City, the Schindlers had three children . . . two boys and a girl. Living at Blackfoot, Idaho, Fred worked as a candy salesman for the Sweet's Candy Company traveling over most of Central and Southeast Idaho. After taking over the mine properties, he made regular trips to do the assessment work and develop the mine, often accompanied by his family. The children loved the country, learning a great deal about nature and outdoor life there.

Fred Schindler, like Bill Soule, cherished the dream of "striking it rich" in one of the mine tunnels, of which the "glory hole" was his favorite. He, too, died without realizing his dream. At his death at the age of 65, in 1960, William (Bill) Schindler, his oldest son, took over his dream and ensuing years have found Bill at the Valley Creek Mine properties at every opportunity . . . often accompanied by his own wife and children.

Fred Schindler, owner of the Valley Creek Mine, with his wife and children. Taken in the 1930's.

THE BUCKSKIN MINE

The Buckskin Mine, on the slope of Buckskin Mountain, in the vicinity of the Valley Creek Mining properties, and a bit southeast of the Cape Horn Landing Field, was located in 1883 by J.A. Dorsey and J.P. Kennan. The Buckskin Mining Company was created by a corporation formed under the laws of the State of Illinois, with Grant Filden as president and Selden P. Spencer as secretary. Ore in the mine was mostly gold and silver.

It is thought this company operated through the summer of 1888, but records are vague and somewhat confused. Recorded deeds of the Buckskin Company, for example, on one page states: The Buckskin Mining Company, on July 30, 1888, sold to William M. Bulkey of Saint Louis, Missouri, for the sum of $300,000. On the following page it states: On July 31, 1888, William M. Bulkey sold to the Buckskin Mining Company for the sum of $299,999.

In any case, the company was on the property and still working in 1889-90. In 1891 Jerry Martin filed suit against the Buckskin Company for a $9,000 debt owed him. The company failed to pay the debt, and as a result the property was sold at a public auction to the highest bidder, who in this event turned out to be Jerry Martin. Then in 1896, the property was sold again, this time for back taxes owed to Custer County, going for $226 to W.H. Silberhorn. Through records of these transactions, no mention is made of a patent. Yet such sales of the Buckskin property would indicate there had been one to someone at sometime during its existence.

Della McGown notes a bit in connection with the Buckskin Mine in her diary kept while the McGown's operated the first store and post office in the early 1890s on the site where Upper Stanley was located later. On the subject she writes: "There was a tall old man with one leg longer than the other. He wore a built-up shoe. He was hauling supplies to the Buckskin Mine with a wagon and two horses. On his trips to and from the mine, he would stop at our place and stay overnight. The children were always glad to see him because he would sit and tell them stories all evening, and they liked that."

"One story he told them was about a Chinaman cook at the Buckskin mine. Seems this Chinaman hid his money near a certain tree there, and then one day a crew of workmen cleared the trees in that area. After that the poor Chinaman could never find his money anymore. Did someone find it? Or is it still there?"

Although Mrs. McGown does not say who the man was, her mention of the "wagon and two horses" was probably due to the bad road conditions throughout the Stanley-Sawtooth country in the early days.

As for the Buckskin Mine, no additional information was found as to whether it was ever worked again after it was bought by Silberhorn for back taxes in 1896.

STANLEY BASIN MINING

In the vicinity of the Stanley Party locations on Kelly Creek in 1863, a year later, rich placer ground was located by another group of prospectors . . . one claim being the "Buckley Bar" and made by James Buckley who had been a member of the Stanley Party. As far as can be determined, the Buckley Bar, measuring 400 by 1,000 feet in size, is one of the oldest sites of mining done in the Stanley Basin.

Mining here was done by ground sluicing, a rather ingenious method considering the wild, remote region, and *the fact* man had little but his hands and back to work with at the time. For example, the Bar was sluiced by channeling creek water through a series of winding rows of hand-placed rock ditches criss-crossing the placer ground. Although tall, lodgepole pine trees grow on the old workings today, some evidence of the ditches can still be found on the site. While there are no legal records available as to the output of the Buckley Bar, mining authorities have estimated it at $250,000 as based on the market price of gold at $20 an ounce.

In Kelly Gulch, then known as Summit Gulch, Alvah P. Challis and Henry Sturkey located good placer ground in 1873. Both men remained in the area for many years and were active in the developement of the Stanley country.

Joe's Gulch, a tributary of the main Salmon River, headed in the mountains over the ridge from where Kelly Creek gathers its headwaters, was another location of early day mining done in the area. Will Casto, in partnership with Pat Hyde and Tim Cooper, made a rich strike here in the late Seventies. In the winter of 1878-79, the men ran a drift, or tunnel, on bedrock, and when the snow melted in the spring providing water for their operation, they set up a series of sluice boxes that enabled them to wash the sands and gravel and save the gold. As a

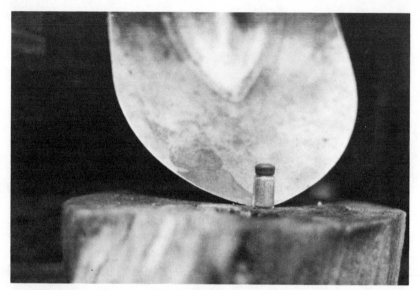

A bottle of gold silhouetted against a shovel. This small bottle of gold sold for over $300 at the old price of gold ($20 per ounce).

result, when clean-up day came, the gold was put into a gold pan and turned out to be so heavy, they placed it on a short plank (board) and two of the men were required to carry it to the cabin where it was weighed and prepared for shipment.

This was at the time when the Sheepeater Indian War was in progress. All the miners and prospectors in the Stanley-Sawtooth region were in constant danger from lurking renegades. One day that spring, while working on the ditch, Cooper was shot in the arm by one of the Indians. Since the Indians camouflaged themselves with cut sagebrush tied around their head and shoulders and lay in wait along the trails, after Cooper was shot all the miners in the Stanley Basin were forced to exercise more caution than ever before until the war ended.

After receiving the money from their share of the gold, Casto and Cooper, with many dreams and aspirations, moved to Vienna in the then newly discovered Sawtooth mining district in the adjacent Sawtooth Valley. Here they went into partnership in the saloon business and did rather well for a time, but the extreme winters and short supplies eventually decided them to go out of business and back to mining. Will Casto moved to Hailey, while Tim Cooper returned to the Stanley Basin.

The next few years saw a great deal of mining activity on Joe's Gulch, and many names were connected with claims there. Dan Murphy and Knox Taylor worked claims there in 1899. Billy Bowen, Con Doty, and Cy O'Dell were there. When the Arthur McGowns (Sr.) moved to Stanley from the Yankee Fork district in 1890, Cy O'Dell often visited their place just above the mouth of Valley Creek near where the town of Upper Stanley is now located.

George Smith was another placer miner who had claims in Joe's Gulch, first about a mile up the gulch from the main Salmon River, then another mile or so farther up. Finally, about 1900, he built a cabin at the mouth of the gulch, and it was here that he lived his last days. Smith lived alone most of the time, sluicing out enough gold each spring during the run-off to care for his needs and wants for the remainder of the year. He had a dog that was his constant companion. He also owned a big black saddle horse about which a little story is told. Seems when he mounted the horse sober, it would invariably become cantankerous, snorting and bucking, and nine times out of ten would throw Smith to the ground. Of course, Smith would not be denied, and usually after several bouts between man and beast, the horse would take him to where he wanted to go. However, if it were to the little community of Stanley, and after a few hours spent drinking with "the boys," when Smith was ready to go home, the horse would show an opposite nature, allowing his owner to mount him without protest and would carry him home, picking his way along the rough trail very carefully.

If George Smith ever talked of his early life, no one still living today remembers. He was an artist, and a good one. Using oils on the back of oilcloth, the kind used for tablecloths and shelf covering in those days, for his canvas, he painted many beautiful landscapes. On one occasion he painted a picture of Redfish Lake as a gift for Edna Niece McGown when she was a small child.

Later, in the Teens, Ora Jones acquired a claim from George Smith and moved onto the property. He built a large log cabin about three miles up the gulch from Salmon River, near the site of one of Smith's old cabins. While living there Mrs. Jones gave birth to twin boys delivered by Mary Marshall. It was here that Jones built a 5-stamp mill a short distance from the cabin. Stamps for the mill were freighted in from the Trent E. & M. Company out of Salt Lake City. What returns were

41

Deserted miner's cabin on Joe's Gulch.

Old stamps still remaining in Jones' mill on Joe's Gulch.

Pulley wheel at Jones' mill on Joe's Gulch.

realized is not known, but it is thought the venture was not overly successful.

Atwood Weeks lived in a cabin and worked a claim on a small gulch known as "Weeks Gulch" near where it intersects at the head of Joe's Gulch (thought to be named for Joe Garadina). Only a foot trail led to the Week's property from the end of the wagon road at the Smith-Jones site until recent years when Dick Pierce extended the road up and over the head of the gulch. This road can still be traveled today by 4-wheel drive vehicles.

Ore throughout the Joe's Gulch region was gold with values of silver and iron and a slight trace of copper. An item in an issue of *The Silver Messenger,* dated September, 1897, reported: "Source of gold found in the Stanley Basin has been found by Frank Montgomery. He has discovered a porphyry vein that cuts across the granite formation on the upper side of the Basin." While Montgomery's discovery applied mainly to the scource of placer gold, the vein he referred to was actually in one of the gold bearing porphyry dykes that cut several creeks and gulches in the Basin . . . Joe's Gulch is one cut by such a dyke.

While Lower Stanley served as the main point of supply for miners and homesteaders in the Stanley Basin during most of the early days, the tiny community also was a kind of hub for all the adjacent locales. A few of these and names of miners can be mentioned here.

Going down the Salmon River from Lower Stanley and the mouth of Joe's Gulch, on Big Casino Creek, Antone DeMartin located the "Goldbug" and "Bruneau" claims in 1900. Two years later he sold these to Peter A. Wagner for $500.00. In 1905, Wagner with William H. Chittenden and Arthur G. Clark, all of Denver, Colorado, organized the Phemspace Mining Company, built a mill of sorts on the property, and offered capital stock at $1.00 per share.

Near the mouth of Big Casino Creek, on the Salmon River, Clay and Priscilla Vance owned "The Donald", the "Alice", the "Priscilla", and the "Glacier" claims which they sold to George Cumine in 1903 for $500.00. Cumine, in turn, sold these to Dave Hershey in 1906 for $600.00. In the same vicinity on the Salmon River, George Cumime with his partner, Thomas Kelly, located "The Gold Cube" claims 1, 2, 3, 4, and 5 in 1905 and which they sold to a Colorado Company for $500.00 in

1910. Later, Hershey sold to a group from Great Falls, Montana, and in 1917 they formed the Big Casino Mining Company in order to work the property. Thomas (Tom) Kelly mined a claim on Casino Creek in the early 1900s. In later years, Tom turned to trapping for a living, and was well known and liked throughout the Stanley-Sawtooth country where he made his home until he died in 1919.

On Rough Creek, some two miles down river from Casino Creek, a man known only as "Whiskey Bob" made a rich quartz strike in 1895. Harry Friend, who was killed in a snow slide in 1910, did mining on Rough Creek in the early 1900s. After his death, his brother, John W. Friend, came from Nebraska to mine the claim. Jack Seagraves, still living, in his late ninties in the 1970's, mined on Rough Creek for many years. One of his claims was called "The Grubstake Placer." In about 1917, Chase Clark and a man named Bunch, are said to have made a rich strike on Rough Creek. *The Silver Messenger,* printed in Challis, Idaho, noted the location to be a talc formation and believed to run $30,000 to the ton. The Rough Creek Mine was also located in this vicinity, but as in so many instances, little information was found in connection with who did the locating, and when.

Across the Salmon River, a short distance from where the Mormon Bend is now located, diggings called "The Mormon Bend Placers" were worked in the late 1800s. Water for this operation was supplied by a hand-dug ditch running one and a half miles from Casino Creek.

Although Alvah P. Challis and Henry Sturkey were partners, each of them often worked alone or in partnership with other miners. The first record of any location made by Sturkey alone in the Stanley country was just before Idaho became a State, and the Stanley Basin was included in the Yankee Fork Mining District. The claim was recorded as in Idaho Territory, in 1890, bearing the name "Vild Hoge Bar" with location cited as at the mouth of Joe's Gulch. Since Mr. Sturkey was German, one is inclined to guess that he meant "Wild Hog Bar," thus explaining the pronunciation.

Back at Lower Stanley, going over Nip-and-Tuck Mountain, on the second creek up the grade, around 1900, Alvah Challis located and worked a small claim. Near Nip-and-Tuck Summit, later, in 1918, W.B. Paul, William (Bill) Soule and Jennie Gleason located the Mayday mine group.

It was in 1895, Sturkey and Challis, in partnership, located one of the largest and best known placer diggings in the Stanley Basin. The site was 12 acres of rich placer ground on the divide where Kelly Creek gathers its headwaters and at the very head of Joe's Gulch. Names of the claims were "The Producer," the "Red Jacket," "The Delight," and "The Bingo." Challis, although a partner, spent most of his time in the area of the town of Challis, and Sturkey was in charge of the mining operations. This was known as "The Sturkey Placer" for many years. The site is thought to have been located originally in 1863 by a man named Mathews, and who, like Alvah P. Challis, had numbered in the Captain Stanley party.

Sign by road leading to old Sturkey Placer at the head of Kelly Creek.

To work the ground, Sturkey, of German extraction and learned in the fundamentals of hydrostaticsm devised a way to turn the operation into a hydraulic works. In doing this, he developed a series of ditches directed to a kind of reservoir at the head of Stanley Creek (located over the ridge) by damming off all the small streams in the vicinity and forcing a heavy flow to a large ditch that followed around the mountain slope and graded down to a 12" pipe and into a canvas hose with a nozzle attached to the end. The large ditch was dug by hand to 15-20 feet deep in places, depending on the contours along the mountainside, and ran a distance of four miles to where it connected with the 12" pipe. When filled with water, this provided ample pressure with which the hillsides of the placer ground could be sluiced down to bedrock. When this was done, the loose gravel and sands were run through a series of sluice boxes, and

Hydraulic placer mining at Sturkey Placer in the early 1920s. Lady in white is Mrs. Lillian Paul. Henry Sturkey manning the nozzle.

thereby most of the gold and associated minerals were saved. While worked this way by Sturkey, one of the claims is reported to have yielded $11,000 and another claim in the same vicinity yielded $5,000 . . . a rather tidy sum in the early days.

The *Challis Silver Messenger* printed a short item in 1897 telling of that years yield: "Sam Tennell came down from Stanley Basin in early November, after mining for Alvah Challis and Henry Sturkey. Messers Challis and Sturkey made a good clean-up on their placer this year. They only hydrauliced 22 days and took out $4,000 in gold dust."

Soon after the location was made and Sturkey began his mining operations, on a flat above the main placer diggings, near the head of the gulch, he erected a barn and corrals for the horses and several cabins for storage and living quarters. The largest of the cabins was used as a cook house that included one room to serve as a kitchen and dining area, with two smaller rooms equipped with bunks for himself and miners who came to work for him. Most of the smaller cabins were generally used by married miners who sometimes brought their families along with them. Oftentimes, a wife of one of the miners would take on the job as cook for the crew. In this case, one of the smaller rooms was usually turned over to the cook and her husband. In this way she was on the premise and able to be up

Henry Sturkey cabins built about 1887. Hand made shakes on the roof, and hand-hewn boards for the floor. Picture taken in 1940.

and have breakfast on the table early without having to come from one of the other cabins in the early morning chill, always so prevalent in this high mountain country.

In 1916 when "Doc" Cothern went to work for Sturkey for the spring and summer, his wife, Affie, took the job as cook. Their two young daughers, Mildred and Virginia, were with them, and in order to provide sleeping space for the children, Affie strung a curtain across one side of the dining area, and at night would draw this curtain to act as a screen for the girl's bed. Other families in other years lived on the premises ... some like the Cotherns, stayed out the season, while others remained only a few weeks.

Sturkey made his last cleanup on the placers in the summer of 1919. As the water began to run low in the ditch, and by now aware of his age, one day late in July he said to his helpers, Cy Davis and Rupert Niece, "That's all boys!" That August he sold out to J.J. Hohman of Pittsburg, Pennsylvania, and moved over to Joe's Gulch at the mouth of Weeks Gulch, mining a little as his health permitted.

What Hohman did in connection with the placers is not known, but eventually the site was abandoned and lay idle until re-located by John Weidman in 1931. It then became known as the "Weidman Camp." Weidman, also German, constructed the reservoir still much in evidence today, a short distance from the Sturkey cabins location. In his operations,

47

Remains of Sturkey cabin. (1974)

Pipe-line to carry water from reservoir to placer diggings.

Headgate on Kelly Creek Reservoir (early 1930s).

All that remains of headgate on reservoir built and used by John Weidman in his mining operation at the head of Kelly Creek.

essentially, he followed the hydraulic method used by Sturkey, except to feed his reservoir he dug a series of ditches in the immediate locale to catch water from the winter snows. He then graded a pipe controlled with two valves at the insert (one just inside the reservoir dike for intake, and the other just outside for pressure) and directed it down to the placer ground at the gulch head. Although no figures are available on Weidman's returns, one old timer said, "At least he made bacon and beans during the many years he lived and worked on the property." At last report on ownership, the ground is still being held by Weidman's daughter residing in San Francisco, California . . . a Mrs. Viola Evans.

Down through the years, prospectors located and mined any number of claims in the Kelly and Stanley Creek areas. One extremely rich placer called "Ham Fat," measuring 200 by 30-40 feet, and deemed a grass roots placer, was located three-fourths of a mile south of Doran Gulch, a short tributary of Stanley Creek. In the early days Doran Gulch alone was the scene of much activity. Even in the Twenties and Thirties, when re-worked by Henry Middleton, in addition to gold, the gulch also produced sizeable amounts of mercury or cinnabar.

On Kelly Creek, Doc Adair and William (Bill) Lutz worked claims in about 1900. In the vicinity of Kelly Creek, a bit of

49

mystery surrounds the name, "Dead Man's Cabin," and is thought to have resulted from the fact that a man named John Taylor was found dead sitting against a tree near his cabin there. About 1890, a small placer was worked near Kelly Gulch by Tony Martena, an Italian, and at the time a good friend to Cowboy Jo, redheaded darling of many of the lonely miners in the region.

While Henry Sturkey was working partners with Alvah Challis, as noted before, he sometimes went into partnership with other miners on claims. One was the "Homestead" claim at the mouth of Kelly Gulch. His partner was Tim Cooper who named the claim, and by so doing, one may wonder if he had intentions of filing a homestead here in view of the fact that he and his wife, Bertha, built a nice log cabin in the vicinity.

All through the early years many mining claims were filed throughout the Stanley district. In some cases records of names, dates, and locations appear much confused as to who did what and where and when . . . such as the "Mountain Girl Mine" located on the northwest side of Nip-and-Tuck up Montezuma Gulch. Doc Adair and Bill Lutz are thought to be the original locators here. Hyde (probably Pat Hyde), Taylor, and Eaton mined on Elk Creek in the north end of Stanley Basin.

Earlyday miners and trappers built cabins in several places in which they lived while working along Elk Creek and in the locale. During the Teens or Twenties, in one of the old cabins on Elk Meadows, a cartoon, hand-drawn, was found that depicted

"All going out and nothing coming in" drawing by Ricky Pierce.

a man sitting on a pot with his pants down, with a caption reading, "All going out and nothing coming in." An oldtimer, in telling about the cartoon said, "I remember it well because the caption was a statement of fact as to the life of most miners in those days."

Pat Rasche worked a claim up a draw near Upper Stanley. He also made a good gold-copper discovery that became known as "The Iron Dyke Mine" in the Stanley Lake area. In the same locale, on the divide above Stanley Lake, the Duquette brothers located claims that in later years became the "Greenback," and which is being worked at the present time.

Many names are listed in the Stanley Mining district as having made discoveries in and around the Basin in early times. Arthur Smith located the Bull Frog and Jumpoff claims. Frank Rapp was there, and at one time was a partner with Bill Bowen. Frank Perry placered there in the early 1890s for about three years. Upon leaving, he started for the Yellow Pine Basin and was never heard of again. Tom Cassidy and Henry Duffy mined in the Stanley Basin. The list of names is long. And whether listed in this chapter, or elsewhere in this book, truly it can be said that each of the miners in his own way had a share in pioneering the Stanley-Sawtooth Country.

STANLEY BASIN DREDGING

While many miners turned their thoughts to hardrock mining as the rich gold placers in the Stanley Basin began to play out, others turned to thoughts of dredging along the creeks in the Basin. The first company was organized in 1890 and was called "The Sawtooth Placer Mining Company" with W.A. Moses as its president. The main office was set up at Kansas City, Missouri, and Matt (Madison) Womacks was the authorized agent in the Stanley field. Womacks had been in the area for some time and was well-liked by other miners in the country. *NOTE: For a brief profile on Womacks, see heading . . . "The Single Ones."*

When the Sawtooth Company was formed, after awhile, but still in the early 1890s, Tim Cooper, Herbert H. Marshall, and Charles Franklin were spurred to prospect and locate 365 acres of placer ground along Stanley Creek. Sid (S.J.) Roberts soon became interested in the ground, said to run 47 cents to the yard from grass roots to bedrock with an average depth of 13 feet, but was unable to come to an agreement with the three partners until 1896. Franklin died that year, however, and the deal failed to culminate. Two years later the ground was sold to Henry Lynn.

Lynn moved in machinery, and under his supervision, a 100 foot dredge boat was built. Completed in August, 1899, the boat was launched and christened "The Pearl L" with Sid Robert's eleven year old daughter, Eva, doing the honors. Meanwhile, the Stanley Basin Dredging Company was formed, setting its main office at Perry, Oklahoma Territory, and making Henry Lynn the president. The company also located 10 acres of placer ground called the "Fisty No. 1" claim, at the junction of Montezuma Gulch and Stanley Creek.

The first dredging done by the Stanley Company was done on part of the placer ground Lynn had purchased from Cooper and

Marshall. Production reports varied from time to time, and finally drew the attention of mining authorities who sent an inspector to check the company's progress. In his report later, the inspector apparently deemed the venture a losing proposition since he said, "In spite of production reports made by the Stanley Company, their attempts to extract gold dust from this ground have proven unsuccessful due to: No. 1 . . . presence of a false clay stratum, called 'robber's clay' by local miners, No. 2 . . . insufficient sampling, and No. 3 . . . inadequate equipment."

Whether the above report was a factor or not, in 1903 the company did rebuild its dredge boat, and when it was completed it was re-named "The Womacks." This was not a floating type boat, but was made mostly of wood and was placed on skids and pulled along with winches.

This dredge and the one owned by the Sawtooth Company both worked off and on for several years in the Stanley Basin. Womacks continued to act as agent for both companies. One of his duties in this capacity was to make out the grocery orders for the company boarding houses. For comparison with today's prices, one such list made by Womacks for the Stanley Company's boarding house is listed below, and is from an invoice dated September 6, 1904 of items purchased from the Pioneer Mercantile Company at Salmon, Idaho.

100 lbs. Sugar	$7.65	25 lbs. Dried Apricots	$3.00
100 lbs. Flour	$3.25	25 lbs. Dried Apples	$3.25
100 lbs. Ham	$16.75	1 case Coffee (24 lbs)	$13.25
50 lbs. Butter	$12.50	1 case Eagle	
		Brand Milk	$8.35
25 lbs. Rice	$2.15	1 case Eggs (30 doz.)	$6.50
9 lbs. Cheese	$1.80	1 gal. Catsup	.45
5 pkgs. Baking Soda	.50		

Many different people living in the Stanley Basin worked on the dredges at different times while they were in operation. Rosemary Hoskins tells of one year when her father, Will Paul, worked the night shift on the Stanley Dredge. "I was a small child at the time, and sometimes my father would take me to work with him," she recalls. "He fired the boiler with cord wood to produce the steam to power the shovels. I would wander around with him until I became tired and sleepy, then he would lay his coat on the floor at the foot of the boiler for me to lie on. Lying there I would watch the fire flicker through the boiler holes and listen to the dredge buckets running as I dropped off to sleep. When his shift was over he would wake me up and we would go the three miles to home." (Note: At that time "home" was the Paul stopping place on the Nip-N-Tuck road where Will Paul and his little family were living with his parents, George and Mollie Paul who operated a stop for freighters and others going to and from the mines in Stanley Basin.)

The Willis Dredge came on the scene in 1909. Henry C. Willis, having been stricken with "mining fever" left a good job with American Steele and Wire Company in New York City, to travel to the Thunder Mountain area of Idaho in 1905. As winter closed in, curtailing mining operations at Thunder Mountain, Mr. Willis returned to his family and home on Long Island. However, he could not put Idaho with it's lofty, snow-capped mountains, broad, grassy meadows, and potential for finding the elusive "pot of gold" out of his mind. The next two summers found him returning to the Stanley Basin to acquire and test ground for a dredging operation.

By late fall of 1908 he had accomplished his purpose, and on January 1, 1909 the placer claims "Willis No. 1," "No. 2," and "No. 3" were recorded at the Custer County Courthouse as being situated along Stanley Creek. Names of the locators were: Henry C. Willis, Jessie M. Willis, Fredrick O. Robinson, Laura B. Robinson, Willis W. Loy, Arthur A. Megget, and Mabel M. Megget.

This group became the Willis Company Incorporated with Henry C. Willis acting as manager. The Willis claims, along with other ground acquired, a total of 480 acres of placer ground, when tested, showed high values in gold, platinum, and mercury sulphides in the black sand residues. Because of the objectionable clay and talcy materials encountered by earlier operations in Stanley Creek, Willis built a bucket elevator type Bucyrus dredge boat, hoping to combat the "robber's clay" the creek seemed to be so lavishly endowed with. He also equipped the dredge with several concentrating appliances. After some experimentation by using an ordinary sluice box method, Willis began his dredging operation in the early summer of 1909.

A camp was erected, and overlooking the site, Willis built his home with the front of the large two-storied house facing the placer ground along Stanley Creek. By so doing, he could see the dredge working from his front windows. Now all was in readiness for his wife and three children to join him.

Front row: Henry and Jessie Willis' children, Muriel, Marian, and Henry Junior. Adults, left to right ... Willis Loy, unknown, F. O. Robinson, Henry Willis Sr. with wife, Jessie in front. Man standing in back is Arthur Megget. On buggy seat ... driver unknown and Ethel Robinson.

Henry Willis home on Stanley Creek (1910).

They traveled by train from Long Island, New York to Ketchum, Idaho where Mr. Willis met them with a team and light wagon at the end of the rail line. The trip to their new home at the dredge camp took three days. The first night was spent at Galena, a small stopping place at the foot of Galena Summit on the Wood River side. The next day, from the top of the Summit, they had their first breath-taking view of the Sawtooth Mountains and Valley. They also began to wonder as they traveled over the narrow, winding, dirt road, pulling a tree behind the wagon to check its speed as they bumped along down the mountain side, just what sort of a wild country this was that Henry was bringing them to. Once down the steep grade, and on the Valley floor, they were able to relax and enjoy the scenery, and in late afternoon reached the Frank Shaw ranch where Henry had made arrangements for them to spend the night. Upon being greeted by the Shaw family, and made to feel welcome as they partook of a tasty dinner, the family began to share Henry Willis' feeling of enchantment with the area.

Early the next morning they started the last lap of their trip. Down through the Sawtooth Valley to Upper Stanley where they stopped at the Benner Place for a short time, then on to Lower Stanley and over Nip-N-Tuck mountain into the Stanley Basin. As they reached the top of Nip-N-Tuck hill, the sun, looking like a huge ball of flame, was sinking in the West, casting a rosy glow over the broad meadowland. Mr. Willis pulled the team to a halt and pointed out the location of the dredge camp. The buildings looked like tiny specks in the distance. The children were so excited that, to quote daughter Marian in later years, "We felt like jumping off the wagon and running as fast as our legs would carry us. We could hardly wait to reach this new home in the wilderness."

That summer was a wonderful one for the Willis family. The children, with memories of their city life lingering, named the trees on the low hill behind the house such places as New York, Chicago, Buffalo, Boston, and Washington D.C. They would ride stick horses and play they were going on a long trip to visit or shop in these places. The family would take time to go on fishing and camping trips, or to picnic at the Lakes, and occasionally make a trip to both Lower and Upper Stanley. As Frank Shaw always said, "Mountain folks never live in haste."

The dredging operation was running smoothly, although they were having difficulty saving the gold. For the next four years the Willis' spent the summers at the dredge camp and the winters in Boise, Idaho, where the children attended school. Each spring as they returned to the Basin, they experienced the same feeling of excitement as they topped Nip-N-Tuck summit and could see the dredge camp in the distance. These were good years for the Henry Willis family.

Nearly everyone in the Stanley-Sawtooth country thought the company was doing well. Then, in March 1913, it came to be known that J.F. Cowan had taken a mortgage on all the Willis properties including ground, buildings, dredge boat, tools, and equipment. Unable to pay off the mortgage, the property was put up for auction by the Custer County sheriff in November 1915. Being the highest bidder, Cowan bought the entire property for $3,180. The following summer the Willis' again returned to Stanley Basin, and Henry, working with Cowan tried once again to make a paying proposition of the dredging operation.

Soon after this, W.W. Challis (nephew of Alvah Challis) entered a claim for back wages against Cowan. Evidently Cowan paid Challis, for things went along without further incident until 1917 when another claim for wages was filed against Cowan by Walter K. Lynch. This was not paid and foreclosure proceedings were started in April, 1918.

Once again, in the spring of 1920, Henry Willis returned to the Stanley Basin. Refusing to give up his dream, he had enlisted the help of some men from Twin Falls, Idaho, and along with W.K. "Walt" Lynch, who now owned the property, they repaired the machinery and tried again to devise a way to save the gold. The Willis family spent a short time at the dredge camp that summer, then thinking that at last they were going to realize a profit from this mining venture, they returned to Boise. There Henry Willis was stricken with cancer and died in November 1921.

In May, 1922, the Sawtooth Company announced in the *Challis Messenger Newspaper,* that the company would work more than five miles of placer ground along Stanley Creek. This was to include some 200 acres, and would take in the famous Buckley Bar discovered in 1863 and from which, it is said, over $250,000 was recovered when worked by crude methods. The article went on to say this dredge would use the latest methods by putting the material through a three foot by twenty-four foot revolving screen. Thus the bright gold would be caught on amalgamating tables fitted with cocoa matting and metal riffles. The principle being that the residue would then be elevated to the top of the dredge and re-screened and pass over riffles and through Neill Jigs built by the Union Iron Works at San Francisco, California. The material caught in the jigs would then be pumped ashore where it would be subjected to a chemical bath in 10 specially built drums. It would then pass over Wilfrey tables where the gold and platinum would be saved as concentrate.

The Stanley Company, like others before this time, continued to work intermittently, but with the stock market crash of 1929 and the Great Depression that followed in the Nation, mining was somewhat curtailed in the Stanley-Sawtooth country as well as in other western locales. During the early days of those hard times many men took to panning gold along the Salmon River and its tributaries, including the Basin area. Then came the "New Deal" under President Franklin D. Roosevelt's administration. The price of gold was raised from $20.67 to $35.00 an ounce in 1934, stimulating new interest in mining throughout the West. The following spring (1935) the Stanley Company announced its plans to resume their operations in the Stanley Basin for the summer. Also, the placer ground that had been located by Henry Middleton at the upper end of Stanley Creek in 1925-28, and worked by the Willis Dredging Company earlier, was leased to C.H. Lord, originally from Ontario, Canada and fresh from Detroit, Michigan in April of 1934.

C.H. Lord's arrival in the Basin was the beginning of the revelation of a promotional scheme that ended in disenchantment for a number of good people who invested their time and money in Lord's project. Altha Davis, wife of "Slim" Davis, a mechanic who worked for Lord, called the event "Operation Gold Bowls."

It seems Lord was a self-styled engineer who thought of himself as an inventor, and who possessed such a "gift of gab he could sell a snow-ball to an Eskimo." At any rate, he sold his idea and plan to a group in Detroit and formed the "Founders Trust Corporation" incorporated under Michigan law. Names of the trustees were; C.J. Wegner, John H. Barrett, Karl Batterman, Arthur Driver, P.S. Strout, and of course, C.H. Lord.

Lord fondly called his invention "Gold Bowls." His plan was to transport machinery and the bowls to the Stanley Basin and

Dragline and hopper used in dredging for gold in the Stanley Basin. (1930).

set up operations on a plot of placer ground he had leased from Henry Middleton, as already noted above. He would "make them all rich" he had promised his stockholders. Lord did arrive at the placer location in the Basin along with some used and badly worn machinery and equipment. Buildings and living quarters were erected on the property, plus one special building to house the "Gold Bowls" when same were trucked into the area in 1935. This building was kept under lock by Lord who carried the only key. Very secretive? "Yes," so said the work crew. By now called the Stanley Dredge Company with C.H. Lord as chairman of the board, the workmen listed on the payroll were Porter Martin, Tim LaPorte, C.J. Landingham, Jack Meeks, (shovel operator) P.S. Strout, Jerry Church, Ivan Perkins, Harry Wright, Earl McBride (cat-skinner), R.W. "Slim" Davis (mechanic), George Walbridge, John Weidman, and Fred Rodman (cook). These names were listed in the Custer County court records on leins filed against the company for back wages due these men. Wages were noted at 50 cents an hour ... pitiful little for experienced hands by today's standards, but all in accordance with times and prices during the Thirties.

No mining was done by the company in 1935, although a dam was constructed across Stanley Creek and things made ready for the trial run of the gold bowls. Even a sawmill was put into operation to cut heavy timbers for derricks and lumber with which to erect housing for the work crew. According to old timers in the region, the frame built to hold the gold bowls was the biggest joke of all. John Weidman called it the "Phinalihopper" inthat it resembled an entanglement of steel rising about 15 feet from a 20 foot square base and tapering off to 8 feet square at the top. This was laced with gears, belts, pulleys, and a motor which was placed at the base of the frame.

The principle here was that the bowls, placed one above the other in the frame, when in operation would employ centrifugal force and throw out the dross, thus allowing the gold to drop into the lower bowl, where by the same process the gold would be washed to almost purity and then drop into a large metal container at the bottom. This would have all been fine if it had worked . . . but when the trial run was to be made a large audience of company stockholders and families of the work crew gathered, Lord gave the signal to start, and, to quote Altha Davis, "All hell broke loose." The "bowls" broke loose from their moorings and the whole contraption ended up in a tangled mass of steel and timbers. To be sure the result was a grave disappointment to everyone concerned . . . including C.H. Lord.

After this an investigation by a number of the stockholders revealed that they "had been took in more ways than one." Naturally Lord promised to rectify the cause of why the gold bowls had failed to work, but distrust had been instilled in those who had put their money and faith in a project that was apparently worthless. Back wages were owed to the work crew who now filed liens against the company. Indications are that these were paid. Then legal action was taken against Lord by the stockholders, who in turn left the Stanley Basin, and if he ever returned it is not generally known.

However, some good did come from Lord's distorted deception in the form of Ivan W. Day, one of the company stockholders. "Doc" Day, as he became known in the Salmon River area, had been a licensed Osteopathic Physician and Surgeon in Detroit, Michigan, and when he came to the Basin in 1936 to take stock of his investment in the gold bowl operation, he and his family fell in love with the Stanley-Sawtooth country and decided to stay. When he noted that a doctor was greatly needed in the area, he straightway went before the Idaho State Medical Board at Boise and took an examination for a M.D. "Doc" Day went on to practice for a few years in the Stanley country, then returned to Detroit.

Many people in the Stanley and Challis regions will remember Doc Day. He was a doctor of the old school ..." old-fashioned, or a horse and buggy doctor," some might call him, for he was the kind of doctor who would come any time he was called no matter what time of day or night it happened to be. Nor did distance or place deter him, whether off up a mountain side, or at a lonely cabin at the end of some back road. While serving in the area he traveled hundreds of weary miles to reach the side of someone who needed him. Several persons around today who knew him said, "Doc Day was a good doctor and we hated to see him go."

Slim Davis, his wife, Altha, and son, Jay, standing by the Ivan "Doc" Day home near the Stanley Dredge.

Jay Davis, the only youngster in camp, and his dog, Towser.

As for the dredge mining in the Stanley Basin, the coming of World War II put a stop to it, as it did to all gold mining everywhere in the West. After the war was over, some mining in the Stanley-Sawtooth area went ahead as before, but never to the extent of the early days. Dredging was another matter. Such proposals met head-on with objections from various sources . . . a number of mining men claimed the method was no longer profitable. Sportsmen declared the entire area would end up devasted like the Yankee Fork of the Salmon River north of Sunbeam, pointing to the massive dredge sitting at the mouth of Jordan Creek as its aggressor. After awhile ecologists and environmentalists joined in the arguments.

Now this is a part of the Sawtooth National Recreation Area, and since restrictions have been put on most mining here, it is not likely the clang of iron buckets scraping against rocks and gravel along Stanley Creek will ever be heard in the Basin again. So ends our resume of mining done in the Stanley-Sawtooth country in days gone by.

WAYS OF PROSPECTORS
AND MINER'S COMMANDMENTS

A fitting tribute to all prospectors and miners, written in an early issue of the Challis *Silver Messenger,* reads as follows:

Every community in the West has its old prospectors and miners still around and about. Our area has many, some of whom are now engaged in other vocations while he still prospects on the side at every opportunity. More often than not, this man enjoys re-living his yesterdays and remembering the *big strikes,* and perhaps some of the little ones he made back in his prime, if only in his dreams. Seems they have an old proverbial saying, "Once a prospector, always a prospector. Watch the way he picks up his ears when someone mentions a new discovery somewhere."

Until late years, people outside the mining world knew very

little about this man's tedious toils, his heroic self-denials, his constant hardships, all borne cheerfully as he devoted his best years to seeking nature's rich treasures in inaccessible mountains and rock-ribbed hills throughout the West. Now he is growing old. His hair is grey, and his shoulders are no longer able to bear the burden of earlier years. In most cases, fortune, like the fabled pot of gold at the end of the rainbow, has eluded him. Yet he continues to hope.

Has this man's life been a failure? No. First as a prospector, then on to mining and back again to prospecting, he had the experience of discovering rich mines which he seldom had the means to develop, and perhaps for only a slight consideration, passed into the hands of those with capital, who in turn, made fortunes from his locations. Through primeval solitude, his findings has enriched the world and enabled our American West to progress to a more comfortable way of life. Because of him towns have been built, and fine ranches now dot this land that was raw and wild until he came to search for the yellow gold so bountiful in the streambeds of the Salmon River and its tributaries. When that gave out, he took to the surrounding mountains in search of the "mother lode."

Yes, the prospector and miner may have missed some of the questionable delights of our society, but no, his life has not been a failure. On the contrary, his constant intercourse with nature has kept his soul clean and uncontaminated. Now on in age, today it can truly be said of this man . . . the ever enduring prospector and miner, living or dead, he deserves the name of being one of the world's greatest noblemen.

How the Miner's Commandments Came to be Written

During the early gold rush days in Northern California, a writer named James M. Hutchings, eager to make his fortune with a pen instead of a pick and shovel, went to San Francisco as a way to begin. There he started a paper, reporting the news and happenings in the Mother Lode Country. To do the job well he often found it necessary to visit the mining camps scattered along the American and Yuba Rivers.

The ways of the prospectors and miners fascinated Hutchings. He noted the way they dressed, how they worked and played, the time they did their laundry and other chores, and most of all, he noted their creed. He liked these rough, yet often gentle men, and in turn wanted them to like him as a writer. As he went from camp to camp, sometimes remaining over night as a guest in the cabin of one of these men, he came to know them as a breed apart.

Then one day in 1853, Hutchings sat down and wrote what he termed "The Forty-Niner's version of the Ten Commandments." This caught the fancy of prospectors and miners throughtout the West. 100,000 copies are said to have been circulated, and miners everywhere proudly displayed a copy tacked on the door of his cabin. For many years thereafter hardly a man who followed mining was unaware of the Miner's Commandments as written by Hutchings.

In later years, because the original version of the Commandments is extremely long, shorter versions have been handed down. The one given here is a condensed version, but follows the original writing done by Hutchings, lithographed by Kurz and Allison in 1887 for the Library of Congress at Washington D.C.

Hutchings wrote:

A man spake these words, and said; I am a miner, who wandered "from away down east," and came to sojourn in a strange land, and "see the elephant." And behold I saw him, and bear witness, that from the key of his trunk to the end of his tail, his whole body has passed before me; and I followed him until his huge feet stood still before a clapboard shanty; then with his trunk extended, he pointed to a candle-card tacked upon a shingle, as though he would say read, and I read

THE MINER'S TEN COMMANDMENTS
I.
Thou shalt have no other claim but one.
II.
Thou shalt not make unto thyself any false claim, nor any likeness to a mean man by jumping one.
III.
Thou shalt not go prospecting before thy claim gives out. Neither shalt thou take thy money, nor thy gold dust, nor thy good name to the gaming table in vain; for monte, twenty-one, roulette, faro, lansquent, and poker will prove to thee that the more thou puttest down, the less thou shall take up.
IV.
Thou shalt not remember what thy friends do at home on the

65

Sabbath Day, lest that remembrance may not compare favorably with that thou doest here. Six days shalt thou dig or pick all thy body can stand under; but the other day is Sunday, yet thou washest all thy dirty shirts, all thy stockings, tap thy boots, mend thy clothing, chop thy whole weeks firewood, make up and bake thy bread, boil thy beans and pork, that thou wait not when thou returneth from thy long-tom weary. For six days labor only thou canst not work enough to wear out thy body in two years; but if thou workest hard on Sunday also, thou canst do it in six months.

V.

Thou shalt not think more of thy gold, and how thou canst make it fastest, than thou wilt enjoy it, after thou hast ridden rough-shod over thy good old parent's precepts and examples, that thou mayest have nothing to reproach and sting thee, when thou art left alone in the land where thy Father's blessing and thy Mother's love hath sent thee.

VI.

Thou shalt not kill thy body by working in the rain, even though thou shalt make enough to buy physic and attendance therewith. Neither shalt thou destroy thyself by getting "tight," nor "stewed," nor "canned," nor "high," nor "half seas over," nor "three sheets in the wind," by drinking smoothly down, brandy slings, gin cocktails, whiskey punches, rum toddies, nor egg-nogs; for while thou art swallowing down thy purse, and thy coat off thy back, thou art burning the coat from off thy stomach.

VII.

Thou shalt not grow discouraged, nor think of going home before thou hast made thy "pile," because thou hast not "struck a lead," nor found a "rich crevice," nor sunk a hole upon a "pocket," lest in going home thou shalt leave four dollars a day and go to work, ashamed, at fifty cents, and serve thee right.

VIII.

Thou shalt not steal a pick, nor a pan, nor a shovel from thy fellow miner; nor take away his tools without his leave; nor borrow those he cannot spare, nor return them broken, nor trouble him to fetch them back again, nor talk with him while his water rent is running on, nor remove his stake to enlarge thy claim, nor undermine his bank in following a lead, nor pan out gold from his "riffle box," nor wash out his "tailings" from his sluice's mouth. Neither shalt thou pick out specimens from the company's pan to put them in thy mouth, or in thy purse; nor cheat thy partner of his share; nor steal from thy cabin-mate his gold dust, to add to thine own, for he will be sure to discover what thou hast done, and will straightway call his fellow miners together, and if the law hinder them not, they will hang thee, or give thee fifty lashes, or shave thy head and brand thee like a horse thief, with "R" upon thy cheek, to be known and read of all men, Californians in particular.

IX.

Thou shalt not tell any false tales about "good diggings in the mountains," to thy neighbor, that thou mayest benefit a friend who hath mules and provisions, tools and blankets he cannot sell, lest in deceiving thy neighbor, when he returneth with naught save his rifle, he present thee with the contents thereof, and like a dog, thou shalt fall down and die.

X.

Thou shalt not commit unsuitable matrimony, nor covet "single blessedness"; nor forget absent maidens, nor neglect thy first love; but thou shalt consider how faithfully she awaiteth thy return; yea, and cover each epistle thou sendest with kisses, until she hath thyself.

And a new commandment give I unto thee; — if thou hast a wife and little ones that thou lovest dearer than life, that thou keep them continually before thee, to cheer and urge thee onward until thou canst say, "I have enough, I will return!" Then as thou journeyest toward thy much loved home, they shall come forth and welcome thee, and in the fullness of thy heart, thou shalt kneel together before thy Heavenly Father to thank him for thy safe return. AMEN.

So Mote it be!

Forty-Niner.

THE FOREST SERVICE

By Presidential Proclamation in 1906, the Lemhi, the Sawtooth, and the Salmon River Reserves of the National Forest were created within the realms of Central Idaho. Two years later, in 1908, and again by Presidential Proclamation, these three Reserves were re-organized into four Reserves. The fourth was named the Challis Reserve in honor of A.P. Challis, one of the early pioneers in the country and the man for whom the town of Challis was named. A part of what is now the Challis National Forest was then the Sawtooth National Forest, including the south side of the Salmon River, down to and including Cold Spring Creek; the west side of Valley Creek up to and including Crooked Creek. These sections were eliminated from the Sawtooth Forest and added to the Challis National Forest in 1913.

While both the Sawtooth and the Challis National Forests take in vast tracts of range and forested land, and their records cover each and all of their districts, our main concern here is

Example of U.S. Forest Service depictive signs.

68

with listings of rangers and locations of stations in the Stanley Basin and Sawtooth Valley. From 1908 down through the years, many local residents have worked for the Forest Service sometimes alongside the rangers helping to fight fires, do road work, and many other tasks. John Thompson, one of the early ranchers, was the first fire guard for the Stanley Basin area. His job was from May 1st to November 1st, 1908 for a salary of $900 for the six month period.

In August of 1908 a law was passed requiring that money be appropriated for the National Forests to be spent on public roads and schools in the different locales. In this way the counties in which the Forest Reserves were located were compensated for the reduction in taxable areas brought about by the creation of the Reserves. This was particularily helpful to sparsely settled Custer County.

The first ranger station in the Stanley Basin was built on the east side of Valley Creek, a short distance from where it empties into the main Salmon River, during 1908-09. Called the "Valley Creek Station," the building was a three-room log house with a small cold storage room off the kitchen. Records state that Edgar P. Huffman was at the Valley Creek Station and was the ranger at that time, resulting in some confusion since several oldtimers say they recall very plainly that Wallin Job was there at the time. Job Creek, near Stanley Lake was named after him. He was married to Emma Malm, a girl who was born in the old mining town of Custer up the Yankee Fork of the Salmon River and who grew up in Challis. After their marriage, the Jobs spent their honeymoon at the Valley Creek Station.

Henry D. Gerrish took over as the Stanley Basin Ranger in 1912. His wife was a sister to Earl Micheal of Challis. Mr. and Mrs. Gerrish had one son, Carlton, who was with his parents at the Valley Creek Station. A niece, Irene Micheal (daughter of Earl and Mamie Micheal), spent the summers of 1913 and 1914 there with the Gerrishes. Later, Irene married Charles Pfeiffer, and they made their home in Challis where Irene still lives today.

The Gerrishes moved in the fall of 1914, and Edgar Huffman spent the winter at the Valley Creek Station. In April, 1915, Leslie Dodge assumed the ranger duties and lived at the Station until 1918. At this time, Edgar Huffman came to replace Dodge, and this time remained six years there.

R.E. Allen, who had lived with his family at the Seafoam Ranger Station, was transferred to the Stanley Basin in 1924, and stayed four years at the Valley Creek Station. Allen was replaced by Merle Markle in 1928. Markle moved in with his wife, Kathleen, and small daughter, Helen, and this was home to the family for nine and one-half years. During this time a large, modern building was constructed on the premises. Mr. Markle cut and hauled the logs and his wife helped with the peeling. A Mr. Dee Thompson and Clifton Connyers were two of the men who helped lay the logs. The new building, completed at a cost of $3,000, composed nine rooms and a bath. When the Markles moved into their new quarters in 1933, the old building was sold to Dave Williams, a rancher in the Sawtooth Valley. He moved it to Upper Stanley for a dwelling for his family to live in during the school terms. Later, the building came to be owned by Marie Sullivan, a daughter of the Dave Williams'. Mrs. Sullivan sold it to the Danners. It now stands empty and forlorn and in need of repair, but rumor has it that a movement is underway to renovate it and use it to house a Historical Museum for the Stanley-Sawtooth region.

Also, while the Markles were at the Valley Creek Station, the natural hot spring on the property was enlarged. The walls were lined with logs and a small bath house with two dressing rooms was added for the benefit of local people and tourists alike. However, in 1971, because too many outsiders, failing to appreciate the facility, were abusing the privilege, the bath house had to be torn down and the pool filled with rock and gravel . . . surely a shame in view of the enjoyment and benefits so many people had derived from the natural hot spring through the years.

When Merle Markle was transferred to the Challis District, he was replaced by Charley Langer. The Langer family, like the Markles before them, took an active part in all phases of the community's affairs. Naturally, the news of his death, April 5, 1943, resulting from a plane crash on Ruffneck Peak, near Stanley Lake, came as a great shock to his friends and neighbors. This mountain was re-named "Langer Peak" later.

After Langer's death, a succession of rangers came to the Valley Creek Station. . . . Paul Grossenbach in 1944, Dean C. Rowland in 1946, Robert Newcomer in 1953, Harold Wadley in 1962, then David Mathis and Tom Kovalicky. Harold Wadley resigned from Forest Service work in 1967 to re-join the Marine Corps.

In the Sawtooth Valley, William Horton helped to build the Pole Creek Ranger Station and became ranger there about 1909 or 1910, remaining for twenty years at the post. Before the Sawtooth Valley Station on Fourth of July Creek was built, at one time a headquarters for the fire guard was set up on the Carroll Foley ranch, located in the vicinity of where the ranger station is now. Foley worked for the Forest Service as did many of the area residents ... some as fire guards, some as fire fighters, and some as trail hands ... whatever the job demanded through the years. One of the first men in the region, Emil (Charley) Grandjean, even gave counsel in the formation of the National Forest boundaries since it was ones like himself who knew the country and realized the wisdom of preserving its watersheds for all generations to come.

A visitor's center was built on the shores of Redfish Lake in the mid-Sixties. Open to the public, here the Forest Service exhibits historical artifacts found in the region and furnishes information to tourists from June through September of every year. Then in 1972, after much Congressional controversy, the entire Stanley-Sawtooth country became a part of what is known as the Sawtooth National Recreation Area. Many changes have taken place since then ... all too numerous to mention in this writing.

It may be noted, however, that Tom Kovalicky was assigned as one of the assistants to the superintendent of the S.N.R.A. in 1972, and at the same time Dave Kimpton was assigned as the zone manager of the Stanley area to assist Kovalicky. Also, in 1969-70, a large rustic building was erected on a low hill overlooking U.S. Highway 93 between Redfish Lake Creek and the town of Upper Stanley, serving as new headquarters for the Stanley Basin Ranger District and supplying information for tourists.

The principles for the National Forests were laid down in 1905 by James Wilson, Secretary of Agriculture then, in a letter to Gifford Pinchot, Conservationist at the time, stated in part, "You will see to it that water, wood, and forage ... are conserved and wisely used." Pinchot, himself said emphatically, "The conservation of our natural resources is the key to the future. It is the key to the safety and prosperity of the American people, and all the people of the world, for all time to come."

Thus, long before multiple use was given recognition by

Congress in 1960, early rangers practiced these principles adhering tightly to the fact that "Water is the lifeblood of the land." So it was and is in the Stanley-Sawtooth country, and may it remain so for all time to come.

Valley Creek Ranger Station, built 1908-09. Courtesy of Challis National Forest.

Valley Creek Ranger Station, built 1933. Courtesy of Challis National Forest.

NAMES OF GEOGRAPHIC FEATURES

Names of many of the mountains, streams, lakes and other geographic features in the Stanley-Sawtooth country were taken from the names of various pioneers and settlers in the region. Some of the ones known are listed here.

In the Sawtooth Valley:Horton Peak named for William (Bill) Horton, the first Forest Ranger at the Pole Creek ranger station . . . there in about 1909 or 10.

Clarke's Hot Springs, first called White's Hot Springs according to a few oldtimers, but changed to Clarke's Hot Springs when David Clarke located there and homesteaded the first ranch in the Valley.

Fisher Creek, named for Frank Fisher who located a mine on the headwaters of this creek, and later homesteaded in the Valley.

Decker Flat, Decker Creek, and Decker Mountain, located south and a bit west of where Obsidian is now, were all named for Ray Decker who lived in the mining town of Custer on the Yankee Fork at one time. He built a cabin and lived on Decker Flat with his family before 1900.

Williams Creek, named for Tom Williams who homesteaded on this creek.

McDonald Peak and McDonald Lake, named for James McDonald, early landowner in the Pettit Lake area.

Horstman Peak, named for Berrhard Deiderich (Dick) Horstman, a German and one of the early bachelors in the Valley.

In the Stanley Basin:

Quite generally known, the Basin itself, the two towns of Stanley, Stanley Creek, and Stanley Lake were all named for Captain John Stanley, oldest member of the first prospecting party to enter the Basin in 1863.

McGown Peak, McGown Creek, and McGown Lake . . . named for the McGown brothers, George and Arthur Sr. Both were in the area before 1900.

Thompson Peak and Thompson Creek ... named for John Thompson, one of the first ranchers and homesteaders in the Stanley Basin.

Tennell Creek ... named for Sam Tennell who filed on land along this creek.

Kelly Creek and Kelly Lake ... thought to be named for Tom Kelly, a miner and trapper, and the first person to be buried in the Stanley cemetery.

Job Creek ... named for Wallin Job, one of the first Forest Rangers in the Stanley District.

Laidlow and Vader Creeks ... both named for sheepmen who ranged sheep in the area.

Marshall Lake ... named for one of the first miners and the man who operated the first mercantile store in Lower Stanley ... Herbert Marshall.

Langer Peak ... first called Ruffneck Peak, but re-named Langer Peak in honor of Charley Langer, well thought of Forest Ranger in the Stanley District who was killed in a plane crash on this mountain in 1943.

LAKES, STREAMS AND FISH

Within the realms of the Stanley-Sawtooth country, the Sawtooth Mountain Range cradles numerous jewel-like lakes in its high recesses and at the bases of its slopes. Big Redfish Lake, one of the most popular in the Sawtooth Valley today, located in the shadows of cathedra Mount Heyburn ... elevation 10,229 feet, covers 380 acres and is approximately seven

Big Redfish Lake.

miles long and three miles wide in size. In recent years its shoreline has become dotted with boat docks and pine-shaded picnic and campgrounds. This lake, regarded as a "Fisherman's Paradise," and the Little Redfish Lake located in the vicinity and covering 40 acres, is the home of the landlocked salmon, called "Red Fish" by the Indians and early trappers.

In the beginning, the Indians and trappers, followed by other trappers and prospectors, miners and first settlers, all found these fish an excellent source of much needed food. The Williams brothers, Dave and Tom, told of how great the salmon runs were in 1900 when they first came to the Stanley-Sawtooth country. Dave's son, Ted, said, "Dad said the salmon were so thick, when we started to ford the Salmon River (there were no bridges then), we had to throw rocks at the fish to make them move off the gravel and out of the way before we could get the horses to enter the water."

Early settlers especially looked forward to the annual runs made by the chinook and sockeye salmon to their place of birth in the headwaters of the Salmon River, where they would spawn and die. Week long camping trips were made to catch these fish. If large catches were made, the fish were shared with neighbors and friends. When the catch was exceptionally large, the surplus was preserved by salting or smoking and was stored for winter.

The day's catch of salmon caught near Cape Horn in the early 1900s. Left to right . . . Clyde Driscoll, Mrs. Alice Olsen, Mae Rose, Savilla Driscoll, and William Rose.

Native trout also abounded at that time in the many sparkling streams in the region. A picture taken by Bennett S. Brown, photographer and outdoorsman of Challis, and printed in the *Challis Messenger* of November 1907, showed the outlet of Redfish Lake. Mr. Brown had stated that as many as 200 speckled trout had been taken from this stream by one fisherman in one hour's time.

For many years there was no limit on catching fish in these waters, even though the Idaho Fish and Game Department was created when Idaho was made a Territory in 1863. No season was put on fishing in Idaho until 1899... nine years after Idaho became a state. Even so, in the sparsely populated Stanley-Sawtooth country, little or nothing was done to enforce that law. In 1903, the Idaho Legislature adopted a license law requiring a fee of $1 for fishing and hunting in the state, but even then nothing of consequence was done in the Sawtooth Mountain region to enforce the law. As a result, by the early Twenties a great many of the game fish were all but depleted from these lakes and streams, not only in this region, but in most sections of Idaho.

Noting this, fish and game officials and district foresters became alarmed, and with the help of local residents, a system of planting fish was started. In the Sawtooth region, first to be planted was the waters of Big Redfish Lake. *The Challis Messenger Newspaper* carried an item in its April 6, 1921 issue reading, "This beautiful lake should be excellent fishing waters, but at the present time contains principally squaw fish, white fish, and red fish, none of which provide sport for the rod fisherman. It is proposed to close fishing in the lake inlets where the new fish are now planted, and it is hoped that the excellent game fish will become established there."

As time went on, other items of interest on the subject appeared in the *Messenger*. One in September 23, 1925 issue read, "Six of the larger lakes in the Stanley Basin and Sawtooth Valley were heavily planted with many varieties of salmon and trout. They were hauled by truck, packed by horse and by man. Lakes planted were Alturas, Big Redfish, Pettit, Hell Roaring, Yellowbelly, and Stanley Lake."

The main fish planted in these waters at first were the Dolly Varden and the Rainbow Trout. A little later the Kokonee and a few California Golden were introduced into the lakes. In August 1934, an item in the *Messenger* read, "Ranger Markle and L.H. Garner, with the assistance of Stanley residents, completed planting 100,000 fingerling fish in the lakes and streams in the Stanley Basin and Sawtooth Valley areas." Then in an August 1935 issue of the *Messenger* a catch of

California Golden was noted. The item read, "Fish planted by A.D. Kelley and others are being caught in the high mountain lakes of the Stanley area. These fish are the California Golden."

Eventually, as the number of fishermen increased in the region, more and more fish had to be planted. The procedure did prove successful, and as far back as the Twenties had become routine for the area. Also, laws on season and limit were put into effect and enforced by game wardens hired by the Idaho Fish and Game Department. Now, although the native trout no longer exist in these waters, one can catch his limit of game fish almost any time during the fishing season set for the locale.

Alturas Lake, mentioned in one of the *Messenger* items, is the largest of the Sawtooth lakes. Covering 480 acres, its principal fish is the Sockeye Salmon, while little Pettit Lake, covering 20 acres, stocks mainly Kokonee and Rainbow trout.

Stanley Lake, in the Basin and covering 125 acres, is about one and a half miles wide and two miles long. Equally as beautiful as any of the other lakes in the region, its fish are mainly Kokonee and Rainbow . . . like Pettit Lake.

According to authorities, fish planted in all these waters find an exacting environment for their production and growth because of the high elevation here. As one writer explains it, "As winter nears, these lakes take several deep breaths, and with the winds turning and mixing the warm surface waters with the colder temperatures of the lower depths, it equalizes the water's density and viscosity. Then once nature has completed this process, the lakes become ice-sealed for their winter stagnation period. In the spring, the process goes into reverse."

For those who see these mountain lakes only in the summertime and marvel at their mirror-like beauty and tranquillity on a still day, they would marvel more so to behold the magic of winter's hand here. Like an artist, he dresses the majestic peaks and stately pines in the miracle of snow. He quiets the land throughout the region. He freezes the surface of the lakes solid, and then without warning breaks the silence with the songs of keening winds. When temperatures drop to marks below zero and the winds lull to soft whispers, another sound rends the fresh cleanness of the atmosphere. This is the loud booming of the ice on the lakes popping and cracking. Oldtimers who lived there in the early days describe it as being like

Snow scene in Challis National Forest.

"The report of a powerful gun that echoes and resounds across the Basin and the Valley floors."

While winter here often imposed hardships on these early residents, hardly one among them would be willing to trade his or her experience of living the year around in the country. One woman said, "You bet it could be plenty rough in the wintertime here without the modern conveniences of today, but if it were possible, I'd go right back and do it all over again. You see, we had good times then too, and life was so much more simple for us in the Sawtooth country then than it is now."

EARLY PROMOTIONS AND PROPOSALS

As far back as 1900, long before the Stanley-Sawtooth country was surveyed and opened to homesteaders, different writers attempted to promote the virtues of the region. With the exception of miners and prospectors, a few trappers and one or two families scattered around the Basin and Valley floors as inhabitants of the area, some parts had yet to feel the footsteps of the white man. In time, if they were still living there and desired, individuals were allowed to present land claims under the "Squatter's Rights" law.

Until that time this scenic, rugged land remained for the most part a virgin wilderness still untouched, its resources intact and its silence broken only by the wind and the voices of the birds and animals. Of the sections they had beheld here, those who came and saw, hardly without exception, fell in love with the scenic wild beauty, and although they were quite aware of how long the winters could be and how bitterly cold they could become, they were also aware of the land's vast potential. Many were wont to sing its praises, and if there were writers and poets among these people, somehow their words found a way into print, sometimes in a magazine, but more often than not in a newspaper.

Nearest to the region was *The Silver Messenger Newspaper* printed at Challis, county seat of Custer County in which the Stanley Basin and part of the Sawtooth Valley are located. One of the first articles to appear in the *Messenger* was primarily on Custer County as a whole, but while intent on pointing out its many advantages, noted the profound beauty of the Sawtooth Mountain Range and the area's great potential.

Another article in the *Messenger* in 1904 read under the heading, STANLEY BASIN, "One of the most picturesque valleys in all Idaho is the Stanley Basin. About 15 miles long and from 3 to 4 miles wide, the valley is traversed by a good

Picturesque scene in the Stanley Basin.

sized stream called Valley Creek. The valley proper is one vast meadow of wild grass growing luxuriantly, and grazing is one of the main industries. Mountains surrounding the valley are thickly timbered with red and yellow fir, spruce, and white pine trees. The Stanley Basin is the center of a highly mineralized section."

Other items sometimes appeared in the news section of the *Messenger,* noting proposals that the Sawtooth region be made into a National Park. The March 12, 1912 issue carried two such items. The first read; "An effort is being made by the people of Boise to get the Government to form a National Park, taking in Redfish Lake, Pettit Lake, and all the other lakes and rivers in the Sawtooth Mountains. There is no grander natural scenery in the world than in the Sawtooths, and it should be reserved as a park." The second item said, "Bennett S. Brown, photographer and collector of ore specimens, Indian relics and other artifacts has mentioned that in his opinion the Sawtooth Mountain area should certainly be preserved as a park."

And so it went. The July 29, 1936 issue stated, "R.G. Cole of Boise, President of the Idaho State Automobile Association and the Idaho Wildlife Federation, urges forming a National Park of the Stanley Basin."

This was followed by an article opposing the park in the September 2, 1936 issue and reading: "The delegation sent to

Boise from Custer County go on record as being opposed to a National Park for the Stanley Basin and Sawtooth area. The delegation was made up of M.L. Drake, E.J. Micheal, A.D. Kelley, Andrew Gini, and A.V. Larter . . . all prominent men in Custer County, along with Forest Supervisor, E.E. McKee and Ranger, Merle Markle."

In his *Idaho Guide Book,* Vardis Fisher, late well-known author, wrote, "Idaho has two resources which can make her rich for many years to come, her phosphate beds and her natural scenery." The *Messenger* carried an announcement of the book's publication in its January 13, 1937 issue, and in ending the item stated: "Fisher says the Sawtooths should be preserved as a National Park."

Through the years, there were many people who were for and against making the region into a National Park. Even today, and since it is now included in the Sawtooth National Recreational Area, the subject continues to come up for discussion. Just what the future of the Stanley-Sawtooth country will be remains to be seen.

BIRDS AND GAME

The first trappers and Indians found the Stanley-Sawtooth country abounding with fish, birds, and game . . . large and small. This was still true when the first prospectors, miners, later trappers, and the first settlers came to the region. In fact, had it not been for the bounties nature provided here, many would have gone hungry in the early days because in this isolated area, with or without money, commercial food supplies were hard to come by. Several of the different oldtimers have told how they often depended on a catch of fish, sage and fool hens, mountain grouse, deer, and if they could take the time to hunt the peaks of the Sawtooths, mountain sheep and goats.

In her diary kept while living in the Stanley Basin from 1890 to 1895, Della McGown wrote, "I sometimes take the children and ride the horse up to the timber after fool hens. They are pretty chickens . . . not as big as sage hens, and have red ears. Fool hen is a good name for them, for they will sit on a limb of a pine tree and I can ride my horse under the tree and knock them off with a stick. If I miss the first time, they just move over a little and let me try again. They haven't got the sense to fly away. I hate to kill them, but they do make good eating for us." She goes on to tell that the fool hen is different from the big gray birds the miners call "camprobbers."

In Mrs. McGown's reference to fool hens, she is speaking of the Franklin Grouse so common in the Stanley country. The so called camprobbers are actually the "Gray Jay" and sometimes confused with the "Clark's Nutcracker" if not closely observed. A wide variety of bird species habit the Stanley-Sawtooth country, all too numerous to mention . . . from the tiniest hummingbird to the largest of the crane family. In recent years "Tarsi," the Great Sandhill Crane especially, has found a sanctuary for its kind here. Gathered in groups in the marshes alongside State Highway 21 during the mating season in June,

83

its clownish antics are a sight to behold. This huge fellow leaps, bounds, hops up and down, flapping and spreading its mighty wings, giving out with a triumphant, shrill rolling, "garoo-a-aa-a" that can be heard for a mile or more. Its voice is as much a part of this country as the lonely wail of the coyote calling to its mate from a hillside, or the spine-tingling bugle of a bull elk deep in the timber in the fall rutting season.

Deer herds have always been common in the Stanley-Sawtooth area. Out of season, even today, small, and sometimes large herds, can be spotted from the roads as they graze in the meadows and foothills. Mountain sheep and goats were also hunted by the pioneer when he afforded the time and gear for the rough climbing in the Sawtooth heights where the animals are known to range. In those years, the head of a Bighorn Ram was just as highly prized as a trophy as it is today.

Dave and Carrie Williams on a mountain goat hunting expedition in the early 1920s.

Cougar, generally called the Mountain Lion, once roamed the region at will, particularily in the Sawtooth Valley. Early stockmen and ranchers found them an animal to be wary of at all times where sheep and cattle were concerned. Being both a predator and an opportunist, the cougar has always been known to stalk and kill whatever prey it can find when it is hungry. As a rule, this excludes man, but not always as various individuals will attest. A magnificent animal, the cougar is graceful and lithe with muscles like a coiled spring. Authorities say it has been known to leap onto the back of a large elk and sever its jugular vein in a matter of seconds. Too, it has been known to stalk and harass man in many ways.

In 1910, A.F. Kavanaugh, resident of Stanley, who was doing some trapping that winter in the Basin told how he was outwitted by a mountain lion. Seems his catches were disappearing from his traps regularly, and finding the big cat's tracks and other evidence at the scene, Kavanaugh decided to set a special trap for the thief. One day he caught what he believed to be the best bait, put it in a sack, and took it to his cabin with the intentions of setting his "special trap" the next day. However, during the night the cougar came to the cabin, and scenting the bait, took sack and all and had a feast half a mile away down the trail. When Mr. K. found the empty sack the next morning, he said he had a feeling he was dealing with a shrewd, big cat endowed with more than normal instinct. M.M. Sweet, editor of the Challis Newspaper, repeated the story in the *Silver Messenger* that spring.

Many strange stories are told of the cougar's stealth . . . some true and some perhaps not. One is told concerning the disappearance of a baby belonging to a family who lived on Decker Flat in the Sawtooth Valley before 1900. As the story goes, the mother placed the baby in a highchair and set it outside in the fresh air and sunshine while she went about doing her chores. Going to check on the baby a short time later . . . the baby was gone! Visible around the highchair, large cat tracks could be seen. The mother had heard no outcry from the baby. A search was organized but the baby was never found. Finally, it was concluded the baby had been stolen by a mountain lion prowling the locale.

Early settlers noted the presence of "numerous bears" in the Stanley Basin and Sawtooth Valley. Later trappers and miners also told of many black bears and of seeing a grizzly on occasions. As the cattlemen and sheep herders came into the country, they found the bears a nusiance around their herds and flocks. Trappers trapped and killed them frequently as the bears became listed as predators, and later regular hunters were brought in by the government to lessen the number.

An item in the 1964 issue of *The Hunting and Fishing Guide* read, "Years ago, in the Sawtooth Valley, the biggest grizzly ever to be captured alive was trapped near Sawtooth City. Branded as a cattle killer, ranchers in the valley called him

"Sawtooth Jack." Old Jack weighed a half ton, and was such a monster, he was taken to New Orleans to an Exposition going on there at the time. But Old Jack soon became so mean, for the safety of visitors, he had to be removed from the grounds."

Bears were numerous during the early days in the Stanley-Sawtooth Country.

In 1890, when she first arrived to live in the Stanley Basin, Della McGown first lived in a crude cabin built previously by her husband, Arthur McGown Sr. In her diary she told of going by wagon to Sawtooth City in the Valley to get doors, windows and lumber to build a new cabin. "We were pretty tired when we got back home," she wrote. "It was such a long, tiresome trip, we went to bed without washing the dishes and went right to sleep. In the night I was awakened by something rattling the dishes. At first I thought it was one of the kids, but as I listened I heard a grunt, and then I knew we had a bear in the cabin. I punched Arthur. Our bed was made of poles with a straw tick over them, and as he started to jump up to grab his gun one of his legs went through between the poles. He let out a yell loud enough to wake the dead, and I don't know who was the scaredest . . . Arthur or that bear! When the bear went through the door where we had hung a blanket over the opening, he was going so hard and fast, he tore the blanket loose, catching it over his head, and went tearing out across the meadow. In the moonlight, the last we saw of him, the blanket was flying in the wind behind him, and the next day we found what was left of it about a mile from our cabin."

A favorite pastime of most of the oldtimers in the wintertime was to gather around the stove in the general store, trade stories and tell tall tales. The Leslie Niece store at Lower Stanley, and later at Upper Stanley, was a favorite gathering place in the Teens and early Twenties. His daughter, Edna Niece McGown recalls the events plainly. Sometimes the subject ranged on bear "Tales." She remembers one evening in particular when a group was sitting around the old wood stove, she being about 9 or 10 years old at the time, her father allowed her to sit on his lap and listen. The men told one intriguing story after another, all true according to the tellers.

Taken inside L.S. Niece store at Lower Stanley (1916). Left to right . . . Dave Williams, Carl Auchenbaugh, David Driskell, Herman Meissner, Hayden Brewer, Claude Gillispie, Preston Shaw, Clyde Gillispie, and Ralph Kyte sitting in front of David Driskell.

One man, a game warden named Apgar, after listening to the others awhile said, "You know fellows, I had the darndest thing happen to me one day in the mountains back of Robinson Bar. Well, you know that's pretty good bear country. So there I was when I spotted this big black bear just standing there like he was waiting for something. He saw me about the same time I saw him, and before I had time to load my gun he came charging straight at me. I threw that gun down and headed for the nearest, tallest tree I could see with the bear close on my heels. I started to climb, but when I looked down over my shoulder that bear was climbing up behind me, his ugly teeth bared. Man, I was so scared I went right on climbing as fast as I could. Suddenly I realized where I was . . . yep, I was fifty feet above the top of that tree and still climbing." It was unanimously agreed by the group around the stove, that Apgar's story was the "tall tale" of the evening.

Ted Williams remembers that his dad (Dave Williams) used to tell about how the bears would come down to the Salmon River in the Sawtooth Valley during the salmon runs in 1900. Bears were so numerous, when the miners from the mining towns of Vienna and Sawtooth City wanted to take a wagon with barrels and salt to catch the salmon for part of their winter's food supply, they found it necessary to carry guns for protection.

Always open season on bear in Idaho until recent years, bears killed and trapped in the Stanley-Sawtooth country displayed by hunters and trappers were not unusual. Naturally they were proud of the animal and their luck in bagging one. Tom Chivers, a cattleman in the area, is credited with killing a large bear in 1943. Nellie Clark Fisher tells of a government hunter bringing a huge grizzly to the postoffice at Obsidian for her to see in 1946. "Being postmistress there at the time, I was busy inside the post office when he yelled through the door for me to come out and see his bear," she said. "When I finished with the mail I went out to his old car. It smelled of bear, the hunter smelled of bear, and the big beast inside the car simply reeked of the bear odor."

Throughout the years, to see bears in any part of Central Idaho has been commonplace. In late years, now and then, especially when the salmon are running, or the wildberries are ripe, and the camas bulbs (the blue Camas Lilly) are prime, bears can be seen on a shaley mountainside, or in a clearing near the timber. In fact, bears were not just numerous in the Stanley-Sawtooth country in the early days as so noted by the early trappers, but also in the valley to the west of the Basin . . . hence the name "Bear Valley." Yes, bears were there in great numbers, and still are to some extent.

TRAPPERS AND TRAPPING

While Hudson Bay trappers found beaver trapping to be a profitable occupation, later trappers found trapping of most fur-bearing animals a way to make a fair living. In the Stanley-Sawtooth country, a number of oldtimers — ones like Trapper Fisher, Tom Williams, Trapper Green, Tom Kelly and a few others, followed the trade as a profession. Other residents turned to trapping on occasion as a way to supplement their incomes. Many were miners and homesteaders in the Basin and the Valley. Prices for prime pelts were good in those early days. Also, for many years a bounty was paid on different predators. In late years, re-classification of the cougar and black bear as game animals has triggered heated arguments among ranchers, stockmen, ecologists, sportsmen, and wildlife people.

Trapping during the early days, however, was a different matter. Although Territorial laws stated in part, "It shall be unlawful to kill game animals between February 1st and July 1st," the law was too vague, and the handful of men who comprised the Idaho Fish and Game Department, created at the time the law was made, had a vast territory, still mostly wild and unsettled, to cover. Thus no season or limits on fish and game actually existed in the Stanley-Sawtooth country for many years. In 1903, the Idaho Legislature finally adopted a license law with a fee of $1 for residents. Nevertheless, Charles H. Arbuckle, Idaho's first game warden, found it impossible to find deputy-wardens in Custer County. It was only after the Challis National Forest came into being and mapped out a plan for grazing and watershed management, that the Fish and Game Department was able to enforce any restrictions on hunting and fishing in the region.

Yet the early pioneers and miners and trappers here did not waste fish and game. On the contrary, it was their food and oftentimes their livelihood, as was the case with the trapper.

To him it was not only a way to make a buck to buy clothes for his back and needed supplies, it also put food on his table and gave him a way of life he came to love. To him trapping was a form of art learned through experience and persistent practice. The type of traps he used, the way the traps were set, where and with what bait, made a difference. Even the way the skinning was done and how the hides were stretched were factors.

The best trapping season extended from October to March or early April while the fur was prime. For the trapper who set out to really make money, late September and October were busy months indeed. Traps had to be cleaned and repairs made if needed. Stretching boards had to be made and in readiness. Scent had to be made, and last but not least, time had to be taken to scout for likely trapping places in the mountains. Traps favored most in the early days were the Victor or the Newhouse, in sizes #1, #2, and #3. Each trapper had his own special method when he set his traps, and true to human nature, each one swore his method was the best.

Many of the trappers established camps or a shelter of sort along their trapline routes. His shelters were stocked with the barest of necessities including a can or heavy box to hold rations of dried fruit, jerky, crackers or hardtack, coffee, and matches. An empty can in which to brew coffee, a blanket and a pile of dry wood were musts. Generally the shelter composed a three-sided affair made with poles and covered with brush, but sometimes a small cave in the rocks could be found and utilized. In all cases stones were placed in a circle for a campfire near the open side of the shelter.

Tom Kelly's design for his shelters, referred to as his "cabins," became a kind of trademark for him. He would cut trees about 16 or 18 inches in diameter, notching the logs to fit together to form a triangle, but with one point left to form about a three foot opening. These cabins would not be more than three logs high with no window and covered over with poles and brush to make a roof. Being low on the ground, Tom would have to crawl into his cabin, but they kept him dry and warm when out running his traplines and caught in bad snowstorms. Tom's favorite locales for trapping were at the head of Elk Creek, along Stanley Creek, and remote parts of the Basin Creek terrain. For many years people who had known Tom would come across one of these shelters in different places, and would know that Tom had been there by the way the shelter was constructed.

A few days after everything was in readiness and the trap-lines were out the trapper began making his rounds, catching mink, marten, weasel, fox, beaver, muskrat, badger, and coyotes. Occasionally he would catch an otter. Different size traps and different sets and bait had to be used for each of the different animals. For example, the mink is a rambler, following the banks of streams in search of food. A water set is best for it, usually just at the waters edge and baited with fowl or fish brushed with a little scent. Beaver and muskrat were trapped much in the same way, although a size one trap was used for mink, and it was necessary to use a size three trap for beaver. Being strong fellows, if a wrong size trap is used, these animals can pull themselves free. To be sure, the trap must be concealed in the runways, dens, or stream banks, and the trapper must wear boots and stay in the water while setting the traps, leaving no sign when he is done.

Oldtimers say the marten was one of the easiest animals to catch, and having one of the nicest furs, if properly skinned and cared for, brought a good price. These animals were trapped in the timber with the trap (size #2) set beneath the roots of a tree or in a sheltered spot under a fallen log. The best bait for them seemed to be a scent made by cutting fish into pieces and placing it in a jar until an oil formed on top.

Trappers in the Basin and the Valley found the fox one of the more difficult animals to catch. A sly, wily animal, he roamed the countryside from late afternoon through the night searching for his food. Like the coyote, the fox is a meat eater, and the trapper often used the carcass of a dead cow or horse placed on some high point to attract the animal to his sets. Ranchers in the area were sometimes bothered with both fox and coyotes around their corrals and chicken houses. When one was spotted here, he could sometimes be caught by placing a dead chicken in a conspicuous place along a near-by trail and setting traps around it. Some even used a bit of chicken manure scattered in the area to camouflage the human scent.

Tom Kelly was known to be exceptionally good at trapping fox. Items appeared in the *Challis Silver Messenger* about him and other trappers from time to time through the years. One in December 1912 read. "Tom Kelly has started his trapping season off with a catch of a beautiful silver gray fox." Another item in the May 3, 1922 issue said, "C.E. Way and L.E. Hawkins were in Stanley from their trap lines on Elk Creek. They are pulling in their lines and camps now; marking the end of a

91

strenous and profitable season for the two men."

According to Rupert Niece, who himself trapped on occasion in the Stanley Basin, Tom Kelly and Trapper (Henry C.) Fisher were the "only real trappers that ever hit the country." The others were more or less amateurs that caught fur if they were lucky. Many tried and some did fairly well, and certainly it was a way to make a few extra bucks. Barney and Webb Lanier, Bud Critchfield, Ted Williams, William Rose and "Dutch" Charley Roschling numbered among the "others." Women and young boys would set a few traps close to Upper and Lower Stanley on occasion. In fact, not many people who lived in the Basin and Valley in the early days failed to try their hand at trapping. Rupert said, "Two of the fur houses I recall that we shipped fur to were the Prowety Fur Company and Mass and Steffan Company, both in St. Louis, Missouri."

Charley Rochling "Dutch Charley," with Faith, Hope, and Charity.

Trapper Fisher was a professional, coming to the Stanley country first as a government trapper and hunter. Everyone loved him. For his story see under the heading, "Ragtime Fiddler, 'Trapper' Fisher." As a trapper, oldtimers said he could catch fur where no one else could.

In any case, a trapper earned his money no matter who he was. After learning to employ the right technique to catch his fur, how he handled the fur made a great difference in the price he would be paid for it. Much care had to be exercised when skinning the animal in order not to cut the hide, break off the tail, feet or ears. The hides then had to be stretched on boards to fit the shape, although beaver were stretched on round hoops. The boards had to be tapered at one end to a blunt point and all edges of the board sanded smooth. This enabled the trapper to slide the board inside the hide with the rounded end at the nose of the animal, leaving the back to be pulled taut and tacked to the board. After the stretching was completed, with the fur side next to the board, any bits of flesh and residue were carefully removed before the skin was set to dry. When this was done, it was checked regularly, and when almost dry, the board was removed, the skin turned fur side out, and laid in readiness for shipping.

Fur companies paid for pelts according to species and condition, prices ranging in keeping with the times. Beaver, marten, muskrat, and mink generally brought a fair price, but fox brought the highest. For example, a silver fox in prime condition and well cared for by the trapper was known to bring as much as $150 in the early Forties. Beaver and muskrat brought as much as $9 and $10 each in the Thirties.

On the predator list, coyote prices continued more or less stable through the years. Reports from the Seattle, Washington Fur Exchange showed a going price of $17 each for pelts in good condition in the year 1973. Mountain lion and black bears

Bear caught in trap by Trapper Fisher near Upper Stanley. (May 1924)

usually brought good prices. Generally hunted by government hunters, when complaints were made by stockmen and ranchers, other trappers and hunters sometimes went to the aid of sheep and cattlemen in the Stanley-Sawtooth region. Considered both a pest and a menace by these men, any of them would tell you that a black bear can go berserk in a band of sheep and do considerable damage, while young calves are always prey for this marauder when he goes on the prowl. The same was said to be true of the mountain lion.

The golden eagle was looked on as a predator for many years in all regions of Central Idaho, and still is by various stockmen in some sections of Idaho as well as other western states. Although opposed by wildlife people and ecologists today, Charley (Emil) Grandjean, one of the first trappers in the Stanley Basin, and who later became Supervisor of the Boise National Forest, once wrote in detail how destructive golden eagles could be. "In the Sawtooths I have seen eagles destroy many bighorn sheep and goats and even fully mature, healthy deer," he wrote. "The attack was very similar each time. The eagle strikes on the back of the head and neck, and thereby frightens the animal; then the eagle continues to strike until the animal is overcome and prostrate."

Bounties were also paid on crows and magpies in the early days. In 1926, the Idaho State Game Warden reported four crow heads taken, 1,738 magpies killed and 8,478 magpie eggs destroyed in the state. Bounties on the birds were one and a half cents each and one cent on each egg. His report included the destruction of 25 eagles, which he said he "reported with pleasure since these birds are one of our greatest menaces to the young mountain sheep and goats." (end of quote).

Oldtimers in the Stanley-Sawtooth country looking back today say, "Yes, hunting and fishing was really something here in the old days, but the trapping our folks did was the greatest of all."

CATTLE GRAZING

Cattlemen were attracted by the heavy stands of lush grasses growing in the Stanley Basin several years before settlers came and a wagon road was built. Thomas Beech was first, ranging a herd of dairy cattle there in the summers of 1881 and 1882. He packed milk and butter over the narrow trail into the Yankee Fork Mining District where he found a ready market at the towns of Custer and Bonanza. As it turned out, Beech's cows failed to thrive the way he had hoped, proving his venture to be unsuccessful.

With beef cattle it was a different matter, as George McGowan soon learned when he began trailing herds to range in the Basin in the late Eighties. These animals grew fat on the Basin's grasses, and when butchered, were sold to miners throughout the region. In 1890, when George's brother, Arthur Sr. moved with his family to operate a stopping place and postoffice for the miners in the Basin, he butchered and delivered beef for George while living there. Every spring, around June 1st, George made the drive from his ranch about three miles east of Challis, up the Salmon River, turned and went up East Fork over to the Germania Basin, then over a narrow pass down into Sawtooth Valley and on to Stanley Basin . . . returning by the same route at roundup time in the fall. After construction of the wagon road from the mouth of Yankee Fork up the Salmon River to the Basin in 1894, the cattle drives were made with more ease and in less time. George McGowan continued to range cattle in the Basin every summer up until the time of his death, September 3, 1903.

Other cattlemen soon followed George McGowan's move to range cattle in the Stanley Basin. The Chivers, George Thompson Jr., and the Ginis were all early cattlemen in the country. The Chivers operation was begun by Tom Chivers Sr. who had been a freighter between Blackfoot and Challis before 1900.

95

Roundup in the Stanley Basin in the 1920s. Roy Chivers on first horse.

After buying land and starting a ranch on the Salmon River, about five miles northeast of Challis, he gradually built up a herd and began ranging cattle in the Basin in 1910. Beginning with his three sons, William, Roy, and Melvin, the Chivers cattle business developed into a family affair, still carried on today by Tom and John, twin sons of Bill Chivers. By starting out at an early age to help their father and Uncle Roy, Tom and John, grandsons of Tom Chivers Sr., both grew up knowing the cattle business from A to Z.

The Piva enterprises were started by Pete Piva from Italy who located a ranch below the mouth of Bayhorse Creek on the Salmon River during the early Teens. Pete and Mrs. Piva had six children ... Lena, Marion, Piero, Bruno, Ruby, and Margaret. Pete began ranging cattle in the Basin in the Forties. In 1928, when he was offered a good price for his herd, he sold all but twenty head and bought a flock of sheep. However, by continuously trading young steers for heifers, by 1941 his herd had increased again, and he sold the sheep in favor of the cattle business. About that time he secured a range right in the Stanley Basin through a trade with Loren Wilson, a Pahsimeroi Valley rancher, while a year before he had purchased the Peters property in the Basin. Then in 1950, the Pivas became the owners of the old Benner ranch and hotel property owned at the time of the sale by Dan Kavanaugh. In addition to this land, they also bought an adjoining 600 acres from the State, including a low bench on the outskirts of Upper Stanley which the family leases for an airstrip.

When age overcame their father, Pete Piva, the sons, Marion, Piero, and Bruno, carried on, with Piero acting as manager

96

in the Stanley area. These boys, like the Chivers boys, grew up in the cattle business. In an interview Piero said when they bought the property in the Basin from Kavanaugh, still called "the Benner place" by some, they tore down the old hotel and used the logs and lumber to build themselves a house in Upper Stanley. In telling about the cattle drives they made to and from the Basin in the Forties, Piero went on to say, "That was while Mac Mckee was the Forest Supervisor, just awhile before he retired. Mac was an oldtime ranger and a fine man. In those days a rancher could get a temporary permit for five years, and if he was still there at the end of that period, the permit could be made permanent. Mac was the one who fixed us up."

In connection with the permits to which Piero referred, Tom Chivers recalled that their permit allowed them to graze about 465 head of cattle in the Basin during the Thirties and Forties. If they had more than that, they were issued a temporary permit for a short time for the number exceeding their allotment of the 465 head. Here it is interesting to note the contrast of fees paid by cattlemen to the Forest Service in early days and now. In 1914, for example, the fee was 26 cents per head for a five month period, and 1974 it was $6 per head. Also, up until 1940, cattlemen trailed their beef cattle out of the Basin over Galena Summit to the railhead at Ketchum for shipment.

Beef cattle being trailed to Ketchum for shipping to market. Picture taken at Salmon River bridge southeast of Stanley in the 1930s.

After Highway 93 was completed, officials began to maintain that cattle should no longer be trailed up and down the Salmon River between Challis and Stanley Basin, saying "it was much too dangerous." As a result, they finally came up with the idea of constructing a large pole corral near Casino Creek on the Salmon River, finished in 1974. This was done for the purpose of holding cattle at roundup time in the fall until they could be loaded and trucked to their winter feeding grounds in the Challis area.

To be sure, an accident while on a cattle drive along the river was always a possibility . . . one hit by a speeding car on one of the sharp curves was always a danger, or a cow making a misstep while wandering up a steep rocky bank, causing it to roll onto the road or into the river. Yet as far as is known, this seldom happened except while the highway was under construction when the Chivers and Gini brothers lost 25 head of cattle over a steep grade while making the drive down the river in late October 1935. The *Challis Messenger* reported 15 head of the cattle were killed outright and the other 10 so badly injured that they had to be killed.

Now it seems cattle drives along this stretch of highway are almost a thing of the past. Piero Piva said he could remember at one time the cattle were trailed along the old gravel road

Trailing cattle up Salmon River before Highway 93 was built. Picture taken just below Clayton, Idaho.

across Salmon River from where Highway 93 is now. "That was before, and while the highway was under construction," he recalled. "The road, beginning above Clayton and up to just below Sunbeam Dam, used to be a part of the first road along the river, and went past Robinson Bar Ranch. But, of course, after the highway was finished we used the new road in making the cattle drives."

Things are changing in other ways too in the cattle business. Tom Chivers says they often hire helicopters now to search for strays in the high country at roundup time, especially in case of unpredicted snow storms in early fall. He told about fourteen head of cattle caught by one of these storms a few years back, and said that after spotting the cattle from the helicopter it took men on horseback several days to break trail through the snow to bring them down out of the mountains.

Tom Chivers ... cattleman.

In earlier days, cattle losses were incurred in more ways than one, and still are to some extent. Aside from storm factors at roundup time and accidents, to keep alert for rustlers is another facet of the cattle business. And of course, cows are forever becoming separated from their calves, called "mismothering" by Piero Piva. In this case, a cow has been known to bawl and wander for miles in search of her off-spring. On a drive, cattle are inclined to lag, and sometimes a rider would have to go back as many as fifteen miles to push the stragglers up with the main herd. In years gone by, a big drive could take

99

Chivers cattle trailing down Highway 93 ... fall of 1973.

as long as ten days to make one way between Challis and the Stanley Basin, and was an event looked forward to by the younger members of the Chivers and Piva families. Working in hand with other cattlemen in the area, the drive has been known to include as many as 3,000 head of cattle, requiring some fifteen riders to keep them together and moving along the road.

In working with cattle, dogs have always been as important as when working with sheep, and hardly a rancher in the Basin or along the Salmon River are without two or three good stock dogs around their ranches. Like the sheep dogs, if a cattle dog was well trained and would act on command the way one owned by Roy Chivers did, such a dog was of great help on a drive. "Roy's dog was so dependable," Tom Chivers recalled, "when we bedded the cattle down on a flat in the evening, Roy would station "Bing" ... that was the dog's name ... at a narrow defile below the bedding ground and say, 'now hold 'em Bing', and the dog would. Roy could go to bed and sleep all night and the next morning Bing hadn't allowed a single cow to stray."

As already mentioned, Tom and John Chivers started out in the cattle business at an early age. Bob Piva, son of Piero and Mabel Piva, is another. He began riding on the cattle drives when he was five years old, cutting quite a figure astride a big black horse and wearing a black cowboy hat turned up in front

100

in pirate fashion. As the drive progressed along the road, Bob's size and attire attracted much attention from tourists driving along the highway. When he complained to his father, Piero told him the next time anyone made a comment to him, if the person happened to be a woman, to say, "Hi ya Babe!" and keep on riding. The very next day while the youngster was riding down the road on his horse, an attractive young woman pulled up beside him, and sticking her head out the car window, said, "You're the cutest little cowboy I've ever seen." Bob looked at her with his dark flashing eyes, and without cracking a smile, said, "Hi ya Babe"! just as Piero had instructed him to, then rode nonchalantly off down the road.

Now the cattle business appears to be reaching new dimensions. Much of the color and glamour as applied to its various segments in the past has faded from the scene. We call it progress. Nevertheless, whether trucked or trailed in, hun-

Cattle grazing on the meadows of Stanley Basin. Fence is the "buck fence" type commonly built by early settlers.

dreds of cattle can still be seen grazing on the broad grassy meadows in the Stanley Basin and Sawtooth Valley. To a cattle rancher the picture is the ultimate of beauty no artist can duplicate. When Piero and his wife, Mabel McGowan Piva, built a modern new home in the Stanley Basin, they designed it with windows to frame the mountains and meadows around them, where as father Pete Piva used to say, "It does the heart good to see all the cows and their roly-poly calves ranging around you." It may be noted here that Mabel Piva is the granddaughter of George McGowan Sr. whose cattle grazed on these very meadows almost a century ago, and that the lovely home where she now lives is merely a stones throw away from the site of the one-room log cabin with the "leaky roof" in which her Great Uncle Arthur and his family lived in 1890. Times indeed do change.

101

RANGING SHEEP

Although cattle and horses were trailed into the Stanley-Sawtooth country to graze the lush, wild grasses growing mostly in the Basin, in the summer months of the 1890s, few, if any, sheep were ranged in the region before 1900. The first item on the subject to be printed in the *Silver Messenger Newspaper* at Challis, Idaho, appeared in the August 6, 1901 issue, reading as follows: "About 60,000 head of sheep are now being grazed in the Stanley Basin. About October 1st they will be trailed back to Ketchum to the Short Line Railroad and shipped to Eastern markets. Each band averages about 2,000 head."

Another item on sheep in one of the September issues in 1905 read: "Assessor Olsen found that there are 86,000 head of sheep now ranging in the Stanley Basin country."

Earlier, throughout the reaches of Central and Southern Idaho, many range wars were fought between sheep and cattlemen, and while the high walls of the surrounding mountain ranges may have been a factor, no trouble of serious consequence ever issued between them in the Stanley or Sawtooth regions. To be sure, there were disputes, but usually resulted more from personal conflicts between the sheepmen themselves. Boundary lines actually never caused too much conflict, as was the case in the sheep-cattle fights, except when the Forest Service was first created and a working program for managing the ranges was introduced in the area.

As it were, many of the first Sawtooth and Challis National Forest Rangers were compelled to spend a great deal of their time during grazing season trying to keep peace between the different outfits. Even in 1914, eight years after the National Forests were created, Bill Horton, ranger in the Sawtooth Valley, found himself kept busy arbitrating their disputes. By that time, the grazing program had been put into motion setting up boundary lines, and allotting each sheepman a certain area in accordance to the number of sheep he owned and the proximity with his winter range. Grazing fees in the National Forests at that time were 5¢ per head. These fees were increased from time to time through the years, and by the 1970s things reached a point where most sheepmen had acquired land of their own, or had gone out of business.

Some of the early sheepmen who ranged sheep in the Sawtooth country were Lemoyne, Ormsby, Skillerone, McCloud, Acuff, Dobush, Brailsford, Killpatrick, Cleveland, and Uranga. These names were listed in Ranger Horton's log book in 1914. A range allotment was made to Uranga up Smiley Creek that summer. His daughter, Alta Horton Ellis, recalls that the Urangas were a Basque family with ten children. Mr. Uranga would bring his family there to camp for the summer, and she would ride horseback up to play with the children.

To the early homesteaders and settlers in the Valley and Basin, coming of the sheep bands and their herders in the spring was an event, and a sure sign summer was on the way. In those days, a great many bands were trailed over Galena Summit in late May and early June from the Wood River side to forage the high mountainous country along the Salmon River headwaters. After there awhile, and the lambs had grown large enough for shipping (about July or August), the ewes and lambs were trailed back to Ketchum where the lambs were fattened and shipped, while the ewes were returned to the summer range. The bucks were also brought to the range for the remainder of the summer.

Most of the herders were Basque, often from Vizcaya in the Pyrennees Mountains of Spain and well adapted to the vocation of sheepherding. Many could speak only a few words of English, or none at all. Nevertheless, they managed to communicate with the various settlers in the region, especially those living along the route they traveled with their sheep. Usually the people were glad to see them come because the herders would often trade half of a freshly butchered lamb for homemade bread, fresh churned butter, milk, cookies, or pie. Such items, home-cooked, were a treat for the herders, and in turn, the fresh meat was a treat for the settlers.

Outfits were made up of the herder, two or three sheep dogs, and about 2,000 head of sheep (a band). His camp was set up and moved from time to time by a camptender. The tender's

Sheep grazing in the Sawtooth Valley area.

duties included a routine check every few days to bring supplies, mail, and other things the herder wanted or was in need of. The herder, on duty at all times, with the help of his dogs, had to be always on the watch to see that the sheep did not become lost or injured. When he was awakened at night by the tinkling of bells fastened around the necks of some of the sheep, or the barking of the dogs, he was up and ready to investigate the cause. Oftentimes he would find a bear or coyote lurking about, or even in the midst of the flock.

Good dogs are a must around sheep, as every sheepman knows. Always considered a valuable asset, these dogs, as a rule, were quick to carry out orders if properly trained, by helping to guide the sheep in the direction the herder wanted them to go, and by keeping a close vigil at night. Generally the dogs were Scotch collies and/or Australian shepherds, but sometimes mixed breeds made good sheep dogs and were used by the herders. Oftentimes when a camptender came across any kind of a dog he thought might be trained as a sheep dog, he would try to bargain with its owner so he could take it to one of the herders in the mountains.

Between 1909 and 1914, when the Leslie Niece family was homesteading in the lower end of the Sawtooth Valley, one summer, Leslie's son, Rupert, about nine or ten years old at the time, did a landslide business with several different camptenders who chanced to notice his part collie dog, named "Hero" that he had raised from a pup. "How much will you take for that dog?" the tender would ask. "Oh, I don't know." the boy would reply. The man would then hand Rupert a 50¢ piece or a silver dollar and say, "Will this do?" After the deal was made the tender would tie a rope around Hero's neck and take him away, while Rupert would go on about his own business feeling almost certain he would see Hero again in a few days. Sure enough, Hero would show up wagging his tail and barking his pleasure at being back home once more. If the tender came looking for Hero, Rupert would let him take the dog again, but usually he never bothered for he guessed it would be the same thing over again.

By late summer this had happened so often, Rupert's transactions with the different camptenders became quite a funny joke in the Valley. The tender, or anyone for that matter, never blamed Rupert, him being only a child, and surely no one could blame the dog because he loved the Niece children the way he did. Long years after Rupert and Edna, his sister, were grown and the incident forgotten by them, Otto Centauras, one of the country's oldtimers, asked Edna, "Do you remember that dog Rupert used to have and sell to the camptenders, and how the dog would always come back to him?" The memory not only brought a chuckle to Otto as he told the little story, but to all who heard him recall Rupert's "sheep dog business" as a boy growing up in the Stanley-Sawtooth country.

Some of the sheepmen still remembered who ran sheep in the Basin and Cape Horn area in the early days were: the Newmans, Keefers, McVeys, Bacons, Laidlows, and Vaders. The latter two had creeks named for them . . . Laidlow and Vader Creeks, both in the Cape Horn area. The Vaders had a ranch and sheep range near the Cape Horn ranger station, and left there to move to the Sawtooth Valley about 1917-18. Their daughter married Maurice Bevins, and for several years owned and operated the Smiley Creek Lodge on Highway 93 in the upper end of the Valley. The Vader family now owns property on Pole Creek Flats. One of the Laidlow boys married a daughter of Brazilla Clark.

Through the years, various sheepmen have come and gone, while some remained and are in the country today . . . the Silvas, Browns, Jones, and the Breckenridges . . . to name a few. With the changing times, any sheepman will tell you that grazing sheep in the National Forests, too, has changed considerably. For instance, where they once trailed the sheep bands to the range, they now must truck them in. Even the

The sheep wagon was a familiar sight during summer months in both the Sawtooth Valley and the Stanley Basin until the late 1940s.

sheepherders can enjoy the comforts of home when they can afford modern camp trailers instead of the old sheep wagons used in the early days. Although many of the herders were of Basque nationality, there were a few who were not. In days gone by in the Stanley-Sawtooth region, one of the country's most colorful, earlyday characters, Henry "Trapper" Fisher came to the Basin as a sheepherder. Also, Henry Middleton, John Weidman, and Jack Seagraves, although all three men soon turned to mining as a way of life.

Numerous articles and stories have been written about the lonely life of the sheepherder while he was on the summer range. But was it lonely? A little perhaps, but with his dogs for company and regular visits from the camptenders, along with his many duties as a shepherd over his flock, it is doubtful if his time allowed loneliness. Oftentimes, he had visitors in the way of other people. One humorous example appeared in the August 27, 1901 issue of the *Silver Messenger Newspaper* at Challis . . . and very pertinent. The article was titled, "Welcome to a Stranger" and read as follows:

Travelers in the Stanley Basin in these times can find shelter and rest in a sheepherder's camp or a prospector's cabin — and are welcome. In one sheepherder's camp, a traveler came across this sign. . . . Hold out for Camptenders, Sheepherders, Miners, Hobos, and Horse Thieves.

Open 6 A.M. to 9 P.M.

Wash your dishes, or make your peace with God before you come again.

Association Camp,
Membership Unknown.

106

STANLEY — TWO TOWNS, FUEDS, FIGHTS, AND POST OFFICES

The question of, "Why are there two towns named Stanley?" followed by, "Which came first?" have been asked by newcomers to the Basin for many years. Almost from the beginning we have had Upper Stanley — sometimes called "Dogtown" and Lower Stanley — sometimes called "Squawtown." Upper Stanley is located one-fourth mile from U.S. Highway 93, on the banks of Valley Creek and on State Highway 21, referred to as the Lowman road by local people. The answers to both questions will be noted here-in.

The first settlement on the site of Upper Stanley was made in 1890 by Arthur McGown Sr. with his wife, Della, and their two small children, Lulu, age five, and Joe, age four. The McGowns were the second family to live in the Stanley Basin. Tim Cooper with his wife, Bertha, and daughter, Daisy, was the first family in 1884, settling on a mining claim in the Stanley Creek area. The McGowns moved to the Basin from the Yankee Fork country at the end of that district's first mining boom for the purpose of establishing a stopping place for packers and miners coming and going through the region. At the time of their move a great deal of mining was being done in the Basin and the Seafoam area. Also, only a horse trail led up the Salmon River from the mouth of Yankee Fork to the Stanley Basin where it junctioned with a rough wagon road coming from the Sawtooth Valley mining district and leading to the many mines scattered about the Basin.

At the junction, on the banks of Valley Creek, Mr. McGown constructed a one room log cabin, very crude at first with pine-pole bedstead and two built in bunks. When he brought Mrs. McGown to be with him soon afterwards, she, of course, added a woman's touch as time allowed and availability of supplies made it possible, and turned the cabin into home-like and comfortable quarters. At first the cabin had no door hung at the opening and no glass panes at the window. In her diary kept during those years, she wrote, "We hung a blanket over the door, and I tacked a flour sack over the window." Later on she tells about how she was able to cook on an old-fashioned wood stove packed in on the back of a mule. Seems the animal had fallen down a bluff on the journey up Salmon River, and, while no real damage was done, the stove damper had been broken off. "I could fix that," she said. "I could take off the back lid and put in a piece of tin when I wanted to bake."

Their first summer in Stanley the McGowns furnished beef to the miners. This was through an arrangement made with his brother, George McGown, who had his son, Wells, and a crew of hands trail cattle from Challis to the Stanley Basin for Arthur McGown to butcher and deliver to the various miners scattered around the mining localities.

After a year the miners wanted the McGowns to establish a post office since their place was centrally located and a post office would be a convenience. Mr. McGown applied for the appointment of post master. However, Arthur McGown was Canadian born, so before he could qualify for the appointment he would have to go to Great Falls, Montana to get his citizenship papers. This he did, but, as it turned out, when the appointment came through from Washington D.C. it named Della McGown for the office . . . dated June 23, 1892. Rather than delay the procedure it was decided she would accept the appointment. Her orders were to go to Sawtooth City in the Sawtooth Valley and in her words, "Get the postoffice from Frank Park, the postmaster there. I went and tended to my business with him in late June." Arthur would erect a small building near their home to house the postoffice. Too, by now he had decided to build a large building for a store-saloon combination. This was all done, and mail was legally directed to the first post office to be established in the Stanley Basin.

The McGowns remained at this location until 1895, and although they endured many hardships the McGown place, called "The Stanley Post Office" and/or the "McGown Store" proved to be most convenient for the miners and packers in the region. Freighters would stop overnight and leave freight or pick up ore as they came and went to the mines. When the family departed the Basin, they sold their holdings to Mose Storher who had operated a store at Wagontown near the foot of Vanity Mountain on the fringe of the Seafoam mining district. The post office was discontinued at this time.

Mose Storher continued to operate the store, but the Stanley Basin was without a post office until 1899 when it was re-established and Henry S. Olds was made postmaster. Mr. Olds kept the office only six months, then was replaced by Benjamin F. Rapp until 1902. The post office was again discontinued. In 1902 Mose Storher sold out to H.L. Benner, and he applied for and received the appointment as postmaster... still on the original site of the McGown place. Mr. Benner kept the office until his death in 1907. During the time Mr. Benner lived, the family had enlarged the store and added a larger building in which to live.

In 1902, about the same time the Benners had purchased the store on Valley Creek (Upper Stanley site), Herbert H. Marshall, a miner and a business man, was building a hotel building at the mouth of Nip-N-Tuck Gulch on the Salmon River. By now a state wagon road had been constructed from the mouth of Yankee Fork up-river to the site of the hotel which Marshall was building. *This was the beginning of Lower Stanley.*

Upper Stanley about 1902

The "Hotel" as local people called it for many years, was a long log building with three rooms and a lean-to bedroom, opening to the outside and attached to one end of the main building. The three rooms in the large building served as living quarters and dining room. The hotel was more like a boarding house, or "eating house" as it was sometimes referred to. It is not known who operated the place first, but a Mrs. Pierce was there in 1909. Mrs. Sadie Merritt tells of staying there when her daughter, Sadie, then a small child, was ill, and how Mrs. Pierce helped her care for the sick child. Later a Mrs. Alice Olsen, nick-named "Red Ollie" operated the hotel. Then in 1912, the *Challis Silver Messenger Newspaper* stated that a Mrs. Strider was running the hotel. Next came Mrs. Leslie Niece, and later Mrs. Affie Cothern, followed by Mrs. Law and Mae Rose. Finally, having served its purpose, in 1931, the building was torn down by Jason Vaught and the logs burned for firewood.

Meanwhile, back in 1907, the year Mr. Benner met his death, Herbert Marshall, with the help of Henry Sturkey, another miner in the Basin, built another large log building near the hotel. This became Lower Stanley's first store and was operated by Mr. Marshall. After Benner's death, the post office which had been discontinued at that time, was re-established . . . this time at *Lower Stanley,* and Mr. Marshall was appointed the postmaster. August Fisher, owner of the ranch across Salmon River from the Marshall store and hotel, (later the William (Bill) Wooley ranch, and now owned by his son, Dan) replaced Mr. Marshall as postmaster in 1908. Fisher was replaced by Leslie Niece, who took over the operation of the Marshall store and received the appointment as postmaster, beginning in 1914.

General Merchandise Store and Boarding House at Lower Stanley (1914)

Herbert Marshall, an outdoorsman and weary of being confined inside four walls, in the spring of 1912, had sold the store, and for a time it was known as the Stanley Mercantile Company with N.S. Powers as proprietor. However, when Mr. Powers failed to meet the note on the property, in January, 1914, Marshall filed notice of attachment and repossessed the store. It was soon after this that he approached Leslie Niece to operate the store for him. Niece, who was homesteading at the north end of Sawtooth Valley, (now the Chuck Hansen ranch) accepted Marshall's offer, moving his family to Lower Stanley where he took over the store and his wife, Ellen, took over the operation of the hotel nearby.

All this time, while Lower Stanley had been building up, Upper Stanley had more or less deteriorated. Mrs. Benner had built a large two-story log hotel, completed in 1912, and soon after opening for business, had closed her store. Her daughter, who had helped her operate the business, had moved to Jerome, Idaho, so Mrs. Benner closed the hotel and sold her property in Upper Stanley to Bartlett and Eva Falls in 1916. The Falls used the hotel building for their home during their first year in Stanley. Mrs. Falls liked to entertain, and gave many parties and dances while living there.

Upper Stanley (1916) X indicates original two rooms of Arthur McGown, Sr. home built 1891. Back rooms added later.

During all this time Upper Stanley was not considered as a town, and Lower Stanley was the one and only *Stanley*. The first schoolhouse in the Stanley Basin country was built at Lower Stanley in 1915. No land survey for a town had yet been made in the Basin. People who lived there and had erected buildings were termed "Squatters," just as all early pioneers were classed in the undeveloped parts of the West. This gave them what was commonly called "Squatter's Rights" or "Squatter's Sovereignity," and, in the eyes of the law, put them in line for title to the land. A recommendation to the Department of Interior from the U.S. Department of Agriculture in November, 1916, requested that 58.01 acres be withdrawn from the National Forest (Challis Division) and surveyed for a townsite, stating in part: "Within the legal subdivisions involved there are approximately 19 acres well suited for building purposes, and the tract is situated at what is believed to be the most logical site for a town, being at the forks of two main roads, one which leads westerly to Cape Horn and Bear Valley, and the other up the main Salmon River to Pierson (Sawtooth Valley Post Office), Wood River and Hailey."

The letter went on to state that there were already a number of buildings constructed at the site: namely, "A store and Post Office, a residence which is used as a roadhouse (the Marshall Hotel), a feed stable, a schoolhouse, and two cabins."

Group at Lower Stanley (1917) Left to right . . . Josephine Thompson, Edward Martin, Mary Marshall, Ellen Niece, Herbert Marshall, Affie Cothern, and Eddie Martin. Girls in front (left to right) Virginia Cothern and Mildred Cothern

Further correspondence on the matter was not filed until April, 1919, when a letter from the Interior Department in answer to an inquiry from Sam Bradford said the land had been withdrawn from the National Forest as had been requested, and that an order for a survey of the land into blocks and lots would be issued in a few days. When the survey was finally completed, July 30, 1921, U.S. Cadestral Engineer Robert A. Farmer appraised the lots and a list was sent to the General Land Office at Hailey, Idaho. Date for the sale was set for August 22, 1922. Notice was posted stating: "Sale to be at public outcry, to the highest bidder, at not less than the appraised value, sale to continued thereafter from day to day as long as may be necessary."

Names of purchasers listed on the opening day of the sale were, Atwood Weeks, Mrs. E.W. Law, T.H. Williams, and School District No. 6 . . . the latter purchased by John Thompson in the name of the School District. This was Lot No. 6 in Block 4, and was the lot on which the schoolhouse had been built in 1915. The lots sold for from $20 to $40 each. Since John Thompson, not being a member of the Board of Trustees, had not been authorized to purchase the lot for the School District, on November 25, 1922, the Board of Trustees of School District No. 6 signed a relinquishment and reconveyance turning the lot back to the Government. This allowed Lot No. 6 in Block 4 to be placed on sale again, and at this time it was purchased by L.S. Niece.

Back at the upper settlement (The Benner Place), Bartlett Falls, the current owner, had been busy developing the land within his domain. Included in his actions was a conditional promise made to Leslie Niece, that if he would build a store and move the post office to the upper settlement, Mr. Falls would present him with a deed to a five acre tract there. Niece accepted Mr. Falls' offer, but in order to be free to apply himself to this new venture, he sold his store in Lower Stanley to Florian Clyde and his wife, Jennie, of Challis, Idaho. Also, Mr. Clyde agreed to take over the appointment as postmaster on a temporary basis. Niece then resigned his post and went on to build his store building at the upper settlement, hiring Tom Williams and Arthur Wright to do the carpentry work . . . the same two carpenters who had built the large hotel for Martha Benner, completed in 1912, and owned by Bartlett Falls.

When the Niece Store was completed and a new home for the Niece family was under construction nearby, Mr. Falls, in the

113

Upper Stanley (1920). Back of Niece Store and the Leslie Niece Residence.

early summer of 1919, set aside a portion of his land for a townsite and a survey was begun. On September 11, 1919, true to his promise to Niece, he deeded (free gratis) the 5 acre plot to Leslie Niece and his brother, Frank "Juggy" Niece. At the same time, with the survey now complete, Falls deeded two lots to School District No. 6, and made a Donation Deed dedicating the streets and alleys of the townsite to the public. This was all entered on the Custer County records dated November 22, 1919. The new townsite was called "Stanley." Now the Basin had two Stanleys . . . Lower Stanley and Upper Stanley.

With all these changes taking place, the lives of the Basin residents were affected in many ways and old fires of discord were rekindled. Could both towns be named Stanley? If so, which would be the rightful Stanley? Could both towns have a post office? If not, could the post office be legally moved from Lower Stanley to Upper Stanley? Each new development tended to intensify the arguments among the Basin people. Location of the school was of great concern. Citizens on one side pointed out that since the upper townsite had been surveyed, approved, and recorded as such in November 1919, and Lower Stanley was not approved and recorded at that time, that Upper Stanley was the rightful Stanley. On the other side, various people maintained that Lower Stanley was the first to use the name of Stanley for their town, and that the post office and schoolhouse were there *at the present time*. The arguments went on and on.

One day, in a joking manner, when the question of "was it

right for both towns to have the name of Stanley" was mentioned, Juggy Niece remarked, "I could settle that controversy. I'd call lower town 'Squawtown' because the women do all the work down there ... and I'd call upper town 'Dogtown' since *that* family with all those dogs moved in here." The names stuck, and for many years the upper and lower settlements were often referred to as "Dogtown" and "Squawtown." Even on the Custer County Court records, Lower Stanley is mentioned as "Squawtown."

Another controversy had arisen during the summer of 1919. By this time the L.S. Niece store at Upper Stanley had been completed and stocked and opened for business. At Lower Stanley, Mr. Clyde had sold his store to Mrs. Elizabeth W. Law of Gooding, Idaho and had tendered his resignation as postmaster in favor of the re-appointment of L.S. Niece at Upper Stanley. He would continue in office until the new appointment was approved. All appeared to be fine until Mr. Niece's appointment came through in July, 1919. The new owner of the store in Lower Stanley, Mrs. Law, had moved in with her son, Hughie, and daughter, Maggie, at the time she purchased the property, and decided she wanted to keep the post office. As a result, when Mr. Niece went to move the post office to his store at Upper Stanley, Mrs. Law refused to allow it to be moved from her store.

Something had to be done. Mr. Clyde was anxious to move back to Challis, but felt compelled to remain in Lower Stanley until he could turn the post office over to his successor legally. The Postal Department at Washington D.C. was notified of the turn of events, and Postal Inspector Dodd was sent in to assist Mr. Niece in securing the post office from Mrs. Law's premises and installing it in a partitioned corner of the Niece Store in Upper Stanley.

Down through the years many exaggerated stories and articles have been written about the episode of moving the Stanley Post Office. One story went so far as to call the move "The Post Office on Wheels," stating that people living and working along the route between the two towns could look and see the post office equipment, loaded on a truck, going one way one day, and the other way the next day. Supposedly, Basinites were never sure of which direction they should go to pick up their mail.

Back at upper town, in the fall of 1918, the Bartlett Falls

family leased the hotel building to the Wells McGowan family from Challis. The Falls then moved into the house that had once been the Benner Store building, and the McGowan used the hotel as their residence. This was while Wells was driving the stage between Stanley and Robinson Bar, located down the Salmon River, a short distance above the little mining town of Clayton.

That winter the McGowan children attended the school at Lower Stanley. When spring opened up in 1919, Mrs. Wells McGowan (Lena), opened the hotel for business. Also, that same spring George Aldredge built a garage across the street (road) from the Niece Brothers Store. The new home of the Niece family was now completed. This was quite a modern home for the time, complete with electric lights, as was the store, with power furnished by a Delco plant installed for that purpose.

Things in both towns went along smoothy for the next two years. . . . Basinites were finally reconciled to having the two towns named "Stanley" and went on to accept upper town as "Upper Stanley" and lower town as "Lower Stanley." Lower Stanley had the school, and Upper Stanley had the post office. The old Benner Hotel became the scene of meetings, dances, parties, and many social activities, and all were well attended from both settlements. Now, with discord diminished, both towns showed signs of rapid growth.

Then the school fight began in the fall of 1921, beginning with a letter from the Superintendent of Schools at Challis, informing School District No. 6 that the Health Department had condemned their schoolhouse, and suggesting that the Trustees find a suitable place to hold school for that term. (*More on this in School Days in The Stanley Basin*). It was at this time that a classroom was set up in the dance hall of the old Benner Hotel at Upper Stanley. Without a dance hall now because of the school being located there, a few of the leading citizens decided to build a new hall for community affairs.

Clyde and Claude Gillispie, William A. Soule, L.S. Niece, and Charley Thompson went together, forming a Membership Association, and put up money for the new structure. A plot was chosen across the street to the east of the Niece Brothers Store. Again, Tom Williams and Arthur Wright were called on to do the carpentry work . . . hired and paid by the Association. The finished building composed a large dance floor with a raised stage at one end for the musicians, and a balcony at the

116

Upper Stanley about 1926.

opposite end where lunch and coffee could be served, or where older folks could just sit comfortably and watch the action on the dance floor below.

When the school fight finally ended, Upper Stanley grew while Lower Stanley declined to some extent. After the postoffice episode, Mrs. Law remained about two years at Lower Stanley, moving when she obtained a government lease on the Alturas Lake resort area in the Sawtooth Valley. On leaving, she sold her store stock to William and Mae Rose and they moved it into a log building bought from Tom Williams, and on the site where "Jerry's Country Store" is now located. After a succession of appointees at Upper Stanley to the postmaster job, Rose applied and received an appointment on February 2, 1925, and the post office was moved back to Lower Stanley. Mr. Rose kept the job for the next eight years.

During that eight years both towns showed substantial growth. In lower town a service station, several log homes, and two motels were additions. At upper town, more homes, a schoolhouse, and a cafe and bar were added. Now, with automobiles becoming more common in the West, more and more tourists were coming into the Stanley-Sawtooth country, creating a demand for cafes, motels (then called tourist cabins), and service, or filling stations. Tourists came in summer, the majority being campers and often in need of groceries and gas, making most trade a seasonal thing. Nevertheless, local people provided enough business to keep both towns on a thriving basis, especially after the event of Highway 93 in 1931.

117

Upper Stanley. Niece Bros. Store with Stanley Dance Hall in the background. Dorothy Taylor and Edna Niece on burros, Punch and Judy.

Back in 1927, at Lower Stanley, Jason Vaught bought the old original Herbert Marshall store and hotel buildings plus several lots in town. When the right-of-way had to be cleared for the highway, Vaught tore down the hotel building and used the logs for firewood. The store building was moved by the Fish and Game Department and set up a short distance to the northeast of the original location, where it still stands and is kept in good repair today. Here, the Vaughts built cabins to rent, and lived on the property for many years. This property is now owned by Jim Jensen.

At Upper Stanley, a large garage, built by George Aldridge in 1919, was sold to Arthur Kavanaugh in 1923, who in turn sold it to Frank "Juggy" Niece in October, 1925. Juggy kept and operated this garage until his death in 1950. The Niece Brothers Store was sold to the Gillispie Brothers in 1926, and Clyde Gillispie ran it for many years. The Leslie "Tink" Niece home had been sold to Mr. and Mrs. Doc Cothern before this time. The Cotherns added on extra rooms and turned it into a hotel which they operated until the building was destroyed by fire in 1932.

Another hotel was built at Upper Stanley in the early Thirties by Lee and Agnes Frakes. This, like many other businesses in both towns, changed hand several times through the years. It is now called "The Sawtooth Hotel" and is owned and operated by Mr. and Mrs. Cole.

118

Garage in Upper Stanley taken in the late 1930s. Owner, Juggy Niece standing by pump.

In 1933, because of ill health, Bill and Mae Rose sold their store in Lower Stanley to Floyd Markle. After the Markle ownership, this business, too, changed hands a number of times. . . . Markle to Savage and Peters, then to Dan O'Conner, and back to Markle who finally sold to Jerry Funderburg of California. At the time Rose sold out to Markle, he also resigned his job as postmaster. Clyde Gillispie was appointed to re-place Mr. Rose, and the post office was again moved to Upper Stanley where it remains today.

Following are the Postal Records of the Stanley-Sawtooth country from the U.S.A. General Services Administration:

STANLEY:

Post Office first established at Stanley (Upper) June 23, 1892. . . .
Della McGown, Postmistress.
Discontinued May 15, 1895.
Re-established October 24, 1899, Henry Olds, postmaster.
Olds resigned and Benjamin F. Rapp appointed April 19, 1900.
Post Office discontinued April 15, 1902.
Re-established November 24, 1902, Henry L. Benner, postmaster.
Next appointment listed is:
Herbert H. Marshall, January 21, 1907 (office moved to lower town).
Marshall resigned and August Fisher was appointed May 2, 1908.

Leslie S. Niece, December 1, 1914.

Florian L. Clyde, July 17, 1918.

Leslie S. Niece (re-appointed). July 21, 1919. Post Office moved to Upper Stanley.

Arthur F. Kavanaugh, October 11, 1922.

Alta I. Moore, August 21, 1923.

William L. Rose, February 2, 1925. Moved again to Lower Stanley.

Clyde R. Gillispie, October 20, 1933 (assumed charge). Appointment confirmed June 23, 1934. Post Office back at Upper Stanley.

Charles A. Gregory, July 1, 1943. (assumed charge). Appointment confirmed, March 30, 1944. Gregory retired in 1965.

Mrs. Lucille F. Denny, December 30, 1965 (acting). Later confirmed.

Upper Stanley Post Office moved into this building with Alta Moore as postmistress in 1923.

A letter from the U.S.A. General Services Administration, dated April 25, 1972, follows:

"The records of the Post Office Department in the National Archives show that a post office was established at Pierson, Custer County, Idaho, on July 30, 1903, with David P. Clarke appointed as its only postmaster. It was discontinued on September 30, 1915. At the time it was established there were 15 people resident in the community that it served. The postmas-

120

ter received the following annual salaries:

1905: $25.25
1907: $57.00
1909: $79.00
1911: $70.00

The postal records do not show why the Pierson Post Office was discontinued."

NOTE: The name "Pierson" was chosen for this post office because it was the middle name of David P. Clarke.

Obsidian, Custer County, Idaho
Established on March 28, 1918

Postmasters

Jennie Buchanan, March 18, 1918
Annie Goaz, March 8, 1919
Frank G. Fisher November 8, 1921
Mrs. Nellie Clark   February 1, 1940 (assumed charge)
                    February 19, 1940 (acting)
                    April 6, 1940 (confirmed)
James M. Decker   January 22, 1947 (confirmed)

NOTE: Earlier under this heading of "The Two Towns," reference and quotes are given from Della McGown's diary in connection with the Arthur McGown Srs. as having established the first post office in the Stanley Basin. As way of explanation, her "business in Sawtooth City" included giving proof to the postmaster there that she could read and write and figure weights and postage. After qualifying on that score, she was then required to take an oath of obligation as her bond to the office, and assume responsibility for stamps in the amount of $50 at a time. No exact proof has been found as to the class of the post office, but evidence indicates that it was either third or fourth class, in that her salary was simply a commission on the amount of business transacted. This was pro-rated on a quarterly basis as enacted into law in 1876.

This procedure for other appointments of postmasters and postmistresses in the Stanley-Sawtooth country continued to prevail until 1938 when Civil Service took over the job of qualifying postal personnel. Before Civil Service, however, bonds and salaries varied with the office class, which in turn was determined by population census and the amount of revenue earned by said post office. The class of a post office is still determined by the population count in the area it serves, and salaries are set accordingly.

SAWTOOTH VALLEY POST OFFICES:

Here it might be noted that Sawtooth City and Vienna, both located in the Sawtooth Valley, and both having post offices in the very early days, were in Blaine County, and were mining camps that bloomed and faded and were practically ghost towns by the time settlers first came to take up homesteads elsewhere in the Sawtooth Valley.

After the Pierson post office was discontinued in 1915, the George Snyder ranch (the Rathmyer place) became a kind of depot where valley residents could drop off and pick up their mail for the next three years. Then, in 1918, the valley residents requested that a new post office be established. Dave Williams suggested the name "Obsidian" because of the location near the base of Obsidian Mountain. The name stuck, and when the post office was officially established in March 1918, it became the only post office in the United States bearing that name.

Jennie Buchanan was the first postmistress appointed, and the office was set up in her home on Decker Flat. This was across the Salmon River from the site where Session's Lodge is now located.

When Mrs. Buchanan resigned the job, the Obsidian Post Office was moved to the Goaz home near the Shaw ranch, in the

Sawtooth Valley Post Office.

vicinity of Champion Creek, with Annie Goaz being appointed postmistress March 8, 1919. A story is told by oldtimers about a robbery supposed to have taken place while she was in office. It was late October, 1921 when Mrs. Goaz was found bound hand and foot. She swore she had been robbed of $25.00 in stamps, and identified the man as having a mole on his neck, leaving the implication that Bert Buchanan was the thief. Investigation proved that Bert Buchanan had no mole, so Mrs. Goaz said, "Well, maybe the man was chewing tobacco, and got a spot of it on his neck." Postal Inspector Dodd came from Washington D.C. to investigate. Enlisting the assistance of Upper Stanley postmaster, Leslie Niece, he soon found Buchanan to be falsely accused, terminated Mrs. Goaz's appointment, and dropped the matter because of inconclusive evidence. Later a jeweler at Hailey, Idaho, is supposed to have told of selling a watch to Mrs. Goaz, saying, "It was funny; the lady wanted the watch for one of her daughters for Christmas, and I sold it to her, but it was the first time I was ever paid with postage stamps."

In any case, Mrs. Goaz was relieved of her duties as postmistress, and on November 8, 1921, the Obsidian Post Office was moved to the Frank G. Fisher ranch and Mr. Fisher took over as postmaster. He kept the post as long as his health permitted, giving over to his daughter, Nellie Fisher Clarke February 19, 1940. Nellie kept the job until January 22, 1947 when James M. Decker took over. Decker moved the post office to the Clarke ranch, and eventually to a location near the Session's Lodge.

Added notes and items taken from *The Challis Silver Messenger Newspaper* concerning carriers and mail service in the Stanley-Sawtooth area relate some of the difficulties faced by residents before a permanent service was established.

The *Messenger* stated in the August 5, 1902 issue:

J.C. Fox returned the fore part of the week from Stanley Basin, where he went to get signers for a petition to establish mail service between Robinson Bar and the settlement of Stanley three times a week, and that H.L. Benner, the merchant, be appointed postmaster at Stanley. Everyone Fox saw signed the petition. At this time there are in the neighborhood of 200 people there, and certainly they are deserving of mail service.

NOTE: According to census reports from the Idaho Historical Society the figure is incorrect ... unless the Messenger reporter was including the many transient prospectors and miners throughout the region, inthat there were only 57 residents listed in 1900, and 74 in 1910.

The December 23 issue of the *Messenger* stated:

H.L. Benner and daughter of Stanley Basin were in Challis. A twice a week mail service has been established between Ketchum and Stanley . . . the government paying the carrier . . . and Mr. Benner has been appointed postmaster. We are pleased to learn there is a service, but the Department is not well informed, for there is a post office at Robinson Bar and a daily mail service over a good wagon road from Challis. The distance from Robinson to Stanley is only 20 miles and it is 60 from Ketchum to Stanley.

March 24, 1903 issue of the *Messenger*:

H.L. Benner, postmaster at Stanley Basin, made three trips to Ketchum on snowshoes during the winter, carrying the mail on his back. One trip from Ketchum to Stanley took five and a half days. Most trips took from 2 to 3 days. Mr. B. reports about 100 men employed at various mines in the Basin this winter.

July 26, 1904, the *Messenger* stated:

Contract let to H. Meachum to carry mail from Ketchum to Stanley. Summer schedule will be twice a week, leaving Ketchum on Tuesdays and Fridays, and leaving Stanley on Mondays and Thursdays. Winter schedule will be once a week.

September 4, 1904:

A move on to discontinue the Stanley Post Office brought protest from the people. About 100 receiving mail there at this time.

July 1910 . . . from *The Messenger*;

Mail route from Ketchum to Stanley discontinued.

NOTE: At this time, mail was sent to Bonanza on the Yankee Fork where the carrier, William (Bill) Merritt, picked it up and took it to Stanley. Merritt, carrying the mail on his back, made the trip on skis from Stanley to Bonanza and back that winter. George Hoffman carried the mail in 1911.

An item from the August 18, 1914 issue of *The Messenger*, signed by Pat Rasche of Stanley said, "The people of Stanley have a complaint or two. They have to carry their own mail or not get any, besides they haven't any roads to travel on when they do go for the mail. Why don't the Custer County Commissioners appropriate some money for roads in this end of the county?"

This was followed by another item on December 29, 1914, in the form of a protest from H.H. Marshall of Lower Stanley: "We have no mail service in Stanley. The route has been advertised for bids three times and turned down three times by our County Democratic Administration. Seems no bid can be small enough to please them."

Apparently the situation was eventually straightened out since no other items appeared in the *Messenger* until September 2, 1925, reading as follows: A bill passed by the legislature to the effect that stages must be bonded to carry passengers brought a protest from citizens of Stanley. They call the bill "unfair and unjust." The Stanley stage is forced to discontinue passenger service because of the high premium on bonds. To many folks in this area, this is their only means of travel to outside points.

After this, for awhile mail service for the Stanley-Sawtooth country continued to be erratic, but in time better road conditions and progress did right the wrong. From 1918 on into the late Thirties, contracts were let for carriers of the mail from Stanley to Obsidian and back. Will Paul was awarded the first contract on this route which called for a twice a week delivery . . . up and back on the same day in summer, and two days for the trip after the roads became choked with snow. As already noted, the Obsidian Post Office was located wherever the postmaster or postmistress happened to live, whether it be Decker Flat, Champion Creek, or the Fisher ranch. Will Paul's contract was for a period of 4 years as were all mail carrier contracts.

Clyde Gillispie had the contract after Will Paul's ended. His term ran from 1922 until 1926. Rupert Niece came next, keeping the contract for two terms . . . 1926 until 1934. His wife, Bonda Critchfield Niece, made the run for him many times when he was working at other jobs. Slim Hendrick took over from Rupert Niece in 1934. By then the roads were kept open as much as possible in the winter, and the trip was made three times a week. When Slim's contract expired in 1938, it was awarded to Harry Fleming, with delivery to be made six times a week . . . still from Stanley to Obsidian. Later the route was extended over Galena Summit to Ketchum in the Wood River area. At that time the Fleming family moved to Hailey where Harry and his wife, Martine, lived for many years. Retiring in 1975 after nearly forty years of service, Harry and Martine returned to the Sawtooth Valley to make their home.

From the Challis direction to Stanley, in the early days, mail and stage service was also erratic, but it too, was eventually straightened out and became more dependable. To be sure, there were a number of carriers and stages on the route from Challis to Robinson Bar and on to Stanley, as well as from Stanley to Cape Horn and the Seafoam Mines. No complete listing is available, and only a few will be mentioned here. Harve Stout, for one, contracted in 1910 to carry the mail from Bonanza, mining town on the Yankee Fork, to Stanley, then hired Bill Merritt to carry it for him during the winter months. George Hoffman was a carrier in 1911. Wells McGowan drove the stage carrying the mail in 1918 and 1919, and I.S. Hardman was awarded the contract for the Challis-Stanley route in 1926. Will Centauras had it in 1927 and 1928 and for some years afterwards.

While many of the earlier carriers found it necessary to travel on webbs (snowshoes) and pack the mail on their backs in the winter time, dog teams were also brought into use. Herman Hoff carried the mail this way from Stanley to Cape Horn and the Seafoam Mines in the Twenties. As young men, Bud Critchfield and Rupert Niece carried the mail to the mines from Stanley during the winter of 1927-28 on webbs and by dog sled. Sandy Brooks used a dog team to carry mail to the Sawtooth Valley, and of course, the heroic efforts of Dave Williams to bring the mail over Galena Summit in the early days during the wintertime is almost legend in the Stanley-Sawtooth Country. There were many such men who were willing to brave the elements. Like "Snowshoe Thompson" the legendary mailman of the old West, they too, did their part to "bring the mail through".

Thus, by the mid-Thirties, the two towns of Stanley were firmly established. Upper Stanley with most of the business houses, the schoolhouse, and the post office, while Lower Stanley went on to be a quiet little settlement on the banks of the Salmon River, where a few people lived the year around, while others spent only the summer months there. This is how it still is today. Travelers on U.S. Highway 93 through the rustic little community are usually impressed with its picturesque setting, often stopping for a few hours, or a few days to enjoy the

Lower Stanley in the 1940s

peaceful aspects of the area.

As Upper Stanley proceeded to come into its own as the main town of Stanley in the Thirties, the year 1938 noted additional business construction and growth. Preston Shaw and his family moved in from the Sawtooth Valley and built a nice home and a large rock combination garage and service station. The Winters family erected a new log home, and several other families moved into town. Doctor Fox of Hailey, Idaho built "The Cape Horn Lodge," and that winter, a new floor was put in the Stanley dance hall. Bill Wall and Larry Peyton did the work. Seems after eighteen years of dancing on the floor, it had weakened to the point of being a safety hazard. Many folks may remember how the floor would bounce when a crowd of dancers were doing a lively foxtrot, or "hoeing it down" while square dancing. Some of the people used to say, "All we need to do is to get the floor to bouncing, then just stand still and let the floor do the rest." By now the hall was called the "Ace of Diamonds" and a small cafe and lunch counter had been added.

And so the changes have continued to go on through the years. All of the first settlers in the Stanley Basin are gone now ... those who first searched for gold, and most of the homesteaders. In fact, the latter's number can be counted on one hand. Even the children who grew up and attended the first schools in the the Basin and the Sawtooth Valley are few in number now. They, like their parents before them, were

127

pioneers in a sense. They, along with newcomers to the Stanley-Sawtooth country in the Teens and Twenties, still found the region to be a relentless, raw land for five or six months out of the year. Only its scenic beauty, its delightful summers and colorful autumns compensated their endurance of the bitter cold winters here. Yet, despite the hardships, most people were content and happy.

The first single prospectors, miners and trappers came, built one room cabins and lived alone or in pairs. Maybe he had a dog for company, and maybe not. He hung his clothes on wooden pegs, or on nails if he had any, driven into the walls of his abode. His bed was made of four vertical pine poles crossed with other poles at bed height and padded with dried wild grass or pine boughs. His table was equally crude with a sawed log for a chair, and, if he were lucky, a packing box nailed to the wall to served as a cupboard. His heat for both cooking and warmth was furnished by either a crude fireplace or a small wood-burning stove.

Men who brought families with them fared little better in the beginning. Nevertheless, their women added a homey touch with curtains at the window and over a corner made into a sort of clothes closet, perhaps a braided rug on the well-scrubbed floor, and hand pieced quilts on the bed. She filled the cabin with delectable odors of tasty foods even though her basic supplies were wild game, fish, dried beans and fruits, flour, sugar, coffee, and a bit of bacon and seasonings. Every household had its food cache or cellar (a hole dug under the floor covered by a trap-door), and its sour dough crock. The sour dough provided leavening for bread, biscuits, and flapjacks. The cache under the floor kept perishables such as canned goods, potatoes, onions, and carrots when they had them. Most families brought in a few chickens and a cow which furnished them eggs, milk and butter.

Two or three places in Stanley had electric lights powered by dynamos as early as the Teens and Twenties, but the average household depended on kerosene or coaloil lamps for night lighting. The housewife had no radio, while television was yet unheard of, and only the forest service and a few business houses afforded telephones. Although homesteads and ranches were generally miles apart, everyone was considered a neighbor. Here, the old adage, "No man is an island unto himself" rang true, perhaps more so than in other regions throughout Idaho during those early days. And anytime anyone happened to come along, he was heartily welcomed and asked to "sit a spell" for a visit or a meal.

Since Highway 93 is kept open the year around now, the Stanley-Sawtooth country is no longer isolated during the winter months, and coming into its own as a summer vacation paradise in recent years, tourists from everywhere pour into the region all through the year. Snowmobile races and cross-country skiing are favorite winter sports, while fishing, hunting, camping, and boating continue as summertime fun for everyone. While Saturday night dances have long been popular with the local people, they now share their fun with any who care to attend the "stomps" or "busts."

Residents are proud of their thriving little communities with their modern homes and conveniences. Today women are no longer beset with the endless chores so necessary in Grandma's day, and although this is true in all parts of the Nation, the Basin-Valley women are kept aware of the fact by the high rugged mountains around them, especially when the peaks are glistening with white and the Basin and valley floors are deep in snow.

WHAT GRANDMA DID ON A WINTER'S DAY

Grandma, on a winter's day;
Milked the cows and fed them hay;
Fed the chickens and saddled the mule;
Got the children off to school;
Did the dishes, scrubbed the floors;
Put out a washing and did other chores;
Split some firewood and then-
Lugged in enough to fill the bin;
Fired the range to cook some fruit;
While she pressed hubby's dress-up suit;
Swept the parlor and made the bed;
Baked a dozen loaves of bread;
Cleaned the lamps and filled them with oil;
Stewed some apples she thought would spoil;
Churned the butter and baked a cake;
Then exclaimed, "For Heaven's sake!"
"The calves are out of that darn pen!"
Went out and put them in again;
Gathered the eggs and locked the stable;
Back to the house to set the table;

Cooked a supper that was delicious;
After this she did the dishes;
Fed the dog and sprinkled the clothes;
Took up her needle to mend some hose;
Then she opened the organ and began to play
"When you come to the end of a perfect day".

(Author unknown)

FIRST SCHOOL DAYS
IN THE STANLEY BASIN

After mining began in the Stanley Basin, settlers were slow in coming to the region as compared to other areas in Central Idaho. In 1900 the country was still very primitive, causing men with families to hesitate before subjecting their wives and children to the long, bitter cold winters. Even in 1910, only a few who had children had come to live in and around the tiny settlements of Upper and Lower Stanley. At the upper end of the Basin John and Josephine Thompson owned a ranch, but did not settle there permanently until the spring of 1910 when Mrs.Thompson had completed a contract teaching school in northern Idaho.

Mrs. Thompson was a dedicated school teacher who loved children, but never had any of her own. After settling down in the Basin she began to fret because there was no school district and no schoolhouse there. As she got to know, and be friends with the few families who had children of, or nearing school age, she fretted even more. Finally, in the fall of 1914, with the help and cooperation of her husband, John Thompson, she did something about it. After discussing her plan with the parents of the children, and making arrangements with the Idaho State and Custer County school boards, she set up a kind of boarding school in her home on the Thompson ranch to conduct regular classes for grades one to four.

She could accommodate four children to live in the Thompson home for a school term of six months ... beginning in late October and lasting through spring. Another little girl, Rosemary Paul, oldest daughter of Will and Lillian Paul who had taken up a homestead about two miles from the Thompson ranch in 1913, would commute to and from school five days a week. This would be on skiis (handmade by Herbert Marshall) after the snow came, and although the child was only seven years old, she was an able skier as well as a responsible little girl eager to attend her first school. The other four children who would live on the ranch were Sadie, age 8, and Myrta, age 6, daughters of Bill and Sadie Merritt who were homesteading near the little community of Upper Stanley, and Rupert, age 11, and Edna, age 8, son and daughter of Leslie "Tink" and Ellen Niece who, at that time were operating the mercantile store at Lower Stanley.

The Thompson home, rustic and picturesque against a backdrop of the Salmon River Mountains, and fringed by a grove of pines, was a large three-room log structure. Looking across the grassy meadows of the Basin floor from the front porch of the house could be seen the majestic Sawtooth Range where one of the peaks now bears the name "Thompson Peak"... and named for John Thompson. It was here that Mrs. Thompson incorporated her class room into the large room that had heretofore served as living room and bedroom separated by a wide archway.

The John Thompson ranch home in the upper end of Stanley Basin.

In this room, against the inner side of the outside wall, she placed a blackboard and bookshelves with an adult desk nearby. Then by placing a row of five little desks facing the blackboard, before a double window looking across the Basin in line with the front porch, she reasoned good light for her students to study by would fall over their left shoulders. For the living room part, Mr. Thompson's chair and table was moved to one corner towards the back by the arch partition and her own chair and table was positioned across from his chair on the other side of the arch.

After all was in readiness and the children arrived, Mrs. Thompson consulted her schedule and started her school. At 9 A.M. sharp the children were seated at their desks, and as in classroom, each student was assigned his and her lessons (according to grade) for the day. Main subjects were reading, writing, and arithmetic with a variety of secondary subjects as outlined by the Idaho Board of Education. Even though Mrs. Thompson was a firm believer of strict discipline, good manners, and most of all, the three R's; she was also very kind and thoughtful and displayed a world of patience with her charges.

At 10:30 A.M. a 15 minute recess was allowed with an hour's lunch break at noon. School was out for the day at 3:30 P.M. Thus for five days a week the children attended classes . . . all without protest. All were eager to learn, and because Mrs. Thompson possessed the ability to make each lesson interesting, her pupils loved every class session. Needless to say, the children learned fast.

Rupert, being the oldest, was in the third grade since he had attended school previously in the Sawtooth Valley (first to ever be held in the Valley) while his parents were homesteading in the area. This gave Edna, his little sister, an advantage since he had first and second grade books, and she had already learned to count, write her name, and read a few simple sentences. Because of this advantage Edna was soon advanced to the second grade while Rosemary, Sadie, and Myrta continued in the first grade.

Although Mrs. Thompson did not have an organ or piano for accompaniment, she also taught the children music. They sang songs, had spelling bees, and coloring and art lessons, played word games, and generally all the things other children did in the schools throughout Idaho. Outside of school hours they had time to play and for other activities. As a part of the household, each was assigned little tasks according to age and capability.

With none of the modern conveniences of our day, there was much to do on the ranch. Wood for the heating stove in the living room had to be carried in from the shed near the back door of the kitchen, and the wood box by the kitchen range had to be filled regularly. Of course, Mr. Thompson had cut great stacks of wood and filled the shed during the fall before the snow came. Water had to be pumped from a well in one corner of the wood shed and carried into the kitchen in pails. Rupert, being a boy and the oldest, took on these jobs as a part of his responsibility.

The water job included wash day and bath day. All water had to be heated on the kitchen range. Saturday was washday, and when Mrs. Thompson was finished, Rupert also carried out and emptied the water used for the laundry. On bath night, usually on Friday after supper in the evening, after each bath, again Rupert carried out and emptied water until all had bathed, a busy time for Rupert, but he never seemed to mind, going about his chores willingly and cheerfully.

After the supper dishes were done, while the bath water was heating in a big tub on the kitchen range, the children usually played games. On one occasion, after the little girls had drawn straws to see who would get the first bath, they were playing hide-and-go-seek through the house. Edna ran to hide in the dimly lit kitchen. In her haste to hide, she had forgotten about the large tub of cold water off in one corner of the kitchen which Mrs. Thompson used to cool each child's bath water. PLOP!! Edna had backed into the tub splattering water all over the kitchen floor. Mr. and Mrs. Thompson, alarmed at the sound, came running in from the living room. He turned up the flame of the kerosene lantern burning low on the kitchen table, and there was Edna, dragging herself out of the tub dripping wet and shivering with cold and looking like a wet kitten. Much to her relief the Thompsons burst out laughing; and that night she got the first bath whether intended or not.

As in all rural areas across the Nation, there were no inside toilets in the Stanley Basin in the early days. At the Thompson ranch the "John", or "Two-holer" as many called it, set out a short distance under the trees from the wood shed behind the house. None of the children minded when they had to go during daylight hours . . . but after dark was a different matter. Yet the trip had to be made every night just before bedtime. Taking the lantern, Sadie, Myrta, and Edna went together, and as the lantern cast eerie shadows along the trail, they would bravely try to reassure one another. The tinest sound would cause them to jump. One would say, "What was that?" Another would answer, "I didn't hear anything."

While Rupert was the water and wood boy, the three girls helped with little chores such as washing dishes, setting the table, dusting, and peeling potatoes; and once in awhile helped to bake a cake. Mrs. Thompson was fair, but she insisted all these little jobs be done properly. As a rule, the three little girls took turns at the different jobs. One day when it was Myrta's turn to dust the living room she called out to Mrs. Thompson in the kitchen, "Why do I have to dust today? It will just get dusty again." Coming to the door, Mrs. Thompson explained very patiently that it would not be the same dust, and that it was a job that had to be done well at least once a week.

To save on washing and ironing, cloth napkins were placed in a napkin ring bearing the name of each child, and in that way could be used several times before going into the laundry (paper napkins were unheard of at that time). Mrs. Thompson was most particular how the dishes were done. She said, "The glasses first, then the silver, the cups and saucers, the plates, and the pots and pans last." Each item had to be washed thoroughly in hot soapy water, rinsed and scalded with hot water, and dried completely with a clean dish towel.

One morning, after it had been Edna's turn to dry the supper dishes the night before, Mrs. Thompson picked up a plate that was wet. Calling Edna she said, "Edna, you didn't dry the dishes very well last night. This one is still wet." "Oh, but I did, Mrs. Thompson," Edna answered. "The water was just so hot it must have caused the plate to steam."

Drawing herself very erect, Mrs. Thompson looked sternly at the child and said, "Dry dishes can NEVER steam," in a cross voice . . . or so it sounded to the frightened child. Away she scooted to Mr. Thompson for sympathy and support, as all the children did when they thought Mrs. Thompson was angry with them. He like her, was most patient and kind to the children. He was a large easy going man who never seemed to hurry or lose his temper, and to Edna he was her pillar of strength when things seemed to go wrong for her.

For sleeping accommodations, Mrs. Thompson strung a curtain down the center of the bedroom which was drawn at night after she had tucked the girls into bed. This separated and provided a degree of privacy for them and the Thompsons. Rupert's bed was placed just off the kitchen in the storage room where food supplies were kept from freezing. Although the kitchen door was left open in the evenings to allow heat from the wood range to escape into the room, essentially it could not be heated too warm in order to prevent the food from spoiling. On cold winter nights Mrs. Thompson heated rocks in the range oven, wrapped them in old blankets, and placed them in Rupert's bed to help keep him warm.

All tucked in bed, the little girls would giggle when they would hear Mrs. Thompson say to her husband as she crawled into bed after a long busy day, "I'm all in but my shoestrings, and they're a'draggin!" Of Irish decent, Mrs. Thompson's good sense of humor often came to the fore this way. Many times situations would develop that might cause her to wonder if her strength was equal to her undertaking. Yet, somehow she managed to rise to whatever the occasion . . . be it good or bad.

After winter truly set in that year, oftentimes during a bad snowstorm, Rosemary would stay over with the other children at the ranch, giving the Thompsons fulltime care of all five students. That meant four little girls in one bed at night; all snuggled down in the covers, whispering and giggling until dropping off to sleep.

Sometimes on Saturdays, if time allowed or company was expected, Mrs. Thompson would say, "Well, I guess I will stir up a cake." Her remark usually acted like an invitation for help from the children . . . Rupert included, for it was he, being larger and stronger than the girls, who could beat the batter to a silky smoothness that, when baked, resulted in the most delicious cake of all. Mrs. Thompson's favorite recipe was for a one-egg white cake that always seemed to turn out perfectly; especially when the batter was beaten by Rupert.

Company did come . . . and often, usually on Sundays. The younger Thompsons (John's son, Charley and his wife, Lottie,) who lived across the way on Elk Meadows, were frequent visitors in the John Thompson home. George Cumine who lived near the younger Thompsons also dropped by often on Sunday for dinner and an afternoon of visiting.

As the holiday season approached that year plans for a New Year's dance to be held at the Charley Thompson home were made. The John Thompsons and Mrs.Thompson's students would attend. The parents would come . . . the Merritts, the Nieces, and the Will Pauls. Will and Mae Rose and George Cumine would join them, and best of all, Trapper Fisher was coming to play his violin. On New Years eve day part of the group would gather at the John Thompsons for dinner, then all would go together across the flat to the Charley Thompson place.

When the day arrived Mrs. Merritt drove a team and sleigh from Stanley bringing Mrs. Niece, Trapper Fisher and Will and Mae Rose. The fathers of the Niece and Merritt children did not come. However, before leaving home, Will Merritt had handed his wife, Sadie, a pint of whiskey and told her, "This is for Trapper Fisher to nip on tonight while he's playing his fiddle." Later, stopping to pick up Ellen (Mrs. Niece) at Lower Stanley, Sadie told her about it. Ellen laughed mischievously. "Let me have that bottle a minute," she said. When Sadie complied, Ellen poured about a fourth of the whiskey out and replaced it with straight grain alcohol. In her words, *"This made a mighty powerful drink."*

At the John Thompson ranch dinner was enjoyed by everyone, and when it was over, readiness was made for the sleigh ride over to the Charley Thompson's place across the way. Mae Rose had brought her bulldog, Toby, along. Rupert had a dog, too. As the group prepared to climb into the sleigh the two dogs got into a fight. With Toby getting the worst of the fight, Mrs. Rose became hysterical and fainted dead away falling into the snow beside the sleigh. Everybody was shouting and trying to separate the snarling, growling dogs. Rupert ran into the house for a kettle of water and was about to douse it on Mrs. Rose when Mrs. Merritt yelled, "STOP!" All the while Will Rose had been kicking snow into his prone wife's face, unmindful of the horse manure mixed in with the snow . . . to him it was handy, and the snow was wet and cold, and it did the trick. She came to in a hurry. Grabbing Toby, she ran into the house, examined him for injury, and after satisfying herself that Toby was unhurt, dried herself off and proceeded to lecture her husband about what a gentleman HE WAS NOT!!

At the Charley Thompson's, Sadie gave the bottle of whiskey to Trapper just before the dance started. In telling of the event later she said, "When we started to dance, every so often he would take time out to go outside for a minute. When he came back in, *LAND SAKES* how he would play that old violin. Kept him going all night, and instead of dancing in the New Year we danced on 'til daylight." Meanwhile, the children had all been bedded down in a cabin at the back of the Charley Thompson home, and checked on every now and then by one of the mothers, to make certain they kept covered and were sleeping well.

After the holidays were over, things on the John Thompson ranch settled again into routine . . . school five days a week for

Mrs. Thompson and her five pupils, and all other routine chores for each, and all normally required to keep everyone fed, clean, and warm. On long winter evenings, when the dishes were done and the kitchen tidied, the children played games. One card game called "Flinch" was a favorite, although they often played "Old Maid," "Casino," and sometimes Dominoes. Once in awhile Mrs. Thompson would have them help her to cut and sew long rag strips from worn clothing which she braided into rugs.

This was a contented, peaceful household most of the time . . . but not all of the time. There was the time John had gone to Stanley on skiis and received a gift of fish from Will Rose when he had taken the time to go down the Salmon River to Sunbeam Dam where Will was the watchman for the winter. The fish thawed and froze and thawed again by the time John returned home. Thinking no harm was done Mrs. Thompson cooked the fish. Since the fish were a rare treat in mid-winter, grownups and children alike ate with gusto and all became deathly ill from having done so.

Then there was the time little Rosemary arrived at school after skiing through cold, wet snow from the Paul ranch with both of her feet frosted. When her shoes were removed, Mrs. Thompson took prompt action. First she had the other children bring in pails of snow to fill a large pan in which she packed Rosemary's feet. After a few minutes she would lift them out and rub them vigorously with a rough towel, then repeat the procedure until the child's feet were warm and the circulation back to normal. As a result, her feet were not even sore, and never bothered her afterwards.

Near spring John made another trip. This time to Challis. Before leaving he told the four girls that if they would be good, study hard, and pass their grades, he would bring each of them a new hair ribbon of their favorite color. Rosemary chose pink, but while John was gone she had disobeyed her mother by remaining overnight at the Thompson ranch when Mrs. Paul had told her to come home after school that day. As a way of punishment for this her hair ribbon was withheld for a few days. After that, Rosemary was careful to do her mother's bidding, needless to say.

On Easter Sunday, a beautiful spring day, Charley and Lottie brought their baby and came for dinner with the John Thompsons. In the afternoon, the older children all went out to play, wandering in the pines a distance behind the house to the site of the garbage dump. While poking around in the rubbish, Little Myrta found an old pair of knee-high rubber boots and pulled them on over her shoes. Cutting silly capers and dancing around all over the place for a time she entertained the other children in a delightful style . . . but when she sat down to remove the boots she could not pull them off. The other children tried to help her, but it was no use . . . the boots stuck. Finally, Rupert ran to the house for help. Charley came, took his pocket knife and cut the boots from Myrta's feet. After that he always called her "Gum-shoe Sal."

In late April school was over for the summer, and the children went home, leaving the John Thompson household to return to normal and Mrs. Thompson filled with pride. Rupert was now ready for the fourth grade, Edna ready for the third, and Sadie, Myrta, and Rosemary ready for the second. Both John and Mrs. Thompson are gone now, and the five students have long since grown up, married, had children and grandchildren. Today when time allows for a visit, each of them find pleasure in recalling those school days on the Thompson ranch . . . as they say, "We have so much and so many things to thank Mrs. Thompson for besides the school lessons she taught us."

STANLEY AND SAWTOOTH VALLEY SCHOOLS

After Mrs. John Thompson conducted the first school session ever to be held in the Stanley Basin at the Thompson ranch in the winter of 1914-15, that spring when school was out, a group of Basin residents petitioned the Custer County Commissioners at Challis (the county seat) for a school district. Mrs. Thompson numbered among them. The petition was granted and Idaho School District No. 6 was created. Now Stanley Basin had a school but no schoolhouse. One was required along with a board of trustees. An election was held electing G.P. Hawkins and Ellen Niece with Herbert Marshall as clerk of the district school board. Members voted to build a one-room log cabin at Lower Stanley, to be completed as soon as possible.

The schoolhouse was started, but was not finished as the time for the school term to begin drew near. Also, a teacher had not been hired. Herbert Marshall, as Clerk of the board, went

139

to Mrs. Thompson and pleaded with her to take the job. If the school did not start on time, Stanley would lose its district. Finally accepting, a week later Mrs. Thompson moved down to Stanley and a school was set up in the bunkhouse owned by Tink and Ellen Niece. Furnishings were made up of a long, rough board table with benches for seats, and a wood heating stove in one corner of the room. Mrs. Thompson went to Challis for the necessary books; and school began at the appointed time. Pupils included the five children who had gone to the Thompson ranch the previous winter and George and Rebecca Sewell, Lulu Kregor, and Johnnie Paul . . .nine in all.

In October the new schoolhouse was compeleted with new desks, a blackboard, and a table for a world globe and a dictionary. Near a large wood heater, installed in a corner to one side of the door, a long bench was placed for the children to sit on while removing their boots in the wintertime. Coat hooks were installed on the wall above for hanging wraps. On the opposite side of the door a wall shelf held a wash basin and water pail, with hooks above to hang each child's drinking cup. The teachers desk was near the back of the room facing the student's desks, and not far from the blackboard. Now Stanley had a real school.

Schoolhouse at Lower Stanley (1915). Pupils (left to right) Johnnie Paul, Rosemary Paul, Sadie Merritt, Rebecca Sewell, Lulu Kregor, Edna Niece, Myrta Merritt, Rupert Niece, and George Sewell. Teacher . . . Mrs. Josephine Thompson.

*Lower Stanley school girls ready for the Easter Party (1918). Left to right ...
Nellie Merritt, Sadie Merritt, Virginia Cothern, Mildred Cothern, Myrta
Merritt, Edna Niece, and Rosemary Paul*

School was held in this little schoolhouse for the next five
years. Mrs. Thompson taught four of those years ... the first
and the last three. Second year was taught by Miss Mary
Kingston who left for Arizona after her marriage to John
Cochran the following summer. Grades were for one through
eight. At the end of each school term, teachers were required to
send in a personal report listing achievements, events, and any
suggestions for improvement that might be of benefit in the
coming year.

Mrs. Florence Rowles tells of an incident relating to Mrs.
Thompson's first report sent in for the 1915-16 term. When
going through the files after she took office in 1921, Mrs.
Rowles found this report sent in to Miss Jennie Kelleher, her
predecessor. Mrs. Thompson had written, "I suggest that the
cracks between the logs in our schoolhouse be filled so the snow
won't blow in on the students."

In early spring of 1921, R.B. Cothern, clerk for the Board of
Trustees of School District No. 6, requested money to either
repair the old schoolhouse, or to erect a new one. Assistant
State Superintendent, R.F. Martin, replied that since the land
on which the schoolhouse sat was in Lower Stanley and did not
belong to the school district, public money could not be used for
repairs or a new building ... letter dated May 3, 1921.

141

Summer passed and nothing was done. Then in September Mrs. Rowles, Custer County School Superintendent, wrote Mr. Cothern, "I have been instructed by the representatives of the County Board of Health to notify you, as clerk of the Board of Trustees of School District No. 6, that the school building located in your district does not comply with the rules of the State Board of Education, and is not suitable for the number of children that attend there, and is therefore condemned and reported as such to the State Board of Welfare." Enrollment had increased to 18 students.

In her letter Mrs. Rowles went on to suggest that since the teacher had already been engaged for the new term, the school board should meet and try to find a suitable place to hold the school.

Reports indicate that R.B. Cothern and C.S. Thompson decided an upstairs room in the old Benner Hotel at Upper Stanley would serve the purpose. Bartlett Falls, owner of the building, gave his permission and the County Superintendent was notified. After being inspected and okayed by Dr. C.L. Kirtley, County Health Officer, on September 30th, 1921, written permission was given by the Superintendent for the school furniture and fixtures from the old school to be moved to the new site, and for classes to begin. Mrs. Sadie Merritt, third member

School children at Upper Stanley. (1921) Left to right . . . Bud Critchfield, Rosemary Paul, Bonda Critchfield, Irma Duffy (teacher), Virginia Cothern, Wilmot Paul, Mildred Cothern, and Johnnie Paul.

142

of the Board of Trustees — District No. 6, later stated that she had not been consulted and had not given her permission for the school to be moved.

In November, that same year, three property owners in Lower Stanley, John Thompson, Thomas Williams, and Ed Huffman, filed suit against the School Board Trustees in the District Court of the 6th Judicial District of the State of Idaho. Hearing for the case was held at Blackfoot, Idaho December 3, 1921, with Sadie Merritt acting as witness for the plaintiffs. The court decided in the latter's favor, ordering the other trustees, Cothern and C.S. Thompson, to pay all costs and to move the school furniture and fixtures back to the schoolhouse at Lower Stanley not later than January 2, 1922.

The Defendants then asked for a dismissal of the case, but same was denied on December 6th, 1921 by Judge Ralph Adair of the Court of the 6th Judicial District of the State of Idaho. Ten days later the defendants filed a motion for a new trial. The motion was also denied by Judge Adair. Notice of appeal was filed January 23, 1922 by the Board of Trustees, Cothern, C.S. Thompson, and W.B. Paul who had replaced Sadie Merritt. Transcript filing time was set for April 24th, 1922, but an extension of 30 days was granted later, allowing school to continue throughout the term in the old Benner Hotel at Upper Stanley.

Soon after school was out that spring, in June, an election was held for the purpose of disposing of the condemned schoolhouse in Lower Stanley, and for selecting a site for a new building. At the time, Upper Stanley was called "Dogtown" and Lower Stanley was called "Squawtown." When Bartlett Falls had the townsite of Upper Stanley surveyed in 1919, he had deeded two lots to School District No. 6 which, up to the time of the election, had been more or less ignored. Custer County Court records recorded the votes taken at the June, 1922 election as follows: Of 53 votes cast, 28 voted to build a new school building on the two lots at Upper town (Dogtown) and 25 votes cast to build a new building at Lower town (Squawtown). On the question of disposing of the condemned building, of 56 votes cast, 29 were for selling and 27 against.

Then, once again, on August 12, 1922, Thomas H. Williams filed a complaint against the Trustees of School District No. 6 charging the June election had been illegal, and that Notice of Election signs had not been properly posted. At the time of

143

filing, Williams posted bond stating he would pay all costs and reasonable fee for counsel incurred conditioning if it finally be determined that said injunction was wrongfully granted. This was issued September 14, 1922 in Chambers at Blackfoot Idaho — 6th Judicial District — Ralph W. Adair as Judge.

At this time Judge Adair disqualified himself, and the case was referred to Honorable James G. Gwinn, Judge of the 9th Judicial District of the State of Idaho.

On September 20, the Defendants, R.B. Cothern and C.S. Thompson filed a demurrer denying the allegation that the election notices were not posted in three public places as required by law prior to the June election. It was also at this time that Cothern and Thompson resigned as Trustees of School District No. 6, and Mrs. Affie Cothern and John Connyers were appointed and qualified as acting trustees.

At the same time, in the Ninth Judicial District Court at Blackfoot, Judge Gwinn ruled that Cothern and Thompson pay the original cost of $500 dating back to the December, 1921, ruling, plus the cost of $125.74 of the current action. Back at Lower and Upper Stanley, questions arose as to the legality of whether seats on the Board of Trustees vacated by R.B. Cothern and C.S. Thompson were rightfully given to Affie Cothern and John Connyers. Finally, after some debate, it was decided that since the two appointees had been qualified for the seats they would be allowed to remain on the Board until the term expired in 1923.

For a time things seemed to be settled, at least temporarily, as to the location of the schoolhouse. But not for long. A Writ of Mandate from the Idaho Supreme Court was served on the Trustees of District No. 6 by F.W. Cummins, Sheriff of Custer County, on February 23, 1923, ordering the school to be moved back to Lower Stanley and set up in the original building. In order to comply with the Court's order several repairs were necessary on the old building. When these were made, on March 23rd, 1923 the furniture and fixtures of the school were moved back to Lower Stanley, and the remainder of the term was completed there.

Still a permanent location for the school continued to be an issue for Stanley Basin citizens. According to one facet of the law the old building did not comply with health standards. If a new one was built, there was the matter of the land on which the schoolhouse sat not being owned by the School District. In any case however, the old building had to be disposed of.

Meanwhile, before this in 1922, after the land survey for Lower Stanley townsite had been completed and Lot No. 6 had been bought by John Thompson in the School District's name (where the original schoolhouse was built) and later relinquished by the School District No. 6 because the site and the building had been condemned by the Custer County Board of Health, the lot had been offered for resale by the U.S. Land Office. At this time, November, 1922, L.S. Niece purchased lots No. 6 and No. 7 — records filed in the Land Office at Hailey, Idaho. *For more on this, see under heading "The Two Towns"*.

Thus, in the summer of 1923, after the school term was finished, Niece advertised the condemned building for six consecutive weeks as required by law, requesting that School District No. 6 move the building from his property. At the end of that time, when nothing had been done, Niece hired Earl and Charley Way and L.E. (Slivers) Hawkins to dismantle the building and haul the logs and place them on lots he owned in Upper Stanley. Here, he used the logs in construction of a home for himself and his family.

His action should have settled the matter of what direction the School District should take. *But did it?* No... since no agreement could be reached by the School Trustees and the citizens to erect a new building, and if so, where? As a result of their failure to act within a given time, the County Commissioners discontinued, or abolished, School District No. 6. However, a teacher had already been hired for the 1923-24 term at the time, and taking this into consideration, school was again held in the Benner Hotel at Upper Stanley, and allowed to finish out the term.

Finally, in October 1924, the case of "The Stanley School Fight" was dismissed in the Idaho Supreme Court, leaving Stanley Basin with no District and no schoolhouse. *NOTE: All legal context contained in this account pertaining to the Stanley School controversy was taken from the files in the Custer County Court House.*

In all evidence, the so-called fight seemed to have stemmed from the letter of condemnation written by Mrs. Rowles (Custer County School Superintendent) to R.B. Cothern (Clerk of the Board of Trustees of School District No. 6) in September 1921. And while the Stanley Basin citizens fought back and forth among themselves in their efforts to solve their school problems, their failure to do so made all of them losers ... particularly their children.

Stanley Basin was without a school until 1928 — a period of four years. At this time the citizens were finally able to organize another school district — this one School District No. 56 as granted by the Custer County Commissioners. First trustees to hold office were Sadie Merritt, Clyde Gillispie, and Dave Williams ... the latter having moved to Upper Stanley from Sawtooth Valley in order to enroll his children in school. There was still no schoolhouse, and once again the dance hall in the old Benner Hotel was allowed to be used as a schoolroom by the State Board of Health. The term that year was of seven months duration with Miss Ida Schadey as teacher at a salary of $100 per month. Miss Schadey taught four different grades with an enrollment of nine students.

School children at Upper Stanley. (1928) Left to right ... back row, Ida Shadey (teacher), Billy Dipp, Chester Dipp, William "Stub" Merritt, Nellie Merritt. Center row, Juana Wooley, and Marie Williams. Front row, Gertrude Gillispie, Stella Merritt, and Morgan Williams.

School continued to be held here in the dance hall of the Benner Hotel until the winter of 1933-34 when the log building that had served as a schoolhouse in the Sawtooth Valley (located on Fourth of July Creek) was moved to Upper Stanley.

The building was placed on lots previously deeded to the school district by Bartlett Falls, and school furnishings and fixtures moved into it. School went on according to schedule, but as the Basin's population increased, enrollment did likewise reaching from 25 to 30 pupils a term.

Then, in 1947 many of the smaller districts in outlying areas, including the Stanley District, were reorganized into one District (No. 181) and put under the supervision of the Superintendent of Schools at Challis, Idaho. A quonset type building was built to replace the log building on the same lots, and is still being used in the Seventies. At the present time a movement is underway to build a new schoolhouse.

Stories about Stanley Basin's "School Fight" have been written and told many times and many ways. In this account we have endeavored to clarify the history and facts as documented by court records, and whether we have succeeded without adding to the confusion, is for you, our readers to decide.

FIRST SAWTOOTH VALLEY SCHOOLS

Although gold seekers had penetrated the Sawtooth Valley as early as the 1880s, establishing the mining camps of Sawtooth City and Vienna at the south end of the Valley, the rest of the Valley remained virtually a wilderness into the early 1900s. By then a few school age children were there, but there was no school until the summer of 1911 when Pearl Haywood held classes in a side-boarded tent near Champion Creek for three months without pay. Students who attended Miss Haywood's classes were; Marjorie and Alden Shaw, Rupert Niece, Nellie Fisher, Alice Van, Iva and Effie Haywood, and two boys named May . . . first names not known.

In recalling the tent school, Nellie Fisher said, "I really never knew how long the school was held there because I was very small and was only able to attend the last month it was held." Nellie then went on to say, "Later a cabin was built farther out on the flat, about a mile from our place (for location see Frank Fisher story). This was the school where my Dad acted as one of the trustees until it closed." No other source of information was found on this cabin school, but Nellie did recall later that while she attended grammar school in the Sawtooth Valley, two of her teachers were Miss Grace Davis and Miss Mary Dunn.

The cabin near the Fisher place that had been built and owned by George Aiken was set up into a schoolhouse in 1919. Meanwhile, in 1918, School District No. 5 had been created; probably petitioned for by Frank Shaw, Dave Williams, Frank Fisher, and a few other families who now lived in the Valley.

Esther Foley taught for the two years that school was held in the Aiken cabin. Her first year, the winter of 1919-20 she taught fourteen students, ages ranging from six to thirteen in grades one, two, five, and six. The term started December 1, 1919 and ended June 11, 1920 . . . a period of six months. The 1920-21 term was more or less the same with an enrollment of sixteen students . . . eight boys and eight girls. Mrs. Foley's salary was $875 for the term.

A new schoolhouse was built on Fourth of July Creek during the summer of 1921, and although Mrs. Foley wanted to retire from teaching in order to work with her husband on their homestead, she said, "I had put up with the crowded quarters at the old Aiken place, so I just had to have the experience of teaching the first year in the new building on Fourth of July Creek."

Her enrollment for that year of 1921-22 was fifteen students. Mrs. Foley kept her word, and after the term was finished, retired from teaching. School continued to be held at the Fourth of July Creek schoolhouse for several years. Names of the teachers are not all known. The 1922-23 term however saw only eight pupils registered . . . 5 boys and 3 girls, as shown on school records. The teachers salary was $865. The term of 1923-24 recorded only six pupils, teachers salary $840 for the term, and eventually the school was closed and the building moved to Upper Stanley.

Prelude to:

HOMESTEADERS

Unlike many parts of the West, the Stanley-Sawtooth Country did not fade and die after the decline of mining done there. True, the towns of Vienna and Sawtooth City in the Sawtooth Valley were ghosted and parts of the Stanley Basin were left dotted with deserted miner's cabins and rusting, mining machinery as silent reminders of the ones who had worked their claims and moved on. But there were those who stayed and, realizing the region's potential as a cattle raising empire and a place to make a home, were there when the land was surveyed for homesteading under the Homestead Law.

This law, called the Federal Homestead Act, was passed by Congress and signed by President Lincoln on May 20, 1862, climaxing a struggle between members of Congress and a Land Reform crusade that lasted for more than forty years. It was during this session of the thirty-sixth Congress of the United States that Galusha Grow of Pennsylvania introduced a homestead law bill that met with approval of Congress, but was vetoed by President Buchanan. Two years later this bill, along with compromises, again passed Congress and was signed by President Lincoln. Horace Greeley, son of a New Hampshire farmer, classed as "a man of the common people," and a member of the National House of Representatives at that time, had favored this bill. When it became law, it was then that he made his famous statement, "Go West, young man. If you cannot buy and pay for a home in the East, go make one in the broad and fertile West."

Under this Federal Homestead Act, any person who was a citizen, or intended citizen, of the United States, twenty-one years of age, or older, and who had never borne arms against the Government of the United States, could file on an open section (160 acres) of surveyed land in their area at the nearest Federal Land Office. In the case of the Stanley-Sawtooth area,

149

the Land Office was located at Hailey, Idaho and remained there until it was moved to Blackfoot, Idaho in 1925. The filing fee was $10. After filing, the applicant was required to establish a residence, build a habitable home, and put at least one-eighteenth of the acreage under cultivation. An applicant had five years in which to make his final proof, and if he could meet these requirements, plus the payment of $1.25 per acre ($200 for the 160 acre tract), the land was his.

Although very few desert entries were made in the Stanley-Sawtooth country in the early days, for a time there were such tracts allotted and open to be filed on. Requirements on a desert entry differed from a homestead entry in that a person was not required to establish a residence if said land was located adjacent to his homestead. Also, he could file on 80 to 320 acres, while the cost amounted to $2.50 per acre plus the filing and final proof fees. From the time these laws went into effect in 1862, many modifications were made on them through the years, but until 1962 both the Homestead Law and Desert Entry Law remained basically the same. In reference to the passing of these laws in 1862, a month before his inauguration, when asked his opinion of the Homestead Act, President Lincoln said, "I am in favor of settling the wild lands into small parcels so that every poor man may have a home."

Needless to say, the settlers who came and stayed in the Sawtooth and Salmon River region were far from being well-off financially, and after filing on a homestead tract, found it necessary to work very hard, not only to meet the requirements, but to sustain themselves while so doing. As one old-timer put it, "Most of us were dirt poor and actually had very little to do with aside from our hands and backs. We did everything and anything we could to make a dollar to help us get by while we were building and working our land. Nothing about it was easy, and I assure you, it took guts and determination to get through those times. But it was a proud day indeed when we walked out of the Land Office at the time we made the final proof and knew the homestead was truly OURS."

As before stated, a number of the first settlers in the Stanley-Sawtooth country made claim to their land through the "Squatter's Rights" law since no Government Surveys of the land in the area were completed prior to 1911. In recalling how they went about measuring the tract of land she and her husband, Bill Merritt, had chosen for a homestead in the Stanley Basin in the late fall of 1908, Mrs. Sadie Merritt said, "We

Crude implement sometimes used by homesteaders to measure land.

just done the best we could. We used a compass and tape and stepped it off. I think some of the folks had a surveyor come in to help them measure theirs, but we didn't. As it turned out, when the Government Survey was finally made, we had almost missed getting our house on the land we wanted. It was within 100 feet of the lines."

Aside from the Merritt's and surveyor's methods, another way was to make a wheel of light material that measured exactly thirty-one and one-half inches in diameter. The circumference of this wheel would come within a hair measuring eight feet, three inches... or one-half rod. By setting this wheel in a frame and pushing it wheelbarrow fashion along two sides of a tract of land, counting the wheel's revolutions at the equivalent of one-half rod each, the number of square rods and hence the number of acres could be determined.

While the following sketches are thought to include the majority of early settlers in both the Stanley Basin and Sawtooth Valley, we feel the list may be incomplete. Yet no one was overlooked intentionally inasmuchas we found it impossible to search out everyone who might have lived there at one time or another during those early years.

Here, too, we point out the distinction between the Sawtooth Valley and the Stanley Basin as did Ruth Niece, currently writing a column in the *Challis Messenger* weekly paper. Quote: "The beautiful valley lying from Stanley south, and including Smiley Creek, is the Sawtooth Valley and not the Stanley Basin as referred to by so many, and even printed in the *Boise Statesman, Twin Falls Times,* and other papers as such. The Stanley Basin lies northwest of Stanley, beyond Nip-N-Tuck Mountain in the Stanley Creek area where Captain Stanley discovered gold over a century ago."

DAVID AND LOUISE CLARKE

As far as can be determined, the David (Dave) Clarke family was the first to settle and homestead in the Sawtooth Valley, filing their claim in 1899. Dave, New York born, was married to Louise Peters who was born of German parents at Boone, Iowa. Before coming to Sawtooth Valley, they had lived several years at Denver, Colorado where Dave's brother, Fred, owned a restaurant. At the time of the couple's arrival in Idaho, they had a nine year old son named Paul ... born November 30, 1890. How the Clarkes happened to choose the then very isolated Sawtooth area, aside from seeking a new start in a new land, is not known. Both man and wife were in their mid-Thirties at the time of their arrival in the Valley.

Dave and Louise Clarke beside their home at the Clarke Hot Springs in the Sawtooth Valley. About 1905.

At any rate, the site they chose for their homestead included a natural hot springs that had been discovered by a Mr. White in 1880. Mr. White is thought to have been related to Mrs. Tommy Reid who at one time lived at Sawtooth City, now a ghost town site on Beaver Creek in the Sawtooth Valley. When the Clarkes came on the scene, the springs, called "White's Hot Springs" had been abandoned. In establishing a residence on their homestead, the Clarkes lived in a large, three-room, log house connected to the hot spring by a long boardwalk where a wooden shelter was erected over the springs. This soon became known as "The Clarke Hot Springs," and even today is so-called by many people who live in the Stanley-Sawtooth area. A barn and corrals for horses and cattle were added nearby.

The first several years in the Valley were difficult ones for the Clarke family, but with hard work and good management they eventually were able to improve their land and acquire a nice herd of cattle. The mineral springs proved to be of great benefit to the Clarkes. As more settlers came into the country and travelers passed through, the Clarke Hot Springs grew in popularity as a stopping place, especially for the Valley residents.

Meanwhile, by 1903, the Frank Shaws had moved into the area and taken up a homestead near the Clarke place. Also, by then, a few single men and/or men whose families were not with them, had taken up land in the area ... at least enough population to merit some form of mail service there. This prompted Dave Clarke to apply for an appointment for postmaster in the Valley; received July 30, 1903. On his property, Dave erected a post office that for many years was known as the Pierson Post office, the name being taken from Dave's middle name ... David Pierson Clarke. This was located on the old dirt road which for years trailed along the foothills on the east side of the Valley floor. Fifteen people were living in the vicinity at the time of the appointment, but as time went by, more came to reside there and use the mail service. The only available records of his salary are listed as follows: $25 for the year 1905, $57 for 1907, $79 for 1909, and $70 for 1911. Dave kept the post office for twelve years, it being discontinued in 1915. Records do not state why this post office was discontinued, but until 1918 when the Obsidian Post office was established the Valley people did not have a regular post office.

Through these years, the Clarkes made many friends. As a stopping place, they extended a warm welcome to all who came their way. In the dining quarters of their home they had a large, round, lazy-susan type table that was made and given to them by Dave's brother, Fred, when they moved to Idaho from Denver, Colorado. This table never failed to draw both comments and compliments from visitors who sat around it to partake of a meal. Being an excellent cook, Mrs. Clarke usually kept it loaded with special goodies ... homemade bread and fresh churned butter, jams and jellies, and pie or cake if ingredients to make them were available. Because of the novelty of this type of table, children especially delighted in gathering around it at mealtime. When a comment was made by a first-time visitor, in reply, Dave, who had a quaint, dry sense of humor, would say, "You know, this is a lazy host's table . . . only one other like it, and it's in Denver at my brother Fred's. He made both of them. Saves time, waiters, and work . . . don't you see?"

Mr. Clarke was not a large man, while Mrs. Clarke, sturdy pioneer woman that she was, appeared to be a bit on the raw-boned side. She was admired and generally well liked by most people who knew her, either because of, or in spite of, her direct open manner. Very outspoken, she talked to the men who stopped there just as another man would, and she could swear with the best of them . . . certainly not considered a lady-like thing in the early days. Even so, if someone displeased her, she could turn the air blue, and woe be unto the offender. Yet she possessed a decided sense of fairness, too. One example lies in a little story told by Dave Williams while he was carrying the mail and made regular stops at the Clarke's. He said Louise Clarke had seemed not to like him from the beginning and didn't mind letting him know it. Then one time he had had an extremely hard, cold trip bringing in the mail by dogsled over Galena summit from Ketchum, and by the time he reached the Clarke place he and the dog were nearly frozen. Taking the dog inside with him where it was warm, and where it stayed right at his side, or lay at his feet, Mrs. Clarke, after observing the dog's actions, in her direct way said to Dave, "Well, there must be some good in you . . . the dog seems to like you."

During these years, Paul, the Clarke's son and only child, grew to manhood . . . about his father's size and with the same dark hair. He was twenty-six years old in 1916, a good hand around the ranch and as yet unmarried. That year, Mrs. Clarke became ill and went to Denver for treatments, and before the year was over, died there. Paul continued to stay on the ranch with his father, working and helping out as best he could.

That winter, since Sawtooth Valley was without a post office at the time, Valley residents had to pick up their mail at Lower Stanley. Snows were heavy and deep by the month of February. Near the last of the month Dave Clarke decided to go to Stanley after the mail even though a warming trend had started snow-

154

slides throughout the Stanley-Sawtooth area. A week later, when he failed to return to the ranch, Paul became alarmed and enlisting the help of neighbors, went to look for his father. Following his tracks to Gold Creek, they found a huge slide blocking the trail with Dave's tracks leading into the slide, but none coming out on the opposite side, giving proof that Dave was buried beneath the deep snow pack. After two days of digging his body was found, frozen and stiff. The body was taken by dogsled over Galena Summit for services at Hailey, Idaho, and subsequently shipped to Boone, Iowa for interment.

Prior to the arrival of Dave's body in Hailey, and keeping in touch by telephone, for several days the *Wood River Daily Times Newspaper* ran items on the accident. The first of these items, dated February 28, 1917, was headlined: "Dave Clarke Gone . . . The Humorist of Pierson Buried in a Snowslide." The item then went on to report the accident as it happened in the Sawtooth Valley. The *Times* continued with the items up to and including the March 4th, issue which carried an announcement of rites and services to be held for Dave that day. Being a 32nd Degree Mason, these included both the Rose Croix and Blue Lodge Mortuary Rites, the latter to be conducted by Herbert McPheters who was then acting as Worshipful Master. Scottish Rite Masons who were to attend Dave Clarke's Rose Croix services were John R. Kelley, Mark Aukema, Hobart Beamer, Drs. Kleinman and Wright, Harold Brownell, Wes. B. George, J.C. Fox, H.R. Plugoff, S.M. Friedman, Emil Friedman, Robert T. Tustin, and J.G. Hedrick. The item also noted that "Other Nobles from Bellevue and Ketchum will come to the services." Note: *No obituary for Dave Clarke could be found.*

After his parent's deaths, Paul remained on the ranch in Sawtooth Valley. In the summer of 1919 he married Nellie Fisher, daughter and only child of Frank and Electa Fisher who lived on a ranch nearby. The couple went on to live a full and happy life. They had no children, but did have one another and the love of her good parents who accepted Paul along with Nellie as their own.

David and Louise Clarke, Paul's own parents, were always remembered as being among the first true pioneers who helped to open the way for other settlers in the Sawtooth Valley.

FRANK GILBERT FISHER

Clarity of name:

Most records refer to Frank Gilbert Fisher as "Frank Fisher," and although quite correct in use, early references tend to confuse his name with that of an uncle, Frank F. Fisher. The mixup is due to the fact that both men held mining interests in the Sawtooth Valley and adjacent areas for a number of years, sometimes together, and sometimes separately. However, Frank F. Fisher was a resident of Boise, Idaho, while Frank Gilbert Fisher resided most of his life in the Salmon River country. The following pertains to Frank G. Fisher, his wife Electa, and the marriage of their daughter, Nellie Fisher, to Paul Clarke.

The Frank G. Fishers:

As a child living in Nebraska with a serious asthmatic condition, when doctors told his parents he would soon die unless taken to a different climate, Frank Gilbert Fisher was promptly packed off to Idaho to live with his uncle, Stant Fisher at Blackfoot. The year was 1874, and at the time Stant Fisher was agent on the Fort Hall Indian Reservation located between Blackfoot and Pocatello.

After awhile, with health greatly improved, and fast growing into young manhood, Frank made his way to the Salmon River country where he learned to prospect and to work at placer mining in the Stanley Basin. At Clayton, a short distance down Salmon River from the town of Lower Stanley, sometime later, he met and fell in love with Electa Brockway. They were married near his twenty-ninth birthday, June 14, 1898.

Both Electa and Frank loved children, but not until October 17, 1903 were they blessed with a baby daughter named "Nellie." Because of Electa's delicate health, Frank insisted she go to Blackfoot for the birth of the baby. Nellie was their only child, and naturally the light of their lives for as long as they lived.

While mining in the Sawtooth Valley and vicinity in the early 1900's the Fishers made friends with the few people who had come to live there ... mainly the Frank Shaws, the Dave Clarkes, and the Dave Williams. As time passed, and seeing a bright future for himself and his family in this scenic, peaceful

Valley, in 1911 Frank took up a homestead claim on the east side of the valley, across the Salmon River from the Sawtooth Mountain range, and in close proximity to what would later become the Dave William's spread. Here he built a large two-story house, several outbuildings and corrals. As he accumulated stock, he began to take an interest in raising beef cattle to butcher for sale in the Basin and the Valley, eventually attaining a herd of 200 head, mostly white-face Herfords and mixed breed red Shorthorns.

When Nellie neared school age, with no school yet established in Sawtooth Valley, Mrs. Fisher, like other mothers with school age children in the region, taught her blonde, petite little daughter at home. Although this would not be considered standard today, in the beginning it was an accepted practice, and relied on in the sparsely settled areas of the West as a way to keep children abreast with education. Surprisingly, many of these children were generally well learned and often more advanced than their contemporaries across the Nation. In Sawtooth Valley, Esther Foley, a teacher for a number of years before coming to live there in 1919, attested to this when she was asked to teach that winter and the two terms following.

New to the country and fresh from Iowa where she had had most all the conveniences of the day at her disposal, at first, Esther said she had some misgivings about teaching the Valley children. "But I was amazed at their general knowledge when I enrolled them that first year," she said later. "That, along with their eagerness for more learning made my three years of teaching there the most rewarding of my entire teaching career."

Nellie, however, in the fall of 1911, just before she turned eight years old, attended classes in a side-boarded tent near Champion Creek, during the last month school was in session there. "Mother and I had been in the mountains with Dad all summer while he worked on his mining claims, and on returning home to the ranch I was able to go for that one month," Nellie recalled in later years.

Like all the Sawtooth Valley children, Nellie delighted in school. In her case, being the only child, aside from her studies, she enjoyed the companionship of other girls and boys. To be sure the Frank Fisher household had numerous visitors who came with their children throughout the years, but to Nellie school was a place for both learning and play. When Nellie was ready for high school, the Fishers rented a house in Ketchum, over the Galena Mountain in the Wood River country, and sent her to school in Hailey.

Soon after that, Nellie married Paul Clarke, only son of David and Louise Clarke. The year was 1919. Alone after the death of both his parents two years before, Paul, now owner of the Clarke ranch, continued to keep and operate it, but built a house for himself and Nellie on the Fisher property so they could be near her mother and father.

In November 1921, Frank Fisher accepted the appointment as postmaster for the Sawtooth Valley and conducted his business in a small building on the Fisher ranch. This was the Obsidian Post Office sometimes referred to as the Fisher Station, or as noted on the Forest Service maps for many years simply as "Fisher."

Frank continued to act as postmaster for the next nineteen years, stepping down only when his health began to fail. Meanwhile, in 1931, Nellie and Paul Clarke had moved to the Pettit Lake area where he worked for Jim McDonald as general manager of his home place on the Clark Miller Guest Ranch, residing there for the next ten years. When Frank's health

Frank Fisher, his wife, Electa, and Bonda Niece. Taken in front of the Obsidian Post Office in 1930.

began to fail, Paul and Nellie moved back to the Fisher ranch in order that she could help her father in the post office. With no one to succeed him, Nellie soon took a Civil Service examination and took over the duties of the post office from her father in 1940. She kept the post for nearly seven years.

Getting on in years now, Frank and Mrs. Fisher decided to move to Bellevue, just south of Hailey in the Wood River country, in the spring of 1945. There the climate was a bit less severe in the wintertime, and they had ready access to medical services in case of need. By now Mrs. Fisher had reached the age of sixty-five and Frank had passed his seventy-fifth birthday, causing Nellie and Paul, still living in the Sawtooth Valley to worry about their welfare, especially in view of illness. As a result Nellie was given permission by the postal department to turn the post office over to Jim Decker (not the Decker for whom Decker Flats came to be named) in the fall of 1946, and she and Paul moved to Bellevue that October. Jim Decker's appointment as postmaster came through on January 22, 1947.

Both Frank and Paul sold their ranches to Bruce Young and his boys after Nellie and Paul moved to Bellevue. The Young family lived in the Fisher home and ran cattle on both ranges, trailing them from the Wood River area for several years. At Bellevue, Paul, being an excellent mechanic, worked for a time in a garage at Hailey, then in the Apache Mine west of Hailey.

Although they missed the Sawtooth Valley, both couples contented themselves at their Bellevue home, growing a large garden and fruit trees on the grounds. Too, Mrs. Fisher and Nellie enjoyed a flower garden like they had never been able to grow before, and they were happy in the doing. Then death came, taking Frank at the age of eighty-four, Paul at age sixty, and Mrs. Fisher at age eighty. All are interred in the cemetery at Ketchum, Idaho.

During an interview in the spring of 1973, Nellie was able to recall names of several people she had once known in the Sawtooth Valley, along with a number of incidents that occurred there in the early days. There was John English, who she said was a "Fine old gentleman" . . . "I don't think he was ever married because he lived alone on his ranch not too far from us when we knew him. Everyone liked and respected John English very much. All of the old bachelors were well-liked. I remember them well . . . Dick Horstman, Herman Meissner, Henry Middleton, and Harry Stroble. Henry and Harry were mining partners and both especially clean men."

Harry Stroble, as Nellie indicated, was meticulously clean and neat, not only about his person and cabin, but in everything he did . . . cooking, growing a garden, mending a fence, or patching his clothes. He grew his own wheat, ground it into flour and made his own bread, and was said to be the best dandelion wine maker in the valley. At Christmas time, being a good neighbor of the Frank Fishers, he always gave Mrs. Fisher a bottle of his wine as a treat to lend cheer on the holiday for all who partook at the Fisher's table. In his garden, even though he had trouble keeping the deer and other animals away, he grew large, luscious strawberries, and peas in season.

In telling of Harry Stroble's stawberries, Nellie was reminded that in 1919 Frank gave a family from Twin Falls permission to plant a section of his ranch in head lettuce. Yes, the lettuce grew . . . huge, beautiful heads, all very solid, crisp and tasty. After selling $3,000 worth of lettuce, the shipment could hardly be missed from the field, the yield was so large. Before frost, Frank and Mrs. Fisher gathered dozens of heads, wrapped them carefully, stored them in a cellar, and were able to have lettuce to eat until well after Christmas.

Tom Kelly, who lived in the Stanley Basin, was a frequent visitor in the Fisher home when Nellie was a child. As a little one she liked to watch him roll a cigarette, and sometimes was able to talk him into letting her try to roll one the way he did with his Bull Durham tobacco. Years later, while attending a dance in the town of Stanley, a man came up and spoke to her, and Nellie recognized him as Tom Kelly, much to his surprise. "I didn't think you would remember me," he told her. "You were such a little tyke when I used to come to your dad's ranch and you pestered me to roll a cigarette. You never did learn to do it with one hand the way I did, did you?"

Another incident Nellie told about involved Mrs. Fisher's fine sourdough bread for which she was quite renowned. A Mr. Dodd from Boise had some mining interests with Frank and came to stay with the Fishers for a few days one summer. "He thought Mother's bread the best he had ever tasted, and when he was ready to go back to Boise, he asked her for a jar of starter to take to his wife so she could try her hand at making bread like Mother's. Mother fixed him up a small jar and told him to be sure to keep it warm or it would go flat." Nellie stopped to laugh. Then continuing said, "He kept it warm alright. He carried it all the way to Boise in his suitcase. When he arrived home, the sourdough had worked its way out of the jar all over his clothes, and really made a mess of everything in the suitcase."

When the news about the trip with the sourdough in Mr. Dodd's suitcase was learned back in Sawtooth Valley, it became a good joke, causing Mrs. Fisher to receive a bit of teasing. However, possessing a delightful sense of humor about most everything, Mrs. Fisher merely smiled, and with a twinkle in her eye said, "Sure I told Mr. Dodd to keep the starter warm, but I never told him to pack it in his suitcase."

More on the serious side, Nellie remembered they were sometimes subjected to severe electrical storms during the spring and summers in the Sawtooth Valley. "The big Fisher home had a tin roof, and the lightening hit it once, bounced down the side of the house and traveled along a clothesline attached to a cabin. There it splintered some of the logs, making a terrific noise, and the family who was working for Dad that summer, and who were sleeping in the cabin at the time, were not harmed . . . not even awakened by the storm. In the big house the entire household was awakened, and even though no harm was done, everyone was thoroughly frightened and alarmed at what might have happened that night."

Nellie was unable to recall anything of consequence in regard to her father's mining projects, but mining reports indicate he made any number of worthwhile strikes through the years, particularly in the early days. For example, near the head of Warm Springs Creek, just over the ridge from Sawtooth Valley from the east side, he located the Silver Bell, the Copper Queen, and the Kansas City Mines, all containing rich veins of copper, lead, and some gold. Assays from the Frank Fisher Mine in the Germania Basin locale showed 6% copper, 28% lead, with values of 52 ounces of silver and running $68 in gold to the ton. This mine sold to the partners of Felt and Coleman in the spring of 1898. Long after he had sold all of his other claims, Frank kept the Aztec, first called the Fisher Mine. He said it was a good mine and he liked to work it, and this he did a great deal. The Aztec was located on the headwaters of a creek in the Sawtooth Valley that came to bear his name . . . "Fisher Creek."

Thus ends the story of Frank Gilbert Fisher and his wife, Electa. Yet their mark is left in the soil of Sawtooth Valley, for surely and certainly these kindly, gentle people had a share in making the Sawtooth region as we know it today.

161

THE FRANK WISE SHAW FAMILY

According to records, Frank W. Shaw was the second man to homestead in the Sawtooth Valley, Dave Clarke being the first. As a mining engineer, Shaw came to the Valley in October of 1902 to expert the Fisher Mine at the head of Fisher Creek. While there, he and his wife, Catherine, came to love the area. Later, when he decided the ore in the mine was not rich enough to merit the amount of work required under adverse conditions of the terrain where it was located, he declined the job.

However, reluctant to go elsewhere, he asked Catherine if she would like to settle in Sawtooth Valley. "We could take up a homestead tract and make our home here if you would like to stay," he told her. Mrs. Shaw liked the idea, and after selecting a site at 6,900 feet elevation on Fisher Creek at the foot of the White Cloud Mountains, he filed on it in the Federal Land Office at Hailey, Idaho in 1904. That spring the Shaws, with their son, Preston, born October 22, 1892 at Deadwood, South Dakota, began their ranch that became known both far and near, as "The friendly house."

Born in EcClair, Wisconsin, February 12, 1859, Frank Shaw moved with his parents, first to Marshalltown, Iowa, then to Los Angeles, California, where after spending twelve years working in the Southern Pacific Railroad yards, he turned to mining engineering. It was during this time that he met Catherine Barter Fitch whom he married at her hometown of Evansville, Indiana on April 29, 1890. From that date until coming to the Sawtooth Valley in connection with his engineering job, the couple traveled from one mining locality to another, mostly in the Black Hills of South Dakota and the Ozark Mountains of the Midwest. Perhaps it was the contrasts of these locales, but whatever it was, Mr. Shaw was already impressed by the beauty and tranquility of the Sawtooth region by the time he was joined by "Kitty," as he so fondly called his wife, in the fall of 1902.

In his diary kept through the years, now in the hands of Martin Pollock of Sante Fe, New Mexico, from time to time he made entries such as: "August 24, 1902 . . . Drove buckboard to Clarke's Hot Springs (Dave Clarke's place) and had a fine bath. A Mr. Burroughs and a Mr. Willis, new people at the Stanley Dredge, came toward evening."

"September 19, 1902 . . . Kitty sent telegram saying she is on her way to join me."

Soon after this he met his wife and son at Ketchum, and while on the way back to the Fisher Mine property, he stopped to rest the team on a rise of ground near a clump of pine trees above Fisher Creek. Mrs. Shaw, looking back across the vast expanse of lush meadow land toward the snow-capped Sawtooth Peaks exclaimed, "Oh, how very lovely it is here!" In way of answer, her husband asked her how she would like that particular spot for a cabin. Her reply reflected her thinking as the wife of a traveling mining engineer, as she had no idea this would become home for the next thirty-four years. "Yes, a couple of years here would be glorious," she told him. Thus, in a

Mr. and Mrs. Frank Shaw . . . early settlers in Sawtooth Valley.

large two-room cabin on this very site, the little family began a new kind of life that would list them among the first hardy pioneers in the Sawtooth Valley.

According to an entry in his diary on December 25, that year of 1902, the Shaws were settled in their new home for Christmas. He told of inviting Will and Frank Jenks, their nearest neighbors, Tom Williams, a trapper in the area, and Dave and Louise Clarke for Christmas dinner with them. He then explained that Frank was the only one who came, saying, "Will did not feel able to make the trip, and Tom had to check on traps to the north. We didn't expect the Clarkes because shoeing (snow shoeing) is bad on our impassable roads. We had a nice dinner: Roast venison and spuds, peas, cheese straws, mince pie, chocolate cake, canned pears, apples and candy. Kitty gave Preston a little spoon she had got in Denver as she came through on her way here, and a pair of socks for me. I had nothing to give but the candy I bought. Weather is nice with sun shining a good part of the day."

Frank Shaw ranch home in winter.

Through the years of 1903 and 4, Mr. Shaw made mention of the Clarkes, Tom Williams and the Jenks brothers quite often. He told of Mrs. Shaw learning to ski, and of her doctoring a back ailment for him with a lard and turpentine rub. He also told of repairs made on the leaky roof of their cabin, difficulty of getting mail in and out of the Valley, especially in winter, and made mention of various people who were living in the Stanley Basin at that time . . . the Benners, Fred and Len Powell and Mrs. Powell, George Smith from Joe's Gulch, and Henry Sturkey from his diggings on the headwaters of Kelly Creek. He also spoke of the Frank Fishers and the fact that Frank was mining in the Valley.

When the decision was made to take up a homestead and the filing done soon thereafter, Mrs. Shaw was expecting their second child. Mr. Shaw became concerned when she developed complications and took to her bed that May of 1904. By late June when she failed to improve and the time for the arrival of the baby drew near, he arranged for the help of a woman from Stanley, made a makeshift ambulance of a spring wagon by padding it with a bedspring and mattress and took her over the Galena Summit to Hailey where she could have proper medical attention. The trip required three long grueling days over dirt roads still breaking up from the spring thaws. From the Shaw ranch to Hailey, the distance was about fifty-five miles, which today, with our modern cars and hard surfaced roads can be made in less than two hours. Back in the early days, however, things were different, but the Shaws did arrive safely in time for the birth of their one and only daughter, Marjorie, born July the 6th, 1904. Their third child, another son named Alden, was also born at Hailey sixteen months later on November 5, 1905.

Mrs. Shaw's health improved considerably after that, allowing her to work side by side with her husband building up and expanding their ranch holdings. They raised and butchered their own beef, pork, and lambs, and ran numerous head of cattle and horses on the range for sale or trade. Cows were milked for milk and butter, they raised chickens and turkeys for the table and for the eggs, they grew strawberries, gooseberries, raspberries, and rhubarb and a large vegetable garden in the summer. To feed the stock they put up enormous amounts of hay every year. In the house Mrs. Shaw did the baking, churned butter, made cheese, rendered lard and grease and made soap, scrubbed and cleaned, washed and ironed, knitted and sewed. Although hands were hired to help both inside and outside whenever possible, her chores were endless. Yet she found time to conduct classes on a regular schedule in order to teach her children the three R's until into the early Teens when a school district was organized, a schoolhouse built, and a qualified teacher hired to teach the few children then living in the Sawtooth Valley.

Despite all the work on the ranch, the Shaws always seemed to enjoy company, extending a warm welcome to all who came their way. In fact, their hospitality became known far and wide to the extent that the Shaw ranch became a kind of guest ranch. Through the years Mrs. Shaw kept a guest register that listed people from every state in the Union as well as several foreign countries, who spent from a few days to several weeks with them in the summertime. Various dignitaries often numbered among the guests . . . Senator William E. Borah, "the Lion Heart of Idaho" for one, during the summer of 1925 and 26.

Meanwhile the children grew and thrived. Together, the Shaw family interests were varied. They hunted and fished, picnicked and boated on the mountain lakes, took hikes and studied nature, learning the habits of animals and the types of flora that grew in the region, and, in so doing came to know well all the trails in the high country. Both parents and children were at home in the saddle. Marjorie, for example, could set a horse and ride like a champion giving her two brothers much competition. Mr. Shaw liked to experiment with the growing of different kinds of grains and grasses. In his diary, when writing of his experiments, he mentioned planting Macaroni wheat and types of barley along with Boomos and Redtop clover, timothy and Alsyke. A Doctor Harry Harlan who worked at the U.S. Agricultural Experiment Station in Washington D.C., spent two summers at the ranch working with Frank Shaw experimenting on a certain kind of grain that, due to the cool climate, proved unsuccessful. The entire family liked and enjoyed music and dancing. Mrs. Shaw played the piano, and beginning as a young man, Preston played the drums for several years with an orchestra organized by Claude and Mary Gillispie.

And so the Frank Shaw family led busy, useful lives. Yet no matter how hard they all worked, they still found time for pleasure and relaxation. Mr. Shaw had a saying for this, "Mountain folks never live in haste." Eventually, both Preston and Alden married, while Marjorie remained single. She chose to stay at home, and when her mother wanted to visit relatives back in Indiana, she took her mother's place as lady of the house.

*Marjorie Shaw and her mother,
Catherine Shaw Rheim. 1933.*

That was the winter of 1929 and 1930. Age was beginning to tell on both the elder Shaws, and although he was not feeling especially well himself that fall, Mr. Shaw insisted that Mrs. Shaw take the trip and spend the winter with her sister. Not well herself, she did go, thinking it would make her feel better. Then, while she was away, on March the 4th, 1930, Frank Shaw died, and as he had requested, was buried on the ranch property.

On her return to the Sawtooth Valley, Mrs. Shaw attempted to operate the ranch alone, but without her husband, and still held back by ill health, things were not the same. As a result, in about 1935 or 36 she divided the ranch between her three children and again went to Indiana where she re-married and stayed for a time. She came back to the Valley later, however, and in December 1942, she died and was buried in the little private cemetery beside Frank Shaw. Three other graves are in this cemetery located on the mesa of the Shaw ranch ... Alden's first wife, and the twin sons of Preston and his wife, Sylvia.

It was in June 1937 that Alden and Preston sold the south part of the ranch, now owned by Dale Reynolds, to a sheepman named McVey, then deeded the remaining parts of their holdings to their sister, Marjorie. As before, with hired help, she continued to live on and operate the ranch until her health too,

167

began to fail. Finally, about 1957, she sold the part of the ranch located on the bench overlooking Fisher Creek to Fred Humphreys and Ernest Day of Boise, Idaho, who own it today. The other part of the ranch, located along Fisher Creek and on the valley floor, she sold to Jack Furey and his brother, Sherman, of Challis and the Pahsimeroi Valley. The following year Louis Racine of Pocatello, Idaho became a partner. During ensuing years homesites have been sold to various individuals, but because of negotiations with the Sawtooth Recreation Area officials, full titles to the sites are yet to be passed into the hands of said buyers.

Many people in the Stanley-Sawtooth country, as well as other parts of the West, can remember different members of the Shaw family, generally agreeing that they were a highly respected family. Certainly they had a host of friends throughout the area who regretted the demise of the "Shaw Ranch" and "The friendly house beside the road in the Valley." Now, like other pioneers and most of the oldtimers of the region, the Shaws are gone, leaving only a few old neighbors and their grandchildren to witness all the many changes which have occurred since they passed on.

Frank Shaw ranch home in summer.

DAVE WILLIAMS

Born in 1880 at Charmersburg, Pennsylvania (near Pittsburg), Dave Williams came West to join his brother, Tom, in Flagstaff, Arizona when he was seventeen years old. Following mining, the two young men traveled over most of Arizona and Nevada. Back in Arizona again, they outfitted a wagon, and traveling through the Pinel Mountains to Utah and Salt Lake City, finally arrived in Idaho and the Sawtooth Valley in 1900. From there they went to Thunder Mountain looking for work, but finding none, returned to the Stanley-Sawtooth country in 1902. *Note: This was just shortly before the Thunder Mountain mining boom began.*

Stopping over where Upper Stanley is now located, Mose Storher, who had purchased the first store there from Arthur McGown Sr. in 1895, was still operating the store at that time (1902), and apparently liked the two Williams boys. He tried to persuade them to remain in the Basin and locate the many acres in the vicinity of his store that later became the H.L. Benner ranch. Both Tom and Dave were impressed and liked the country, but declined to stay since both were young and still filled with a sense of adventure for the more populated areas.

In 1904, Dave went to work in the smelter at Mackay, Idaho in the Lost River country, taking up a homestead nearby. That spring he put in a field of potatoes and one of alfalfa, and bought a few head of cattle. One day the cattle found the alfalfa field and ate so much that they all bloated and died. Dave felt the loss and said, "One of these days I'll go where alfalfa won't grow."

In the meantime, still trying to make a go of it in Mackay, Dave started a dairy, operating it for two years during the time the Mackay dam was under construction. When he sold his dairy, he took the profit and invested in the Vienna Mine and soon went broke. Finally, in 1910, Dave gave up and went to Robinson Bar on the Salmon River where his brother, Tom, was doing some mining. After working here with Tom for awhile, in 1912, he filed on a homestead tract of 160 acres in the Sawtooth Valley just over the mountains west of Robinson Bar. That year, because of his mining interests at the Bar, he could only make a showing of living on the homestead (location adjacent to the Frank Shaw ranch) by traveling back and forth by way of Warm Springs Creek. On his trips to the homestead, he would throw out a few empty tin cans and a few egg shells as a way of showing some semblence of evidence that the land had been taken up until he could get moved onto it. This he did in 1913.

At Mackay, that early spring, Dave packed a wagon with his goods, and taking his oldest son, Ted, age seven, and little daughter, Vella, a toddler, he started out, going by way of Spar Canyon to the East Fork of the Salmon River. It was a wet spring, making the wagon roads deep with mud and causing the wheels on the wagon to become solid disks of the thick gumbo as they plied through the Spar Canyon road. Ted, although a mere lad at the time, rode a horse and drove a small herd of cattle that would be needed on the homestead while his father drove the wagon.

They stopped to rest a day at Robinson Bar, then followed on up the Salmon River to Sunbeam, then Lower Stanley, and on to their new home in the Sawtooth Valley. At first Dave and the two children lived in a kind of dugout cellar that had been dug and used by someone who had filed on the site earlier and then had abandoned the claim. "The home ranch" as Ted now calls the site was just north of the Frank Shaw place.

In recalling the move later, Ted said, "It was all sagebrush at the time, and sage hens were thick everywhere. We lived in the cellar until Dad could get a house built."

At last Dave Williams was settled where "alfalfa was not growing," but times were hard in the Stanley-Sawtooth country in those days, and like the other settlers who lived there, he did everything he could to make ends meet. Aside from feeding and caring for his children and trying to build up his homestead, he must have money saved to pay for his land ($1.25 per acre) along with the filing fee and other requirements at the given time of proof as stipulated under the homestead law. With the scarcity of money and goods in the isolated region, this was not easy for any of the settlers. Too, in Dave's case, he still owed money from his Vienna Mine venture, but he was both hard working and honest.

By now in his mid-thirties, Dave did indeed work long, hard hours, seven days a week, fifty-two weeks a year. In the winter time, he took his turns carrying the mail on his back over Galena Summit between the Valley and Ketchum. In the spring he often took on the job of shearing sheep, leaving the children with the Frank Shaw family for a month or so at a time during his absence from the ranch while he did jobs for various sheepmen.

On his homestead, Dave cleared sagebrush, dug irrigation ditches, and put up hay. Eventually, he proved up on his homestead, paid off his mining debts, and succeeded in building up his cattle and horse herds. Needing to enlarge his house, he went to the old mining town of Vienna at the base of the Sawtooth Mountains on Smiley Creek, now deserted, and tore down an old building, marked the logs and hauled them to the ranch, and erected an addition to the ranch house. Very sturdy, this house is still standing and now used as a storage shed.

After Dave's marriage to Carrie Casto (daughter of Bill Casto of the mining town of Custer) in 1917, on entering the house her first time, Carrie exclaimed, "Dave! Where did you get these logs?" She had recognized the logs in the addition as having been used by her father in his cabin at Vienna because he was the only man in the mining camp who squared the logs to the inside walls.

About a year later, Dave and Carrie built a large, new home in the near vicinity of the old one. When it was completed, a house warming was given, and although it was late fall and the weather very cold, everyone in the Valley and the Basin came for the event. Folks began arriving in their wagons early on the date set. Horses were unhitched and put in the barn, and the fun began with music, dancing, games and refreshments for all. According to those who remember the event, "What a time they had!" Everyone stayed until daylight, and many remained for breakfast before taking their leave for the long trip back to their homes scattered long distances apart in the country.

During the next several years, Dave acquired more land . . . the Perry place, the John English place, and a part of the George Achen place. Also, with his son, Ted, he bought the Clark place (not the David Clarke at Clarke's Hot Springs) for back taxes. Later, Ted traded cattle for Dave's half interest in this place, and it is where Ted and his wife, Phyllis, have lived for many years.

As Mrs. Dave Williams, Carrie bore three children . . . two daughters, Marie and Norma, and a son named Morgan, in that order, along with mothering Ted and Vella, Dave's children by his former marriage. Dave and Carrie were good parents to the five children and saw to it that each of them received a good education. Time passed, and the children grew up, married and made homes of their own. In 1947, with his health beginning to fail, and now in his late sixties, Dave retired. In way of preparation Dave divided his ranch holdings between the five children. Ted was given a tract of what is now a part of the Rocky Mountain Dude Ranch, Vella received the Perry place, Marie the place now owned by the Cutler family, Norma's place was the tract now owned by Marvin and Fern Larson, and Morgan got the "home place."

After the division was completed, Dave and Carrie Williams moved to Challis where they bought a house and began a slower pace of life. However, Dave had always been too active and energetic to be idle, even though he was far from being well. For awhile he sold Watkins products. This enabled him to get out among people and was something he enjoyed until he became too ill to make his calls and deliveries to his customers. Dave was bed-fast the last few months of his life . . . he passed away December 30, 1950 and is buried in the Stanley Cemetery.

Carrie recalls that after Dave's retirement from ranching, the two of them spent two winters in Arizona before they

Dave and Carrie Williams

172

finally settled down to living permanently in Challis. She also adds that she and Dave were married at Custer, Idaho by Judge A.R. Smith, who figured prominently during the second mining boom on the Yankee Fork of the Salmon River above Sunbeam. "Bill Centauras and Della (Mrs. Arthur Sr.) McGown stood up with us," Carrie remembers. "For a part of our honeymoon we went on a camping trip over on the Loon Creek before we went home to the ranch in Sawtooth Valley."

Like his brother, Tom Williams, Dave was a rugged outdoorsman, especially in his younger years. When he first came to the Stanley-Sawtooth country and still unmarried, he hunted in the high reaches of the Sawtooth peaks and in Bear Valley with Tom. Both were friends of Charlie (Emil) Grandjean, a naturalist and later a forest ranger in the Boise and Payette areas adjacent to the Sawtooth region. Although the men hunted a variety of game animals, grizzly bear headed the list. At the time, the huge bears were roaming the country in great numbers and were looked on as predators, presenting a threat to man and to other animals.

After Dave was well established on his homestead in the Valley, he operated a kind of dude ranch, guiding hunters into surrounding mountain ranges. At the time more mountain sheep were said to habit the White Cloud peaks than any of the mountain ranges in Idaho. Dave's son, Ted, remembers hearing his dad tell about when he and Tom hunted together as young men, how they often bagged rams with heads that made beautiful trophies, selling many such heads for a good price. Several of these were mounted and hung in Perk's Saloon at Mackay, Idaho.

Through the years, despite Dave's struggle to make ends meet and to get ahead, and regardless of his own circumstances, he never seemed to be able to refuse a helping hand to anyone in need. Ted tells a little story concerning a family who came to the Valley and settled for awhile on the Salmon River not far from the William's ranch. In Ted's words, "They were a very poor family and had one boy and a girl. Everyday, they would wade the river and come to our place for something to eat, and we would give them milk and eggs to take back with them. The girl didn't have enough clothes to wad a shotgun, and Dad felt sorry for all of them. One day he dug through a trunk of things he had and found some pieces of clothing that fit the girl, fixing her up pretty good. He gave the boy some clothes, too."

"Dad helped these people all he could, and they made it through the winter, but they finally left the next summer. There were other families, too. One time a Spanish family lived near us for awhile, and the man worked for Dad some. Then Dad had a lot of friends among the Indians that used to come from the Fort Hall Reservation at Pocatello to fish and camp along the Salmon River during the summer. There was one old Indian named Johnny Williams. He used to stay in the old Rathmeyer house. Well, Dad would lend him traps to catch ground squirrels for him. Dad told Johnny he would give him 2¢ a tail for every one he caught, and that Indian pret-near broke Dad. When he left he gave Dad a pair of buckskin gloves that fit just perfect."

"One time Johnny had his son and his family with him up there, and the son's little girl got an infected tooth. Her little cheek was puffed out something terrible, and she was in awful pain. The old Indian got some balsam and made a poultice and put it on her cheek. Then Dad took his car and took that Indian family clear over to Dr. Wright at Hailey. When the Dr. looked at it, he said, 'Why I can't do much with this. You have already done what is necessary by drawing the abcess to a head, and it's broken and drained. I'll just sterilize it and clean it out good, and the child will be well in no time.' Dad brought the family on back home, and sure enough, in a day or two, the little girl was all healed up. I, myself, through a friend, got Johnny a red buckskin one time. He was sure tickled with that."

"But Dad made lots of friends with all kinds of people. You know, no matter who a person was, if he happened to stop by the ranch close to meal time, he was always asked to eat. It was that way everywhere in the Stanley-Sawtooth country in those days ... when somebody stopped, he was invited to stay for dinner or supper, whichever it happened to be."

Ted also relates an amusing story that points out the scarcity of necessary things to work with in those early times. "The winter Dad was carrying the mail from Ketchum to the Valley, on the Wood River side, he carried a washboard, the only one in the country then, from one ranch to another, dropping it off at one place on his way to the Valley and picking it up on his way back. While he was gone, the women would get their washing all caught up and the washboard was ready to go on to the next place."

"Dad could carry an eighty pound pack on his back when he

174

skied over the summit, and lots of times had heavy mail order catalogs in his pack. When the snow began to soften in the early spring there was always the danger of snowslides." *Note: For more on snowslides, refer to heading: "Snowslides" in this book.*

Dave Williams, like the Dave Clarkes, the Frank Shaws, the Frank Fishers, and others who numbered as the first settlers in the Sawtooth Valley, knew the country from the primitive, raw land it was. Dave Williams built what he had by the sweat of his brow, and Ted, as his oldest son, and there at the start, was particularily aware of how it was. Needless to say, Ted has many treasured memories of those early years in the Stanley-Sawtooth country, as does his stepmother, Carrie Casto Williams.

RANGER WILLIAM HORTON

One oldtimer who, with her husband, worked with Bill Horton in the Sawtooth Valley during the Twenties, said that Bill was an old time Forest Ranger. "In fact, I sort of thought he was like one of the characters in a Zane Grey novel . . . one of the good guys, you know," she said. In describing him as she remembered, he was in his mid-Forties when she knew him, a slender, erect man, wore batwing chaps made of curly, white goatskin, high-heeled boots, red shirt and bandanna around his neck, and always carried a yellow slicker (raincoat), coiled lariat, and a pair of horse hobbles tied onto the saddle. Usually he spoke in a soft voice, was very alert and had a dry sense of humor.

William "Bill" Horton began his career with the Forest Service early in life, coming first to Idaho's Wood River country with his mining engineer father, John Horton, who had taken a job to expert a mine there. Bill's mother was dead, but his paternal grandmother was still living back East. As it turned out, father and son had barely arrived in the Wood River area when word came that she had been taken critically ill. Thinking he would be gone only a short while, John left his young son with the Billingsley family at their farm in the vicinity of Hailey and went to his mother's side. He never returned, however, since he too became ill and died, leaving Bill an orphan.

After his father's death, the Billingsley farm became home to Bill. He stayed around, helping with the farm chores and doing odd jobs for the Forest Service during the summer months until he finished school. He then went to work full-time for the Forest Service, helping to build the Russian John and the Flowers Ranger Stations in Blaine County. In about 1909 or 1910 he was sent over the Galena Summit to build the Pole Creek Ranger Station in the Sawtooth Valley and was made Ranger there.

Meanwhile, Bill had married the Billingsley's eldest daughter, Elizabeth Jane, and the couple had a daughter named Alta. Bill acted as Pole Creek Station Ranger for twenty years, and while so doing the little family maintained a home at Carey, Idaho where they spent their winters after the busy summer in the Sawtooth Valley. Coming ahead of his wife and daughter, Bill would always come on snowshoes over Galena Summit in the very early spring in order to get the station open and his

William "Bill" Horton inside the Pole Creek Ranger Station. (1910)

work lined out for the summer. Later, when the snow melted on the pass, Mrs. Horton and Alta would join him, coming by horse and buggy. Since three days were required for the trip, Bill would usually go over as far as the Russian John Station to meet them.

A great deal of Bill's work concerned sheepmen who had National Forest grazing rights in the Sawtooth Valley area. From a log of his activities, now in the hands of his daughter, Alta, he often noted having to arbitrate disputes over range boundaries. He also had to keep check on the water and feed conditions, and sometimes acted as a messenger and all around helper to the herders. Most of the herders were Basque who had little, if any, knowledge of the English language.

One amusing story Bill liked to tell about one of the herders is as follows: It was late fall when the sheep were being trailed back over the summit from the Valley to the Wood River area. Doing his job of keeping check and helping if needed, he came upon a herder trailing his band of sheep on the narrow dirt road instead of on a sheep trail marked for that purpose. Bill tried explaining that the sheep should not be on the road, but the herder would only shake his head and shrug his shoulders and say, "No savvy." It was a cold rainy day, and finally, in desperation, Bill set about to turn the sheep onto the regular sheep

177

trail, all the while making motions and pointing in an effort to get the herder to understand what had to be done. Soon the herder began to help him, and the sheep were on the trail where they were supposed to be. Although the rain had stopped and the sun was trying to break through the clouds, both men were cold and dripping wet. Bill paused before departing the herder to try again to establish communication with him. The herder broke into a big smile and in very good English said, "It sure don't rain here like it does in Oregon."

In the early days in the Sawtooth Valley, bears were most plentiful causing the herders to always be on their guard against them. Bill kept traps set around the Pole Creek Station and caught several. One was supposed to be the largest ever caught in that part of the country.

Forest and range fires were always a threat . . . then even as now. Lookouts and firefighters were kept ever alert in dry seasons since they knew full well even the smallest blaze could quickly become an inferno and cause great destruction in the Valley and on the mountainsides. However, if a fire did break out in an isolated area, it was allowed to burn itself out as a matter of practice. In this way, grass and forage would grow and be more abundant for the following year. Also, after herds and flocks had been trailed out in the late fall, oftentimes range fires were purposely set for this reason by the sheepmen. In the Twenties telephones were installed at strategic locations, and when short wave radios became popular, several were placed on the different ranches in Sawtooth Valley. This way messages could be relayed to the Ranger Station real fast. Bill developed a code which the ranchers soon learned meant different things. For example: If Bill said "Everything is going fine," the meaning was just the opposite. If he reported "Coyotes straying up to the district headquarters" it meant some official was headed that way.

In the course of his duties, Bill often visited with the ranchers in the area, and now and then Mrs. Horton would accompany him, trading newspapers and magazines with the different ranch wives they visited. He liked to tell "bear tales" and often told some good ones. His daughter, Alta, remembers her growing up years while her father acted as Ranger at the Pole Creek Station. In her teens she often rode horseback for many miles with him as he went about his duties. She came to know most of the Sheepmen and the herders who came and went in the Valley, and was a welcome guest in their camps. As a child she was allowed to ride her horse over the summit, if the weather was good, to the Galena Store to buy herself some candy . . . usually about once a month.

Bill Horton retired in 1930 and moved to California. Alta Horton had married Boyd Ellis and was living in California at the time. She and her husband brought Bill back to the Sawtooth Valley for a visit. Not well at the time, his activities were somewhat limited, but he enjoyed seeing so many familiar places and faces once again. On this trip Alta and Boyd decided to buy some land in the Valley for a home there in the future, ending up with the old George Achen ranch which they were able to purchase through a bank in Burlington, Vermont. Back in California, Bill Horton passed away in 1936.

In time Alta and her husband, Boyd, did return to make their home in the Valley. For years the old log dwelling on the Achen place, now theirs, had been used for a cattle and horse shed. Noting the good timber in the old building, Alta and Boyd decided to incorporate it into their new home and thereby preserve the original ceiling beams in the two main rooms. When this was done they built a large rock fireplace in a corner of one of these rooms, and then added other rooms to complete the overall structure. Across Highway 93 from their home, they remodeled an old building that had once been used as a schoolhouse, making it into a store which they call "The Trading Post." For many years now, Alta and Boyd Ellis have operated The Trading Post, selling Indian jewelry and curios and leather goods to tourists and others who stop by. At first they spent only their summers in the Valley, but after a time decided to stay the year around. At this time they still do. They gave their ranch the name "The Running Springs Ranch," all very picturesque alongside U.S. Highway 93 there on the Valley floor at the foot of the even more picturesque Sawtooth Mountains.

THE C.M. FOLEYS

When Carroll Foley was teaching school and in other fields of endeavor in Texas, long hours of study and lack of fresh air and exercise impaired his health to the extent friends suggested he should take a vacation to recuperate. He did so, coming to the Sawtooth Valley in early 1916. Here the land was still raw and very sparsely populated. Nevertheless, he found it to his liking. Soon he made many friends, fell in love with his surroundings, and wrote glowing letters about it all to the girl he was engaged to back in Cedar Lake, Iowa.

That is how it all started for Carroll and Esther Missman Foley. His health improved a hundred fold. Would she come with him to live here in this scenic valley? She would. He filed a homestead claim on 160 acres adjoining the Frank Shaw ranch on the north, the Snites place on the west, and Forest Service land on the south and east. As a start on "proving up," with the help of Preston (oldest son of Frank Shaw), he constructed a crude 16' by 18' log cabin with a pole roof.

Meanwhile World War I was declared, and both Carroll and Preston, being young, enlisted in the Armed Forces. When the war ended, Carroll went to Iowa where he and Esther Missman were married January 9, 1919. Esther, one of ten children, and also a schoolteacher until near the eve of her marriage, had her first glimpse of the Stanley-Sawtooth country a short time later. Needless to say, Esther felt like the tenderfoot she was ... but not for long. Together, for over forty years, the Foleys found happiness and peace beyond measure in this picturesque land that tended to remain much on the wilderness side until the event of U.S. Highway 93 through the area. To use Esther's words, "The happiest, busiest years of our lives were spent here."

Moving into their makeshift home in mid-February, 1919, since the government had allowed his time spent in the service, Carroll was able to "prove up" on his homestead that same summer. In a relatively short time, working alongside her husband, Esther had learned to wrangle horses, build fences, and all manner of ranch work. She even learned the how-to of log home building, designing and helping Carroll build a spacious three room house on their ranch. In connection with their new home, they also built a barn, shop, and garage, and corrals for their stock.

In later years the Foleys built three other homes . . . one in the Pettit Lake area that became a part of the Clark Miller Guest Ranch, and two in the Stanley Basin in the vicinity of Job Creek on what is now known as the Lowman Road (Highway 21) going toward Boise. The latter they called their "Mountains Meadows" ranch, while their first homestead was fondly referred to as "Mesa Del Monte." Carroll and Esther did all the work on the different houses, even to constructing the large, efficient rock fireplaces that contributed much to their comfort on cold winter evenings.

Carroll and Esther Foley's Mesa Del Monte ranch in Sawtooth Valley.

Going back to the early fall of 1919, Esther, prevailed upon by Frank (Dad) Shaw, who was president of the school board for district No. 5 at the time, reluctantly and with some misgivings, accepted the position of school teacher. "But just until you can find a replacement for me," she told him.

Due mainly to the region's isolation during the winter months, finding qualified teachers for their children had long been a problem for Sawtooth Valley residents. Because of this and the small number of students, no particular building had yet been designated as a school house in 1919. In fact, the few terms that had been held up to this time were conducted in whatever happened to be available. For example: one school term was conducted in a tent with boarded sides located in the vicinity of Champion Creek.

Esther Foley knew these things. She also knew the George Aiken's old two room homestead cabin on Fourth of July Creek was to be used for the school house that year. Packrats had occupied the premise for some time, necessitating a great deal of scrubbing and cleaning to rout the odor and make the cabin usable. However, the Foleys went to work with a will. Carroll, thinking it best that he do the commuting between their Mesa Del Monte ranch and the school that winter, said they would live in the back room of the cabin. This involved even more work and preparation, but neither Esther or Carroll minded. That summer, with Preston Shaw, Carroll made a trip over Galena Summit road from Ketchum with two pianos . . . one for the Shaws, and one for Esther.

As they told it later, "Carroll had one on a concord stage, and Preston had the other on a springless wagon. With all that weight, they had to tie heavy logs on the back ends of both the stage and wagon to slow their descent down the steep grades . . . but they made it without mishap."

Esther's piano was crowded into one corner of the schoolroom, and in ensuing months gave much pleasure to both students and teacher. Opening school on schedule, December 1, 1919, Esther's students ranged in age from six to thirteen years old. An end of the term program printed June 11, 1920 listed her students as follows:

School District No. 5
Custer County, Idaho
June 11, 1920

Trustees: Fred E. Gray — F.W. Shaw — C.M. Foley. Teacher: Esther M. Foley
Pupils:

Sixth Grade

Alden Shaw	Marjorie Shaw
	Clara Smith
Elliot Williams	Lillian Young
Fineous Young	Eva Young

Fifth Grade

Estella Smith	Guynnie Young

Second Grade

Vella Williams	Ida Mae Smith
	Symore Young

First Grade

Edwin Young	Constent Young

School held in the old Achen ranch house winter of 1919 & 1920. Teacher was Esther Foley. Students from left to right ... Back row ... Clara Smith, Lillian Young, Marjorie Shaw, Alden Shaw, Middle row ... Elliot "Ted" Williams, Eva Young, Guynnie Young, Estella Smith, Fineous Young. Front row ... Edwin "Eddie" Young, Vella Williams, Ida Mae Smith, and Seymour Young. The Smith girls were better known as the Goaz girls.

Esther found her students eager for knowledge, and they learned fast, completing nine months of school in seven. All of them were self-reliant and took hardships of the country and times in stride. They walked to school, rode horseback, came on sled, skiis, or whatever the weather dictated, but they came, seldom missing a day. Although Esther kept them busy with studies, she also managed for them to have time for story reading and singing accompanied by the piano. She worked in various handicrafts too, . . . needlework for the girls and leathercraft projects for the boys.

The boys prepared their own leather from cowhides, a fact reported by Florence Rowles, Custer County School Superintendent, after she had paid a surprise visit to the school. "When I arrived," she said, "there were the boys down on the floor scraping the hair off of the hides. Later Mrs. Foley showed me beautiful things the boys made from hides ... horse whips, bridles, hackamores. They were experts at making horsehair ropes too. I felt proud to witness such industry in our Sawtooth Valley young people."

On the horsehair ropes, the boys presented Esther with one for a Christmas gift during her second year of teaching in the Valley. "Certainly a treasured possession for me," she commented afterward. "Knowing the amount of work and good will that went into that rope made it one of the nicest, and most valuable gifts I ever received from any of the boys and girls I taught in all my years of teaching before I came to the Valley."

Yes, Esther taught the second term . . . and the third. A new teacher was hired to replace her the second year, but became ill and had to leave soon after the term started, causing Esther to fill in again. And the third year, a new schoolhouse had been built in the vicinity of the Aiken cabin where she had taught the first two years, and Esther said she just had to have the experience of teaching the first term in the new building before she went back to the fulltime job of ranch housewife.

Through the years, Esther kept a kind of log, or diary of sorts, including her teaching years in Sawtooth Valley. A few of the entries were: "Getting the old house cleaned, blackboards put up and repainted. Seats and desks brought from other old school." "Went to Pierson for more seats P.M." and so on. She noted all the names and ages of her students on the dates of their enrollment, and from day to day made brief references as to their activities and progress throughout the school term.

Later, the Aiken homestead cabin that housed the school where Esther taught first came to be owned by Boyd and Alta Horton Ellis who remodeled it into living quarters. This is near the Trading Post, also owned and operated by the Ellises. Alta's father was William Horton for whom Horton Peak, located in the edge of the White Cloud Mountain Range on the northeast side of Salmon River, is named.

The Foleys were good friends of the Hortons. For that matter they were good friends with almost everyone in the Valley and in Stanley Basin, especially the oldest residents . . . John English, the Paul Clarkes, the Frank Shaws, the Dave Williams, the Cal Youngs, Henry Middleton, Herman Meissner, Tom Williams, Trapper Fisher, to name a few.

When Esther completed her teaching commitment in 1922, the following year Carroll went to work for the Forest Service with the Foley Mesa del Monte Ranch assigned as headquarters for the fire-guard. As such, and on call 24 hours a day, both Carroll and Esther had many varied experiences during ensuing years. Fires were frequent in the Valley, and on more than one occasion Esther found herself involved in helping out . . . once by hauling men and tools to a fire site, and often by relaying messages to rangers and firefighters in the area.

As time went by, the Foleys accumulated several head of cattle, horses, and sheep, and in doing so, learned the value of good dogs around a ranch. All black, their first dog, named "Coalie," was given to them because he did not like sheep, by a sheepherder passing through the valley one spring. "Bird" and "Guess" came next, and although Bird was not as good with stock as Guess, he was Esther's favorite, and was trained exceptionally well as a watch and sled dog.

Esther Foley and old Model-T. Taken in the early 1920s.

"Bird was my dog and somewhat jealous of Guess," Esther said in relation to a fight between the two dogs. "Fur was flying, and they were going round and round. Bless Bob, I was so excited. In my attempt to stop the fight, I threw a pan of water on Carroll instead of the dogs. It was funny and he teased me about it for sometime afterwards, but it was the only real fight the dogs ever had."

In 1929, when the Foleys sold Mesa del Monte and moved to land they had purchased from Ottis Wells two years earlier, in the Pettit Lake area, they got another dog named "Try." With Bird and Guess, the three worked excellent in sled harness with other dogs. While carrying mail and supplies to miners still hanging on at Vienna that winter, Carroll said he found them as dependable as a team of Alaskan huskies. On leaving

185

the Valley for a time, the next fall Esther and Carroll gave Bird to Sandy Brooks who used him along with his own dogs.

As the great Depression of the Thirties advanced, the Foleys moved about a great deal. In Hailey they built another house (still standing today), and Carroll went into the real estate and abstract business for awhile. They took a trip back to visit relatives and friends in Iowa, and even went to live in Boise for a time. Yet they could not forget, and grew very homesick for their beloved Stanley-Sawtooth country.

"Come Back Country," Esther said Frank Shaw had called it in the early days . . . and come back they did, in the late Thirties. This time to settle in the Stanley Basin area. On the Lowman Road (Highway 21) going toward Boise, about four miles from Upper Stanley, they bought property and built a spacious log house with a large stone fireplace, and rented cabins to tourists. After awhile, in the same locale, they built another similar house . . . both with their own hands, calling both places their "Mountain Meadows" ranch. Here, they spent many winter evenings before a cozy, blazing wood fire, reading and listening to the radio, and generally enjoying the fruits of their labors.

Carroll and Esther Foley's Mountain Meadow ranch home about four miles west of Upper Stanley. (1938)

186

However, not all was enjoyment, even in the September years of their lives. Chores still had to be done, and snows piled just as deep as in the early years. Too, there seems to have always been a kind of unwritten law in this rugged high country that if possible, one goes to the aid of his fellowman in case of accident or trouble. While living there, and in the Sawtooth Valley, Carroll helped with more than one such rescue mission.

One such incident occurred while they still lived at Mesa del Monte when Esther was called to the Williams ranch to give first aid to a hunter who had broken his leg. With arrangements made for a doctor to meet them on the Galena Summit road as near as he could on the Wood River side, Carroll and the Williams men started out with the injured man bedded down in a wagon. But at the foot of the mountain, on the Sawtooth side, they found a herder with a flock of 2,000 sheep stalled in his attempt to trail them over Galena pass. Although it was only mid-October, an early snow storm had moved in, and already the pass was beginning to be choked with snow. What to do?

Discussing the situation with the herder, the men quickly transferred the hunter to the herders warm wagon, the Williams men went back to their ranch for horses to haze over the road as a way of packing the snow enough to trail the sheep and get the herder's wagon, carrying the injured man over the pass. Carroll went on foot over the mountain to let the doctor know of the delay. When it was all done, and the man delivered to the doctor, none the worse for the ordeal, back in the Sawtooth Valley, the Williams and Carroll merely looked on what outsiders might term an act of heroism as part of their duties to their fellowman, and as far as they were concerned, "it was all in the day's work." Such an attitude has always been of prevalence in the Stanley-Sawtooth country, for here neighbor helps neighbor and stranger alike without thought of reward or praise, especially in the early days.

Every once in awhile Valley residents and Basinites found themselves "snowed in" during the winter months, even in later years. Esther recalls how it was in 1943. "Bless Bob, we had one blizzard after another that year. The snow got so deep we could hardly do our outside chores. It kept me busy trying to keep a trail packed from the house to the corrals, haystack, and cabins on my snowshoes while Carroll shoveled snow from the cabin roofs and tended the stock. It was an endless job for both of us. The worst storm that year lasted for five days, and the temperature dipped to 54 below zero. We thought it would never moderate again."

187

Carroll Foley on his way to cut wood.

Yet despite various tragedies, the atrocious winter weather, and adversities, the Foleys found their lives in the region filled with a great measure of happiness. Although both were voracious readers, Esther did a bit of writing too, once in the Fifties with Ferris Weddle; Idaho author and writer of wildlife. And for her own enjoyment, she wrote poetry now and then. In younger years, while she and Carroll were designing and planning their first home in the Sawtooth Valley, she wrote one entitled "Dream House". It is as follows:

DREAM HOUSE

I'll dream of a house I'll build
Somewhere upon a hill,
A little cabin made of logs,
A life that's sweet and still.

I see it all within my mind,
As someday it will look,
The cozy rooms where one may rest
And read a favorite book.
A fireplace to gather 'round
As twilight shadows fall,
And many dreams will come to life
In hours that never pall.

So much of life this house will hold,
I could not ask for more,
Except a path, well worn and wide,
That leads up to the door.

However, one of Esther's favorite poems was written by Alexander Smart, titled:

BETTER THAN GOLD

Better than grandeur, better than gold,
Than ranks and titles, a thousandfold,
Is a healthy body, a mind at ease,
And simple pleasures that always please.
A heart that can feel another's woes,
And share his joys with genial glow,
With sympathies large enough to enfold
All men as brothers, is better than gold.

Better than gold is a thinking mind
That in the realm of books can find
A treasure surpassing Australian ore,
And live with the great and good of yore;
The sage's lore, and the poet's lay,
The glories of empires passed away,
The world's great drama will thus unfold,
And yield a pleasure better than gold.

THE CRITCHFIELD FAMILY

Andrew Critchfield, born at Tooele, Utah, April 8, 1865, saw the Sawtooth country for the first time while helping to drive a herd of horses to range there in the early 1900's. At that time he was ranching at Oakley, Idaho, and running sheep in the Muldoon and Martin areas. Back there after the trip with the horses to the Sawtooth Valley, he was unable to put the sight of the jagged, snow-capped peaks, the pine-studded foothills, and the crystal clear lakes out of his mind.

So it was in the summer of 1912, Mr. Critchfield brought his wife, born Leafey Ann Kimpton at Bingham, Utah on December 19 (year not known) and their children to the valley. Here, on the site where Sessions Lodge is now located, they staked off a homestead and took up a desert entry. Meanwhile, Mr. Critchfield had sold his partnership in the Golden Rule Store at Kimberly, Idaho which he had operated in connection with his ranching business. Both Andrew and Leafey had children by a former marriage as well as two of their own... Andrew Jr., always called "Bud," and a daughter, Bonda. When Leafey and the children beheld the majestic Sawtooth range and Valley floor, lush and green, spread before them as they topped Galena Summit overlooking the scene, they too, fell in love with the region.

On the homestead ground, in the spring of 1913, Mr. Critchfield erected a nice one-room cabin. Leafey peeled small poles

Mr. Andrew Critchfield, son Andrew "Bud," a daughter, Bonda, and Mrs. Leafey Critchfield. Grandaughter, Berdina Buchannan in front. Taken in front of the Critchfield ranch cabin about 1915.

190

to enclose the porch, which, when finished, not only looked attractive but provided ample storage space for wood and other things.

That fall, traveling in a covered wagon pulled by two horses called "Dave" and "Fanny," the family returned to spend the winter in the Oakley locale. Then in the spring of 1914 they came again to their homestead in the Sawtooth Valley. By driving in the daytime and camping at night along the way, the one-way trip required a full week. One of the children's favorite places to camp was in the vicinity of the Fleming Sawmill, near the Russian John Ranger Station on the Wood River side of Galena Summit. Knowing this, when they were nearing the Fleming place, Mr. Critchfield would turn to his little brood and ask, "Well, where shall we camp tonight?" In one chorus the children would answer, "Let's camp by Fleming's so we can have bread and milk for supper!" It seems Mrs. Fleming made excellent bread which she would sell to them, and she always had extra milk on hand. This was a special treat for the children after days of traveling without fresh bread or milk, making the stop one of the high-lights of the trip.

That fall it was decided they would stay the winter in the Valley instead of returning to Oakley again to reside until spring came. And stay they did ... Mr. and Mrs. Critchfield, Bonda and Bud, joined by the Buchanan family; Jennie, (Leafey's daughter by her former marriage) Jennie's husband, Bert, and their little daughter, Berdina ... making seven people in all living out the winter of 1914 and 1915 in the one-room cabin in Sawtooth Valley. Nevertheless, the two families managed to survive the deep snows and sub-zero temperatures remarkably well.

When spring came (1915) the younger family, the Buchanans, built a cabin on the desert entry land located on Decker Flat and moved there to live. Both the Buchanans and the Critchfields set about improving their ranches. Supplies were purchased at Stanley from the Niece's Store. A round trip from the ranch to Stanley and back required a full day. Usually, on these trips, Mr. and Mrs. Critchfield took along their children, Bonda and young Bud. Even today the two of them remember those trips. Bud said, "The folks would always buy lunch stuff at the store, and when we started home we would stop somewhere along the Salmon River and eat." Bonda liked sardines, and said that when they had them, she would never forget how good they tasted, then went on to remark, "The sardines were

191

The Andrew Critchfield family and the team and wagon which was their mode of travel (1915).

always kind of gritty." In reply to that, Bud laughed and said, "That was the fish's insides. You know they don't clean the little fish they make sardines of."

Hay for their stock was bought from the Hellsinger ranch near Upper Stanley and had to be hauled before the snow came. Mr. Critchfield would buy enough to last through the winter because once the roads were closed by drifting snow, they remained closed until spring, limiting travel except on snowshoes or skiis. Consequently, little traveling was done by any of the Stanley-Sawtooth country residents during the wintertime in the early days before blacktop roads and motorized snowplows.

Needing to put Bonda and Bud in school, and with none established yet in the Sawtooth Valley, the Critchfields went first to Buhl, then to Twin Falls to spend the winter of 1916-17. The following fall both the Critchfields and the Buchanans left the Valley to spend the winter at Oakley. That was the year the bad influenza epidemic spread across the Nation causing the deaths of many hundreds of people as it continued on through the winter months of 1918. Mr. Critchfield was the first in his family to be taken with it, and in late November of 1917 he passed away. On the day of his funeral, Jennie and Bert Buchanan's baby boy died. Both were buried in the Oakley cemetery.

For a time after her husband's death, Leafey worked as a cook at the Vipont Mine near Oakley, while the Buchanans brought Bonda and Bud and came back to Decker Flat to spend

192

the rest of the winter. In order to support the family, Bert was compelled to work away from home, leaving Jennie and the children alone. At the time the mail was directed to the George Snyder place which was across Salmon River from Decker Flat. Once a week Bud would go on snowshoes to pick up their mail, usually staying overnight with the Snyders. In the morning, as he prepared to leave, Mrs. Snyder would slip some treat for him and Bonda and little Berdina Buchanan into his pack. Sometimes it was a container of sugar, a can of fruit, a nice cut of meat for Jennie to cook for them, or perhaps some candy, but whatever it was, it was looked forward to and deeply appreciated by those waiting on Decker Flat. These were hard times for the family and supplies at the cabin included only the barest of necessities that winter.

When Leafey returned to Sawtooth Valley in the spring of 1918, she sold her improvements on the homestead to George Snyder, and it was he who made the final proof on that parcel of land. Then for several years, taking her two children, Bud and Bonda, with her, she traveled in the covered wagon to and from the Valley every spring and fall. In the Oakley area, or the Wood River country during the winter months she worked at different jobs. In the Valley during the summers she did the same. One summer she operated the Redfish Lake Resort for Dick Horstman who owned it at that time. Finally she bought lots in Upper Stanley, built a cabin, and lived there the year around. Bonda and Bud attended the Stanley school, grew up and both married natives of the country . . . Bonda became the wife of Rupert Niece, and Bud the husband of Stella Merritt, all still living and classed among the oldtimers left in the Stanley-Sawtooth Country at this time.

Leafey lived on in her home in Upper Stanley, her health failing in the late Thirties. In spite of the loving care given her by family and friends, on September 30, 1940, she passed away, and was taken to Oakley where she was buried beside her husband, Andrew Critchfield. In recalling their parents, Bonda and Bud remember their mother's jolly disposition. "But she had a firey temper, too," they say. "She loved the outdoors, and would rather do a man's outside jobs anytime than to stay in the house and do woman's work."

Bonda, as well as other oldtimers, say Mrs. Critchfield was a rather short, heavy set woman who always wore high-necked black sateen dresses with long sleeves. By contrast, Mr. Critchfield was a tall slender man . . . rather quiet and reserved. He

193

often spent hours whittling dainty doll furniture and trinkets for his children when he was living. Both Bonda and Bud have inherited their mother's jolly disposition, as well as some of their father's traits, and both are grateful to their parents for their pioneer heritage that continues to serve them today.

OTHER SETTLERS AND SQUATTERS
IN THE REGION

Ray Decker:

Besides the people who took up land and homesteaded in the Stanley-Sawtooth country, others also came to settle there ... some buying land and becoming permanent residents, while others simply selected sites and lived there a short time before moving elsewhere. Today a few of the geographic features in the region still bear the names of various ones of these people. Decker Flat, for instance, derived its name from Ray Decker who was the first man to build a cabin and live on the flat. Before coming there, he had lived at the mining town of Custer on the Yankee Fork of the main Salmon River.

The May Family:

Later, a family by the name of May came to live on Decker Flat in the vicinity of Hell-Roaring Creek. Very little is known of this family except that they had two boys who attended the first school that was ever held in the Sawtooth Valley. This was in 1911, and the classes were conducted in a tent set up across Salmon River from their home. The boys are remembered having been seen fording the river on horseback as they went to and from school that summer.

Henry Middleton:

Another who built a cabin and lived on Decker Flat for a time was Henry Middleton. Little is known about him other than at one time he had been in partnership with Harry Stroble on some mining claims. Like Harry, he was a single man, and well liked by the Valley residents. In later years he moved to the Stanley Basin area.

Henry Middleton

The Haywoods:

The Haywood family came into the Valley in the spring of 1910. They had four daughters . . . Iva, Effie, Pearl, and Hilda. Pearl was the teacher at the tent school in 1911, and Iva and Effie, the youngest girls, numbered among the students in her classes. Hilda married Jack Seagraves, a miner in the area. After three or four years in the Valley, the Haywood family moved to another locale.

Jack Seagraves:

Jack Seagraves, after having lived some fifteen years at Mountain Home, Idaho, and while on his way to Montana with a herd of sheep in July of 1910, stopped and stayed in Sawtooth Valley. Here he married Hilda Haywòod, and homesteaded on a part of what is now the Breckenridge place. He raised cattle and did some mining. Jack and Hilda had six children. When the couple divorced, Mrs. Seagraves kept the ranch, and Jack went on with his mining. Later, she sold the ranch and she and the children moved to the Wood River country. Through the years Jack traveled a great deal, spending time in Alaska, Nevada, Arizona, and California. Although now past ninty years old, he still holds mining claims on Rough Creek, north of Stanley, where he spends his summers.

The Auchenbaughs:

Coming from Wyoming, the Auchenbaugh family moved into Sawtooth Valley in 1912. They homesteaded and spent several years there. Eventually, they sold their ranch to Carroll M. Foley. This is a part of the Breckenridge holdings at the present time. Ray Auchenbaugh, one of the sons of the family, has spent many years in and around the area.

The Buchanans:

The Bert Buchanans were related to the Andrew Critchfield family, coming to live in the Sawtooth Valley in 1914. Bert's wife, Jennie, was Mrs. Critchfield's daughter by her first husband. They settled on Decker Flat, where they took up a desert entry on 160 acres of land. It was while living there that Jennie acted as postmistress during 1918 and '19. Bert and Jennie had one little girl named Berdina. Several oldtimers remember that Berdina was unable to pronounce her R's when she first started to school, and how at a school program in Stanley, she recited a rhyme that went:

> Pitty little panties,
> Hanging on the line,
> Uffles on the bottom
> And gas stains on the hind.

The Rathmyers:

The Rathmyers settled on a ranch near the Dave Williams' place. Mrs. Rathmyer was a sister to Mrs. Frank (Electa) Fisher. To use the words of one oldtimer when she described their home, she said, "The Rathmyers didn't stay too long in Sawtooth Valley, but when they first came they built a tall funny looking house. It looked just like a tall box . . . had two rooms upstairs and two rooms downstairs . . . and no porches."

The Youngs:

The Youngs were made up of three families, George, Bruce, and Calvin. Just when they first came to the Valley, and exactly how many children were in each of the three families is not known. However, they did live there and several of the children attended one of the first schools conducted there. One teacher, Esther Foley, took a picture of her class in which seven of the children appear during the winter of 1920. They are Lillian, Eva, Martin, Guynnie, Fineous, Seymour, and Eddie . . . all thought to be children of Bruce and George. Aside from the ones mentioned above, there were two boys, Lawerence and Joseph, and two girls, Constent and Hazel. Hazel Young Barber was a daughter of Bruce Young, and at last report, resided at Hailey, Idaho. Lillian Young married and lived for many years near Clayton, Idaho. In the late Forties, when Frank Fisher sold his ranch, the families bought the property and lived there, where they ranged their cattle during the summer months, trailing them out for the winters.

Gillispie Families:

James Gillispie brought his family to live in the Sawtooth Valley in 1911, where he worked at the Vienna Mine. After a short while, they moved to Bellevue, Idaho, but about 1915, Mr. Gillispie, with his two sons, Claude and Clyde, returned to the Valley and settled on land that had once been the John English ranch. After service in the Field Artillery during World War I, Claude returned to the Valley, where soon after, he married Mary Snyder, daughter of George and Lizzie Snyder. Clyde, the younger of the two boys, born in Bellevue in 1900, remained on the ranch awhile, then married Reva Moore of Stanley, Idaho. . . .ceremony performed by Judge Palmer who resided in the upper end of Sawtooth Valley. After the ceremony, going back down the Valley, the couple stopped at the Dave Williams' ranch where Mrs. Williams prepared the wedding supper.

Both Claude and Clyde were well thought of, and together and individually, worked at various enterprises during their years spent in the Stanley-Sawtooth country. As young men, they worked on their father's ranch or hired out to neighborhood ranchers. Clyde got the contract to carry the mail from Stanley to Obsidian about the time of his marriage. Clyde is said to have asked the Stanley merchant and postmaster, Tink Niece, for a loan with which to buy the marriage license. "My God boy!" Tink said, "If you don't have the money to buy your marriage license, what are you planning to live on?" With all the assurance of youth, Clyde replied, "Oh, I have a job, and besides, we can live on love for awhile." Ironically, the Niece Brothers Store was sold to Clyde and Claude Gillispie in 1926. Clyde ran the store, and in 1933 became the Stanley postmaster, remaining so until 1943 when the store again changed hands.

In the 1930's Claude established a dude ranch in the vicinity of the Rocky Mountain Guest Ranch, and on what was locally referred to as "the Dick Horstman" property. Here he acted as guide for tourists going on pack trips and trail rides in the Sawtooth Mountains.

Claude and Mary had two daughters, Mae and Evelyn. In

later years they moved to Salmon, Idaho, where they bought ranch property, and where in 1974, Claude passed away at the age of eighty-four. Clyde and Reva were the parents of three children ... Gertrude, Doris, and Jack. They too, moved to Salmon where they lived for many years before moving to Boise, Idaho, where they reside at this time.

The Snyders:

George Snyder, wife Lizzie, and daughter Mary, moved from Salmon, Idaho to the Sawtooth Valley in 1917, settling on the old Rathmyer place. Not long after their arrival here, the family gave a housewarming party that was thoroughly enjoyed, and long remembered by people of the area. Mary played the piano and her father, George, played the violin, and the rafters of the house shook that night with the music and dancing. The Snyder home soon became a favorite gathering place for both Stanley and Sawtooth Valley residents. After Mary's marriage to Claude Gillispie, Claude learned to play the violin and his brother, Clyde, learned the saxaphone. Soon joined by Preston Shaw, who played the drums, the little orchestra made quite a name for itself playing for dances and community affairs in the Stanley-Sawtooth area for many years. The elder Snyders, George and Lizzie, sold their ranch to Dave Williams and returned to Salmon, Idaho in 1922.

The Flemings:

Although it was 1929 before Harry Fleming came to live in the Sawtooth Valley, as a youth he had made many trips into the region during the very early days. In fact, some of his earliest memories include those trips made with his father, Ed Fleming, who operated a sawmill near Ketchum, Idaho, and who delivered lumber with his freight teams for many of the buildings in the Stanley area ... the large Benner Hotel in 1911 for one, and later the Niece Brothers Store, Stanley Dance Hall, and other buildings. In any case, young Harry vowed to return some day. Four years after settling on what had formerly been the Herman Meissner place, Harry married Martine Pierce. Martine's parents lived on a neighboring ranch, and her father made the rustic furniture that became so popular in the area in the Thirties and Forties.

Misfortune seemed to follow Harry and Martine for awhile. First a baby daughter was taken from them by death. Later Harry had an accident in which his leg was badly mangled when his truck skidded on ice near the Sunbeam Dam and went over the grade on a cold, wintry night. As a result he lost his leg, but was thankful to be able to get around on an artificial limb.

Then one day while the family were away, their home and all its contents burned to the ground . . . everything they owned. Neighbors and friends came to their aid, helping to rebuild a house, but even today, Martine laments the loss of several pieces of beautiful antique furniture and other unreplaceable items and family mementoes. Nevertheless, the Harry Flemings survived. They raised five children while Harry carried mail in the region and maintained their ranch which they fondly call "The Poor Farm." Having retired recently after forty years service as a mail carrier, the Flemings are at home in the Sawtooth Valley. Both Harry and Martine keep busy with their hobbies. . . . Harry making furniture, and Martine making quilts and doing other fancy handwork, and they enjoy frequent visits from their children and grandchildren.

Harry's brother, Fred Fleming, bought the ranch that was homesteaded by Leslie "Tink" Niece located in the lower end of the Valley. It was here that Fred died. Later his wife, Mattie, was married to Chuck Hansen, and the couple still live on a part of the ranch today.

In reference to the freighting trips Harry recalled having made with his father over Galena Summit from the Wood River country to the Sawtooth Valley in the early days, Harry tells one story concerning a huge boiler the elder Fleming con-

Ed Fleming's bull-team leaving Hailey with the boiler for the Fisher mill in Sawtooth Valley.

tracted to haul up a mountainside to the Fisher Mine. It had been a wet, cold spring. Melting snows had swelled all the streams in the area, washing out bridges and making roads a muddy mire. Ed was using bull teams to do the job. One day some other freighters found him camped along one of the streams on his way to the mine with the boiler, and they swore he would never be able to make it with that heavy load. Ed just laughed and said, "I'll bet any one of you $100 that these bulls can pull it through." No one took the bet, however, and Ed's bull team did pull the boiler to the mine.

Ed Fleming died in 1922. The Fleming boys continued to operate their father's sawmill until 1925 when they closed it down.

Charley Grandjean:

Emil Grandjean, known as Charley Grandjean in the Stanley-Sawtooth country was born in Copenhagen, Denmark, where his father, Daniel L. Grandjean, had served as Chamber Councillor. Charley came with his brother, Sophus, to the new world in 1884. The two boys were soon joined by their mother, Nathalia Hansen Grandjean, and sister, Ingeborg. Settling first near Plum Creek, Nebraska, the sister met and married Otto H. Leflang there. Spurred by stories of rapid growth and rich opportunities in Idaho's Wood River country, the family, with the sister's new husband soon moved to the Bellevue area. Already schooled in forestry back in Denmark, Charley and Sophus found the then primitive region of the Stanley-Sawtooth country more to their liking, and in the early 1890s moved there with their mother. On what later became the Matt Womack and Henry Duffy ranch, they built a cabin where they lived until Mrs. Grandjean died on December 3, 1895. At the time the snow was deep throughout the area, and the boys, wanting to take their mother to Ketchum for burial, loaded the body on a hand sled, donned snowshoes, and pulled the sled some seventy miles through the Basin and the Valley and over Galena Summit for interment in the Ketchum cemetery.

Charley, being a naturalist along with his interest in hunting, trapping, and forestry, stayed on in the Stanley-Sawtooth country. In so doing Charley Grandjean played an important part in the formation of the National Forest boundaries in the region and the management thereof. Eventually he became the Idaho State Supervisor of Forestry and went to Boise, Idaho to live. In the early Twenties he married Mary Bushfield. The couple had two children ... a son, Donald, who now lives in Twin Falls, and a daughter named Ruth who lives in Boise. Charley also has a niece, Elizabeth Leflang Sliger, who lives at Twin Falls, Idaho, and who visits the Stanley-Sawtooth area quite often. Charley Grandjean, "Grand Old Man of Forestry," died in 1961.

Tom Williams:

Thomas H. Williams, always called "Tom" in the Stanley-Sawtooth country was born in Pennsylvania in 1870, coming to Idaho in company with his brother, Dave Williams, when he was thirty years old. While following mining, Tom found time for his many other interests. He hunted bear in Bear Valley with Charley Grandjean, he explored the rugged Sawtooth

Thomas Williams

202

Mountains, being the first man known to have scaled their jagged peaks and crossed over into the Payette River country, he acted as guide for a Geodetic survey crew, and he set long traplines in winter. Tom was also a carpenter and millright, and good at the building trade. In fact, many of the business houses and homes in Stanley were built by Tom. He sometimes worked with Arthur Wright, and it was these two men together who constructed the large Benner Hotel completed and opened for business in 1912. This building is no longer there, but for years it loomed large and outstanding on the landscape in the Stanley locality.

Tom had gone to school in Pennsylvania, but he was mostly a self-educated man. He was an accurate student of history, and would spend long hours reading the classics, such as Shakespeare, often by the flickering light of a campfire. He could quote Shakespeare's "As You Like It" or "The Taming of the Shrew" fluently.

When his brother Dave settled down to ranching in the Sawtooth Valley, Tom took up a homestead on a small creek that now bears his name, near Dave's homestead. Unlike Dave, Tom was never married.

In an article, Ferris Weddle, a long time writer and resident of Idaho, once wrote on the Stanley-Sawtooth country, he made several mentions of Tom. In one paragraph he said, "Tom likes people in small groups, and only once in a great while did he venture to Challis or the town of Salmon. And if he was feeling particularily nervy, he went to Gooding or Twin Falls. The pavement hurt his feet he said. What did Tom have? asks the man from teeming main street. Well, he had an unspoiled wilderness for his backyard, plenty of hunting and fishing, scores of friends, a small cabin . . . and no radio."

The cabin writer Ferris noted in the above paragraph was located up the East Fork of the Salmon River near the George Yacomello ranch. It was here on the day of February 18, 1942, that young Tony Yacomello found Tom on the ground a short distance from his cabin, dead from a heart attack. Tom Williams was buried in the cemetery at Mackay, Idaho, at the age of seventy-one years.

Dick Horstman:

Dick Horstman who lived in the Sawtooth Valley in the early days is well remembered by several people in and around the area today. In her diary kept in the 1890's while the McGown family lived in the Stanley Basin, Della McGown sometimes referred to different single men there as "Dirty old batches," and even though she never knew Dick, he could have fitted such a description. In fact, Ted Williams, who knew him very well, said Dick was considered dirty indeed . . . or untidy, if you will, by all his neighbors and friends. And yes, despite his lack of cleanliness, Dick had a great many friends in the Valley and Basin.

Dick was born Berrhard Deiderich Horstman in Germany on August 5, 1858. He arrived in the United States June 15, 1889, coming to the Sawtooth Valley in the early 1900's. Choosing a site which included a natural hot spring near the Salmon River, he built himself a cabin and took up a homestead. Being an especially nice location, Dick raised a garden every year in a plot near the hot spring, producing fresh vegetables that were always a real treat to those living where the growing season is cool and short. Like everyone who tried to grow a garden in the area, Dick had trouble protecting it from the wild animals. Deer were particularily difficult to keep away, and even when Dick enclosed his garden plot with a high fence, he often found the culprits inside nibbling away at his lettuce and other produce.

Dick loved the outdoors, and would work endless hours in his garden and at making improvements on his homestead land . . . but he was no housekeeper. The unswept cabin floor, table and cupboard piled with dirty dishes and cooking utensils, and unmade bed failed to bother Dick whatsoever. Sometimes things would go undone for days before he would make any attempt to do a little cleaning. Yet he was the soul of hospitality. When anyone stopped by to see him, as was the custom in the region, if it were mealtime he would ask them to eat with him. "And if you did, you were sure taking a chance on getting sick from it," Ted Williams recalled. "My land, Dick's table was so dirty if a fly tried to light on the sugar bowl, he'd skid and break his neck."

"I remember one time Dick stopped at our place (the Dave Williams ranch not far from Dick's property), and Dad had cooked some rice and put raisins in it. Dick always wore little wire-rimmed glasses. He wore a goatee and had a mustache, and he was sitting there at the table carefully picking the raisins out of his bowl of rice. Finally Dad said, 'Dick, don't you like raisins or currants in your rice?' Dick laid down his spoon, adjusted his glasses, and said, 'Soo ... I tonk dey vas flies!"

Whether Dick's untidiness caused him to have health problems or not, he was a great hand to read ads in the newspapers and send through the mail for all kinds of patent medicine cure-alls. The postmaster (Leslie Niece) noticed this when Dick would come to pick up his mail at Stanley, and on more than one occasion told him, "Dick, if you don't quit taking so much of these damn patent medicines, they're going to kill you."

About 1920, Dick moved from his homestead to the Redfish Lake. Here he secured a life-time lease from the Forest Service, built himself a cabin for living quarters, rented boats to fishermen, and a short time later, built a large two-story log building (still in use today) that was the beginning of the Redfish Lake Resort. On his leased ground, Dick paid an annual fee of $35.00 to the Forest Service. All appeared to be going well for him until the spring of 1928. He was not feeling well, and then on June 13th his cabin was destroyed by fire and he was taken to the Challis Hot Springs where he could receive care. On September 22nd, that same year, Dick Horstman passed away shortly after his seventieth birthday and was buried in the Challis Cemetery.

At the time of Dick's illness, Custer County took over caring for him, and subsequently the burial expenses when he died. As a result, his possessions were sold at county auction. When all bills were paid, the amount of monies left over was divided and sent to Dick's surviving relatives ... one sister, one brother, and one nephew living in Germany, and one nephew living in Brooklyn, New York. In the meantime, a Mr. Lewis E. Megoewn held a three year lease on the Dick Horstman property at Redfish Lake. When the lease expired, the buildings and boats were sold to a Mr. George S. Krom.

Dick Horstman had become a naturalized citizen of the United States on April 2nd, 1913 with Arthur McGown Sr. and Albert Colter of Challis as his witnesses.

Herman Meissner:

Herman Meissner, like Dick Horstman, could be termed as another one of those "dirty old batches" who lived in the Stanley-Sawtooth country. Born May 28, 1855, at Erfurt, Prussia, he came to the United States and on to the Sawtooth Valley, where in 1916, he filed on 160 acres of land on Gold

Creek under the Desert Entry Act. He lived here in a one-room cabin, kept a few horses for transportation and to do his ranch work, and occasionally did outside jobs to earn money to keep him going.

Since his ranch was not far from Dick Horstman's place, the two men soon became very close friends. Both being in their fifties, and both being bachelors, they found much in common. Like Dick, Herman was no housekeeper. And also like Dick, he was the soul of hospitality and was well liked by the Valley and Basin residents. Herman's untidiness is noted in the following story as told by Nellie Fisher Clarke:

"Dad's ranch (the Frank Fisher ranch) was not too far from Herman's place, and one day when Mary Gillispie and I were going that way, we stopped to say hello. He had a pot of beans and bacon simmering on the stove, and of course, asked us to share some with him. In those days people always washed any mold off of bacon that had gotten old with vinegar. Well, apparently Herman didn't do that because we ate some of his beans and bacon, and that night I was awfully sick. My husband, Paul, said I should have made some excuse to keep from eating Herman's cooking since everyone knew Herman and Dick were two of the dirtiest cooks and housekeepers in the Valley. 'Dirty old Bohemians' most folks called them. Anyway, I did know better, but Herman was such a good old man, I didn't want to hurt his feelings by refusing his invitation. But believe me, after that when we happened to stop by his or Dick's places, I found all kinds of excuses to keep from eating anything they had cooked. You know, we all liked Herman and Dick even if they weren't as clean as they could have been."

Recalling Herman's different characteristics by oldtimers today is always inclined to bring chuckles, and more than one funny story about him. One has to do with a time when he was helping Clyde Gillispie with his haying. Clyde was driving the team and Herman was sitting in the back of the wagon very relaxed and paying no attention whatsoever to what Clyde was doing. Noticing this, and always ready to play a prank on someone, Clyde hit the horses causing them to start with a jerk. Herman went flying through the air to land prone several feet behind the wagon. Old Herman picked himself up, shook his fist at Clyde and shouted, "By de Holy Christ der, you'd kill a man der!"

When Herman Meissner died, at his request, he was buried

on his property. Today, only a few persons are living who know the exact location of that grave. After his death the ranch was sold to Palmer G. Snedecor of Twin Falls, Idaho, for the sum of $1,100. When indebtedness from his illness and the funeral expense was paid and deducted from the amount above, the $700 that was left was sent to his only living relative, and sole heir, a niece living in Potsdam, Germany.

Harry Stroble:

Although it is not known for sure just when Harry Stroble came to the Sawtooth Valley, he was there in the Teens and Twenties and on into the Thirties. An Englishman, Harry had been a sailor in the King's Navy. In contrast to the untidiness of Dick Horstman and Herman Meissner, Harry Stroble was a meticulous housekeeper . . . almost to the point of fanaticism. From habits learned in the English Navy on board ship, he scrubbed his cabin floor with a scrub brush every day, rain or shine, and it is said the floor was so clean that it appeared new and white anytime and every time anyone went to his place. Phyllis Williams (Mrs. Ted Williams) says she finds herself laughing even now when she remembers how Harry would grab his mop and mop up behind her when she visited him at different times. She said, "My feet weren't that dirty, and I wasn't tracking up his floor."

Harry homesteaded on Champion Creek, or in the vicinity thereof. And while he was an immaculate housekeeper, he was also very clean and neat about his person and everything he did, going about his chores and projects in a very systematic manner. Along with his ranch work, Harry raised a fine garden every year, growing exceptionally large, lucious strawberries, and peas in season. He grew his own wheat, ground it into flour, and made his own bread. Too, he was said to be the best dandelion wine maker in the Valley, and those who were fortunate enough to be presented with a bottle of it at Christmastime found it a treat indeed. Mrs. Frank Fisher received a bottle of this rare wine from Harry every Christmas for several years, and her daughter, Nellie, said, "It always lent a special air of festivity to our holidays."

Nellie then went on to say, "Harry was a fine old gentleman and perhaps the most respected bachelor in the Valley. At one time he had been a mining partner with Henry Middleton in and around the country, but while Henry went on with his mining, Harry preferred his ranching and gardening."

207

In reference to Harry baking his own bread, Ted Williams remembered that when you stopped by Harry's place he always asked you to eat with him whether you had eaten or not. "In fact, Ted said, this was true of any of the ranchers in the Valley." Ted's wife, Phyllis, then went on to tell about one time when she and Ted were out for a drive and stopped in to see Harry. "Of course we ended up eating with him, and I sat and watched him slice a piece of bread. He kept the loaf and knife right by his plate, and if you wanted bread he would cut off one slice at a time. I knew this was to keep the bread from drying out, but it seemed so different when we were used to cutting several slices at a time and placing them on a plate on the table for everyone to help themselves."

Just how old Harry Stroble was when he came to Sawtooth Valley, or when and where he died is not known; yet he did number among the early residents in the Stanley-Sawtooth country, and certainly he found a place in the hearts and memories of those who knew him there.

John English:

John English was as English as his name would indicate. He ranched on land adjacent to the Dave Williams' property during the late 1900's and on into the Teens. Those who can recall John, say he was a fine old man, and a highly educated man. Before coming to the Sawtooth Valley he had been a school teacher somewhere in the Eastern United States. He loved children; the few who lived in the area when he was there were always happy to see him when he happened to visit their parents, for John usually had some tiny gift and or time to stop and talk with them. No information could be found as to whether he was ever married, or where he went from the Sawtooth region.

Sandy Brooks:

Many people may consider Sandy Brooks as one of the old-timers of the Stanley-Sawtooth country. Sandy, well known throughout the region and still living there today, owns a ranch in the Sawtooth Valley and is a packer and guide in the area. After his arrival there, sometime in the Twenties or Thirties, he and his dogteams became rather famous in a way. Not only did he carry mail in the winter time to isolated communities and ranches scattered at the base of the Sawtooth mountain range, but was also on standby to carry passengers in emergency cases. At one time he worked for and with the Frank Shaw family on their ranch which was located in proximity to the one he now owns in the Valley.

After doing service in the Armed Forces during World War II, Sandy returned to the area and accepted a job at Sun Valley. Here he took lodge guests for rides during the winter season on his dog-sleds over the snowy mountain trails in the vicinity of Sun Valley.

Sandy Brooks' dog team.

A Few Others:

And of course, there were many others who came and stayed awhile in the Valley before moving elsewhere. There was a family by the name of Van who were related to the Frank Fishers. They had a daughter named Alice who numbered among the students at the tent school in the summer of 1911. There was Arthur Wright, a bachelor, who homesteaded in the lower end of the Valley near the Leslie Niece homestead property. Arthur was a carpenter who worked with Tom Williams at times when the town of Upper Stanley was starting to build up. There were the Fred Goaz family, the Palmers, the Dipps, the Lannings, the Wilcoxs, and the Duffys. Then there was a black man named George Blackman who came regularly to pick up his mail at the post office in the Valley. George lived just over the ridge in Washington Basin, appearing there in the 1890's, and living there for fifty years or more. *Note: For special story on George Blackman see under title; "Scrapbook."*

209

Excluding all the above named people, no doubt there were any number of others who lived in the Sawtooth area in the very early days, but whoever they might have been is unknown to us as this writing goes to press.

THE BENNERS

The Benner hotel on the outskirts of where the town of Upper Stanley now stands, just off the Lowman road above Valley Creek, was completed and opened for business the summer of 1912. Constructed by Tom Williams and Arthur Wright, the large, two-story log building was rustic in every detail and presented an impressive view from a distance. At the time lodging in the Stanley country was at a premium. Residents were proud of the hotel. Then the following spring marked a special event when the new hotel afforded electric lights, powered by a dynamo installed on the premises. *This was the first electricity in the Stanley-Sawtooth area.*

For the hotel owner, Mrs. H.L. Benner (Martha) the event was kind of a dream come true. And while residents were proud, visitors coming to this section of the country delighted in the clean, comfortable accommodations she provided at the hotel. They thanked her for her hospitality and complimented her cooking ability. A tall, handsome woman, Martha Benner was noted to be many things . . . resourceful, energetic, good-hearted on impulse, and sometimes a very unorthodox person.

Mrs. Martha Benner (winter 1912 and 1913).

"Eccentric," was the way several oldtimers who knew her came to describe her in later years, especially after the mysterious disappearance of Mr. Benner.

Going back, the Benner's story begins on their arrival in the Stanley Basin in early 1902. They came from Fillmore, Utah, where she had been born Martha Meacham. Before Mr. Benner, she had been married to a man named Speed, by whom she had a daughter christened Sarah, but called "Sadie" in the Basin area. The exact date of Martha's marriage to Mr. Benner, or just where he was born, is not known, but it is thought he was from Denver, Colorado since he had two spinster sisters living there at the time of his disappearance.

In the Basin, they purchased the store and buildings erected and first owned by Arthur McGown Sr. from Mose Storher for the sum of $500. At this time Mose was somewhere around 78 years old. He moved into a small cabin between the two bridges on Valley Creek, directly across from the store. On August 27, 1910, Mose committed suicide and was buried on a knoll about two hundred yards behind the hotel. A brother of Martha Benner's had also committed suicide and had been buried at this site earlier.

The Benners were accepted and liked in the Stanley Basin. H.L., of Cuban extraction, dark complexioned and stocky-built, soon made many friends with his genial ways and general good humor. He enjoyed the company of the miners and prospectors scattered here and there in the Basin, and paid the different ones visits whenever the opportunity arose. Within a few months he was considered an upright, community-minded citizen by those who knew him. The August 5, 1902, issue of the Challis *Silver Messenger Newspaper* noted that J.C. Fox had circulated a petition to establish mail service between Robinson Bar and Stanley with H.L. Benner to be made postmaster at Stanley. Service was granted and Benner appointed. Yet the whole thing turned out to be quite a mixup and no dependable service was established for some time. Meanwhile it was necessary for Mr. Benner to make three trips on snowshoes to Ketchum for the mail the winter of 1902 and '03. NOTE: For more on mail service see under heading, *"Two Towns."*

Sadie, a lovely young woman by now, had met George Hoffman, and on November 11, 1904, they had been married. The Reverend George McDougall performed the ceremony at the Small Brother's ranch near Clayton, on the Salmon River.

From the beginning the marriage was a stormy one. This worried Mrs. Benner since she feared Hoffman would do bodily harm to her daughter. On one occasion Mrs. Benner swore out a warrant for the arrest of Hoffman, claiming that he had tried to kill both she and her daughter. The case was tried before Judge Horton in Challis, Idaho. Evidence being insufficient, Hoffman was dismissed and the costs were assessed to the complaining witness. The young couple, being of different temperaments, separated several times, divorced once and she married George Hyde. Later she divorced him and remarried George Hoffman. When she died of pneumonia at Jerome, Idaho, in 1915, Sadie had borne two daughters and one son.

Thought by some to be related to Mr. Benner, Harve Stout appeared in Stanley Basin in the fall of 1905. An item in the *Silver Messenger Newspaper* printed in Challis, Idaho, dated September 18, 1905, read as follows: "Harve Stout, an alleged horse rustler from Big Hole, Montana, was arrested at Woods Livestock ranch on Pahsamaroi one day last week." No mention of the outcome of this action was found, but soon after this Stout went to work at the Benner place as a kind of all-around hand, and as time went on, both Mrs. Benner and H.L. came to rely on him in many ways. The Benners prospered. Mr. Benner was made Deputy Recorder at Stanley in 1904 in which office he served for two years. Mrs. Benner helped out in the store and provided room and board for wayfaring travelers stopping over in the tiny settlement, and as more people came into the Basin, Mr. Benner filed on a homestead in the area.

Harve Stout delivering supplies by dog team (1912 and 1913)

Then in June, 1907, H.L. Benner suddenly disappeared. The June 25th issue of the *Challis Silver Messenger* ran the following article:

Henry L. Benner, merchant and businessman of Stanley Basin, and well known in the western portion of Custer County and on the Wood River, has disappeared very mysteriously.

The last seen of Mr. Benner was near Casino Creek. He was on horseback and seen by several persons that afternoon. When near Casino Creek, Mr. Benner got off his horse and was tracked to the bank of the Salmon River, and whether he fell or jumped into the river with suicide as intent will never be known. The horse was found the next morning where Benner had left him standing with his bridle and saddle on. Mr. Benner had on hip boots, and it is thought by some that he endeavored to cross the Salmon River on foot, as at this point there is a wide shallow crossing, but current is very rapid now on account of the high water, and it took Benner off his feet and carried him into an eddy of deep water 100 feet below before he could regain control of himself. He had some cattle on the opposite side of the river, and it is thought he was crossing over to look after them. But why didn't he ride the horse over instead of trying to ford the river on foot? No trace of Mr. Benner had been discovered.

On June 10th, four days prior to his drowning, Mr. Benner sent a letter to Recorder Henderson to record, giving his wife, Martha Benner, power of attorney to all his property. Mr. Benner has been in the general merchandise, mining, and stock business, etc., at the Basin for several years, and was pretty generally liked. He was supposed to be in good circumstances financially. He leaves a wife and daughter. His wife offers a reward of $100 for the recovery of Mr. Benner's body.

End of Article

News of Mr. Benner's disappearance came as a shock to Stanley Basin residents . . . particularly to the persons last to see him that fatal afternoon.

As one oldtimer tells it, Benner left home that morning intent on visiting prospector and resident friends as he so often did when his time allowed, stopping first to visit with Mr. Herbert Marshall at his cabin at Lower Stanley. Riding his big black horse, from there he went on down to Casino Creek where

214

he stopped awhile with George Cumine and Tom Kelly who were doing some placer mining there. Noting the time on his big watch with its distinctive chain, made up of gold nuggets, and watch fob designed in a circle about two inches in diameter divided into pie shaped sections, each set with a different kind of metal such as gold, silver, and copper, he remarked, "Well, I better be going or I will never make it home before dark."

After taking leave of his friends, nothing more was heard of him until Harve Stout found his horse standing beside the river. Mr. Benner's body was never found, and later there were many conjectures as to the cause of his disappearance and/or death. Yet no one was ever sure if he died by his own hand or otherwise . . . or for that matter, if he died at all.

Several people claimed to have seen the big watch in question in Mrs. Benner's possession sometime later, but no issue was made of it and in time the matter was dropped. Nevertheless, for years thereafter, people who had known the Benners pondered Mr. Benner's strange disappearance, and even today the incident is remembered as strange and tragic.

Also, down through the years, many stories have been told of Mrs. Benner's unorthodox behavior. In connection with Mr. Benner's disappearance, one goes that while the new hotel was under construction, the carpenters, Tom Williams and Arthur Wright roomed and boarded with Mrs. Benner. Not always being able to sleep well, Arthur would go stand at his window, and on moonlight nights told of seeing her stroll to a site behind the large new building and kneel on a knoll where her brother and Mose Storher were buried. Naturally he told Tom of what he saw, jokingly mentioning the ghost of Mr. Benner one morning at the breakfast table. His remark was overheard by Mrs. Benner who flew into a rage and fired him then and there. Arthur said he was curious to explore the site, but was never afforded the opportunity in the ever presence of Harve and Mrs. Benner.

Another story has to do with the store and the fact people in the Stanley-Sawtooth country relied on credit as much as they do today. The Merritt and George Sewell families both lived within two miles of the Benner place, and both traded at the store. Mrs. Benner would allow them credit, although she would not charge groceries to the Merritts, but would gladly let Mrs. Merritt have clothing, dress materials, and other items on account. With the Sewells she acted in quite the opposite

215

manner ... allowing them groceries on credit, but no clothing or other such items. Trading confidences on the matter, unknown to Mrs. Benner, of course, the two families would trade commodities when the need arose.

Between 1902 and 1916 the *Challis Silver Messenger* carried numerous items on the affairs of the Benner family. One noting the cost of construction of the hotel was printed June 25, 1912, briefly stating: Mrs. Benner is constructing a $5,000 hotel at Stanley. On March 11, 1913, another item said, The Benner Hotel in Stanley is being wired for electric lights from the hotel's private lighting plant. Again, in August, 1915, the newspaper stated: Harvy Stout is in Challis, and has sworn out a warrant against Mrs. Robert Finley, charging her with shooting some 20 head of horses owned by Mrs. Benner.

And so from time to time such items found their way into the paper for all to read ... some good, and some not so good. Another of the latter was a lengthy story involving Harve Stout and an Italian. Seems this young man rode in on a beautiful horse with a fine saddle, a bridle inlaid with silver, and wearing two guns on his hips. He was looking for work, but Harve, who did the hiring, was not around. Mrs. Benner told him he could stay there and wait for Harve's return. This turned out to be two or three days. Then Harve told the man that he had no work for him, but that he owed Mrs. Benner $15 for room and board. The man had no money, so Harve kept the horse, saddle, and bridle in payment. Feeling this to be unfair treatment, since any one of these would be of more value than the amount of the bill, the Italian started walking up the road. A few minutes walk brought him to the Imeson ranch where the William Merritts were staying. Here he stopped, and while telling Mr. Merritt his story, asked to borrow $15 in hopes of getting back his horse and outfit. In Mrs. Merritt's words, "We didn't have a nickel, let alone $15."

The young man spent the night with the Merritts, and during the evening tried to trade his two guns for a high-powered 44 revolver owned by Bill Merritt. During the course of the conversation Mr. Merritt made some remark about the Italian using his gun to get his horse back. Evidently this remark sparked the idea, for the following morning the man returned to the Benner place and confronted Harve in the store, demanding his possessions at the point of his gun. Harve refused, the man fired, Harve fell behind a counter, and thinking he had killed Harve, the Italian rushed back to the Merritt's, burst

216

through the door, shoved the gun at Mrs. Merritt, and shouted, "Take it! I've just killed Harve Stout!" Being alone at the time and not knowing what to do, the poor woman took the gun, and the man ran off up the road. After he was gone, Mrs. Merritt decided she must hide the gun . . . but where? In desperation she put the gun in a sack, tied a rope to it, and hung it down inside the hole of their outdoor toilet.

Soon a regular manhunt was on. The acting deputy marshall, George Smith, and his assistant, tracked the Italian to the Merritt place through a light skift of snow that had fallen the night before. Upon being told he was not there, they soon found his tracks leading up the road, and following these, sighted the man on some cliffs above the trail where he had taken a stand with the one gun he had left. Deciding they would need more help, the two lawmen returned to the Benner place. Pat Rasche was there and offered his assistance. Mrs. Benner allowed Pat to ride the Italian's horse since Pat was on foot. By this time it was known that Harve Stout had only a slight head wound and was not seriously hurt.

On returning to the cliffs where the Italian had taken his stand, Pat called out to him, telling him that Harve was alive and not seriously injured, and proceeded to persuade the man to give himself up. The young Italian accompanied the three men back to Herbert Marshall's place at Lower Stanley where he was to await being taken to Challis, the county seat of Custer County, for a hearing. George Smith then rode up to the Benner's to consult with Harve Stout and Mrs. Benner as to what charges they wished to bring against the man. While George was gone, Pat was to guard the prisoner.

However, as soon as George was out of sight on his way to Benner's, Pat turned to the Italian and said "You better go feed and curry your horse. I rode him pretty hard." The horse, still saddled, was tied to the corral fence nearby. As the man went out the door Pat handed him a few dollars. When George Smith returned from Benner's, naturally, Pat was blamed for allowing the prisoner to escape. Mrs. Benner was very angry with him, and one day soon after that, as Pat was passing the Benner store, she came sailing out to the road, hurling threats and calling him vile names . . . even threatening to run him out of the country. Pat was not one to scare easily, and being a stubborn man, made it a point to walk up past Benner's place often just to see what Mrs. Benner would do. She did nothing, and of course, Pat went on to live in the Stanley Basin for many years.

Meanwhile, on the date of the alleged escape, a man coming down the Nip-and-Tuck road told later of having met the young Italian "tearing up the road like the devil was after him!" A few months after the incident it was learned that the Italian had carried mail into Thunder Mountain that winter, and on one trip had frozen both of his feet, developed infection, and had died there.

According to various oldtimers, Mrs. Benner could be an artist at fleecing people too . . . and literally on several occasions until the sheepmen became wise. In those early years the old wagon road came down across the flats from way of Sawtooth Valley to cross Valley Creek near the Benner place. At one point, where the terrain rose rather sharply at the hotel location, a kind of tunnel had been dug facing the barn just across the road. While it is assumed the tunnel was for the purpose of storing supplies, as the story goes, it seems Mrs. Benner and Harve Stout found the tunnel and barn locations could be quite handy in another way.

In the spring and fall, when sheep were being trailed to and from range in the Stanley Basin, Mrs. Benner would position herself, holding a long stick with a hook attached to the end, just inside the entrance to the tunnel while Harve would do the same just inside the barn door across the road from her. Then as the sheep bunched through the narrow defile Mrs. Benner and Harve would select nice, fat lambs, snake their hooks out from their hiding places, grab the animal by its leg and drag it into the recesses of the tunnel and/or the barn. By the time the flock of sheep passed through the defile, Mrs. Benner had added at least a half dozen woolies to her assets.

Inasmuchas many large bands of sheep were grazed in the Basin in the early days, usually with one herder and his dogs to a band, the Benner scheme went undetected for sometime. When the ruse was finally suspected, sheepmen stationed two men in the area of the defile as watchmen when trailing their sheep in and out of the Basin, thereby putting an end to Mrs. Benner's sheep rustling days in the Stanley Basin.

No one ever knew what caused Mrs. Benner to be the way she was. On one side she was a woman of many fine talents. She could be kind and gentle, and often performed deeds of goodness. One example lies in the fact that many times when she heard of someone being ill and alone, she would go bring him to her place, nurse and care for him, and when he was well enough to be on his feet, would say, "You are all right now. GET OUT! I don't want to ever set eyes on you again!"

She proved up on the homestead Mr. Benner had filed on, the notice appearing in the *Wood River Times,* July, 1908. After Sadie's death she took her two granddaughters to care for, keeping them for a time. Then for some reason, she sold her place and returned to Fillmore, Utah, where she died some years later. Harvey Stout remained with her to the end.

The last item to appear in the *Challis Messenger* was November 15, 1916, reading: Bartlett Falls purchased the Benner farm in the Stanley Basin last week; consideration $16,000. The Falls are moving to Stanley.

Thus ends the Benner story.

THE LESLIE S. "TINK" NIECE FAMILY

On their way to the Stanley Basin mines, Leslie Niece and his wife, Ellen, beheld the Stanley-Sawtooth country for the first time from the old wagon road atop Galena Mountain in the summer of 1906. To the tired, desert-weary travelers, in company with Ellen's oldest sister, Ruth, and her husband, Aaron Slothower, the picturesque valley below appeared as a paradise after the long, dusty miles by wagon from Rambler, Wyoming. Camped on the headwaters of the Salmon River a short time later, the two young women, burned and parched by the winds and sun while coming through the vast stretches of wastelands, thought they would like to remain beside the cool, noisy, little stream forever.

Leslie and Ellen Niece (1903)

Their husbands said, "No, we stay here for a few days and rest and give you girls time to do a washing, then we will go on to the Stanley Basin the way we planned."

With that, Ellen and Ruth busied themselves washing clothing, airing bedding and cleaning their wagons. Each of the

220

couples had a little three year old boy.... Rupert, son of Leslie and Ellen, and Roy, son of Aaron and Ruth. Within two or three days, while the children ran and played and the men repaired their gear and did some fishing, the women were able to rest and truly enjoy their surroundings. During this time the two families became acquainted with the few settlers who were living in the Valley. Dave Clarke and his wife, Louise, and son, Paul were among them. The Nieces and Slothowers soon learned that Dave Clarke was the Valley postmaster and had a small post office called Pierson (for his middle name) on his homestead. They learned too, that the Clarkes operated a stopping place for travelers like themselves, and that they owned the hot springs, first called "White's Hot Springs," with a bath house built over the pool. After relaxing in the warm mineral waters and enjoying one of Louise Clarke's fine meals served on her unusual, lazy-susan type table ... a pleasure afforded them many times in years thereafter ... the two families moved on.

On the first day from the Clarke's place, they camped near the lower end of Sawtooth Valley where a broad, grassy meadow was bordered on one side by the Salmon River with the other side nestling against the foothills of the Salmon River Mountain Range. Leslie and Ellen fell in love with the site immediately. They lingered here for many days, planning how they would take up a homestead here as soon as they could, even to where they would build their home and put up their fences. Yes, someday they would make a home here, but at present Ellen was expecting her second child within a few months, and it was imperative that they move on to where the menfolks could find work and to find someone to care for Ellen when her time came.

At Stanley the Nieces learned that a midwife by the name of Molly Paul, with her husband, George Paul, operated a stopping place for travelers on Nip-and-Tuck Mountain a short distance above lower town. This was on the main road leading to the Basin mines and Bear Valley at that time. Going to the Paul place, the Nieces discussed their problem with Mrs. Paul. She agreed to take care of Ellen, and because Ellen was not well in her condition, Molly thought it best that she and little Rupert remain with her while Leslie went on to the mines with the Slothowers.

At the Valley Creek Mine, in late September that year (1906), both Leslie and Aaron secured jobs and set up housekeeping in two, one-room cabins provided by the mining company. Snow came early in the high country that fall. On their days off at the mine the two men hauled supplies for the Greyhound Mine over Vanity Mountain with their teams and sleighs in order to make extra money.

Back at the Paul Place, under Mrs. Paul's care, Ellen did fairly well, and on the cold, snowy morning of November 22, 1906, gave birth to a baby girl whom they named Edna Rosella. A short time later, she was able to join her husband and the Slothowers at the Valley Creek mining properties. It was a bad winter that year, and instead of Ellen gaining strength, she grew weaker, finally developing a nervous disorder common in the early days called St. Vitus Dance.

Eventually, Ellen did improve, although her health was never good after that. But during the next two years, both the Niece and Slothower families did take up the land they had chosen the summer of 1906 while at their campsite in the lower end of the Sawtooth Valley. By now they had been joined by Frank Niece (Leslie's older brother) and his wife, Mary, along with Will and Charley Martin, brothers of Ellen and Ruth. While Will and Charley spent most of their time prospecting the surrounding mountains, Frank, called "Juggy" by everyone who knew him, took up a homestead adjoining Leslie's.

Working together, the men built cabins, barns, corrals, and other outbuildings on each of the three ranches, centralizing most of the out-buildings on Leslie's place which was between Frank's and the Slothower's. They also made most of the furniture for their new homes. This included bedsteads, chairs, tables, and a large wooden rocking chair for each of the Niece homes.

After many months without much income of any kind while they were establishing their homestead home, times became difficult for Leslie and Ellen. Money was badly needed in readiness at the alloted time for proof on their place, so when Leslie's sister wrote from Spokane, Washington in the fall of 1909 that work was plentiful there, it was decided he would leave Ellen and their two children and go seek a job. Starting out to hitch-hike to Spokane, he ended up by walking all the way . . . but he did get work and stayed out the winter there.

Meanwhile, in August of 1909, Ellen had helped to deliver twin daughters to Frank and his wife. Early that fall Will and

Charley Martin and the Aaron Slothowers departed the Stanley-Sawtooth country in search of greener pastures elsewhere.

That was a lonely winter for Ellen and the two children alone in the homestead cabin. However, with Frank and his family nearby, she managed. Many times she blessed the big, handmade rocker with its wide arms. Here she would sit to do hand sewing and to read stories to her little ones with a child perched on each arm. Naturally the energetic little boy and girl found all kinds of games to play on the chair, sometimes pretending the arms were horses, rocking back and forth shouting, "Giddee. .ee up old Johnson!" (Johnson was the name of their father's big, white saddle horse).

From the ridgepole, or the main stringer of the roof (called a beam today), Leslie had hung a swing for the children to play on. Oftentimes their vigorous swinging would land them on one or the other of the two homemade beds topped with high, straw-filled mattresses . . . on purpose, of course, and hard on the beds, but great fun for the children.

Things were some better for the little family when Leslie returned from Spokane, and even though there were other times when he had to be away from the ranch, his absence was of shorter duration. For the children, life was never dull in the Sawtooth Valley. In the spring they looked foreward to watching the great bands of sheep file by their place on the way to range in the Stanley Basin. Oftentimes, it ended up in profit for Rupert and Edna in way of money and meat for the family's table.

This came about when the children, waiting at the fence after hearing the tinkling bells and the baaing of the sheep, would be offered what the sheepmen called "Bum lambs" (ones with sore feet, or for some reason or other were holding up the flock) by the herders. Most of the sheepherders were Basque brought from the old country by the sheepmen, and while many could speak only a few words in English, if at all, somehow Rupert learned to communicate with them by gestures and signs. When a herder did give the children a bum lamb, they would run happily to the house where their mother would fix a nursing bottle to feed the lamb until it was old enough to eat grass. One fall the two children netted $30 each when their "grown-up" lambs were sold at the going price that year.

Liking the out-of-doors, and being a boy, Rupert liked to

223

trap. Even at an early age, he set traps for ground squirrels so numerous in the Valley. In the summer of about 1910, Leslie was pasturing a small herd of horses for some sheepmen, and one time while he had to be away for two or three days, the horses broke fence and wandered up behind the ranch. Ellen knew she must get them back in the pasture. Edna, then about three and a half years old, was taking her afternoon nap. "Rupert," Ellen instructed, "You keep an eye on the baby in case she wakes up before I get back." "Alright, Mama," the little boy replied.

On foot, Ellen was hardly out of sight when Edna woke up. Rupert took her outside to play with some toy pans in the dirt, and thinking she was content, he went to check on some traps he had set. By the time he reached the first trap, Edna was at his heels, and spotting the pan part of the trap, cried out, "My little pan!" reaching for it at the same time, before Rupert could stop her. BANG! The trap snapped shut on her hand. She screamed with pain and fright. Rupert tried to comfort her, but she would not hold still to let him spring open the trap to release her hand.

Quickly, Rupert got her to the house, put her inside, and ordered her, "You stay here while I find Mama!" He then took off running up the trail. Through her tears the little girl saw him go and tried to follow, but already exhausted by the pain and crying, her steps lagged, and on wobbly legs she wandered away from the trail.

Ellen had seen Rupert coming and ran to meet him. Back at the house, they found Edna gone and began a search for her, calling her name as they followed her tracks in the soft dirt along the trail. Where the tracks stopped, they searched the sides of the trail, but the missing child was nowhere to be found. All the while Ellen was wishing she had not changed her little girl's dirty red dress to a grey print one before she had put her down for her nap. With the sun dropping low behind the Sawtooth peaks, the poor mother was beside herself with fear for her child's safety as she and Rupert scoured the area, calling out frantically.

Finally, just at low dusk Ellen glimpsed a movement in the sagebrush as Edna came crawling out from beneath a clump of sage where whe had cried herself to sleep. Gathering the sobbing child in her arms she saw that the little hand had swollen so badly that the jaws of the trap were no longer visible. She was sure the bones must be broken. Back at the house she found it necessary to soak the hand to lessen the swelling before she could remove the trap. When it was done, she bandaged it with a cloth soaked in Arnica Linament. Fortunately, in a few days Edna's hand was healed . . . and no broken bones.

Another summer, when Leslie had to be away for a few weeks, Ellen was again a woman alone with two children. One evening a sheepherder made camp near the Niece ranch. While the herders were usually courteous and polite, this fellow was a big, burly man who came to the house acting a bit obnoxious. His actions made Ellen jumpy and nervous. That night she was awakened from a restless sleep by a thumping noise. By the moonlight filtering through a crack at the bottom of the door, she could see a moving shadow that appeared to be a man squatted against the outside of the door. Quietly she slipped out of bed and carefully pulled a long hat pin from one of her hats in a box nearby. Then creeping to the door, very cautiously, she inserted the point of the pin in another small crack at what she judged to be about rear-end level. When she had it aimed just right, she gave a mighty jab with all the strength she could muster. What a surprise she got! Instead of a lusty "OUCH" in a man's voice as she had expected, Rupert's poor dog let out a pain-filled "Yelp!" that could be heard for miles and went tearing down across the meadow howling like he was being pursued by a thousand banshees.

During the winter of 1910-11, Leslie took his family to be with him while he was on a short job in the mines at Jarbridge, Nevada. The trip proved most taxing on Ellen, and in February she became very ill and had to be taken to the hospital in Twin Falls, Idaho for surgery. When it was over, due to her critical condition, she had to remain there for several weeks. In order to be near her, Leslie rented an apartment where he could take care of the children. Working nights in a livery stable, he sent Rupert to school and took care of Edna during the days.

Finally, back on the ranch in Sawtooth Valley that summer, for the next three years things seemed to go better for Leslie and Ellen. With Frank's help he was able to build a nice barn where they kept a good milk cow, and a chicken house for a few chickens. By spring of 1914, he had proved up on his homestead, and felt a certain satisfaction in knowing that at last he owned the title to this land which he and Ellen had once termed "their dream ranch."

In June, that year, Herbert Marshall, the merchant at Lower Stanley, paid the family a visit to ask Leslie if he would take over the management of his store for him. Mr. Marshall had known since their first meeting that Leslie had been well educated and posessed a good business head. Also, in a conversation one day, he had learned that Leslie had worked at bookkeeping and had been a bank teller at Cedar Rapids, Nebraska, before coming to Idaho. But with his ranch free and clear now, it took persuasion to win Leslie's consent. After some consideration, he did accept, and the family moved to Lower Stanley.

L. S. Niece Store at Lower Stanley (1914)

Left to Right ... Ellen, Rupert, Edna, and "Tink" (Leslie) Niece. Dave Foster in foreground at right. Taken inside boarding house at Lower Stanley (1914)

When Leslie took over the store there a short time later, Ellen took on the job of running the boarding house next to the store, also owned by Mr. Marshall. August Fisher was the Stanley Postmaster at that time, but was not well and wished to give it up if Leslie would apply for the appointment. Leslie did, receiving said appointment December 1, 1914. Mr. Fisher died in a Salt Lake City hospital the following spring, May 8, 1915. August Fisher had relocated the ranch directly across the river from Stanley in 1902 that had first been located by Edgar Huffman Sr. This later became the Bill Wooley ranch.

In the early days to operate a mercantile business, particularily if it was the only store, as in this case, in the Stanley-Sawtooth area was not easy. In the fall before the first snows fell, large orders had to be placed and brought from the nearest railway at Hailey by wagons and teams. This was imperative because once the dirt road became choked with snow, in those years, the entire Stanley-Sawtooth region was cut off from the rest of the world for at least five months out of the year. Deliveries were made by freighters with outfits made up of two wagons and six horses.

Arrival of these freight wagons was an exciting event in the lives of the people who lived in the tiny Stanley community. Menfolk and children would gather at the store to help unload, exclaiming with delight at the many cases of canned fruits and vegetables, jams, jellies, pickles, and the like as they stacked them in every nook and cranny available inside the store and storage room. Without refrigeration, no fresh meats, fruits or vegetables could be stocked, but there was always plenty of cured meats, canned fish such as salmon and sardines, condiments, cheese, Eagle Brand milk, and canned cream, butter, dried fruits, sacks of flour, sugar, coffee and other such staples. Too, orders included tobacco, candy, hardware items, some ready-made clothing, and all items usually stocked in any general merchandise store in that day and time.

In the store, Leslie soon proved himself to be most capable and efficient as manager and postmaster. His personality won him many friends and things went well. That winter, 1914-15, Rupert, now eleven and Edna, eight, numbered among the "live-in" students at the John Thompson ranch . . . first school to be conducted in the Stanley Basin.

In the fall of 1916, Ellen still beset by ill health, took Edna and went to Vancouver, Washington to seek medical aid and to

227

visit with one of her sisters who lived there. Another of her sisters, Affie Cothern, and her husband, "Doc," with their two daughters, Mildred and Virginia, came from Encampment, Wyoming, to take over the boarding house at Lower Stanley for Ellen. After spending the winter at Vancouver, Ellen and Edna were on their way back home, stopping off to change trains at Blackfoot, Idaho, when the first group of Idaho Volunteers of World War I boarded a train enroute to their training camps. Naturally, the mother and daughter delighted in the exciting experience amid the cheering, flag-waving crowds, listening to the bands and watching the big parade.

In 1917, Leslie bought the store from Herbert Marshall. Also, he purchased a Republic truck inasmuchas freight teams were now being replaced by trucks, and Leslie wanted to haul as much of his own freight as he could from the railway at Hailey. His brother, "Juggy," and his son, Rupert, both learned to drive the truck, helping to save on freight and expand the Niece enterprises.

Meanwhile, Bartlett Falls from the Pahsamori Valley had purchased the Benner ranch holdings in the area where Upper Stanley is now located. During the winter of 1917-18, Falls approached Leslie, offering him clear title to five acres of land in the location where he proposed to plat a townsite, providing Leslie would build and operate a new general merchandise store there. Accepting Fall's offer and taking his brother, Frank, in as a partner, he hired the carpenters, Tom Williams and Arthur Wright, to build a store building, a residence for his family, and a small building to house a power plant for electricity for the store and home. The following April, Leslie sold his store at Lower Stanley to Flo Clyde of Challis, Idaho, in order to help with the building of the new store. When it was finished in the early spring of 1919, while waiting for the new house to be completed, the family lived in a small building behind the Benner Hotel. In the fall, when they were able to move into their new home at last, the family was indeed proud and happy, for to have seven large rooms and a bath instead of an outside "John," all lighted by electricity was surely a great convenience at that time in the Stanley-Sawtooth country. In fact, this residence was the first of its kind to be constructed in the immediate area.

While by now a school district had been established and a schoolhouse built, it was still at Lower Stanley a mile and a half away. Rupert and Edna walked the distance every school day, no matter what weather condition prevailed. One morning in January, 1920, when the temperature dipped to 50 below zero, the two youngsters insisted on going to school against their parents protests. "Aw! Dad," Rupert told his father, "We'll hurry and be there before you know it."

Giving in, Leslie finally said, "Alright. But whatever you do, don't stop . . . and walk as fast as you can."

Promising they would do just as he instructed, the two started out. The wind was bitter cold, penetrating their heavy, woolen clothing as they hurried along. Being the younger and smaller of the two children, Edna soon fell behind. Rupert took her by the hand and pulled her along yelling, "Come on!" By the time they reached a place below the Valley Creek Ranger Station where they sometimes stopped to rest on their way to and from school, the little girl had decided she was going to rest. "NO, Dad told us not to," her brother shouted, "Come on!" With that, Rupert had to practically drag her the rest of the way.

Their teacher, Mrs. Josephine Thompson, was watching for them, and when the youngsters did reach the school, she hurried them inside where they had to lean over the stove to thaw their frozen scarves away from their mouths and noses. Even their eyelashes were crusted with ice and had to be thawed, the children were so cold. The warmth of the big woodburning stove soon warmed them, making them like new again . . . not even a frosted finger or toe resulted from their frigid walk to school.

Both Rupert and Edna graduated from the eighth grade that year, going on to school at Pocatello for a short time that fall. Edna also attended school at Challis for two years. During this time, Rupert had met, fallen in love with, and married pretty dark-haired Bonda Critchfield.

That was the year that Leslie and Ellen began having marital problems. After taking Edna, now sixteen, to enter school in Boise that fall, by spring they had sold their nice home and moved into a smaller house that had once been the schoolhouse at Lower Stanley. By this time Leslie was mixed up in the school fight and the post office fight between the two towns as well as his own troubles at home. Things went from bad to worse in their marriage, and in August, 1924, the couple was divorced. Dissent over the property resulted, causing the store to be sold to the Gillispie brothers, Claude and Clyde, in June,

1926, in order to settle debts.

In November, 1924, Edna had also married, and she and her husband, Arthur "Tuff" McGown, had gone to live at Challis, Idaho. After their divorce and property settlement, Leslie departed for Nevada and Ellen went to Oregon, both working at various jobs for the next few years. Finally in 1932, they settled their differences and remarried, and again established a home in Upper Stanley. Leslie declined to start another business, but went on to work at mining and for the Highway Department and the Forest Service.

The winter of 1936-37 found Leslie and his son, Rupert, working on some mining claims on Red Mountain, about ten miles from the old mining town of Bonanza, up the West Fork of the Yankee Fork. While here Leslie was taken critically ill. Rupert hurried to Bonanza on snowshoes for help. Jimmy Cearley and Frank Casto went back with him to bring his father on a hand sled to Sunbeam where Ellen and Edna and her husband were waiting to take him to Stanley. From that time on until his death in June, 1939, his suffering was constant.

The following notes are exerpts from his obituary as it appeared in the *Challis Messenger Newspaper:*

Leslie S. Niece was born at LaPeer, Michigan, October 30, 1876, one of the nine children of Oscar and Rosella Ann Niece. At the age of ten, he went to live at Denver, Colorado with his mother's brother and his wife who had no children of their own. There he received a good education, and by the time he reached the age of seventeen, had secured a job at a bank in Cedar Rapids, Nebraska.

Feeling the call of the West, in 1900 he traveled on to Rambler, Wyoming, where he went into the store business with his brother, Frank Niece. Here he soon became postmaster, and within the next few years a bond was welded between the two brothers never to be broken as long as Leslie lived. On Christmas Eve, 1902, Leslie took Ellen Martin, originally from Nebraska where she had been born in 1886, as his bride.

Still feeling the urge to explore farther west, Leslie and Frank sold their interests in Rambler in 1904, stopping off at Encampment, Wyoming, until the summer of 1906 when they first appeared in the Stanley-Sawtooth region. The obituary went on to note that Leslie had been a well-to-do merchant and the postmaster at Stanley, and at one time had homesteaded in the lower end of Sawtooth Valley. The fact that he and Ellen had two children, a son, Rupert, born November 14, 1903, at Shepherd, Michigan, and a daughter, Edna, born November 22, 1906, in the Stanley Basin, was also cited.

The obituary ended, "Leslie S. Niece passed away on June 17, 1939, and was interned in the Stanley cemetery. "Tink," as his friends and neighbors called him, was an upright and honest citizen. Through the years, he has lent a helping hand to many people, and has always worked for the betterment of the community. At the graveside service, a fitting tribute was made to him by Charley Langer in the reading of 'A House By The Side of The Road,' for no kinder man has yet to live among us."

After "Tink's" death, Ellen stayed on at Upper Stanley until World War II. At that time she went to the state of Washington to work in the shipyards. Later, she returned to make her home in Challis, Idaho, buying a house, fixing it up and doing gardening until again she was overcome by failing health. In 1957, she was told by her doctors that she had cancer. She then went to be with her sister, Affie Cothern, in Nevada, before she finally entered the hospital at Twin Falls, Idaho. On May 1, 1959, Ellen died there, and is buried in the Memorial Park Cemetery on the outskirts of town.

Like all the early pioneers in the Stanley-Sawtooth country, Leslie "Tink" and Ellen Niece had a part in the making of its history. And like all of the others, they too, suffered hardships, but learned to cope with their problems. His daughter, Edna, remembers two of her father's favorite sayings. One is, "If a thing is worth doing at all, it is worth doing well"; and the other is, "After breakfast work awhile, after dinner rest awhile, and after supper walk a mile."

HERBERT H. AND MARY MARSHALL

On a morning in April, 1915, the little community of Lower Stanley was pervaded by an air of excitement and expectancy. Herbert Marshall, one of Stanley Basin's pioneers, was bringing home his bride. What would she be like? Would she accept as her friends the folks who knew and admired Herbert, and were his friends?

An elderly lady today, who at that time was but a small child, remembers that morning well. It was one of those sparkling, clear mornings when the warmth of the April sunshine was erasing the last of the winters snows from the flats and the low hills, and the Sawtooths, still snow-covered, gleamed in the background. The stage from Challis was to arrive at noon. Ellen Niece had prepared an extra special meal to be served at the "boarding house" that day. Ellen's daughter, Edna, with her dark hair smoothly brushed and fastened in braids with ribbon bows, and her dress freshly starched and ironed, was ready to help her mother serve. Mr. Marshall was one of her favorite people, so between small chores assigned to her by her mother she would dash to the door and look down the road to see if the stage was coming yet.

Finally the light, two-seated wagon, drawn by a team of matched bay horses, arrived and halted in front of the post office adjoining Leslie Niece's store. Mary Marshall, a woman about five feet five inches tall, a little on the plump side, dressed in a stylish black coat and a straw hat tied firmly over her grey hair with a white scarf, was helped from the wagon by her bridegroom, who said, "Mary, these folks will be our neighbors and friends." He then introduced her to each of the little group gathered to welcome them, including the children. Her blue eyes sparkled as she smiled and acknowledged the introductions in her soft, pleasing voice. That day Mary Marshall, later to become familiarily known as "Mother Marshall" won the same admiration and respect that the people of this isolated village held for her husband.

Herbert H. Marshall was born in Vermont in 1845. When just a child he moved with his parents to Iowa, and it was here, while still a young man that he learned the carpenter trade. It was here also, that he met and fell in love with Mary (her maiden name not known). It was a Mr. Baxter, a close friend and working companion of Herbert's who first introduced Herbert to Mary. As time went on, Herbert realized that Mr. Baxter too was in love with Mary. This, however did not hinder their friendship. It was one of those "May the best man win" situations.

Herbert Marshall, being of a rather adventurous disposition, had often told both Mary and Baxter of his desire to travel West. This idea did not appeal to Mary, so eventually she made her decision to marry Baxter. After the wedding Herbert was often a visitor at the Baxter home, and continued to work with Baxter for a time. Then, late in the 1880s he headed West, arriving in the Stanley Basin in 1888.

At that early date there was no opportunity in the Stanley country for a carpenter to work at his trade, so Herbert became interested in mining and trapping. He spent one winter in partnership with Tom Kelly trapping at the head of Joe's Gulch and Basin Creek. During the 1890s he was in partners with various placer miners in the Basin. When the Arthur McGown Sr. family moved to Stanley in 1890, Herbert had settled on a piece of meadow land across Salmon River from where Valley Creek empties into the main river. Here he had built a snug little one room cabin. It was here too that he plowed the first ground ever to be plowed for ranch purposes in the Stanley country.

As the years passed Herbert came to love the remote, rugged beauty of the country, and could visualize the possibilities for development. In 1902, having the know-how to build, and with house logs easily available, he decided to enter into a new venture. He built the first stopping place in what later became Lower Stanley. Located at the mouth of Nip-N-Tuck Gulch where the State road left the Salmon River to wind its way over the Nip-N-Tuck hill and into the Stanley Basin, this hotel, or "boarding house" was a long log structure of three rooms with a lean-to bedroom attached to one end. Many mining men and prospectors going and coming from the mines in the Basin and the Seafoam area found this a convenient overnight stop.

During the next five years a number of ranches had been located and more permanent people had settled in the country. The future for both quartz and placer mining looked promising. It was then, in 1907, that Herbert Marshall and Henry Sturkey formed a partnership and built and stocked a general merchandise store near the hotel building. Herbert ran this business himself until 1912 when, tiring of the confinement, he sold to N.S. Powers and it became known as The Stanley Mercantile Company.

While Herbert was confined to running the store he was far from being inactive in other fields. He made homemade skiis, turned and grooved to exactly the right proportions. As a result, his skiis were much in demand by area residents. He liked to build furniture, and some of the pieces he built are still in use. Then too, even at sixty-six, his adventurous spirit inspired him to purchase a motorcycle, and often the stillnes of the Basin or Upper Stanley would be shattered by the roar of this cycle as Herbert came to drop off small grocery items, deliver the mail, or just to drop in and pass the time of day with the neighbors. Local people referred to Herbert's motorcycle as his bronc, and would say, "H.H. is out on that noisy bronc again today."

After selling the store Herbert built a two-room log cabin across Salmon River from Lower Stanley, just south of the August Fisher ranch (now the Wooley ranch). Working in partnership with Bill Merritt, they started a sawmill up behind the Merritt ranch. Mr. Marshall was free again to live and work in the great outdoors that he loved.

Then, in January, 1914, Herbert filed notice of attachment against N.S. Powers for payment of debt, and by June of that year was back managing the grocery store. It was at that time that he prevailed upon Leslie Niece and his wife, Ellen, to take over the store and boarding house. When they had moved from their ranch in the north end of the Sawtooth Valley and were settled in Lower Stanley, Herbert once again was free of his business obligations.

During the winter of 1914 and 1915 Mr. Marshall busied himself by building a workshop behind his cabin across the river. He repapered the walls of his two rooms, built in cabinets, and finished off by building a covered porch across the front of the house. Friends would jokingly say, "Old H.H. sure is busy these days. Looks like he might be planning on getting married." Little did they dream how near to the truth they were. It came as quite a surprise when the word came out that he had gone to Challis to be married.

Over the years Herbert had continued to correspond with the Baxters back in Iowa. Word had come about four years earlier that Mr. Baxter had died. Since that time Herbert had written regularly to Mary Baxter telling her of his business ventures, the people who lived in the area, the snug little home he had built, and painting a glowing picture of this rugged, beautiful country that he loved. Finally, as Mary told later, he wrote asking her to come, saying, "If you don't come, I'll have to come back to get you." She came. She met Herbert in Challis, Idaho, and on April 12, 1915, Mary's fifty-eighth birthday, they were married by Judge Dougherty. After thirty-five years of waiting, Herbert, now seventy years old, could finally claim this woman he loved as his bride.

The next seven years saw the Marshalls content and happy in their little home. Herbert spent long hours working in his shop, or sitting in his easy chair by the window reading. Mary, always an industrious lady, liked to cook, kept her house immaculately clean, spent many hours knitting, and was ready on a moments notice to go to the aid of a needy neighbor or friend. Acting as a midwife, she helped to deliver several babies in that vicinity. The Marshalls both took an active interest in the affairs of the community. One winter Ted Williams, whose parents lived on a ranch in the Sawtooth Valley, boarded with Herbert and Mary and went to the Stanley school. Each spring, as the last of the winter snows disappeared, Herbert could be seen wandering over the fields with a shovel on his shoulder, and the area residents would comment, "There goes Herbert . . . a sure sign of spring."

The passing years took their toll and Herbert's health was failing rapidly. It was decided that they should sell the ranch and build a cabin across the river and near to Will and Mae Rose, who at that time owned the Stanley Grocery, now Jerry's Country Store. This they did, and it was here on June 12, 1924, that Herbert H. Marshall passed on to the Great Beyond. Mrs. Josephine Thompson was in charge of the graveside services, and gave a glowing tribute to the old pioneer. As had been his request, Edna Niece and her friend, Thelma Hodell rendered the songs for the service. So ended the life of a grand old man who had spent more than forty years in Central Idaho in the labor of building a country where he might live in peace.

So far as is known, at the time of his death, Mr. Marshall had just one living relative, a niece, Mrs. Fred Wheeler of Layton, Utah. She and her husband had visited the Marshalls occasionally, and came to be with Mary and to attend the funeral.

Mary stayed on in the home she and Herbert had shared for several years. Friends would come to visit or to take her to their homes for a stay of a day, or sometimes several days. Mrs. Sadie Merritt was especially good to Mary, and Mary, in turn often helped Sadie with cooking during busy times on the ranch.

Many years passed before ill health finally made it necessary for Mary to have constant care. By now the small savings that Herbert had left to her was gone, so she was taken to Challis, Idaho, in the late fall of 1940 to be cared for by Custer County. She spent the winter at the home of Mrs. Alice Osborn, but was a very unhappy, lonely little old lady.

It was during the early summer of 1941 that Mrs. Merritt was in Challis and dropped by to visit with Mrs. Marshall. Before leaving she asked, "Mother Marshall, how would you like to go back to the ranch with me?" Needless to say, Mrs. Marshall was overcome with joy. Straightway Mrs. Merritt went to the County Commissioners, and after a short time received permission to take Mary Marshall home with her. For the remainder of her life, Mary lived at the Merritt ranch and was cared for by Sadie Merritt.

All during her adult life Mrs. Marshall had had the habit of drinking a glass of warm water with a half teaspoon of epsom salts dissolved in it each morning before her breakfast. On the

Mrs. Lizzie Snyder Bohney standing, and Mary "Mother" Marshall in rocking chair. Taken at Merritt ranch in 1941.

236

morning of August 10, 1942, Mother Marshall surprised Mrs. Merritt by appearing in the kitchen fully dressed while Mrs. Merritt was preparing breakfast for her son, Stub, and young Leslie Niece who was there to assist Stub with the haying. As Sadie saw her come in she said, "Land sakes, Mother Marshall, why are you up so early?" Mary answered, "It is such a beautiful morning, and I feel so much better, I thought I'd like to step outside into the sunshine for a minute. I'll just take my glass of water and go out the back door here." Sadie fixed the water, then said, "Now don't go far," and went on making breakfast for the boys. The back door stood open. Mary walked to the door and stepped outside. As the screen door closed behind her Sadie and the boys heard her fall. They rushed out, but it took only a glance to tell them she was dead. The boys picked her up gently and carried her inside.

Mary "Mother" Marshall, who had been born in Bremer County, Iowa, on April 12, 1857, and who had journeyed to a strange land when well past middle age to join the sweetheart whom she hadn't seen for thirty-five years, had taken her last journey. She was laid to rest beside her husband in the Stanley cemetery.

WILLIAM AND SADIE MERRITT

J. Davenport Merritt, who was known in the Stanley-Sawtooth country as William or "Bill" Merritt, and his wife, Sadie, arrived in the Stanley Basin in the late summer of 1908. At that time they had two small daughters, little Sadie, almost two years old, and Myrta, less than a year. Traveling in the company of a congenial man named Cobb, the Merritts came by wagon and team, leading a few extra horses, from Ely, Nevada, where they had been living for about a year. Prior to Nevada they had lived in Wyoming . . . first in Green River where they had met and married, then in Jackson Hole for a time.

For information on the Stanley country, Mr. Cobb had been advised to see John Thompson as soon as they arrived in the area. However, Mrs. Merritt was so tired from traveling with the two babies through the endless miles of dust and desert to get there, when they stopped to camp at Redfish Lake, she was ready to settle there rather than travel farther on to the Basin. The men felt impatient, deciding that Cobb should take a horse and ride on to the Benner place, located at Upper Stanley, to learn where John Thompson might be found. While he was gone Mrs. Merritt would wash some clothes and rest. A few miles from camp Cobb met two men the Merritts had known in Wyoming, John Cherry and Paul Imeson. Cherry recognized the horse Cobb was riding as one that had formerly belonged to Bill Merritt. Pulling rein, he asked Cobb, "Where did you get that horse?" When told that the horse belonged to Bill Merritt, and that the Merritts were camped at Redfish Lake, Imeson said, "Go back to camp and tell them to pack up right now and come to my place. I have a ranch about a mile and a half from Upper Stanley."

The next day the Merritts did go to the Imeson's, and liking the locale, chose a homestead site in a protected nook at the foot of the Sawtooth Mountains, a mile distant from the Imeson ranch. Here it is noted that none of this land had been surveyed as yet, and those who settled there retained what was commonly referred to as "Squatter's Rights."

After staking their homestead, it being late in the season, both Bill and Mrs. Merritt were anxious to have a roof of their own over their heads as soon as possible. Therefore, a spot was chosen, and Bill, with some help from Paul Imeson and Mr. Cherry, built a log cabin that, when completed would have

Winter at the Merritt ranch home (1911). Left to right Mr. William Merritt, Mr. Cady, Mrs. Sadie Merritt, Mrs. and Mr. Wertz. Little girls ... left to right ... Myrta and Sadie Merritt.

three large rooms. Meanwhile the little family stayed at the Imeson place until they could move into their new home. Although one of the rooms lacked completion, when the roof was on and they knew the finished part would be livable, one day in December, with the temperature 30 degrees below zero and eight inches of snow on the ground, they moved in. It was a snug home built of logs with floor and roofing boards hauled from the old mining town of Vienna in the Sawtooth Valley. The roof was a "dirt roof," but didn't leak the way most dirt roofs did, inasmuchas Bill nailed a double layer of boards to the ridge logs, covered them with six or eight inches of soil and sod, and then covered that with another layer of boards. In recalling this home, Mrs. Merritt said, "That year we had two rooms and a PATH ... the path led to our outside 'John.'"

Sadie also recalled their first winter there as being the hardest they ever had to endure. Before spring they were out of money and down to bread, rice, and coffee. Finally, after several days of such fare, Bill announced that he was going to either the Benner Store, or on down to Marshall's Store where Lower Stanley is now located, and "run his face" for some groceries. When he returned they had food for awhile longer. Then in March they ran out of feed for the horses. Snow was deep on the ground at that time. Even so, to provide a bit of forage for his stock, Bill, with Sadie's help, shoveled a wide path down to the creek where the horses could nibble on the brush and willows growing along the banks. This sufficed until Bill could move them to the Imeson ranch and across the Salmon River to the bare foothills behind the Frank Hellsinger ranch. Spring was welcome indeed that year.

The summer of 1909, Bill contracted to cut one hundred cord of wood for the Willis Dredging Company working in the Stanley Basin at that time. Making camp in an old cabin on Kelly Creek, thought to belong to Henry Sturkey, he got the wood cut and was ready to deliver it when it started to rain. It rained for days. As a result, every time he loaded his wagon and prepared to start, the wheels would mire down before he could get off the loading spot. He decided to wait until it snowed, then use a sled to haul the wood. When it did snow, he took his little family, set up camp in the cabin, and went to work. He was able to deliver only a few loads when a bad storm came, snowing and blowing with such a vengence he became afraid they would be snowed in at the cabin. Acting accordingly, in the early morning they began the journey homeward through the snowstorm, requiring all day to travel the distance of six or seven miles.

That November Mrs. Merritt was expecting her third child. Since no doctor was available in the Basin, and Molly Paul, living on Nip-N-Tuck mountain where she and her husband, George, operated a stopping place for travelers, was a midwife, Bill took his wife to her. As it happened, the roof over Mrs. Merritt's bedroom leaked quite badly, prompting Bill to buy a large piece of oilcloth to go over the bed. On the date of the delivery, November 23, 1909, Mrs. Paul thought to move Mrs. Merritt into her own room which did not leak. Somehow, in the moving Mrs. Merritt fell against the bed, and it was thought caused injury to the unborn child because when it arrived, a short time later, there was a deep crease in its forehead. The baby, a little girl, was named Peggy. She lived only a few weeks and it was a sad day when baby Peggy was buried near the Merritt home on their ranch.

During this time the post office was at Lower Stanley with August Fisher as postmaster. Harve Stout, who lived at the Benner place at the Upper town, had contracted to carry the mail from the post office at the mining town of Bonanza on the Yankee Fork of the Salmon River to Stanley, and that winter (1909 and 10), hired Bill Merritt to carry it for him. Although Bill knew he would have to go on snowshoes carrying a

50-pound mail sack and a way sack for each, Dave Hershey at Casino Creek and Pat Lynch at Lynch Creek, over snow choked roads, never kept open in the wintertime in those days, he took the job because he needed the money badly. On one trip in February, snowslides were coming down on both sides of the Salmon River all the way to Sunbeam. On arriving there, all but exhausted, Bill met Will Centauras who carried the mail from Challis to Bonanza. With Centauras on his way to Bonanza, and thinking to rest at Sunbeam, Bill asked Centauras if he would bring him the Stanley mail there to save the trip up the Yankee Fork and back. At Bonanza the postmaster refused to release the Stanley mail to anyone but the regular carrier, in this case, Bill Merritt. When Centauras returned to Sunbeam and relayed the Bonanza postmaster's message, Bill had to make the trip after all, causing him to be a day late returning to Stanley.

Back at the ranch, alone with her little ones, Mrs. Merritt worried, fearing her husband had been caught in a snowslide. Hoping to get to Stanley to find out why he was late, she hitched up the team and attempted to drive there, but soon found it impossible for the horses to travel through the deep snow. Managing to get back to the house she resigned herself to wait. About eleven o'clock that night, looking out the window, she saw a light bobbing along coming toward the house. She just KNEW it was someone coming to tell her that Bill had been caught in a slide. As the light drew nearer, she opened the door and waited with pounding heart. When the someone came into full view, *it was Bill,* his snowshoes caked with ice and snow, and he himself half-frozen and tired to the bone. All the way home he had kept thinking about a drink from the bottle of whiskey he always kept around for just such occasions, but when he finally got there he was so weary he forgot all about it. It had been a tough trip with poor visibility due to the ground blizzard, losing his way on the trail part of the time, falling into drifts, and being overtaken by darkness. The light he carried was a candle secured in a can cut to give the flame air and hooked to his belt, called a "hobo lantern" by the miners and prospectors who devised it.

While Bill worked for the Forest Service off and on, and in partnership with Herbert Marshall in a sawmill operation, cutting and delivering lumber to the Seafoam Mine and other places in the area, the Merritts made many improvements on their ranch in the following years. They built fences, added

241

outbuildings, and completed the unfinished bedroom in their home. Too, they had their fourth child, another little girl whom they named Nellie.

The Merritts were very hospitable people and loved company. A large woman with a jovial manner and a hearty laugh, Mrs. Merritt was an energetic person ready for a dance, party, or any activity that happened to develop in the community. In telling about the first dance she ever attended in the Stanley country, she said, "It was late fall, as I remember. Bill was away working and I was staying at the Benners for a few days. Will Paul and Bill Soule came with a sleigh pulled by a four-horse team to take us to the Willis Dredge place where the dance was to be held. Lucy Sewell, Mrs. Benner, Mary Niece, Preston Shaw, John and Josephine Thompson, Ellen Niece, and a few other people were there. The dredge watchman, a Mr. Cady, loved to dance, and had a Victrola graphaphone. Someone played a mouth organ too. You know, we danced to any kind of music that anyone in the crowd could play. Anyway, we danced until daylight and had a wonderful time. On the way home, Preston Shaw, sitting up front, jumped off the sleigh, slipped around back to where Mrs. Benner and Mr. Cady sat talking and dangling their feet. Grabbing Mrs. Benner's feet he pulled her off into the snow. He knew it would make her mad since everyone was aware of what a bad temper she had. Well, she got mad alright. She picked herself up and called Preston every unlady-like name she could lay her tongue to. She really had a temper!"

Sometimes when Mrs. Merritt stayed at the Benners, Mrs. Benner would help her do sewing for her little girls. On one occasion she was making dresses from material stocked in the Benner store, and Mrs. Benner took the time to make the dresses very pretty with ruffles and lace. Mrs. Merritt had gone to the Benner Hotel a couple of days early to be there for a big dance planned to be held in the upstairs ballroom which had been built especially for such events.

Being a very rugged and resourceful woman, Mrs. Merritt went any and everywhere she wanted to, or could, whether Mr. Merritt was able to go with her or not. In the summer of 1915 there was to be a carnival at Hailey, Idaho, over the Galena Summit in the Wood River country. Mrs. Merritt loaded her little girls and two little neighbor girls, Edna Niece and Rosemary Paul, into the wagon and went, taking two days to make the trip one way and camping out at night along the way.

Left to right ... William (Bill) Merritt, Edna Niece, Rupert Niece, George Sewell, Rebecca Sewell, Mrs. Sadie Merritt holding daughter, Nellie, with daughters, Sadie and Myrta Merritt in front. Taken on old road leaving Lower Stanley (1914)

Since one of the team she drove was a mare with a colt, she simply allowed the colt to tag alongside the wagon as she drove. In camp, the four oldest girls would invariably get into an argument as to who would lead the mare and colt down to the river for a drink of water, resulting in Mrs. Merritt acting not only as teamstress, but as nursemaid, camp-tender, cook and peacemaker as well.

At Hailey she and the children had a delightful time. One incident relating to the trip which Mrs. Merritt told about later occurred when they stopped in Friedman's General Store to buy a few things. Seeing a large watermelon at one end of the counter, little Rosemary Paul said in an excited voice, "Oh, Mrs. Merritt! Look at that great big cucumber!" Looking at Mrs. Merritt in astonishment, and not knowing it was the child's first time to ever see a watermelon, Mr. Friedman asked, "Where in the world has that child been raised?"

On the way back to Stanley Basin from Hailey, Mrs. Merritt stopped to camp for the night at Pole Creek. Sometime before morning it rained, and awakening at daybreak she could see the horses off at a distance heading toward home. She jumped out of bed, and without taking time to put on the corset which she always wore, pulled on her stockings and shoes and started after them on a dead run. "I had to run like the devil," she said, "But I rounded them up and got back to camp alright. By that time my stockings had worked down around my shoes and were a wet, muddy mess."

243

After the Hailey trip, things went along much as before at the Merritt ranch ... both man and wife working hard to improve their property and with Bill continuing to work at outside jobs in and around the area. Their first son, named William, and nicknamed "Stub" was born, and later joined by another sister whom they named Stella. In 1917 Bill built a cabin at Lower Stanley in which Mrs. Merritt could stay and send the children to school in the wintertime. The following year, Inez Binkley, Mrs. Merritt's younger sister, came from Wyoming to live with them. That winter Mrs. Merritt remained at the ranch and Inez stayed in town with the children who were going to school.

In 1919 Inez and Chester Lloyd were married in an unusual ceremony performed by a judge in Challis, Idaho, by telephone, the young couple at Stanley repeating the wedding vows over the line as instructed by the judge. After the wedding they went to Alaska to make their home, but the event of their marriage was long remembered in the Stanley Basin.

As the years passed, all the Merritt children grew up and married, and for a time, all lived in the Stanley area. Later, Sadie, the oldest, and her husband, Garner Warner, moved to Salmon, Idaho. When Myrta's first husband, Henry Dougherty of Challis, Idaho died, she remarried and moved to Arizona. He too died, so now Myrta spends part of her time in Arizona, and part back in Idaho. Nellie married Barney Lanier and lived in Stanley for several years before moving to a ranch near Challis. After Barney's death sometime ago, she continues to live on the ranch while she works in town. Stub (William) and his wife, Vella, live in Montana. The youngest daughter, Stella, is the wife of Bud Critchfield, and they are still living in Stanley.

Bill Merritt began to fail in health about 1936. Although urged by his wife and family to go to a doctor, he flatly refused. By November, 1938, he became very ill and was confined to bed. Yet he still refused the aid of a doctor. Becoming very concerned, and over his protests, Mrs. Merritt called Dr. Fox in Hailey. When she explained Bill's symptoms, he told her to get Bill over to Hailey as quickly as possible. But Bill still refused to go. That night Ellen Niece stayed at the Merritt home assisting Mrs. Merritt in every way she could with her sick husband who appeared even worse the next day. "You go call Dr. Fox again," she told Mrs. Merritt. "I'll stay with Bill while you are gone." On the way to Stanley, Mrs. Merritt met her son, Stub, coming home from work. When told that his father was worse, and that she was on her way to make another call to Dr. Fox, Stub said, "Come on back home, Mother. Dad will go to the doctor."

Back at the house, Stub walked into his father's room, talked to him a few minutes, then said, "Get dressed Dad. We are taking you to see Dr. Fox as soon as we can get there." That was all it took to get him up and ready to go. On the way to the car, walking through the kitchen to the back door, Bill Merritt paused and looked around as though to say, "I want just one last look." At Hailey the doctor diagnosed his condition as cancerous. A short time time later he died there in the Hailey hospital and was buried in the cemetery at Stanley.

Stub stayed on at the ranch with his mother until he married Vella Williams Lee. In 1949 when the Merritt ranch was traded to Selby Hansen for another ranch some three miles from Challis, Idaho, Stub and Vella moved there to live. Mrs. Merritt also stored many of her belongings there while she worked at various jobs in the region, sometimes cooking, and sometimes caring for aged persons in need of help. Things on the ranch went fine for a time, then the house burned destroying everything in it, including Mrs. Merritt's things.

For as long as she was able, Mrs. Merritt continued to work, drove her own car and traveled around a great deal. In 1965 she moved into a little home of her own located on the ranch owned by her daughter, Nellie. Even though the years have advanced upon her, she puts in her time doing fancy handwork and crocheting beautiful afaghans which she sells. On December 1, 1975, she celebrated her 86th birthday at a dinner given in her honor by her daughters.

Beginning in 1970, the Merritt children and their families, with their mother, gathered at the old homestead which their parents had carved out of the wilderness, for a reunion. With all the grandchildren attending that were able to come, the family counted sixty-five members present. In 1972, when the event was repeated, eighty-one members attended. When another reunion was held in 1974, one grandson came from as far away as Anchorage, Alaska. This event was held at Crooked Creek near the location of the old homestead. Although not all of the family were able to be there, Mrs. Merritt counted that she had eighteen grandchildren, sixty great-grandchildren, and five great-great-grandchildren. At the time she noted over sixty members of the Lanier family alone... Nellie being the mother of nine married children, each with children of their own. In fact, one of the group at the large gathering in 1974 remarked that it was more like a Lanier reunion.

Mrs. Merritt enjoyed each of these events to the fullest, and while age prevents her from being as active as in yesteryears, she keeps busy. In recollecting her life, she said, "Despite all the hardships of the early days, my years have been good years." Chances are, like the other oldtimers who are still living today around the Stanley-Sawtooth country, if she could, she would gladly do it all over again . . . making a home in a new land and raising a family.

The Merritt ranch, traded to Selby Hansen in 1949, is now in the hands of Jack Furey of Challis, and Louis Racine of Pocatello. Both Jack and Louis have erected rustic log cabins on the property where they spend some time in the summer enjoying all the aspects of the rugged Sawtooth region.

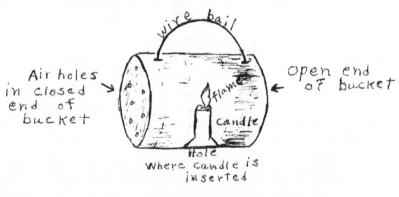

Hobo Lantern designed by early miners and like one used by Bill Merritt.

THE GEORGE AND WILL PAUL FAMILIES

Going from Lower Stanley in a north-westerly direction, a gravel road leads over a mountain called "Nip-and-Tuck," so named, as oldtimers will tell you, "because in the early days it was sure nip-and-tuck to get over that grade with a loaded wagon." For many years this was the only road going to and from Bear Valley, and the Capehorn, Seafoam, and Stanley Basin, and the mines in that direction.

In 1905, where the road grades down onto the grassy meadows at the foot of the summit, George Washington Paul and his wife, Mary Mannix (Molly), and their son, Will Paul, came to build a home that soon became a popular stopping place for miners, freighters, and other travelers coming and going that way. Although only ruins remain today, the "Paul Place," as it was called locally, once constituted a large, one-story log house of four rooms with a cellar, a small woodshed, and two large structures across the road; one of which served as a blacksmith shop and barn for the horses, and the other used as a saloon and bunkhouse to accommodate travelers stopping there.

George Paul . . .early settler in Stanley Basin

Molly Paul ... wife of George Paul.

The story of George and Molly Paul began on a romantic note. Born in Massachusetts, she met George on a boat while sailing around the Horn to California, about 1876. Later, in California, she became engaged to another man and may have married him, but seems on the eve of the wedding while being treated to a party by friends, her intended over-indulged in drink, causing Molly to call off the wedding. Later she and George met again, and the attraction that had begun on the boat trip soon blossomed into a deep and lasting love. It mattered very little that George too drank, sometimes causing hardships for them during the years of their marriage. George and Molly's only children were a set of twins, one that died in infancy, and the other, their son, Will, born April 14, 1878.

From their home in Stockton, California, the Pauls went to Virginia City, Nevada, where he worked in the mines until 1888, at which time they came to Bayhorse, Idaho, to work. Later, about 1898, they took up a homestead on the East Fork of the Salmon River, remaining there until 1905 when they sold the ranch and moved to make their home in the Stanley Basin.

Molly, always an industrious and resourceful woman, aside

248

Remains of the George and Molly Paul stopping place in Stanley Basin. (1973)

from serving wayfaring travelers, did all the cooking, baking, laundry, and all of her own sewing. While the dining room that also doubled as a living room, opened toward the road, Molly's kitchen faced the Sawtooth Mountains to the South. She loved these mountains, never failing to gain inspiration from their majestic beauty as she worked at her kitchen chores.

Molly's granddaughter, Rosemary Paul Hoskins, tells a little story about what was probably Molly Paul's only vice. After breakfast each morning Molly would make her morning trip to the outside "john," and while attending to nature's call, would roll herself a cigarette with coarse paper and tobacco, and sit back to relax and enjoy the view of the Sawtooths through the open door. As far as anyone ever knew, this was the only time she smoked . . . just her one cigarette each morning in the outside toilet.

Molly had two parrots given to her by a seafaring brother. Both of the birds were called "Polly." The first was thought to be female since it was quite gentle and liked to be fondled and petted. Soon after it became a part of the Paul household, this "Polly" learned to call the cats and dogs that strayed around the neighborhood. Thinking Molly was going to feed them, the animals would come running. Then Polly would "sic" the dogs on the cats . . . and when the chase began, would squawk and chuckle with delight amid all the din of barking dogs and squalling cats.

The second "Polly" was believed to be a male since it was the exact opposite in nature, never allowing itself to be petted by anyone, and at times would be quite mean, especially with children. This parrot too could talk, and generally showed an uncanny awareness of what was going on around the Paul Place. Also, this bird loved desserts, and when Molly baked pie or cake he would refuse to eat a bite of any other food until he had been served his dessert first.

In 1905, Will, the only child, and son of George and Molly Paul, married Lillian Sullivan Webb of Clayton, Idaho, and went to live on Spud Creek near that town. That fall Will contracted to carry the mail between the towns of Clayton and Challis. On January 6, 1907, Lillian gave birth to their first child, a little girl named Rosemary, delivered by Lillian's mother, Mrs. Jason Webb.

Molly Paul too, was a midwife, aside from her many other talents. While living on Nip-and-Tuck she delivered two baby girls in her home there ... first a child for Ellen and "Tink" Niece, and the other for Sadie and Bill Merritt.

After a time Will and Lillian Paul went to live at the Valley Creek Mine property where he worked for the company. They had three more children ... all boys. Johnnie B. was born November 21, 1909, Wilmot W., born August 11, 1913, and one son, Chester, passed away in infancy. Will continued to work at the mine until about 1913 when his parents decided to return to Stockton, California. At this time the older couple turned their home over to Will and Lillian. Traffic on the Nip-and-Tuck road had declined somewhat by now, so the younger Pauls did not operate the stopping place for travelers as Molly and George had done.

Instead, to earn a living, Will and Lillian did whatever they could — Will working at mining whenever work was available, and carrying mail if a contract became open, usually during the winter months. Aside from caring for her home and family, Lillian often took work at the Benner Hotel in Upper Stanley. In 1913 Will filed on a homestead adjacent to the Sam Tennell place, seven miles northwest of Upper Stanley on the Valley Creek Mine road. While continuing to work at their various jobs, and putting in long, hard, extra hours at home, the Pauls were able to build the ranch up in time, running cattle and sheep, and raising chickens.

Their oldest child, Rosemary, being eager to learn, could do

William Paul on homemade skiis with canvas housings (1912 and 1913)

Mrs. Lillian Paul helping with the haying on the Paul ranch in the Stanley Basin; driving burros, Punch and Judy.

many kinds of household chores at an early age . . . washing, ironing, cleaning; and could even milk a cow when she was seven years old. This little girl's efforts to help her hard working parents was typical of most children living in the Stanley-Sawtooth country back in those years. Times were hard then in this still-new land where people had to work and manage in order to survive, and to be sure, even the help of small hands was appreciated.

Molly and George Paul, in California, missed the Sawtooth mountains, and were lonely for their son and his family. Finally, in 1919, they came home. At first they lived on the ranch with Will and Lillian. Soon, however, although getting on in years now, Molly, always active and industrious, decided to open a bakery at Upper Stanley. Rosemary, age twelve that year, would be her helper while attending school in Lower Stanley. Molly, always renowned for her bread-baking, turned out bread and rolls almost daily for the next three years, never lacking for customers. Aside from local trade, mainly bachelors and men who lived alone in the Stanley Basin, her trade included many tourists as well as sheepherders trailing their flocks to and from the summer range. Molly also made doughnuts and fudge candy to sell on occasion.

Up before dawn, she would set her dough to rise, and throughout the day would have three or four bakings of bread . . . baked in the oven of a large Majestic, wood-burning range. Bread sold for 25 cents for a one pound loaf, and fudge for 15 cents a pound. When Rosemary started to help her grandmother in the bakery, she soon learned to cut off a piece of dough that would weigh out to exactly a one pound loaf the way Molly could do.

In 1922, Molly Paul closed her bakery when Rosemary left Stanley to go to work for her maternal grandmother, Mrs. Jason Webb, who operated a mercantile store in Clayton, Idaho. A short time after this Mrs. Webb passed away, and in 1924 the Paul family . . . Will, Lillian, and their children, and Molly and George . . . all moved to Clayton where Will and Lillian worked in the store.

By this time George and Molly's health was failing, and on October 11, 1924, both George Washington Paul and Mary Mannix (Molly) Paul died within one hour of one another. Both are buried in the Clayton cemetery.

After his parents passed away, Will and Lillian went on to operate the store at Clayton for many years. They had a good trade with the local people and those traveling through the country. Many of the travelers were regular customers. Fred Schindler, who was a partner with Bill Soule in the Valley Creek Mine in the Stanley Basin was one. He often took his wife and children with him on trips from their home in Blackfoot, Idaho, to the mine, and would stop at the Paul store for supplies. The young Schindler boys loved to fish while their father was working at the mine, and knowing this, on one occasion, Mrs. Paul had made the boys each a small leather pouch in which to carry their fish hooks. Bill, the oldest boy, in telling about it in later years said, "Mrs. Paul made my brother and I very happy with the leather pouches and we used them for years. She was a good and kind woman, and apparently loved children very much."

The years passed. The children of Will and Lillian Paul had long since grown up, married, and gone to make homes of their own. Then Will became ill and was taken to the hospital in Salmon, Idaho, where in March, 1949, he passed away, and was buried in the Salmon cemetery.

Soon after Will's death Lillian sold the store in Clayton to Fred and Catherine Leuzinger and went to live at Salmon where her youngest son, Wilmot, was living at the time. Later she moved to Twin Falls where she lived until her death, May 22, 1963. At her request, her children returned her remains to Salmon and laid her to rest beside her husband and their father.

The Paul children, all three, attended school in both Lower and Upper Stanley. Rosemary attended her first grade on the John Thompson ranch in 1914 when Mrs. Thompson conducted classes in her home. (Story told elsewhere in this book.)

Of course, Rosemary married in young womanhood and had children of her own . . . three of them still living today. Rosemary herself is one of the few remaining oldtimers who enjoy visiting and reminiscing with others who grew up in the Stanley Basin in the early days. Together they note the many changes that have taken place, and sometimes lament the way it used to be when both they and the country were young, and the people who lived there were all neighbors and friends.

JOHN AND JOSEPHINE THOMPSON

John Howard Thompson, born December 16, 1864, near Roseburg, Oregon, one of ten children, got his first look at the Sawtooth Mountains and the Stanley Basin in the late 1890's. John, trailing a herd of cattle, coming from the Boise Basin where he had engaged in stockraising buisness, was looking for a new place to settle. As he came from out of the timber and mountains by way of Bull Trout Lake and beheld the broad upper valley of the Basin spread before him like a lush green carpet, he wanted to stay. But could he?

John looked around this scenic land still much a wilderness at the time. Noting the isolation, and finding the area's inhabitants to be only a handful of miners and trappers, and realizing he had to consider his wife and two sons, with reluctance, moved on down Salmon River. Over the range from the little town of Challis, he finally selected a site in the Pahsimeroi Valley. Here he built a house and started a ranch.

In 1902 his marriage ended in divorce and John came back to the Stanley Basin, this time alone, to start again. Although surveys for homestead tracts had not yet been made in the Basin, he chose 160 acres at the upper end, built a large three room house, dug a well, built fences and outbuildings, and soon had a good ranch going. The country began to build up as a few families moved in. John was joined by one of his sons, Charley Thompson.

In the meantime, John had met the school "marm" at the little mining town of Clayton, a short distance down the Salmon River. In 1908, on June 17, they were married at Hailey, Idaho, over in the Wood River country. Her name was Josephine O'Day. Before she met John, her life almost reads like a tale out of the old west... where the young school teacher dreams of coming west to teach and help educate the sons and daughters of the pioneers, and finally meets her prince charming.

However, to begin at the beginning, this school "marm" was born in Fredricksburg, Iowa, May 10, 1875. As a child she loved history and geography, particularily that of the western United States. Stories of the early settlers intrigued her, and she began to dream of the day when she could go West.

Liking school work very much, Josephine also wanted to be a

teacher. She studied hard, and at the age of seventeen she taught her first school. She saved her money towards her dream of traveling West. Yet it was ten long years before she was able to realize that dream. But in 1902, when a contract was let for a teaching job in the tiny settlement of Chilly, Custer County, Idaho, she was ready. Her excitement knew no bounds.

Coming up through the Lost River Valley by wagon from the mining town of Mackay, she drank in the beauty of the golds and reds of the cottonwoods along the stream and the quaken aspen and scrub maples in the foothill draws. To her right towered the rugged peaks of the Lost River range, already tipped with white by the season's first snows, while on her left the White Knob Mountains spread shrouded in deep purple shadows. Yes, the West was all Josephine had dreamed it would be. That is until she saw the small log building where she was to teach.

With flagging spirits, Josephine entered the log cabin hung with a homemade door and lighted only by two small windows. In one corner she saw a wood-burning heating stove ... no blackboard, no desks, no books, not even a table and chairs. Soon she learned that she was to live at a farm house one and a half miles away, and on school day mornings, would have to walk the distance early in order to build a fire and have things ready when her eleven students, ranging in age from six to sixteen, arrived from the neighborhood farms.

In telling of this experience later, she said, "If I had had money enough left from my trip out there, I think I would have taken the next stage back home. But I didn't, so all I could do was to try to improve the situation."

Josephine appealed to the people in the community, and before many days had passed, they brought tables and chairs and all the items they could spare that would help facilitate a school room. School started and was going well when word came that her mother was seriously ill. Could she come home? Reluctantly, she resigned and with her first paycheck, returned to Iowa.

In 1904 Josephine was able to come to Idaho again ... this time to teach in the little mining town of Clayton, on the Salmon River. This was where she met her prince charming, John Thompson, and where she taught school for three years. Like John, she had fallen in love with the Stanley Basin coun-

255

Left to right . . . Sister of Mrs. Frank Shaw, Mrs. Frank (Catherine) Shaw, Mrs. Paul Strieder, Mrs. Josephine Thompson, Preston Shaw, and John Thompson. Children are Marjorie and Alden Shaw. Taken on the porch of the Thompson ranch home about 1910.

try, but because she was already committed, after their marriage, she went to teach at Mullan, Idaho, the winter of 1908-09. John went to be with her. When school was out for the holidays they took a trip to Iowa to visit Josephine's family, returning at the end of the term to the Stanley Basin ranch. Josephine taught one more year at Mullan before the couple could settle permanently in the Basin.

By 1911, homestead tracts had finally been surveyed in the region and John was able to file legally on the 160 acres he had chosen nine years prior . . . final proof made in 1917. During the years between the filing and proof dates he had added to his holdings, eventually owning 480 acres that made up what was called the "Lower Ranch," aside from 103 acres where the Thompson home was located. Here, in the edge of the timber at the foot of the Salmon River Mountains, the house looked out across a grassy meadow, cut by a small stream now named Thompson Creek, towards the jagged peaks of the Sawtooth Range.

John and Josephine Thompson were a devoted couple. They loved living on their ranch at an altitude of 6,500 feet where winters have always been long and cold, sometimes with snow depths reaching five to six feet on the level. How did John raise cattle, horses and sheep there in those days without modern conveniences? He built many sheds, barns and corrals, and in summer stocked the buildings with wild hay cut from his meadow lands; and thereby cared for his stock very well.

Although Josephine contented herself as a ranch wife, she loved children, and not having any of her own, began to miss teaching. A school district had not yet been established in the Stanley Basin in 1914, and knowing that three families with school age children now lived there, she worried. That fall, with John's consent and cooperation, she brought one boy and three girls to the ranch. Another little girl was to commute to and from a ranch two miles away. That winter she taught these five children on a regular class schedule in her home for six months . . . like a boarding school of sorts, and all with the approval of the Idaho State Board of Education. Note: For more details on this, see under *First School Days in the Stanley Basin*.

Josephine's venture proved to be most successful. By the summer of 1915, the Stanley School District had been established, and when a schoolhouse was built in Lower Stanley, she taught there. In ensuing years, Josephine, now always addressed as "Mrs. Thompson," taught three generations of several families who lived in the Salmon River country. She was a good teacher and a strict one, with very definite ideas on discipline in the schoolroom. Nevertheless, she made the lessons interesting for her pupils, and many persons still living in the area today have fond and pleasant memories of their school days with Mrs. Thompson as their teacher.

The years passed all too quickly for this happy, dedicated teacher and her tall, handsome husband. Their summers were filled with a combination of work and pleasure . . . work preparing for the coming winter, punctuated with special dinners, picnics, camping trips into the mountains, and other outings with friends and neighbors.

In 1937, John, beginning to feel his age a bit (73 that year), decided to sell a large part of his land and go into the packing and guiding business for tourists and hunters. Making their ranch home the headquarters, the Thompsons packed to many isolated areas. The Seafoam Mine, where the Thompsons had built a cabin, was a favorite spot for the tourists, but regardless

Sunday dinner at the Thompson ranch. (About 1912) Left to right ... William "Bill" Lutz, George Cumine, Grover Cearley, unknown, Matt Womack, Frank Hellsinger, Standing ... Mrs. Josephine Thompson and her husband, John Thompson.

of the area, John and Mrs. Thompson soon gained fame for their hospitality and efficiency. An article published in the *Idaho Farmer Magazine* in 1940, as told by one of their guests, gave a glowing account of a trip taken with the Thompsons; dwelling at great length on "the delicious homecooked meals served by Mrs. Thompson."

Reading in part, the article said, "After arriving at the ranch we were served a dinner of perfection ... lamb chops, young and tender, a large baked Idaho potato with milk gravy, freshly baked bread with home churned butter and all the fresh milk we could drink. The next morning, after a breakfast of crisp bacon and golden brown sourdough hotcakes, butter and syrup and piping hot coffee, we mounted our horses and hit the trail. As we rode along, Mrs. Thompson told us many little interesting stories about the Stanley Basin country and pointed out different species of trees, shrubs and wildflowers. Both John and Mrs. Thompson were lovers of wildlife, and certainly he was a knowledgeable man when it came to animals. When we made camp, Mrs. Thompson again set out a delicious meal."

The Thompson's guide business was due to be short lived, however, because of John developing an illness in 1939. As this illness worsened, he was taken to the hospital in Hailey, Idaho, where he died March 2, 1940. He was laid to rest in the Hailey cemetery.

After John's death Josephine bought a home in Challis, and was living there when World War II was declared. Teachers were scarce, and although in her mid-sixties at the time, she went back to teaching, still holding to her principle of strict discipline in her classroom. These ideas were now considered outmoded and old-fashioned by her students. They stood in awe of her, and some even called her "old sourpuss," behind her back, of course. Even so, all of them came to admit that she was a good teacher, and after awhile someone in her class would say, "Oh, Mrs. Thompson ain't so bad."

Until the last few years of her life, Josephine Thompson kept active. At age sixty-six she went on a trip into the Sawtooth

Mrs. Josephine Thompson ready for a pack trip.

back country with Claude Gillispie's Trail Riders, and when she was in her seventies she took a float trip down the Middle Fork of the Salmon River, referred to as "The River of No Return." John's oldest son, George, and his wife lived at Plummer, Idaho, and in 1962 Josephine went to live with them, remaining there until he passed away in 1968. By now 93 years old, her mind clear, but her eyesight and hearing failing, she returned to the Salmon River area and entered the Cassabello Nursing Home at the town of Salmon, Idaho.

On learning of her residence at the Salmon Home, many of her friends and former students visited her from time to time. She loved their company, and even then, keeping abreast of the times, enjoyed chatting with them about world affairs and current events. On one occasion, one woman who had numbered among the four little girls who had been her students that winter of 1914-15 on the ranch, remarked, "I hardly see any reason for all this fuss about going to the moon." Mrs. Thompson quickly retorted, "Why, my dear, you should be ashamed. Goodness, if I were only twenty years younger I would delight in going there myself!"

As she continued to live, Mrs. Thompson began to worry. "I have now out-lived all my savings," she said. "Now I am afraid there will be no money to take me to Hailey so I can be laid to rest beside John." In all evidence, this was a great source of concern to her since she mentioned it several times that day to a group of former students who had come to visit. Before leaving they told her not to worry anymore; that if she desired to be buried at Hailey, they would see that it was done.

Soon after this, the group went to the First National Bank at Salmon and set up a Memorial Fund. Needless to say, her numerous friends and former students were very generous, and when Josephine O'Day Thompson passed away at the age of 99 in July, 1974, the fund contained enough money to take the remains to Hailey to be buried beside her beloved husband, John. Those who donated each were gratified to know they had had a part in paying a final tribute to this dedicated teacher and great lady.

CHARLEY THOMPSON

Charley Thompson, son of John Thompson by his first marriage, came with his wife, Lottie Way Thompson, from the northern part of the State to the Stanley Basin in the early spring of 1914. Choosing a homestead across from his father's ranch, near Elk Creek and the George Cumine ranch, he built a large one-room log cabin. The young couple were expecting their first child at the time, and on June 1, that spring, their baby girl, named Dorothy, was born at the town of Challis, Idaho.

Times were hard for the young couple. Charley was a handy carpenter, and worked at the trade whenever such work was available. Other times, in the summer he worked on the roads and in the mines, and in the winter did some trapping. With her husband away at work, Lottie and little Dorothy were often alone on the homestead. Their neighbor, George Cumine, was a kindly old man, and on occasion the young couple exchanged visits with him as well as the senior Thompsons, John and Josephine.

Two years passed. Then in the spring of 1916 Lottie was expecting a second child. One day when Charley was away working, in the afternoon, Lottie realized that the baby was going to arrive sooner than expected. She was alone with little Dorothy (not yet two years old), and with no way to call for help, so decided she had better try to get across the Basin to her mother-in-law, Mrs. Josephine Thompson. The distance was about a mile, but the spring thaws had softened the snow making it difficult to travel. With Dorothy in her arms, Lottie started out. Her pains began coming closer together and she would have to stop and rest often.

By the time Lottie came to Elk Creek, she realized that she would never reach the Thompson ranch in time. She would have to try for George Cumine's place since it was nearer; but to get there she would have to cross a narrow footbridge over Elk Creek that she knew would be slippery and wet with the melting snow. Without hesitation, she took the trail leading in that direction. At the bridge she paused long enough to gather her strength, and to clasp little Dorothy more tightly in her arms, and started across. About halfway on the bridge her foot slipped and she fell into the icy water.

Still clutching the little girl, Lottie gasped for breath and managed to drag herself out onto the bank. Shivering with cold, and holding back her tears while attempting to comfort the whimpering child, she started along the trail again. As she neared George's cabin she began to call out to him for help. After just a few minutes he heard her and hurried to meet and help her inside.

George too, would have to travel by foot, and it would take him a few minutes to reach the Thompson ranch. Once there, he stated his mission, and after quickly gathering up a few things she would need, George and Josephine, together began the return trip to his cabin. All the while, Lottie's pains had become more intense and closer together; and although it seemed like an eternity to the anxious, painridden young woman, it was hardly more than an hour from the time George left until he and Mrs. Thompson arrived back ... and barely in time. The new baby, a little boy, arrived in short order, and when Charlie returned from work that evening, he found himself the father of a fine healthy son. Lottie got along well, but since in those days it was believed a new mother must stay confined to her bed for ten days, she remained at George's while he, Charley, and Mrs. Thompson managed to care for her, the new baby, and Dorothy.

The following summer, Lottie's father, Willis (Bill) Way, and her two brothers came to live in the Stanley Basin. Bill Way was an oldtime fiddler who often helped play music for the dances and parties while he lived in the region. His sons, both fine-looking young men, loved to dance and sing, making their company much enjoyed by residents attending these affairs. Bill and his sons, like Charley Thompson, all worked at various jobs that happened to be available in the summer, and trapped during the winter months. In this way they managed to live, but were unable to accumulate much in the way of money.

After a year in the Basin, Bill Way met Grace Hansen, a school teacher at the mining town of Clayton, a ways down the Salmon River. In September, 1919, they were married and went to make their home at the Thompson ranch. Despite the hard times which prevailed throughout the Stanley-Sawtooth country they managed and appeared quite happy together. Then, about a year after their marriage, Grace was taken seriously ill and was rushed to the home of Leslie "Tink" and Ellen Niece in Upper Stanley. A doctor was called from Challis, but to no avail. Grace died and was the second person to be buried in the Stanley cemetery.

After Grace's death, Bill returned to the Thompson ranch. Within the next four years wages continued to decline in connection with the Nation's flagging economy. His son-in-law, Charley Thompson, found it more and more difficult to earn a living for his little family. Then, thinking he might fare better in a more moderate climate, in 1923 he moved to Oregon. Bill Way and his two boys, Earl and Charley Way, also departed the Stanley country soon after... sometime in the summer of 1924.

Thus the Charley Thompson homestead stood vacant and forlorn until 1926 when it was sold by Custer County for deliquent taxes. Accordingly, the family did leave a mark in the Stanley Basin; even though a small one. All were well liked, and it was with regret that their friends and neighbors saw them go.

Lottie Thompson and daughter, Dorothy, at Will and Mae Rose cabin in Stanley Basin, about 1920.

OTHER STANLEY FAMILIES

Who were the first families to face the hardships of establishing a home and raising a family in the isolated, rugged land of the Sawtooths? As near as can be determined it was the Timothy Cooper family, followed by the Arthur McGown Sr. family who are mentioned in numerous places throughout the pages of this book. True, other women had lived in the area . . . Mrs. Wells, the widowed sister of Will Casto, with her two sons, Hod and Will Wells, had spent the winter of 1878-79 at Joe's Gulch where she had cooked for her brother and his partners who were placer mining there. Della McGown told of a Mr. and Mrs. Cochern and their three teenage daughters who had lived at Upper Stanley in the 1890's, and Charley Grandjean's mother, Nathalia, had kept house for her son in a tiny log cabin in Stanley Basin prior to her death there in 1895. However, up until 1900 the Stanley-Sawtooth country had been principally a man's world.

Timothy Cooper:

Timothy Cooper had placer mined on Joe's Gulch in 1878-79 (see Stanley Basin Mining), after which time he spent a few years at the mining camp of Vienna in the Sawtooth Valley. It was while there that he met and married Bertha, a widow woman with a young daughter whose name was Daisy. As mining activity declined in the Vienna area, Tim Cooper and his partner, Will Casto, sold their saloon business, and Tim, Bertha, and Daisy packed up their household goods and moved to the Stanley Basin.

Records show that in 1890 Tim, in partners with H.H. Marshall and Charles Franklin, located placer ground in the Basin, and that in 1894 he and Henry Sturkey located "The Homestead Claim" near the mouth of Kelly Gulch. It was on this claim that the Coopers built the home in which they lived during their years spent in the Stanley country. Built at the base of the hills near a small stream that flowed into Stanley Creek, the

Winding trail traveled by Daisy Cooper on her way to the McGown Place.

remains of the log structure can still be seen today. There were two rooms about twelve feet apart with doors, each facing the other, and the space between roofed over and enclosed on one side to form a sort of a breezeway area. Nearby were barns and corrals for the horses, for both Tim and Bertha loved horses and had acquired several good work and saddle animals. The wild hay that grew so luxuriantly on the Basin floor was cut and stored for winter feed. Bertha, being a strong, sturdy pioneer, worked side by side with her husband whether he was placer mining, cutting hay, getting firewood for winter, or doing other outside chores. As daughter Daisy grew older she became an excellent horsewoman. She learned to ride bare-back, Indian fashion, and would spend happy hours galloping over the countryside or traveling the narrow trail that wound around the mountainside to the McGown place at Stanley where she would go for the mail.

In 1892, a daughter, Francis, was born to Tim and Bertha Cooper, and in 1896 they sold their property in the Stanley Basin and bought a ranch near Clayton, Idaho. Being reluctant to leave their comfortable little log home after the sale, they spent one last year there enjoying their life in the beautiful Stanley country. They moved to their new home in November 1897.

The years on the ranch and in Clayton brought many changes for the Cooper family. Daisy was married to James

Papworth who owned a ranch on the East Fork of the Salmon River, and Francis married Charley Ernst who was mining on Peach Creek. In 1910 Bertha and Tim were divorced, only to remarry in 1911. By 1914, with both girls married, and things not going well for the Coopers, they decided to sell the ranch and leave Idaho. This decision took them to Florida where they spent the next seventeen years. In 1931, Tim and Bertha, both well along in years, came back to Clayton for a visit with Daisy and her family. While there Mrs. Cooper fell ill, and on September 2, 1931 she died and was buried in the Clayton Cemetery. Just two short months later, on November 25, 1931, Tim too, was called by death and was laid to rest beside his wife. Timothy and Bertha Cooper's intended visit had brought them home to stay.

Looking back to daughter Francis, it is noted that after leaving Peach Creek she and her husband took up a ranch in the Middle Fork region. Their land was rocky and hard to work, and with little money with which to make ends meet, the two looked with envy at the nice ranch and comfortable cabin of their bachelor neighbor, "Jake" Reberk. Jake and Francis soon became very friendly, and finally Francis divorced Charley and went to live with Reberk. Weeks passed and Charley brooded. Then one morning as Francis prepared breakfast for Jake, Charley came to the cabin, a shot rang out on the still morning air, and Jake Reberk lay dead just outside the cabin door. Conflicting stories were told, and it was never proven conclusively whether it was Charley or Francis who had fired the fatal shot. Some thought the whole affair had been a plan between Charley and Francis to get Reberk's property. At the trial, letters from Francis to Charley hinted at this. As a result of the shooting Charley Ernst spent three years in the penitentiary, then Francis signed a confession stating that it was she who had shot Reberk. Charley was pardoned, and Francis spent nearly five years in prison before being pardoned when she agreed to leave the country.

Driskell Family:

James B. Driskell and his family settled on land a little to the northeast of the John Thompson ranch, in the vicinity of Hanna Creek, in the early 1900s. Besides their two sons, Clyde and David, two married daughters, Elsie Wertz and Alice Olsen, also lived in the same neighborhood. It was in 1911 that Mr. Driskell, age sixty-four, was taken ill and died. He was buried at the ranch, as that had been his last request. Not long after his death the land in that area was surveyed for homesteading, enabling the widow, Savilla Driskell, to file a claim on the land in 1912, making final proof in 1917.

Soon after the final proof was made, Savilla sold the ranch to John Thompson, and she, son Clyde and Alice Olsen moved away. During these years Elsie had divorced Wertz and married Oscar Lerow who was homesteading about a mile west of the Benner Place. The younger son, David, also stayed on in the Stanley area. In 1919 he and Helen Huffman, daughter of Forest Ranger, Ed Huffman, were married, and shortly after their marriage left for Canada to make their home. No one living today remembers the location of the lonely grave of the husband and father, James B. Driskell.

Several families were involved in the settling of the area south of Upper Stanley. All of these people, for one reason or another, moved away after a short time, but the buildings they built remained to be used by numerous other folks for the next three decades.

Paul Imeson:

Paul Imeson, his wife and young son, came to the Stanley region about 1905 or 1906 from Jackson Hole, Wyoming. Upon arriving at the Benner place, Paul learned that there was unclaimed land to the south, and adjacent to the Benner ranch. He immediately measured off a homestead tract of 160 acres and set about building a sturdy log house, barns and corrals about a mile and a half distant from the Benner Store. This done, he measured off another 240 acres on which he planned to file a desert entry claim. This was situated between his homestead and the Benner ranch, and was later sold to George Sewell.

It was early fall of 1908, when Mrs. Imeson was expecting her second child, that Paul decided they should move to Challis. William and Sadie Merritt, whom the Imesons had known in Wyoming, had just arrived in the Stanley country, so arrangements were made for them to stay at the Imeson place and care for the stock until Bill Merritt could build a house on the land he had chosen for his homestead. The Merritts moved to their own home in December of 1908, and Jess Baker, a bachelor from the East Fork of the Salmon River, spent the remainder of the winter as caretaker at the Imeson property.

In those days a man's only claim to land was "Squatter's Rights," which according to law did "Secure Homesteads to actual settlers on the Public Domain," thus giving them the first right to file on land as soon as the Government survey was completed. However, if a settler was to leave his property abandoned for any length of time, another person could move in, claim the land and improvements, and there was nothing the original owner could do to repossess his holdings. Consequently, settlers either stayed on their land, or had friends or hired help to care for things until they could return. In many areas of the West this ruling caused feuds, and even bloodshed, but no instances of this nature ever occurred in the Stanley-Sawtooth country.

By spring of 1909 the Imeson family returned to the ranch for a short time. Paul, being a restless, easily discouraged person, soon tired of the effort involved in improving the homestead. He became associated with Frank Shaw of the Sawtooth Valley in a sawmill operation. Arguments and disagreements followed. Finally, Frank Shaw won out, and it was then that Paul Imeson sold his homestead holdings to F.L. Clyde of Challis, Idaho, and moved on.

When Mr. Clyde moved to Stanley to take possession of his newly acquired property, he brought his adopted daughter, Miss Mattie Mott, with him. Since there were very few young people living in the area at that time, Mattie's first year there was a long, lonely one.

Then in 1909 *Perry Franklin* came to stay and work at the William Merritt ranch. Perry was young and had dreams of developing a prosperous ranching operation in the Stanley country. He and Bill Merritt had agreed that Perry should locate land adjoining the Merritt homestead, then, since Perry was single and had no family obligations, he would go out to work for wages, and would send money each month to the Merritts to help with their living expenses. In return Bill Merritt would build a cabin and make the necessary improvements on Perry's homestead.

As is so often the case, the well laid plans of Bill Merritt and Perry Franklin failed to materialize. Perry met and fell in love with the neighbor girl, Mattie Mott. After a year's courtship, November 24, 1910, was set for the wedding date. The young couple planned to travel by team and buckboard to Bonanza City on the Yankee Fork, where they would be married at the Dellen Hotel, with Judge A. R. Smith performing the ceremony. When the day arrived, a fall blizzard was raging, but nevertheless, Perry and Mattie set out on the twenty-two mile trip, reaching Bonanza late that evening, cold and tired, but in time to recite the wedding vows as planned. Thus the newlyweds embarked upon a marriage that proved to be fraught with trouble and heartaches.

Back at Stanley, the young couple were to share the home of the aging F.L. Clyde, and Perry would take over the ranch work. Times were hard, and Mattie, never having enjoyed good health, was unable to cope with the hardships encountered as the wife of a pioneer homesteader. During the next few years a son, Clyde, and two daughters, Ida and Fay, were born to the Franklins. Mr. Clyde died, leaving the ranch and all cattle and horses to Mattie and Perry. More people moved into the country and with all these changes Perry hoped that Mattie would be happier.

But this was not to be. During the winter of 1917-18 tragedy struck the Franklin home. Mattie, always high strung and nervous, had grown thin and pale, and on several occasions had threatened to kill some of the neighbor ladies. One day she had walked over to visit at the home of Sadie Merritt. As the two women sat talking, Sadie picked up her crocheting and starting to work on it. Suddenly Mattie leaped up from her chair, grabbed the crocheting out of Sadie's hands, threw it across the room and screamed, "All you do is sit there and stab, stab, STAB, at that damned thread!" Thoroughly frightened by her distraught, wild-eyed look, Sadie was relieved when Mattie announced, "I'm going home!"

After several such outbursts and threats, Perry feared that Mattie would do bodily harm to the children, herself, or someone else. He enlisted the help of Dave Williams, and the two men set out to haul Mattie on a hand sled over Galena Summit to Hailey where she could consult a doctor. It was on their second day out as they paused to rest while climbing a steep incline on the Valley side of the mountain, Dave, from the corner of his eye, glimpsed a flash of a shiny object. Turning, he was just in time to see Mattie pulling a long, sharp butcher knife from under the blankets tucked around her on the sled. As she attempted to rise with the knife in her hand, Dave and Perry grabbed her and relieved her of the weapon, but had to tie her in the sled for the remainder of the trip.

In Hailey Mattie was pronounced insane and was sent to the asylum at Blackfoot, Idaho.

Perry then moved his family to Mackay, Idaho, and it was there, while still a young man, that he passed away on June 14, 1919. His homestead was incorporated into the holdings of Dan Kavanaugh and later sold to Pete Piva.

The marriage of *George Sewell,* age 26, and Lucy Bowman, age 22, took place at Challis, Idaho, in April, 1902. George had worked in the mines at Butte, Montana, before coming to Custer County to work at the General Custer Mine about 1900. By 1906, due to the decline in mining activities in the Yankee Fork region, George and Lucy moved to the Stanley Basin.

After nearly two years spent working at various jobs, George bought the desert entry land claim of Paul Imeson, located about a mile south of the Benner Store. There he built a cabin, and in the late summer of 1908 the Sewell family moved to their new ranch home. Two children, George Jr. and Rebecca, had been born to the Sewells during their years at the mines.

Three years passed, then the effects of his years spent working in the mines began to take their toll of George's health. He developed what in those days was called "Miner's Consumption," caused by breathing the mineralized dust from the ore. The family moved to Salmon where he could have the medical aid needed, and it was there, when not yet forty years old, that George Sewell died.

In June, 1915, his widow, Lucy, married Robert Finlay of Salmon, and they, along with Lucy's children, George and Rebecca Sewell, returned to the ranch at Stanley. There a daughter, Mary Ellen, was born in 1918. She was named for the two ladies who ushered her into the world; Mary Marshall and Ellen Niece. A short while after this baby's birth, the Finlays moved back to Salmon. The ranch they once owned is now a part of the Piva property.

Hawkins:

Another name added to the list of homesteaders in the Stanley country was Gardner P. Hawkins. G.P., as he was called, and his grown son, Lancelot, settled on a piece of land about a mile and a half west of the Benner place in 1914. Like other residents of the region, the Hawkins' had quite a struggle to keep the wolf from the door. While G.P. worked at the necessary improvements on the homestead, raised what garden stuff that would grow, and kept a few chickens and a cow, his son worked at any available jobs to provide the family finances.

Lancelot was a tall, long-legged, gangly young man fittingly nicknamed "Slivers" by Stanley folks. He and his father both loved to dance and managed to be in attendance at all community gatherings. Slivers was an expert square dance caller, and when calling would mingle with the dancers, guiding some of the younger or more inexperienced through the changes ... never missing a word of the call, and always ending with, "Promenade all, to you know where and I don't care." G.P., however, although an excellent dancer, was not always so popular at the dances. He invariably partook of a supper well seasoned with garlic before arriving at the dance hall.

Oldtimers who recall Slivers in those days say he always wore a gun belt and holstered six-gun, even to the dances. As he called and danced, his long legs, clad in tight Levis, looked like they might become tied in knots, his six-shooter would be bouncing on his hip, and his high tenor voice would ring out above the music of old Trapper Fisher's fiddle. Indeed, Slivers Hawkins was a character to long remember.

In 1919 Slivers was married to Florence Reynolds, the oldest daughter of a family who had taken up residence on the former Frank Helsinger ranch (now the Arrow A) near Upper Stanley. At that time he located a homestead adjoining his father's and built a two room log cabin. The windows on one side looked out upon the lofty Sawtooth Peaks, while from the other side could be seen the grassy meadowland along Valley Creek. A cold spring bubbled from a knoll nearby: a beautiful setting, but unfortunately, no way to earn a living for a wife and family. After a few years the young couple sold the ranch to John Brown, a sheepman, and departed for the Wood River area. The remains of their cabin still stands at the time of this writing, and can be seen by travelers passing on Highway 21.

Left alone after his son's marriage, G.P., being lonely, chanced to read the "Lonely Hearts Column" in a magazine, and began corresponding with a woman who lived in Arkansas. This was a case where two lonely people sought companionship, and since she had expressed a desire to come West, it was not long until G.P. purposed that she do so. On her arrival in Hailey they were married and came to make their home at the ranch near Stanley.

Hallie, the new Mrs. Hawkins, was totally deaf, but could read lips readily and was able to converse to a limited degree with neighbors who came to call. When a baby boy came to bless the Hawkin's home, knowing Hallie could not hear his cries, her husband hired Bonda Critchfield to stay at their home and help care for the baby.

As time passed, Hallie persuaded G.P. to sell the ranch and take her back to Arkansas. Some fifty years later the son who had been born at Stanley returned to see the old homestead that had once belonged to his parents, and to gather information that would help him to obtain a birth certificate. No birth records had been kept. Mary Marshall, the lady who had cared for his mother at the time of his birth, as well as his parents, had long since been dead, and no doctor had been in attendance. Bonda Critchfield Niece signed a notorized statement for him, but it is not known if this had been of any help.

Calling the square dance.

Rose:

A couple who spent many years in the Stanley country, and who are well remembered by a number of folks living today, was Bill and Mae Rose. It was in 1906 that William (Bill) Rose came from Meadsville, Pennsylvania, the place of his birth, to visit an Uncle, William Oster, who at that time was working as an engineer for the Sunbeam Consolidated Mining Company on the Yankee Fork. Bill stayed two years in Idaho before returning to the East where he married Mae Thomas.

Born in Buffalo, New York, Mae had grown to young womanhood there. She was a gay, vivacious person, quite heavy-set, always neat and clean... and she loved to tell stories of her growing up years in New York. She told of a time, when she was a small child and had been taken to a circus. Being intrigued with the antics of the clowns, she decided she would try some of their tricks. At the time she was perched on the top rail of the fence around her parents property. Hanging onto the gatepost, she managed to work her leg up until she could put her foot behind her head as she had seen the clowns do. After sitting in this position for a minute or two, she found it impossible to get the leg back down. So she sat, screaming for help, hurting and embarrassed, until a passerby came to her assistance.

Another of her favorite stories was about an event which happened when she was a teenager, and was present at a reception given in honor of President William McKinley, at Buffalo, N.Y., on September 6, 1901. Mae was standing just a few feet away from the President when he was shot by a terrorist, Leon Czolosz. The President died eight days later, and his Vice President, Theodore Roosevelt, became President.

At the time Mae met Bill Rose, she was working as a whiskey taster for the Fleischmann Whiskey Company. She told friends later that she had come to like the taste of the whiskey so well that she feared she might become an alcoholic. It was about this time that she met Bill, so she quit her job, and after a whirlwind courtship they were married and came to Idaho.

Bill and Mae spent their first years in the Salmon River country at the Sunbeam Dam. Bill worked on the construction project and Mae cooked for the crew. After completion of the dam and power house, the Roses stayed on as caretakers for the Sunbeam Consolidated Mining Company until 1915 when they moved to the homestead Bill had located earlier in the Stanley Basin.

Mr. and Mrs. Rose lived for about five years at the homestead, but made frequent trips to town. Always glad for the opportunity to earn a few dollars, both Bill and Mae worked at various jobs. Mae was called upon many times to run the boarding house in Lower Stanley when Ellen Niece would be sick. The Niece children liked to have this jolly lady there bustling around the kitchen, telling them stories or singing snatches of songs as she worked. She and Bill loved children and wanted a family of their own, but their only child, a baby girl, born at Challis, Idaho in 1921, died at birth.

Ready for a hay-ride at the Thompson ranch. Left to right ... Preston Shaw, Alden Shaw, John Thompson, Josephine Thompson, Mae Rose, Mrs. Frank (Catherine) Shaw with daughter, Marjorie, in front, next lady and man unknown, William Rose.

After the death of their baby they no longer wanted to live on the ranch. They took a trip back to visit relatives in Pennsylvania and New York, but like so many before them, the Roses could hardly wait to return to the Stanley-Sawtooth Country.

They did return. In 1922 they sold their ranch to Theodore (Dad) Cameron who was working for Roy Chivers at the Cow Camp. A section of this ranch became known as the Stanley Rodeo Grounds, and is a part of the H.H.H. ranch today.

With the homestead sold, Bill and Mae purchased a log

building at Lower Stanley from Tom Williams, enlarged it, bought the stock of merchandise from Mrs. Law's Store, moved it to their building, and started The Stanley Store. This business has changed hands many times through the years. It is now Jerry's Country Store.

In 1925 Bill Rose was appointed as Stanley postmaster, and for the next eight years, while he held this position, the post office was in the store at Lower Stanley. Mr. Rose was an enterprising business man, and his fun-loving, congenial disposition endeared him to his many friends. Mae Rose, after a time, became reconciled to the death of her baby and was once again the robust, jolly little lady her friends had known.

Floyd W. Markle bought the Stanley Store in 1932. Bill and Mae moved into a small log house nearby, and Bill continued to serve as postmaster until October of 1933. Not content while idle, Bill, in partners with Jason Vaught, built the first Service Station at the Y below Upper Stanley (now the Harrah property). They also built The Pine Knot Service Station across Highway 93 from The Stanley Store. These businesses kept Bill busy and content for the next few years, and Mae was happy in the lovely new log home built near the station at Lower Stanley.

During the Thirties, neighbors and very close friends of the Roses, Wallace, and Laura Lightfoot, and their two sons, Phillip and Douglas, had moved to Ketchum, Idaho. Missing the Lightfoots, especially the boys who affectionately called Mrs. Rose "Auntie Bill," Bill and Mae decided to spend a winter at Ketchum. Bill got work at Sun Valley, and they stayed there for over a year. Then shortly before World War II, the Roses went to San Bernadino, California, to make their home. They made one last trip back to the Stanley country in 1945 to finish settling business transactions in connection with the sale of their property, and as Bill said, "To breath the clean mountain air and look once again at those grand old Sawtooth Mountains."

A few years later Bill passed away and was buried at San Bernadino. Mae stayed on in their home for several years. The Lightfoot boys, both grown and living in California, found time occasionally to visit their "Auntie Bill," and to check on her welfare. Finally, sick and alone, Mae was taken to a rest home near Los Angeles where she lived out her remaining years. Mae Thomas Rose found her final resting place beside her husband in the San Bernadino Cemetery.

Cothern:

Adding to the influx of families into the Stanley region was the Cothern family. R.B. (Doc), his wife Affie, and two daughters, Mildred and Virginia, came from Encampment, Wyoming in the late summer of 1916. Affie, who was a sister of Ellen Niece, was to run the boarding house in Lower Stanley for Ellen whose health no longer permitted her to do the work. Doc drove the stage between Stanley and Robinson Bar that winter and the girls attended school. Virginia was only five years old, but being a bright, eager child, she was allowed to enroll in the first grade.

When spring came Ellen was again able to take over her duties at the boarding house, so the Cotherns accepted employment at the Sturkey Placer Mine. Doc worked in the mine and Affie cooked for the miners, but fall saw them again at the boarding house in Lower Stanley. They stayed there then until 1918 when Doc leased the ranch across the river from Lower Stanley from Charles Fisher of Spokane, Washington. (Now the Wooley ranch.)

The Cotherns enlarged the original house and would often have paying guests who would spend several weeks at the ranch. Both Doc and Affie were kindhearted, genial people, and Affie was a wonderful cook, making a stay there with them a most enjoyable experience. There were horses to ride, mountains to climb, lakes and other scenic spots to explore, fishing in the Salmon River just in front of the house, swims in the natural hot springs less than a mile distant, and of course, the Stanley dances, and pleasant evenings in the hospitable atmosphere of the Cothern home.

In 1920 the Wells McGowan family who had been running the Benner Hotel at Upper Stanley moved to Boise. Affie Cothern then took charge of the Hotel, and her meals, served family style at long tables, became quite renowned throughout the country. Doc still kept the ranch and his cattle, enabling him to furnish the hotel with a plentiful supply of fresh beef, milk, and cream. Affie churned her own butter, did all of her baking, and made cottage cheese that was an exceptional treat to her guests. Big kettles of skim milk would be soured, then placed on the back of the wood range on which she cooked, where it would heat slowly. When the curds were of just the right consistency the cheese would be poured into a cloth sack and hung to drain. After draining it was ready for use. The amount needed for a meal would be placed in a bowl, salted lightly, and covered with thick, freshly skimmed cream. Affie was a generous person, and many a container of this delicious cheese was carried home by friends and guests.

After three years at the Benner Hotel, the Cotherns bought Tink and Ellen Niece's large home which was located directly behind The Niece Brothers Store in Upper Stanley. They added on more rooms and moved their hotel business there. By then their two daughters were popular teenagers, a great help to their mother during the busy summers, and away to high school through the winter months.

Hotel Stanley with owner, Affie Cothern, and daughters, Virginia and Mildred, standing on porch.

It was in 1930 that Mildred, the oldest daughter, was married to Ward (Slim) Hendrick and the young couple went to make their home on the George Cumine ranch in the Basin. And it was on November 16, 1932, that tragedy struck the Cothern family. Their hotel burned to the ground.

It was early morning, still dark, and the temperature down near the zero mark. Doc had kindled a fire in the wood-burning heater in the dining room, and had gone back to bed to wait for the house to warm. A short time later Affie was awakened by a crackling sound and the smell of smoke. Jumping from her bed, she dashed into the living room and could see one corner of the dining room completely enveloped in flames. Terrified, she screamed for the family to get up and out of the house . . . and to get help. In a matter of minutes most of the Stanley residents

277

Group on porch of Hotel Stanley. Left to right ... Wallace Lightfoot, George Cumine, Virginia Cothern Lightfoot and husband, Dick, Laura Lightfoot. Girls in front ... Gertrude and Doris Gillispie. Taken in the 1930s.

were there, but their efforts to save the building were futile. No fire fighting equipment was available. The buildings water supply was from a hand pump in the kitchen area, and in no time at all it was impossible to reach that. A water brigade was formed to carry pails of water from neighboring homes, but that too, was a hopeless effort. A few pieces of furniture, some clothing and small articles were carried to safety, and luckily, no lives were lost.

Disheartened and depressed, the Cotherns once again set up housekeeping in the Benner hotel building. Friends and neighbors came to their aid by bringing any pieces of furniture, dishes, or other household items they could spare. Quilting bees were held, and dozens of other acts of kindness were shown the family. With the coming of spring, through their own efforts and with the help of their many friends, Doc and Affie were well enough equipped to start the hotel again.

The next year, 1933, Virginia Cothern was married to Dick Lightfoot. She and her husband established a home at Upper Stanley, and Virginia continued to assist her mother at the hotel. Then, the fall of 1936, the Cotherns were dealt a tragic blow when their daughter, Virginia, died. She had been in poor health for some time, and Dr. Fox of Hailey had been consulted by telephone. Often in those days people living in remote areas

278

would call the doctor and he would advise them as to how to treat a patient, or would send medicine if he felt it necessary. Affie was exceptionally good at caring for the sick, so Virginia was cared for as the doctor instructed, but as she grew steadily worse it was decided that she must be taken to Hailey. The roads were rough and she was in great pain, making the long trip one of excruciating agony for her. Immediately upon her arrival at the hospital in Hailey Doctor Fox performed surgery. Her condition seemed to improve at first, but after a few days she gave up the struggle and the end came. Affie said, "She suffered so much on the trip over; I can't bear the thought of taking her back. We will bury her here and let her rest." She was buried in the Hailey Cemetery.

Soon after Virginia's death Doc and Affie purchased the ranch across Salmon River from the Y below Upper Stanley. They built a beautiful home on the banks of the River, and there they spent their remaining years in the Stanley area.

Doc became interested in mining claims near Beatty, Nevada, and for a number of years he and Affie spent the winters there and returned each spring to their home at Stanley. Eventually they sold their holding in Stanley, and bought a small ranch on the outskirts of Challis. This was also sold after a short time and the Cotherns moved to Nevada to make their home. It was there that Doc passed away in 1956, and that Affie still lives at the time of this writing.

Soon after the Cothern family came to Idaho in 1916, Edward Martin Sr. and Edward Martin Jr. had followed. The senior Mr. Martin was the father of Ellen Niece and Affie Cothern. Edward Jr., or Eddie, as he was known, had been deaf since having had a serious case of measles when only five years old. Due to this handicap, school work had been difficult for Eddie, and though seventeen years of age, he had not completed the eighth grade. Mrs. Josephine Thompson, teaching in Stanley at that time, encouraged Eddie to start to school, and with her help and patience, he was able to finish his elementary education.

Mr. Martin mined, worked on ranches, and at one time planned to homestead near the old dredge workings on Stanley Creek. He tore down one of the abandoned Henry Willis buildings, moved the material to his homestead site, and built a cabin that was later moved to Lower Stanley. Due to illness, Mr. Martin was unable to continue with his plans, and in 1929

279

his daughter, Ellen, took him to the home of another daughter at Portland, Oregon where medical aid would be available. He died of cancer there in 1931.

Eddie Martin lived for years with the Cothern family. When Lee Kerr of Challis Idaho, opened a pool hall at Upper Stanley in 1930, he hired Eddie Martin and Joe Woods to run it for him. This was during the time of Prohibition, and apparently Eddie and Joe were doing a little bootlegging on the side, for an item in *The Challis Messenger Newspaper,* dated September 24, 1930, stated: "Federal men raided Stanley and took Eddie Martin and Joe Woods in for violation of the National Prohibition Act."

Later Eddie owned and operated The Alamo Club in Upper Stanley, and at one time also ran a cafe. He married and moved to Beatty, Nevada, where he and his wife reside at this time.

"Doc" and Affie Cothern.

Law:

Mrs. Elizabeth Law, Irish, and with all the traits of the Irish people, the quick wit and humor, and also the firey temper, moved to Lower Stanley with her two children, Hughie and Maggie Bradford, in 1918. Coming from Gooding, Idaho, she bought the General Merchandise Store from Flo Clyde . . . the store formerly owned by Tink Niece.

When Mrs. Law learned that Mr. Niece had been reappointed as Stanley postmaster, and that the post office was to be moved to Upper Stanley, a real feud erupted between the two. Mrs. Law refused to allow Mr. Niece to set foot on her property, and threatened him with dire consequences if he dared. How was he to move the post office from her store building? After much arguing, correspondence with the Postal Department, and consultation with lawyers, Tink Niece finally won. Postal Inspector Dodd was sent in from Washington D.C. to accompany Mr. Niece and help him in moving the post office.

Elizabeth Law's stay in the Stanley area was of short duration. After about two years there, she secured a lifetime lease on the Alturas Lake Resort area from the U.S. Government, and it was she and her son, Hughie, who built the tourist cabins, lodge, and other buildings there. A humorous little story is told about her by a Sawtooth Valley resident. One day he and his wife stopped by Alturas Lake to chat with Mrs. Law, and as they were leaving she walked to the car with them. Standing beside the car, she glanced down at her feet, a surprised expression came over her face, and she started to laugh. With her Irish brogue she said, "Well faith and begorra, would you look at that! I got on one sock of one color and one of another. Oh, well . . . just pr-roves I got two pair-r-r!"

Hughie and Maggie Bradford were very popular young folks in the Stanley area, energetic and full of fun, and ready on a moments notice for any lark that was suggested. They worked and played with equal zest . . . and at the dances were the envy of other young people when they skipped gaily through a two-step or a heel and toe polka together. Maggie lived for many years in the Twin Falls vicinity, and at the present time Hughie owns a home near Smiley Creek in the Sawtooth Valley.

Rowles:

A young man from Challis, Donald Rowles, was another who had hopes of developing a homestead in the Stanley Basin. Having worked at the Stanley Dredge during the early Teens, he became acquainted with Bill and Mae Rose who were living on their homestead nearby. In 1917 Donald located the 160 acre tract adjoining the Roses, built a cabin, and spent two summers there as a bachelor. After his marriage to Florence Gridley, a school teacher from Pennsylvania, in 1919, Donald established a permanent home in Challis, but the homestead in the Basin could not be forgotten. Donald and Florence spent two summers there in the little log cabin after the birth of their first son, Gridley. Recalling these summers in later years, Florence said, "Those were summers we thoroughly enjoyed. It was beautiful there in the Basin, and we didn't mind not having modern conveniences. We went on picnics and fishing trips with the Roses and the Charley Thompsons . . . they were our nearest neighbors. I would like to have stayed, but there was no work there for Donald."

Donald Rowles was a carpenter by trade, and even though there were more people moving into the region, there was very little opportunity for him to get work. Consequently the ranch was sold to the Huntingtons, and the Rowles' gave up their dream of living in Stanley Basin.

As a little boy, Gridley Rowles plays with dog, Toby, owned by Mae Rose at the Rose's cabin in Stanley Basin.

Moore:

George Moore, a widower with two attractive young daughters, Reva, blond and blue eyed, and Alta, a vivacious brunette, came to Stanley about 1918. Originally from Missouri, they came to the Stanley area from the Snake River Valley.

Mr. Moore was one of the many who drove stage between Stanley and Robinson Bar during the Twenties. The girls kept house for their father, and took advantage of any opportunity to work. Alta served as postmistress from 1923 to 1925, after which time she moved away. Reva became Mrs. Clyde Gillispie and lived for many years at Upper Stanley.

Although George Moore lived only a few years in the Stanley country, he is thought of as one of the oldtimers.

George Moore

Lanier:

Ohio born, but living in Virginia when, because of family discord, Mrs. Luna May Lanier and sons, Barney and Webb, decided to come West. Mother and sons arrived at Hailey, Idaho, in 1917. Barney, then sixteen, went to work at the North Star Mine in the Hailey vicinity. They came to the Stanley Basin about two years later, settling on what was locally known as the "old Thomas Kelly place," and where Mrs. Lanier filed a homestead claim in 1921.

Both Lanier boys were popular with old and young alike. Barney, tall, broad-shouldered, and dark-complexioned was of a happy disposition and full of fun. He loved parties and dancing and seldom missed these affairs in town, riding horseback in summer and skiing in winter to cover the twelve miles between the Lanier ranch and Stanley. In contrast, although equally as handsome as his older brother, Webb was of slighter build, lighter complexion, and on the quiet reserved side, and while Barney was generally always in attendance at town socials, Webb would accompany him only on occasion. At these affairs he preferred to just sit quietly as on on-looker, while Barney enjoyed being in the middle of the activity.

Barney Lanier standing by enclosed sleigh used to transport the Merritt and Lanier children to and from school on cold winter days.

Mrs. Lanier, also a rather reserved person, rarely came to town, but visitors were welcome in her home on the ranch any time they chose to come that way. When she became ill in the spring of 1926, Mrs. Lanier was taken to Mackay, Idaho, where, at age fifty-one, on May 18th that year, she passed away. After their mother's death the two boys remained on the ranch only a short time. Both were married in 1929 . . .Barney to Nellie Merritt of Stanley and Webb to Mrs. Merle Smith who had been working at the Hotel Stanley for Affie Cothern. The Lanier boys and their wives established homes and went on to live in the Stanley area, but after a few years, Webb and Merle moved elsewhere. Barney and Nellie remained there until into the early Forties when they moved to Challis. At the time of Barney's death, he and Nellie had raised a family of ten children. Today, these children, all living and married, are very devoted to their mother who still lives on the home ranch near Challis.

Mr. and Mrs. Barney Lanier and family at home ranch in Stanley Basin.

Wooley:

William (Bill) Wooley had traveled over much of the Western United States before he reached the age of twenty-five. Born in Missouri in 1888, the first move was to Texas, then to Washington State, coming to Idaho in 1913. While living in Boise, Idaho, he met and married Lela Mae Harbaugh.

Still young and still seeking the land of opportunity, Bill and his wife traveled into the Stanley area. There they decided to homestead land adjacent to Redfish Lake in the vicinity of where the Redfish Lake Lodge and the Forest Service Visitors Center is now located. However, this venture proved unsuccessful. The continuous lapping of the waves along the lake shore bothered Lela, causing her to be discontent. Because of this, the Wooleys once again moved on.

William "Bill" Wooley with his pet cougar.

Bill got a job as a game warden for the State Game Department and was sent to the Middle Fork of the Salmon River where he and Lela lived on a ranch near Thomas Creek. Bill, being an outdoorsman, enjoyed his work and the wild remoteness of the area, but could not forget the idea of homesteading in the Stanley country. A year passed. As the winter of 1920-21 drew near, the Wooleys, with baby daughter Juana, came back to Stanley. They lived that winter in the house on the Perry Franklin ranch about a mile and a half south of Upper Stanley. By spring they had purchased the ranch formerly owned by August Fisher from his brother, Charles Fisher, of Spokane, Washington.

This ranch, located across the river from Lower Stanley, was to be home to the Wooleys for many years. Here Juana grew to young womanhood and married; here their son, Daniel, was born, grew up and was married; and here Bill Wooley lived on alone after Lela left him. Bill cultivated more land, built up a large herd of cattle, raised horses for packing and riding, and acted as guide, taking numerous tourists, hunters, and fishermen into the "back country," a term used by guides for the remote Sawtooth and Middle Fork areas.

Then came the spring of 1972. Snow had laid unusually late in the high mountains, and as the warm spring days passed the Salmon River became a wild tumultous torrent that swept rocks, trees, and even bridges along with its raging tide. Bill Wooley, it is conjectured, went to the river's edge to dip up a pail of water, and the force of the water caused him to lose his balance and topple into the churning current. The river he had watched flow by his door for over fifty years had claimed his life. His son, Dan, now owns the Wooley ranch.

The Salmon River, sometimes called "Idaho's River of No Return" can be treacherous in the spring when the snow melts too fast.

287

Connyers:

Mr. John Connyers, his wife, Olive, and their five children arrived at Upper Stanley in time to start the older children to school in September, 1920. Prior to that time they had lived in a remote section of Bear Valley, located to the northwest of Stanley Basin, where Mr. Connyers had planned to homestead. He had given up the idea, however, when the question arose as to whether the land there would be forest service controlled, and because of there being no way for the children to attend school. At Stanley they moved into the log house that had been built by Arthur McGown Sr. in 1891. Here the Connyers' home soon became a favorite gathering place for the children in town. Many happy evenings were spent there popping corn, making candy, and playing games when the weather was too cold to play outside. After the snow melted in the spring, the Connyers' front yard became the playground where children loved to skip rope with baby Evelyn Connyers sitting in her highchair, watching and clapping her little hands and squeeling with glee.

In 1922 the family moved to Challis where they bought a home, and where both John and Olive passed away. Eva, Viola, and Bryan married and raised families and still live in Challis. Evelyn also married, but spent many years in Alaska. When she and her husband retired they returned to Idaho and now live in Boise. Clifton was never married. In 1973 he suffered a severe stroke, and now lives with his sister, Viola, in the old family home at Challis.

Bryan tells a little story about a family named Carrigan who lived near the John Connyer's family during the time they were in Bear Valley, before coming to the Salmon River area. "They were a large family and real old Irish people," he said. "They had several children and were so poverty-stricken they couldn't even buy shoes for all of them. In fact, they had one pair they used as community property which sat just inside the door. Anyone who had to make a trip to the outside "John," out to get wood, or to go outside for any reason, would slip them on as they went out, and when they came back in would take them off and leave them for the next member of the family who had to go out."

The Carrigan family was there in February of 1920, and

when their food supply ran low, several men from Stanley hauled food to them with dog sleds through the deep drifted snow. One of the party told later of a little boy, perhaps four years old at the time, running around outside in the snow with nothing on but a little light shirt . . . no pants, no socks or shoes, no coat or gloves . . . just that little shirt. "He was a tough little bugger" this man said. "After awhile he went to the cabin door and said to his mother, 'Gee Mom, my hands are cold.' " As soon as the snow thawed and the road was open, this family left the country.

"Gee, Mom my hands are cold!"

Winters:

Coming from Shoshone, Idaho, William and Flora Dell Winters, with their family of five boys, arrived in the Sawtooth Valley in 1932. William was employed on the State Highway, and after living in the Valley for a short time, they moved to the Stanley area and built a nice log home on the outskirts of Upper Stanley. While they lived there three more children were born to them . . . another little boy, a baby girl who came to be the pride and joy of both her parents and her older brothers, then another baby boy. Flora Dell was a wonderful mother, and her death, three weeks after the birth of this last baby, came as a tragic blow to the family. After her burial in Stanley, William's sister came and took the baby and the little girl home with her to care for them. William and the older boys stayed on in Stanley for a short time, then moved back to Shoshone.

As the Winters boys grew up they managed to come back to the Stanley country at every opportunity. Norman, the oldest, worked on the William's ranch for several summers. He and three of his brothers also worked on the Yankee Fork gold dredge in the Forties. One boy, Vernon, and his family moved to Challis in 1966 and still reside there at the time of this writing.

Yankee Fork gold dredge worked in the 1940s.

Maag:

Dan and Violet Maag and two young children came to Central Idaho from North Dakota in the late 1930s. Dan's mother and Marie Ray (Mrs. Walter Ray) had been traveling companions enroute from Germany as young girls and had kept in touch with one another through the years. Thus, it was from Marie Ray, whose husband, Walter, was employed by the Challis National Forest Service, that the Maags learned of the Salmon River country. Times were lean in the Dakotas due to extreme drought and heavy dust storms, deciding Dan and Violet to try for a new start in Idaho near the Rays.

The Maags spent their first winter in the country on Sullivan Creek, near the Sullivan Hot Springs. With the coming of spring Dan got work with the Bureau of Public Roads . . . "picking rocks," he said. It was while working here that he became acquainted with Tom Campbell of Clayton who was instrumental in helping Dan secure the job as watchman on the Dan Kavanaugh ranch (generally referred to as the Benner ranch) in the Upper Stanley vicinity. During their first two years at Stanley, the little family lived in the old Benner hotel building, and while there Violet gave birth to their third child. During her confinement she was cared for by a neighbor, Laura Lightfoot, and a nurse, Fern Scharff.

When Dan went to work for Custer County on road maintenance and repair, the Maag family moved to Challis where they make their home at this time. Dan and Violet raised a family of seven children, all still living in Idaho. June, their oldest daughter, is married to Bill James, an employee of the Challis National Forest Service, and they have made their home in Stanley for many years.

The preceeding brief sketches cover a number of the families who lived, worked, played, and helped in the development of the Stanley country up to the 1930's. Those who came in later years are far too numerous to mention.

TRAPPER FISHER

Henry C. Fisher, the grand old man of the Salmon River Wilderness and always called "Trapper" Fisher, was perhaps the most colorful pioneer to ever put down roots in the Stanley-Sawtooth country. His life reads like one long adven-

Henry "Trapper" Fisher out on the trapline in winter.

ture, beginning with his birth on March 10, 1847, in New York City, until the day he died at the ripe old age of 103 at Salmon, Idaho on March 23, 1950. Sheepherder, prospector, government trapper, fiddler and homesteader, he loved and wore loud colors, was endowed with exceptional humor, had a brogue all his own, and could play a fiddle so well not even a lame man could resist kicking up his heels when Trapper wielded his bow across the strings.

In 1852, Trapper's well-to-do parents caught the California gold fever. That spring they sold their holdings, packed up their son, booked passage on a ship, and sailed around the Horn to San Francisco. In California, they bought more property and enrolled their son in school. As the lad grew, he became restless. He loved the out-of-doors, and with his mind in the mountains while he warmed a seat in a schoolroom was not to his liking. He endured such confinement until he reached the age of fifteen. Saying goodbye to his parents, he became a government trapper . . . a job that led him to Montana, Canada, North Idaho, and eventually to the Sawtooth region. He had learned to play a fiddle and carried one with him wherever he roamed, even into the far reaches of the wilderness.

In line with his job, Trapper hunted and trapped grizzlies, wolves, cougar, and other predators so prevalent in the Northwest in the early days. He moved sheep, and somewhere along the line took up prospecting. A little color in his gold pan every now and then, as he went from one locale to another exterminating wild animals, gave him a diversion as well as an extra dollar on occasion. Too, he usually turned a profit by selling the furs from prime animals caught in his traps. In fact, that is how he won the sobriquet of "Trapper Fisher." It happened one year on the South Fork of the Payette River in Central Idaho when he just missed the world record by one-quarter of an inch in length on a premium silver fox.

Trapper had his first look at the Stanley-Sawtooth country in 1877 when it was still very primitive and yet unsettled. Coming by way of Hailey, Idaho, with a pack string, he followed down the Salmon River as far as Sheep Creek near North Fork where he did some placer mining and trapping. From then on he made many trips in and out of the Sawtooth area, making several friends in the Stanley Basin.

During this time, Jack Sheek of Salmon, Idaho, met Trapper in 1897 up in Montana where he was trapping wolves that had moved into the Wolf Creek region and were preying on cattle ranging there. Jack was driving stage over a 100 mile route between Lewiston and Fort Benton that year, and the way he told it later, Trapper had been sent to do the job because the great wolf packs had moved down from Canada after the buffalo herds had been killed, leaving them lean and hungry enough to migrate southward to Montana's Judas Basin in search of food.

After all his years of roaming the wildernesses and back countries of the great Northwest, Trapper came back to the Stanley Basin, and in 1919 located a homestead on Iron and Goat Creeks. On his property he built a small cabin with a dirt floor, then went on with his trapping and doing a little mining . . . and, of course, some fiddling. In all of his travels his beloved fiddle had been his constant companion, always protected in his saddlebag. Now in the Basin and in his seventies, when he played at the community dances, or just in his cabin, anyone within earshot was challenged to action by the laughing notes of his fine old fiddle. He fiddled like the veteran he was, setting young folks and old alike to bouncing out the figures of a square dance, or gliding across the floor to the strains of "The Missouri Waltz," or some other tune. Needless to say, Trapper's zest for life, his cheerful personality, and his colorful charm endeared him to everyone who knew him.

A brief item attesting to his stamina and endurance that appeared in the May 3, 1922, issue of the *Challis Messenger Newspaper* read: "H.C. Fisher, who lives in a scenic spot near Stanley is a frequent visitor to town. "Dad" or "Trapper," as he is called, is a spry chap of about 76 years, but doesn't mind walking. He often plays for dances all night long, then goes home and milks his cow before breakfast."

While Trapper lived on his homestead, he shipped and received payment for his furs through the Stanley Post Office. Sometimes when he cashed his check at the store, the storekeeper teased him as he counted out the money to him. "Here, you old son-of-a-gun is more dough to stash away in your old tomato can." Trapper would chuckle and answer, "Yea, don't you wish you had my old tomato can?"

No one knew if he really did hide his money, of course, but it was generally believed that he did . . . especially after he made a deal to buy the William Soule ranch. It was wintertime. The price was $1,500. "I can't pay you until spring," he told Mr.

Soule. "What's the matter, you old rascal . . . got your money buried somewhere under the snow?" Soule asked. "Heh, heh, heh," Trapper chuckled, "Don't you wish you knew?" Sure enough, when the snow melted that spring, Trapper showed up with the $1,500 to close the deal.

In the meantime, while still on the homestead, he had as his constant companion a female dog named "Shaky." One fall he had killed a deer toward his winter's food supply. Bonda Critchfield and her half-sister, Jennie Buchanan, went up to help him cut up the meat. Shaky sat near the table in the cabin to watch the process. Jennie dropped a piece on the dirt floor. "Just give it to Shaky," Trapper said. Jennie, not knowing the dog's name, thought he said, "Just give it a shake," promptly picked up the meat from the floor, and with a questioning glance at Bonda, tossed it into the pan with the other meat. Bonda said, "Oh, don't do that. Trapper said to give it to the dog." Trapper merely laughed and said, "Oh, that's all right. We all have to eat a little dirt sometime."

In about 1925, a Dr. Terrell and his wife, Dora, came to Stanley and established a summer residence. The Terrells became very good friends with Trapper, and even after the doctor's death a few years later, Dora remained a friend to Trapper. She built a number of tourist cabins and operated a tourist court called "The Rest Haven" at Lower Stanley, continuing to spend a great deal of time there. Once when Dora made a trip to Salt Lake City, she took Trapper along for a treat to him. Since Trapper had not been far from Stanley country in several years, the big Utah city overwhelmed him. While shopping in a large department store with him one day, Dora became so embarrassed by his loud remarks, she began to walk a little distance ahead of him. Trapper, being somewhat deaf, and much to Dora's agitation, called out to her, "Hey Doree! This sure is a big store. Why I bet they sell a hundert dollars worth of stuff here every day."

Trapper always wore Levis, a bright plaid shirt, an old grey felt hat, and a blue bandana tied around his neck. For special occasions, such as playing at a dance, he would wear a bright silk scarf instead of the blue bandana. Not a large man, he usually created quite a stir wherever he went with his snow-white whiskers, casual dress and picturesque speech. It seems he did not always pronounce his "A's" when he talked, especially when he called someone by name. He called Edna McGown "Ednee," for example.

In August of 1927, Edna went with her husband, Tuff McGown, to Trapper's place to help him put up hay. While the two men worked in the field that morning, Edna tended her baby, little Arthur Jr., and cooked dinner in Trapper's cabin, fulfilling a promise to bake a lemon pie for Trapper. When the men came in at noon, Tuff was dead tired. "Whee," he told his wife, "This old Coot has about worked me to death." Trapper was eighty years old that year, making Tuff fifty years his junior.

When dinner was over, Trapper said. "Ednee, your mother used to cut my hair . . . do you think you can?" "Well, I can try," Edna replied. "Good," the old man said, "It's too hot to do more in the field right now, and Tuff can nap with the baby while you cut my hair."

When the job was done, Trapper inspected his haircut carefully in a mirror, then turned to Edna and matter-of-factly declared, "You do a pretty good job cutting hair; but by cracky, you can't bake a pie the way your mother can."

"Trapper" Fisher fiddlin' a lively tune.

Trapper then brought out his fiddle and began to play, rousing Tuff and the baby. Soon Edna and Tuff were dancing as the baby lay watching and cooing happily. As the afternoon wore on and time drew near for the McGowns to leave, Tuff told Trapper they had better get back to the field if they expected to get any more hay in that day. "Oh, that's alright, Tuff," Trapper said. "We did a pretty good job this morning and I think I can finish now. Besides, you dance a heck of a lot better than you pitch hay." A short time later, when preparing to go home, Edna asked Trapper if he wanted the rest of the pie. Trapper laughed and answered, "I can eat it, even if it ain't as good as your mother can make."

In 1936, when he was eighty-nine years old, Trapper sold his ranch in the Basin to Arthur Silva of Shoshone, Idaho. He then bought a cabin near the Bill Merritt home on their property. Here, he spent his time doing little chores, fishing, trapping, and just visiting with "folks." Trapper truly enjoyed being with people.

While he lived on the Merritt ranch, the family looked out for him in any way they could. Knowing Trapper liked sourdough hotcakes, Mrs. Merritt would fry six for him, and while the cakes were still hot off the griddle, her son, Stub, would run with them over to Trapper's cabin. Whatever Trapper ate, his dog also ate. If he had steak, his dog had steak. If the fare were beans, dog and master shared alike. And so it went. One of his favorites was dried apricots stewed and sprinkled liberally with sugar. When he cooked the fruit, he filled one bowl for himself and one for the dog.

One day Trapper came over to the Merritt home and said to Mrs. Merritt, "Sidie, will you come give Shaky some salts? She sure is sick." Mrs. Merritt did what she could, but the dog died. Grief stricken, Trapper asked, "Will Stub come and help me bury Shaky under that lone pine tree behind the house?" Then, wiping a tear from his eye, he added, "And when I die I want to be buried there beside her."

After Bill Merritt's death in 1938, Mrs. Merritt and her son, Stub, stayed on the ranch until his marriage to Vella Williams Lee. Then the newly married couple took over the management of the ranch and continued to look after Trapper Fisher while Mrs. Merritt went to work at different places. In 1940, now at age ninety-three, Trapper began to worry some about his health, remarking to friends that his father had died of cancer when he was 108 years old, "And I certainly don't want my life cut short like that," he said. Since he had developed a tumor, he called on his good friend Dora Terrell to drive him down to Ogden, Utah, to have the growth removed.

While at Ogden, Trapper attracted more than a little attention by his manner and the way he dressed in his tight western levis, plaid shirt, high heeled boots, and old felt hat, and griping a new ornate pipe in his mouth. The trip proved a delightful event in the ninety-three year old man's life, and all in all, he found city life much to his liking after his years of trapping, hunting gold, and playing his fiddle all over the Northwest. "A hermit's life can get mighty wearisome sometimes, and I like people," he told Mrs. Terrell.

Back at the Merritt ranch, things went along for awhile much as before. . . . Trapper still fishing, trapping, and playing his fiddle, and Stub and Vella keeping an eye on him as he came and went. Then for some reason, Trapper started wearing rubber shoes both winter and summer. Finally his feet were in a bad condition and emitting a foul odor. Stub could not convince him to stop wearing the rubber shoes, and it got to the point where the old man, now ninety-nine, could hardly walk. In his concern for Trapper, Stub notified the sheriff who took him to the Silbaugh Nursing Home in Salmon, Idaho. Trapper was not happy there, but realizing the limitations of his old age, he made the best of the situation. As his feet improved he took long walks with cane in hand along the Lemhi River, soon becoming a familiar figure to the residents and ranchers who drove the route. Despite his years, he remained in comparative good health and was a hearty eater until he was stricken with pneumonia about the thirteenth of March, 1950.

He died ten days later at the age of 103, at the nursing home in Salmon. His last request was that he be given a simple burial without fanfare. His creed as he said was, "God is in His Heaven, and His church is the vastness of nature's wilderness." Truly this fine old man of the mountains had lived in peace with his Maker and with his fellowman. Yes, in compliance with Trapper's wishes, his body was attired in his favorite loud colors and laid on the gentle slopes of a hillside in the Salmon Cemetery . . . many miles apart from the grave of his dog, Shaky.

Although Trapper has been gone for well over two decades now, there are those who still remember his rousing renditions of Pony Boy, Over the Waves, Golden Slippers, Moonwinks, Snow Deer, Silver Bells, the Clarinet Polka, and other tunes he played at dances they attended in the Stanley country in bygone days. Nor is it likely that any one of them will ever forget this beloved old man's color and character.

THE SINGLE ONES

Early pioneers . . . they came from far away places, and for many reasons. Some came in search of gold, some seeking the land of opportunity, some looking for adventure, and some hoping to find peace and quiet in which to forget troubles and disappointments. There were those who came that very little is known about, and many who came that even their names are not known, or have long since been forgotten. Wherever they came from, or for whatever reason, they did come. A few had at one time been married, but at the time they pioneered the Stanley Basin they were classed as "The Single Ones."

Alvah P. Challis and Henry Sturkey

Alvah P. Challis and Henry Sturkey were two who located placer ground in Kelly Gulch (then known as Summit Gulch) in 1873. Mr. Challis, past forty years of age at the time, and a veteran placer miner who had tried his luck in the Mother Lode country of California, along the Frasier River in British Columbia, in the mining camps of the Boise Basin, and at Leesburg near Salmon, Idaho, in 1872 had finally settled in the Round Valley near where the town of Challis is now located. Alvah Challis had made money in mining, but, being a generous, big-hearted man had never saved any of it. However, his name and credit were good, and he had a friend, Henry Sturkey, who had accumulated a small savings. The two men decided to buy a few head of cattle and settle on a piece of land along the Salmon River. Both having the "mining bug," they would prospect on the side. Thus the spring of 1873 found them prospecting in the Stanley Basin and ultimately locating placer ground. *For more on the mining see Stanley Basin Mines.*

Alvah P. Challis in his late years.

For the next several years the partners worked the placer claims during the early summer months and spent the winter months at their ranch on the Salmon River. Both made many friends, and the tall, stately Mr. Challis, with his shock of greying hair and his handle-bar mustache, and the short, stocky little German, Henry Sturkey, became a familiar sight in both Stanley and Challis. Then in 1878 the town of Challis, Idaho was laid out and was named for Alvah Challis. From then on he became more involved with the Challis area, making only occasional trips to Stanley.

Years passed, and in the fall of 1902, Mr. Challis had a longing to return to Rosedale, Indiana, where he had been born in 1832. On his way, he visited a brother who lived in the Black Hills of South Dakota, then he journeyed on to Carbondale, Kansas where he planned to spend Christmas at the homes of another brother and two sisters. While in Kansas he was taken ill and was hospitalized, suffering first from Mountain Fever, then he had gall bladder surgery, and finally developed cancer of the stomach. He died there in Kansas on April 17, 1903, never having reached the place of his birth in Indiana.

Upon receiving word of his death, M.M. Sweet, then the publisher of *The Silver Messenger Newspaper* printed at Challis, Idaho, wrote, in part: "Alvah Challis was a noble character, generous to a fault, and as straightforward and honest a man as I have ever known. The earth that bears him dead, bears not a truer gentleman." And in Stanley, when Della McGown heard of his passing, she wrote in her diary: "This was a noble and a good friend, and no better man ever lived than Alvah Challis."

After the death of Alvah Challis two of his nephews, W.W. Challis, and a Mr. Crow came West to take over his holdings. Henry Sturkey worked with them through the summer of 1903, then, in December of that same year, he sold his half interest in the Challis-Sturkey Placer to Mr. Crow. It was at that time that Henry Sturkey went back to visit relatives in Germany where he had been born on November 15, 1846.

A few months later, with the coming of spring in the Stanley-Sawtooth country, Henry Sturkey returned. After having lived for thirty years in the shadow of the grand old

Henry Sturkey.

302

snow-capped Sawtooth Mountains, he had missed the friends he had made, the quiet of his own little cabin among the pines, and most of all, the activity of the placer mining. Back in the Stanley country he again worked with W.W. Challis and Mr. Crow, and on the various other claims he had an interest in. Then in 1908 he purchased back the half interest in the Challis-Sturkey Placer that he had sold to Mr. Crow. Since by now W.W. Challis had decided to move on to other fields, Henry once again became manager of the placer, each year making a profitable clean-up at the end of the season. It became known as The Sturkey Placer, and some oldtimers refer to it as such today.

By the 1920s Henry spent much of his time in Boise, Idaho, and on May 30, 1931 he made application to enter the Odd Fellows Home in Caldwell, Idaho. There he spent his last days, passing away on May 28, 1933 . . . cause of death listed as 'old age.' He was buried in the Caldwell cemetery. At the time of his death he had one sister, Mrs. Marie Hall, still living at Cookhaven, Germany

Rubble continues to remain in drain ditch at Sturkey Placers near headwaters of Kelly Creek in Stanley Basin.

B.F. Rapp:

Benjamin Frank Rapp came to Stanley Basin in the late 1880s from Bonanza City located on the Yankee Fork of the Salmon River. While active in both quartz and placer mining, he also located a homestead at the upper end of the Stanley Basin, but did not live long enough to make the final proof on the land. Records tell of Frank Rapp and partners (no names) making a clean-up of gold which netted them $3,000 during the summer of 1894.

Mr. Rapp took an active part in the development of the Stanley area. An item in *The Silver Messenger Newspaper* of Challis, Idaho, dated August 15, 1899, read: "At a meeting of the citizens of Stanley Basin on July 17th, B.F. Rapp was duly elected as Deputy Mining Recorder for the Stanley Basin Mining District. Then on April 19, 1900 he received the appointment as postmaster at Stanley, and was also awarded the contract to carry the mail once a week over Galena Summit from Ketchum.

Frank Rapp was living in the Stanley Basin when the Arthur McGowns arrived there in 1890. They had also known him in Bonanza, and Della McGown, in later years, would tell the following story about him. "Frank liked to stay up late and watch the poker games or whatever else might be going on. He never went to bed until all the lights in town were out. One year he decided to spend the winter in Salt Lake City, but it was not long after his departure until he was back in Bonanza. Old "Banjo Bill" asked him why he had come home so soon, and Frank replied, "Well, I'm used to staying up until all the lights go out, and in Salt Lake they never go out. I had to come home to get a little sleep."

Benjamin Frank Rapp was born in Pennsylvania, and died at Bonanza, Idaho on October 28, 1901 . . . age about sixty years.

304

Dave Hershey:

Dave Hershey came to Idaho from Utah in search of gold, and stayed on as a bachelor because of a disappointing love affair.

According to oldtimers who knew him, Dave worked a placer claim near Casino Creek on the Salmon River in the 1890s and made some "mighty fine clean-ups." When he decided that he had a pretty fair "stake" he returned to Utah intending to be married. On leaving Stanley he had said to Della McGown, "I'm going to marry the sweetest girl in all the world. I am having a home built in Ogden, Utah, and we will live there. I'll not be back to Stanley." Della remarked, "You've been away a long time, Dave, and there's many a slip between the cup and the lip." Dave just laughed, said his goodbyes and left.

It was only two or three weeks later that Dave Hershey again came to the McGown Store in Upper Stanley. Della, much surprised to see him there, said, "Well, hello Dave. Where's that sweet girl?" Haltingly Dave told her that his girl had married another man, then he said, "I've come back to Stanley to spend the rest of my life. I'll never trust another woman."

Hershey went back down the River to Casino Creek, and weeks, or sometimes months would pass when no one would see him. Only the smoke coming from his stovepipe would let the stage driver or others who passed know that he was there. Occasionally he would be forced to make a hurried trip to town for supplies. Then, in the early 1900s George Cumine, Tom Kelly, and several others were mining in the area, so became acquainted with Hershey, and once again he seemed to enjoy company. In 1906 he bought George Cumine's mining claims on Casino Creek, and in 1912 he filed on a homestead, making the final proof in 1917.

By now Dave Hershey was considered "the dirtiest old batch" on Salmon River. His cabin had two rooms . . . one in which he lived, and the other used as his chicken coop. The door between stood open most of the time, and often the chickens would have to be "shooed" off the table before the food could be set on. Mr. Hershey, like nearly all the folks in the early days, would invite anyone who happened to be there near mealtime to eat with him . . . no one ever did.

Besides his chickens, he kept a few head of horses and put in a field of hay. and on a sunny slope behind his house he raised strawberries. When ripe they were large, sweet, and lucious, and a treat to anyone who bought them from him. Each spring during the years that the Niece family lived at Lower Stanley, Dave would pick the very first ripe berries and make a special trip up to the store (about five miles) to give them to Tink and Ellen Niece's little daughter, Edna.

Dave Hershey lived at Casino Creek for nearly thirty years. Finally old and ill, he was taken to Challis for medical attention, and was to be cared for at the Challis Hot Springs. There they gave him a bath, and according to some oldtimers, "Old Dave just couldn't stand that." He died there and was buried in the Challis Cemetery.

Cabins could be found up any of the creeks in the Stanley-Sawtooth region during the early days.

Cyrus Odell:

Cyrus, or Cy Odell, was another "old batch" who didn't take kindly to soap and water. He had a placer claim at the head of Joe's Gulch which he was working at the time that Arthur and Della McGown lived at Upper Stanley. He made frequent trips to their store. To quote Della McGown, "He was a sight to behold with his hair standing on end, and he himself so dirty that he looked like he had been sleeping in a coal bin. The two kids were scared of him, but he was pretty well read, and he was one who helped me get the post office in Stanley."

She went on to tell of the Christmas of 1893 when they were snowbound at Stanley. "There were not many presents to put in the kids stockings. Herbert Marshall had made a doll out of wood for Lulu, so I made a rag doll for Joe. I used some old yarn for the hair. The kids hung their stockings over their bed, and I put those dolls in them. Just at daybreak Joe raised up in bed and saw that doll, and he yelled, "Cy Odell," and dived back under the covers. Lulu played with her doll, then took Joe's doll out of the stocking and started to play with it. After awhile he decided it wouldn't bite, so he played with it too, but both kids always called it "Cy Odell."

An item in a December 1894 issue of *The Silver Messenger Newspaper,* printed at Challis, Idaho, stated, "Cy Odell, a placer miner from Stanley, has been judged insane and taken to Blackfoot."

A year and a half later, in June 1896, relatives of Cyrus Odell contacted *The Silver Messenger Newspaper* office wishing to learn the whereabouts of Cyrus Odell. They gave his description as being five feet five inches tall, brown eyes, and brown hair streaked with grey. Upon inquiry it was learned that Cy had been released from the asylum in September of 1895, and that his whereabouts were unknown.

Madison (Matt) Womack and Henry Duffy:

Early mining in the Stanley-Sawtooth country brought two more men into the Stanley Basin that were to live out their remaining years there among the mountains and the valleys that they both came to love.

Madison (Matt) Womack, born in Missouri on June 1, 1849, was one of a family of ten children. When only fourteen years old he joined a band of guerrilla troops called Quantrill's Raiders: named for their organizer and leader, Clarke Quantrill. This band had been organized at the start of the Civil War in 1861, and by 1862 had been mustered into Confederate Service, but was allowed to continue to operate independently. On August 21, 1863, Quantrill and his men burned most of the town of Lawerence, Kansas, and many people were killed. Matt Womack, as well as Frank James, a brother of Jesse James, was riding with the Raiders that day. Matt could tell some thrilling stories of his adventures while with Quantrill's Raiders, but unfortunately, none of them are remembered.

In 1881, Matt Womack, then thirty-two years old, arrived in the Central Idaho area and purchased a sawmill on Mill Creek, a few miles west of Challis, Idaho, from A.P. Challis and Benjamin Blackburn. While engaged in the sawmill business, Matt became interested in mining, and in 1886 he bought a one-sixth interest in a claim located in the Seafoam Mining District known as The Sulphur Mine.

This mining venture led him to the Stanley Basin area, where in 1890 he was appointed as the authorized agent for the dredging operation of the Sawtooth Placer Mining Company whose principal office was in Kansas City, Missouri. A second dredge was built in 1899 by The Stanley Basin Dredging Company, and Matt was also appointed as agent for this company. Acting in this capacity he managed to keep both dredges operating intermittently until 1910 or '11. Matt, being a cheerful, friendly person, made many friends among the men who worked for him through the years.

One of these men was *Henry Duffy*. Henry, a complete opposite of Matt, was a quiet, reserved man, of medium build and always neat and clean. He came originally from Illinois, and the first record known of his life in Idaho was in 1894. At that time he was working at the Singeiser Mine near Salmon, Idaho. From there he moved up the Salmon River to the mining town of Bayhorse where he worked in the mines for several years before coming into the Seafoam and Stanley areas. There, while working on the Stanley Dredge, he became acquainted with Matt Womack and the two men formed a lasting friendship.

Henry Duffy and Matt Womack located adjoining homesteads in the Stanley Basin in 1913. They bought the buildings and improvements on the B and B Ranch (called The Cow Camp today) from George McGowan and moved them to Matt's land. Later they built a two-storied log house near-by, but on Henry's homestead.

During this interval Matt had started a small sawmill on Anderson Gulch near the Womack and Duffy ranches. This, along with tending their few head of cattle and horses, putting up wild hay for winter feed, and getting their winter's wood, kept the partners busy through the summer months. Henry was the housekeeper and did most of the household chores and cooking for both, and as was the custom in the early days, always welcomed guests at their table. Even the youngsters from Lower Stanley would occasionally walk over Nip-N-Tuck hill road and have dinner with Matt and Duffy.

Little more is known of Henry Duffy except that in 1926 when he was taken ill he deeded all of his property to his friend and partner, Matt Womack, leading one to the conclusion that he had no living relatives. Shortly after this transaction he died and was buried at Mackay, Idaho.

Matt stayed on at the ranch through a long, lonely winter, and by spring he had decided to deed the property to his niece, Cozette Peters, who was living in Montana. In May, 1927, he went to Challis, Idaho to take care of this business, and while there was visiting at the home of Donald Rowles, another close friend from his days at the Stanley Dredge. It was there that Matt became ill. Doctor C.L. Kirtley was called, and everything possible was done for the old man, but he passed away on June 3, 1927, at the home of Donald and Florence Rowles, two days after his seventy-eighth birthday. He was buried in the Challis Cemetery.

George Cumine and Thomas Kelly:

George Cumine was another who wandered far from his homeland in search of adventure. George was born in Wichlow, England, on November 14, 1855, the son of Reverend and Rosalie Cumine. When seventeen years old he had an opportunity to come to America with friends of the family. His parents were reluctant to give their consent, but seeing that nothing they could say would dissuade him, they allowed him to quit school, and wished him God Speed on his journey. He crossed the Atlantic, landing in Virginia in 1872. After a short time there his pioneering spirit urged him to travel farther westward. He worked his way across the continent to California. There he worked on ranches for a time, then became interested in mining.

Hauling in the winters wood supply. Right to left, George Cumine, Juggy Niece, and Doc Cothern on load.

In search of the ever elusive gold, he traveled over most of the southwest, down into Old Mexico, and back to Florence, Arizona. There he got a job driving stage-coach from Florence through the Pinel Mountains to Globe, Arizona. Along this route bandits were numerous at that time and his coach was held up on several occasions, making the run both exciting and dangerous.

It was while in Florence too, that George met and fell in love with a beautiful Mexican girl and was considering getting married and settling down. However, when he learned that the girl of his dreams was a married woman, he pulled up stakes and traveled on.

Stopping to work awhile in Wickenburg, Arizona, he met *Thomas Kelly,* a wiry little Irishman, and the two became close friends. Together they traveled to Idaho, arriving at the then busy mining town of Bayhorse in 1903. After working in the mines there that winter, they moved on up the Salmon River to Casino Creek, where George bought a placer claim from Clay and Priscilla Vance, and Tom located The Humbug claim nearby. A year later George sold his claim to Dave Hershey, and he and Tom together located the Gold Cube Claims a little farther to the south, but still in the Casino Creek area. They built a cabin and worked their claims profitably for the next five years before selling to a mining company from Colorado. While working their placer through the summer months, the two men trapped during the winter season and became quite proficient at catching the mink, marten, fox, and other fur bearing animals that roamed the area.

After selling their placer ground, George and Tom moved to the Stanley Basin. George, now well past fifty years of age, decided to file on a homestead in the northwest end of the Basin near Elk Creek. Tom, still preferring to mine and trap, built himself a cabin a few miles farther west on a small creek now called Kelly Creek. Tom wandered the hills in the summertime, then as the first snows and the cold days came, making the fur prime, he would spend long days setting out his trap lines. He came to be considered the best trapper in the Stanley country outside of Trapper Fisher.

Meanwhile, George had built a comfortable three-room log cabin, a barn and blacksmith shop, and other necessary outbuildings, and had made final proof on his land in 1916. The two friends often visited and worked together. Then in August

311

of 1919, Tom was found seriously ill in his cabin. Before a doctor could reach him he died ... cause of death was acute uremia. His death was a sad blow to George Cumine, his friend of many years. When word that he had died reached Stanley, the towns-folk decided they should set aside a plot of ground across Valley Creek from Upper Stanley, on a slope overlooking both Valley Creek and Salmon River as a cemetery. This they did, and Thomas Kelly was the first person to be interred in the Stanley Cemetery.

George Cumine, the slender, grey-haired, distinguished looking English gentleman, stayed on at his ranch until the fall of 1930. Then Slim and Mildred Cothern Hendricks moved onto the ranch to care for George's home and his few head of horses, and George went to spend the winter at Upper Stanley in the home of Doc and Affie Cothern.

By 1933 George had decided that he wanted to make just one more try to find that rich gold mine that, as he said, "Must be waiting for me somewhere." He sold his ranch to Slim Hendricks, and although now seventy-eight years old, he went prospecting. He located a placer claim near the West Fork of the Yankee Fork and spent the summer there camping out under the pines and doing a little work with his sluice boxes. However, by fall the old man abandoned the effort saying, "I just can't work like I could thirty years ago." He returned to the Cothern home and spent most of his remaining years with them.

As time passed George became feeble and ill. He was taken to consult Dr. Fox in Hailey, Idaho, and it was found that he had cancer. Affie Cothern, with the help of Ellen Niece, Mary Marshall, Mrs. Josephine Thompson, and other kind neighbors, nursed George through a long seige of intense suffering. He passed away at the Cothern home in April, 1938, and was buried in the little hillside cemetery near his old friend, Tom Kelly.

George Cumine, through all the years had not visited his native land, and had never married. At the time of his death he had but one living relative ... a sister then living in London, England.

Walter and Lemuel Lynch:

The Lynch family, the father and six grown sons, traveled from Glassport, Pennsylvania to Idaho in 1903. These husky young fellows came with dreams of the fortune they would reap from the mines of Central Idaho, only to be so disappointed that four of the boys had returned to Pennsylvania before three years had passed.

Their first mining venture after arriving in the Stanley country was near the Valley Creek Mine, then operating on the northwest rim of the Stanley Basin. This proved unsuccessful, and after only a short time *Walter and Lemuel,* or Walt and Lem, as they came to be called by the Stanley folks, found a promising prospect on Potato Mountain. They located claims and did extensive work through the years, but failed to find the rich gold vein they had felt was there.

By this time the father, Pat Lynch, had tried his luck at placer mining on Joe's Gulch, then had moved a few miles north on the Salmon River to a small creek that now bears his name . . . Lynch Creek. There he built a cabin and lived, washing out enough gold to care for his meager needs, but never finding the El Dorado he had hoped for. After a few years he too, returned to Pennsylvania. Walt and Lem stayed on in the Stanley-Sawtooth country.

Lemuel Lynch had been educated as an electrical engineer, but there being no opportunity for him to work at his trade in the Stanley area, and being disillusioned with mining, he turned to working on ranches, cutting wood, or just any 'jack-of-all-trades' types of work. He was a good workman, pleasant and agreeable to work with, so managed to make a living. Then, in the early Twenties, people began to notice that Lem acted queer at times. He was living alone in an old cabin on Stanley Creek, and would tell about hearing beautiful music. He insisted that he could wash his dishes in a metal pan, throw the water out and hang the wet pan on a certain nail outside his cabin door, then he could sit and listen to the Metropolitan Opera, Jenny Lind, Carrousa, and other great artists in the musical world. Radio was unheard of in the area at that time; but who knows? Perhaps the air waves were just right there in the Basin, and Lem was really "tuned in."

One hot afternoon in August 1927, Lem was cutting wood for

Lemuel Lynch

a young couple who lived at Upper Stanley. He was to have his lunch and dinner as part of his pay for the work. Late in the afternoon the lady of the house and a friend were sitting on the porch in the shade visiting, and Lem, being hot and tired joined them. The young housewife asked, "Lem, would you mind having a cold meal this evening? It is so hot that I hate to build up the fire." Lem startled the ladies by answering, "Oh, don't worry about it. When I get hungry I just write what I want to eat on a slip of paper and toss it in the wind, and there is my meal . . . all set on a table and ready for me to eat."

The things that Lem would say and do became quite a joke in the community and people would remark, "Poor old Lem. He's crazier than a hoot owl, but he's harmless." One fall in the late Twenties Lem, still living in the old cabin on Stanley Creek, was found to be destitute and ill. His condition was reported to the authorities, and Lem was taken to the asylum at Blackfoot, Idaho.

Through all the years Walt had continued with his mining. He held the claims on Potato Mountain and also worked for the dredges and other mines operating in the Stanley Basin. In 1918, not having received the wages due him for work on the Stanley Dredge, he filed a lein on the property, and eventually

314

came to own the placer ground along Stanley Creek. It was while he was working this ground that he was credited with discovering some radium ore. He and William Soule experimented with the rock, and by placing a key and a coin on a piece of heavy paper, covering them with another piece of paper and a piece of metal, then laying the rock on top, they developed a perfect picture of the key and coin on the top piece of paper. The rock would glow in the dark, so one evening Walt brought it to a dance at the Stanley Hall to show it to interested persons. In order to see the strange glow it had to be taken into a dark closet under the stairway leading up to the balcony. Several people had been in and were exclaiming over it, so Leafy Critchfield decided she too, would have a look. As she started toward the closet, her daughter, Bonda, called out, "Mamma, don't you go in there with old Walt." Mrs. Critchfield was very embarrassed, and the crowd had a good laugh.

During the early spring of 1939 Walt and his nephew, Jess Lynch, were working at Walt's mine on Potato Mountain when Walt was taken seriously ill. There was no road to the cabin. Jess made a hurried trip to the Stanley Dredge for help. Doctor Ivan Day who was living near the dredge, and the dredge crew, went up the mountain and carried Walt the four miles out to the road. There he was put in a car and taken to the hospital at Hailey, Idaho. His health improved somewhat and he was able to be back in Stanley for the summer. However, late that fall of 1939, Walt's condition worsened, and he finally gave up the battle. Another old miner was laid to rest in the Stanley Cemetery.

The nephew, Jess Lynch, went into the service during World War II. After his discharge he returned to the Stanley country to follow in the footsteps of his Uncle Walt. It was there that he died and was buried near his Uncle.

A year or so after Walt's death, the couple whom Lem had cut wood for in Upper Stanley were in Blackfoot and decided to visit Lem. They doubted that he would know them, and were amazed when Lem was brought to the visiting room at the asylum, to have him recognize them and call them by name. He was delighted to see them, and told of his activities there in the gardens and grounds . . . was "The overseer of the work force," so he said. The couple were really amused when they asked Lem if he knew Mattie Franklin, a woman who had lived in Stanley many years before, and was at that time confined in

315

the asylum. He answered, "Yes, she's here, but you don't want to see her. She's crazier than hell."

A few minutes later Lem asked about his brother, Walt. On being told that Walt was dead, he immediately became irrational. Taking a note-book from his pocket, he began to scribble figures and to talk about all the millions of dollars that had been stolen from he and Walt, and about Walt staying on to guard their property while he, Lem, was away. The attendant came then to take him away, and the visit was over. Lem died there at the asylum.

Road sign to Joe's Gulch where much mining was done in the early days.

William (Bill) Soule:

William A. Soule, a long time resident of the Stanley country, was born in Nebraska in 1869. He seldom spoke of his life before coming to Idaho, but it was known that he had been married and had a son, Claude L. Soule, and that he was a relative and heir of the Soule family that first made "None Such Mincemeat."

Bill Soule was a small man . . . about five foot eight inches tall, slender and well built, with dark hair and grey eyes. He was usually clean and neatly dressed, and his soft-spoken, cultured manner made him quite a "ladies man." He was an excellent dancer, knew all the chords and could play a few tunes on the piano, so was popular at the Stanley social gatherings.

William "Bill" Soule

Mr. Soule was a natural genius where electricity was concerned. He had helped to install one of the first electric light plants in Hailey, Idaho before coming to the Stanley area. He installed all of the battery powered home lighting systems in and around Stanley in the early days. When radios were invented Bill Soule sent for books and materials and built several sets. He was also a photographer . . . did his own developing

317

and enlarging. He made beautiful panoramic views of the rugged Sawtooth Mountains and the numerous crystal clear lakes in the area. For many years these pictures were for sale in the Niece Brothers Store, and later in the Clyde Gillispie Store in Upper Stanley.

In 1912 Bill filed on a homestead in the Stanley Basin and established his residence there. Being quite a speculator, he formed partnerships with many different mining people through the years. In 1918 he was a partner of W.B. Paul and Jack and Jennie Gleason on what they called The Mayday Group, located just over the Nip-N-Tuck hill from Lower Stanley. At other times he was interested in claims on Valley Creek, in the Stanley Basin, and even extended his mining activities to the Red Mountain and Yankee Fork areas. However, with all the work and enthusiasm he put into his mining ventures, he failed to realize any large profits.

Packed and ready for a prospecting trip. Bill Soule between burros, and Will Paul by saddle horse. Taken in front of the Bill Soule home about 1914.

After fourteen years on his ranch in the Basin, he sold to Trapper Fisher and built himself a small log house in Upper Stanley. Now free of his ranching chores, he devoted all of his time during the summer months to mining. Through the cold, snowy winters he would work at his photography and spend some time visiting friends in Challis or Hailey. As far as is known, he never returned to Nebraska, but his son, Claude, came to Stanley to see his father during the summer of 1937.

It was in 1933 that he bought the old Valley Creek Mine. Later that same year he sold an interest in it to Fred Schindler of Blackfoot, Idaho. *(See Valley Creek Mine in Mining Section.)*

Like so many others in the Stanley-Sawtooth country, after years spent tramping the hills in search of a fortune, the dapper Bill Soule finally gave up. By the early 1940s he spent much of his time alone in his cabin at Upper Stanley. Then one stormy day in January 1945, a neighbor remarked to the sons of Barney and Nellie Lanier, "I haven't seen Bill around for a day or two. Wonder if he went somewhere?" The boys went to investigate. When there was no answer to their knock, they peeked in the window and could see Bill lying on the floor beside an overturned chair. Friends were called, but they found the door locked. Sheriff Lee Clark was summoned from Challis, and when the door was opened it was determined that Bill had been dead for several hours. The date of his death was listed as January 6th, 1945. After nearly forty years spent in the Stanley country, Bill, like many other oldtimers, found his final resting place in the Stanley Cemetery. At the time of his death he was survived by his son, Claude, of Grand Island, Nebraska, a nephew, George Dickson, of Nampa, Idaho, and a grandson, Howard Soule, of Denver, Colorado.

Old gold rocker on display at Custer Museum on Yankee Fork and is like ones used by early miners throughout the West.

Frank A. (Juggy) Niece:

Frank Niece was born on August 30, 1874, at Lapere, Michigan, the eldest of a family of ten children. While still in his early twenties he came west and went into the general merchandise business at Rambler, Wyoming. In 1900 he was joined there by his brother, Leslie (Tink), who worked with him in the store for the next four years. At that time the business was sold and they moved to Encampment, Wyoming. Leslie had married before leaving Rambler, and after two years in Encampment, he and his wife left for Idaho. Frank spent another two years at Encampment. By 1908 Frank had married Mary Peterson, bringing her as a bride to the remote Sawtooth Valley in Central Idaho. He located a homestead adjoining his brother's, built a large one-room log cabin, and settled down to improve the property. Mary was not accustomed to the lonely life of a pioneer lady so was discontent and often insisted that they go to Stanley, Pierson, or just to spend a day or two visiting other ranchers in the area. Their first winter together was spent at their cabin on the ranch. That was a long, difficult winter for Frank and his wife. When spring opened up, Frank got work at the Casino Creek placer mine and took Mary with him. By mid-summer they were back at the ranch, and on August 12, 1909, two darling little red-headed girls, Margaret and Francis, were born. Ellen Niece helped to deliver the babies and cared for them and their mother. When Mary was able to be up and around, she found that caring for twins with none of the conveniences of today was a difficult chore. Shut in with their two babies, Frank and Mary spent another winter at the ranch. Mary seemed to be adjusting to this way of life. With the coming of spring the need for money made it necessary for Frank to work away from home. It was then that Mary laid her plans to leave. One day in early summer when the twins were not yet a year old, Mary took the babies and caught the mail stage to Hailey, Idaho. There she was met by a man she had known before she and Frank were married, and returned to Wyoming with him. As soon as she and Frank were divorced, she married this other man.

Frank, now alone, made his headquarters at the ranch, but spent much of his time away at work. He sent money regularly to Mary for the girls. While on the ranch he would occasionally saddle up the old white horse, Johnson, and go to the Benner Place for an evening with the boys. The next day Tink and

Ellen Niece's children, Rupert and Edna, would wait and watch for their Uncle Frank to come home. He never failed to bring them a treat. Sometimes it would be candy, but the favorite thing was a box of puffed rice. Dry cereals were a luxury in the homes in those days, and the only kinds available in the stores were shredded wheat, corn flakes, grapenuts, and puffed rice.

When the old white horse and his rider would finally be sighted turning into the road that led across the field and up to the house, the children could tell if Uncle Frank had imbibed too much at the Benner Saloon. If old Johnson appeared to be doing a balancing act, zig-zagging across the road in whichever direction his rider swayed, they knew that their Uncle would go to the barn, unsaddle Johnson, and go directly to his cabin. They would have to wait until he had "slept it off" before he would bring them their treat.

When his brother and family moved to Lower Stanley in 1914, Frank stayed on to run the ranch. As Rupert and Edna got older they spent a few weeks each summer there with their Uncle. During haying season he would hire one or two men to work in the fields and the children would fill in by doing odd jobs that they were capable of. Juggy loved his niece and nephew, and they always enjoyed being on the ranch with him.

For several years the ranch was home to Juggy. Then in the early Twenties it was sold to Barney Lanier, and Juggy moved to Upper Stanley. Deciding to get out of the snow for the winters, he went to Nevada and worked in the mines, and one winter was spent in Death Valley where he worked on the construction of Death Valley Scotty's Castle. But always, with the coming of spring, Juggy was back in the Stanley-Sawtooth country.

In 1925 he bought the Stanley Garage from A.F. Kavanaugh. He built a long lean-to room along-side the large log building and used one end of it for his office and supply room, and the other end for his bedroom. All of his time and energy were devoted to this garage business. For the first few years the gasoline was hauled from Hailey in fifty-four gallon drums and pumped out with a hand pump. It sold for forty-five cents a gallon. Later a large under-ground tank was installed and Bob Horn of Hailey delivered the gas. As tourist trade increased Juggy was busy through the summer months, since his was the only service station or garage in the area at that time.

Frank "Juggy" Niece

Frank (Juggy) Niece was a stocky built man who took little short steps when he walked, causing him to sort of rock along like a little fat jug ... hence the nickname of "Juggy." He always wore blue bib overalls ... well patched for everyday wear, and for dress-up a new pair of his favorite blue bib overalls sufficed. He was an honest, upright citizen, and his cheerful good humor could brighten up the dullest day. He loved children. Phyllis Williams tells of one winter when she and her husband, Ted, were living at Upper Stanley. Juggy would offer to baby-sit with their little daughter, Mitzi, when they had occasion to be out for an evening. To quote Phyllis, "When we would get home Mitzi was *never* in her bed. Juggy would either be playing with her on the rug in front of the fireplace, or they would both be sound asleep in the big chair by the fire. Her tiny body would be draped over his fat tummy, and her little red head snuggled down on his shoulder."

Through all these years Juggy had kept track of his own daughters, but didn't see either of them from the time they were babies until they were grown. During the Thirties, Margaret, being separated from her husband, brought her daughter and came to Stanley to see her father. She spent a year or more with him, making him very proud and happy. Francis and her husband also came for a visit at that time, so after more

322

than twenty years Juggy became acquainted with his twin daughters.

It was in the late 40s that Juggy made arrangements with Susie and Russell Vaughn, who lived across the street from the garage, to have his meals with them. On the morning of October 2, 1950, when Juggy failed to arrive at their home at the usual time for breakfast, Russell went to check on him. He found him sitting in his favorite chair with his feet propped up on his desk . . . but he was dead. Since Juggy had been in exceptionally good health most of his eighty-four years, his sudden death was a shock to the enitre community. He was buried near his brother, Leslie (Tink), in the little cemetery overlooking Valley Creek. Besides his nieces and nephews, he was survived by his two daughters, three grandchildren, and his mother, who at age 103, lived in Michigan. This jolly little man was greatly missed by friends both near and far. It can truly be said that Frank (Juggy) Niece was a man who lingered in the memory of all who knew him.

View of the Sawtooth Mountains that is admired by everyone who has ever seen these jagged peaks.

Patrick Rasche:

Patrick (Pat) Rasche, a native of St. Paul, Minnesota, came to the Stanley Basin in the early 1900's. Mr. Rasche was a well educated man, having attended Notre Dame College at South Bend, Indiana, while a young man. Later, in St. Paul, Minnesota, he had been business manager for Dennis Ryan of the famous Ryan Addition which included the Ryan Hotel, Ryan Drug Co., Ryan Cigar Stand, and various other enterprises. It was in St. Paul also, that he met and married a beautiful French girl. There is a conflict on information here . . . one old timer says Pat and his wife had two daughters, another says it was one. Regardless, after a time, Pat and his wife divorced due to his excessive drinking.

With family ties broken, Pat quit his position with Dennis Ryan and became a wanderer. After traveling extensively through most of the midwest and western states, he settled in Utah for a time where he worked as Secretary-treasurer for the Ham Silver Mine. It was after this sojourn in Utah that he wandered into the Stanley Basin and fell under the spell of the towering Sawtooth Mountains. He built himself a snug log cabin near the shore of Stanley Lake, and there he began a new life-style.

Because Pat enjoyed people, and to quote one oldtimer, "He also loved whiskey," he made frequent trips to Lower Stanley, the Benner Place, or to the dredges and mines then operating in the area. Becoming interested in mining, he soon decided to "try his luck," so spent long days tramping over the mountains in the vicinity of Stanley Lake. Finally, in 1912, he located the Iron Dyke Mine. The vein assayed high in gold and copper, but even though Pat worked at it for several years, he never developed the bonanza he had hoped for.

Pat Rasche was perhaps one of the first to have the foresight to realize the full potential of the Stanley-Sawtooth Country. It was after one of his infrequent trips to Challis, Idaho, in the spring of 1913 that the following paragraph appeared in *The Challis Messenger Newspaper* printed at Challis: "Pat Rasche is a gentleman of the old school, and believes in standing up for his home country, which he does to the full extent of his six feet two inches and weight of two hundred and fifty pounds. He has been in all parts of the West and declares that the mineral wealth of Central Idaho can beat them all. He says that if we were alive to our interests we could bring thousands of people here to view the scenic grandeur and develop the golden resources of Central Idaho. We must admit that a dozen men like Mr. Rasche would raise a boom even in the midst of a dry and thirsty desert, to say nothing of Custer Country which has such natural facilities for development."

With the passing of time Pat became disillusioned with his mining venture and moved to the deserted Oscar Lerow cabin about a mile west of Upper Stanley. Since this cabin was but a short walk from town, Pat often stayed late visiting, playing cards, or having a few drinks of his favorite beverage. When he would light his "hobo lantern" in readiness for the walk home, Pat would sometimes say, "Well, its pretty late. I guess I'd better go home and throw my hat in and see if the old lady throws it back out."

One summer a daughter whom Pat hadn't seen for many years came to Stanley to visit her father. She was a pretty, dark complexioned girl who showed her French ancestry. This girl married a banker and lived at Salt Lake City, Utah.

In his last years, Pat Rasche, unable to survive longer without aid, drew Public Assistance. He moved back to his cabin near Stanley Lake, and it was there in late fall, 1940, that he was found dead.

A few other early-day Stanley-Sawtooth residents can be mentioned briefly:

August Fisher, who came to Stanley from Dillon, Montana, located land across the Salmon River from Lower Stanley. It had formerly been located by Ed Huffman who later became a forest ranger in the area. While living there, Mr. Fisher served as Stanley's postmaster for six years. In 1915 he was taken to Salt Lake City, Utah, for medical treatment, and it was there that he died. A brother, Charles Fisher, of Spokane, Washington, fell heir to the property at Stanley.

Another who came into the Stanley Basin in 1894 was *Charles Franklin*. Leaving Bonanza City, located on the Yankee Fork of the Salmon River, because of the death of Lizzie King, the woman he loved, he traveled with wagon and team to Stanley Creek. There he located placer ground, built a small cabin in a secluded little gulch leading off Stanley Creek, and spent his remaining years. In June, 1896, he was found dead in his bed by two prospectors who happened to pass that way. In

Remains of the Charles Franklin cabin (1973). in Stanley Basin.

his hand was clasped a locket which held a picture of Lizzie King. His body was wrapped in his blankets and buried beside his cabin. After his death it was discovered that through all the years he had lived in both Bonanza and Stanley, he had been living under an assumed name. His real name was Charles Michealson. He had a brother, who at that time lived in Pioneerville, or Centerville, in the Boise Basin. Charles Franklin, or Michealson, was about sixty years old at the time of his death.

Joseph Boggs, a short, stocky built man with a bushy beard, was well known in the Stanley area in the early 1900s. He had owned a sawmill in the Loon Creek country which was burned at the time of the Chinese Massacre there in 1879. Since it was supposed to have been the Sheepeater Indians who massacred the Chinese, Joe put in a claim to the Federal Government for reimbursement for the loss of his property. However, it was never proven conclusively who killed the Chinese and burned the buildings, so Joe was unable to collect.

From Loon Creek he moved to Bonanza City on the Yankee Fork where he spent many years before coming to live in the Stanley area. In later years Joe established no permanent home. He loved to travel the mountain trails on foot or on horseback, and no one knew where he might show up next . . . Loon Creek, Bonanza or Custer, Stanley or Challis. During the time Henry Willis operated the Stanley Dredge (see Stanley Dredging), Joseph Boggs spent much of his time there. An old

326

man by then, he worked at various tasks that he was capable of doing. The Willis children loved him, and soon came to affectionately call him "Uncle Joe." Where he went after leaving Stanley is not known.

Coming to the Stanley country in 1897 was *Cornelius Doty*. Little is known about "Con," as he was called, except that each year for some twenty years, he washed out a little gold from his Klondyke Claim, located on the divide between Joe's Gulch and Kelly Creek. Before coming to Stanley he had owned the Mamie Mine on Squaw Creek near Clayton, which he had sold to David Dupont in 1892.

Con had two loves in his life . . . his horses and his whiskey. Having been educated as a minister, he died an alcoholic. At one time he offered his services as the teacher for the newly organized Sunday School at Lower Stanley. (See Scrapbook chapter in this book.)

During the summer months Con's horses were pastured at the Womack and Duffy ranch in the vicinity of his Klondyke Claim, but were taken to the William Oster ranch south of Clayton for winter care. Con had a cabin at Mill Creek, which was nearby, where he spent the winters. After his death in 1919, Matt Womack and Henry Duffy were appointed as administrators of Con's estate. He had willed the only treasures he owned in this world, his horses, to people he knew were kind and who would take care of them as he had. Matt and Henry were to have five, Mae Rose, three, Affie Cothern, one, and David Driskell two mares and a colt . . . twelve horses in all.

Some of the names he chose for his horses, such as, Teddy, Dennis, Eva, Cammie, and Minnie cause one to speculate. Were these family names, or names associated with his past? Without a doubt, if it was known, his life story would fill the pages of a book. However, the one thing that lingers in the memory of the few folks left living today who knew him is the following remark, "God made water to run under bridges and for fishes to swim in. It rusts the stomach of man."

Records show that as early as 1898 *William Lutz* was interested in mining in the Stanley Basin. Where he came from, or why, no one remembers. He was a small, dark-complexioned man whose only interest seemed to be mining. He worked at the Valley Creek mine for several years, and later located the Mountain Girl Mine on Nip-N-Tuck Mountain. His last years were spent at the Sullivan Hot Springs near Clayton, Idaho.

There were those who came to the Stanley region to homestead, but for one reason or another, stayed only a short time. One of these was *Ulysses S. Pless*. In 1914 he filed on a tract of land near the John Thompson ranch. Upon making his final proof in 1919, Pless sold to Mr. Thompson, and moved on.

Two others, *Ralph Kyte* and *Elmer Focht*, came from Oakley, Idaho, and located adjoining ranches about three miles west of Upper Stanley in 1917. An amendment to the original Homestead Act was passed in February 1919, allowing homesteaders to make final proof at the end of three years providing all requirements could be met. This enabled Ralph and Elmer, both strong, husky, energetic young men to make their final proof in 1920. It was only a short time later that Elmer Focht was killed when his car ran off a narrow grade on Galena Summit. Ralph Kyte sold the property to Carroll and Esther Foley and moved to Salmon, Idaho, where he lived out the remainder of his life.

Another who came about this time was *Arthur R. Smith*. Born in Plattsville, Pennsylvania in 1861, he arrived in Idaho in the late 1880's. He lived for many years in the mining towns of Bonanza and Custer. It was while acting as Justice of the Peace at Bonanza that he acquired the nickname of "Judge Smitty." After forty years spent in the Salmon River country, Arthur R. Smith died at Stanley in September 1929, and was interred in the Stanley cemetery.

Henry Middleton with hand on his "T-Model," as he always called it, and Walt Lynch with hands in pockets.

Henry Middleton, another oldtimer, had settled first in the Sawtooth Valley. Later, after moving to Stanley Creek and locating placer ground, he became a familiar sight around the little town. He had a Model-T Ford which he called his "T-Model," and which he said could "pass anything on the road." Quite often after he had visited the Bar in Stanley for a few hours, Henry's friends would worry about him driving home, but he would say, "Oh, don't worry about me. 'T-Model knows the way. She'll take me home.'" However, on one occasion Henry's trusty old car failed him. He rolled it over a grade a short distance from his cabin, and although Henry was not injured, his "T-Model" was a total wreck.

In 1948 Henry deeded seven claims located along Stanley Creek to a Mrs. Mary, or Mamie, Martin, of Hagerman, Idaho, for the sum of "Love and affection," as the deed stated. Mrs. Martin was either a sister or niece of Henry Middleton.

First coming into the Stanley Basin in the early 1920s as a sheepherder for the Bacon and Goodman sheep men, *John Weidman* became intrigued with the idea that there was still "gold in them thar hills." The ground at the head of Kelly Creek that had once been The Sturkey-Challis Placer was open for location, so John took advantage of the opportunity, located the claims, and moved into the old Sturkey cabins.

John Weidman working at old Sturkey Placer in 1940s.

Buildings at site of Sturkey Placer used by John Weidman.

It was John Weidman who had the large dam and reservoir constructed, the remains of which can still be seen today, and it was due to his mining there in later years that the original Sturkey-Challis Placer came to be called "The Weidman Camp."

Through the many years that Weidman lived in the Stanley area, he became known as quite a character. Being exceptionally strong for his size and age, he delighted in challenging younger men to feats of strength such as arm wrestling or weight lifting, and nine times out of ten he would be the victor. And John made home brew that, according to those who sampled it, "Had a kick like a Missouri mule." He could also be classed as one of those "dirty old batches," especially in his later years.

By the early 1860s John moved from the Sturkey cabin to one of the cabins left vacant at the Stanley Dredge camp where he lived for a few years. Finally, old and unable to care for himself, he was taken to the Cassabella Nursing Home at Salmon, Idaho where he died. He was survived by a daughter, Mrs. Viola Evans of San Francisco, California, and a niece at Hagerman, Idaho.

Another... not really an oldtimer, but one who came to Stanley country about 1923, was *T.R. (Trapper) Green*. Born at Clay, Missouri, on July 10, 1869, he had worked for a railroad company in Canada for many years before coming to Idaho.

T.R. "Trapper" Greene with some of his winters catch.

Trapper lived in a cabin at Upper Stanley, but spent much of his time out in the mountains. He guided hunting parties through the hunting season and trapped during the winter months. Trapper Green passed away at Mackay, Idaho on April 3, 1940, and was buried there.

William (Bill) Wall is another oldtimer who spent more than fifty years in the Stanley Basin country. A carpenter by trade, Bill came to the area while a young man. He worked in the mines for a time, then as more people moved in, he worked on the construction of numerous homes and other buildings throughout the region. Living in his own home at Upper Stanley today, Bill still recalls "the way it was in the 'Good old days.' "

Now we come to the end of our long list of "The Single Ones," who, each in his own way shared in the making of the history of the Stanley-Sawtooth country.

EARLY DAY HOLIDAYS

Long before automobiles and radios became common, as in other rural areas across the Nation, people who lived in the Stanley-Sawtooth country made their own entertainment. Outside of the small town of Stanley, the majority of residents found themselves isolated for weeks at a time on their home-steads or at mine properties. Consequently, when they did get together, they made the most of it. National Holidays were always something to look forward to and plan for . . . especially the Fourth of July. By then the winter snows had melted, spring work on the ranches was caught up, and the weather nice and warm, making the occasion an ideal time for a real celebration. This, as well as all the community affairs, was simple, clean entertainment enjoyed by both young and old folks. One example of the way the Sawtooth people went all out to ensure a good time for all is shown in the following story.

In the summer of 1917, when the United States was caught up in the midst of World War I and every American citizen was feeling a sense of patriotic duty to their country, Stanley Basin folks began to plan for their Fourth of July celebration. It was decided a large open air pavillion would be built that would afford plenty of room for eating and dancing. Once the decision was made, Charley Thompson, who at that time was operating a sawmill back of the Thompson ranch, furnished the lumber, and every person who could spare the time gathered at Lower Stanley to help erect the building. The men each brought their own saws, hammers, squares, and nails, pitched in with a will, and when the pavillion was completed, measured about 20' x 30' with boards extending three feet up from the outside edge of the floor and railed on the top. Around the inside of the board siding benches were made and nailed to provide seating space. The floor was constructed of rough lumber, but when the boards were fitted tightly together and nailed down as smoothly as possible, it would serve as a nice dance floor. On the day before the celebration, several loads of freshly cut pine boughs were hauled in and laid over the top of the framework to form a roof of sorts. The inside of the framework was draped with red, white, and blue bunting to lend a festive air, lanterns were hung for lighting, and a long table, draped with bunting, was set up down the middle of the floor.

The next day (Fourth of July) dawned sunny and clear. Residents from everywhere in the Basin and the Valley came in wagons, buckboards, buggies, and on horseback to get there. Friends greeted friends, and the women piled the table high with plates of sandwiches, salads, cakes, pies, pickles and other various goodies. As pre-arranged, Mrs. Leslie Niece made and furnished the coffee. The Finlay family had filled their ice house with ice the previous winter, enabling Mrs. Finlay to set up an ice cream and lemonade stand. Actually, the ice cream was more like sweetened milk that had been flavored with vanilla or chocolate, but the children loved it, keeping their parents passing out dimes with which to buy a dish. The lemonade lacked enough fresh lemons for true flavor . . . probably a half dozen lemons to a gallon of water, sweetened and a bit of lemon extract added. Nevertheless, the drink sold too, because it contained ice and was cold.

By mid-afternoon a large crowd had gathered in and around the pavillion. Mrs. Josephine Thompson started things off by leading the group in the singing of The Star Spangled Banner. Pat Rasche followed her with a heart-felt rendition of the Gettysburg address. This was followed by other songs, speeches and recitations, and then the contests began. Foot races caused much merriment . . . especially the fat ladies race. Mrs. Mae Rose, Mary Marshall, and Sadie Merritt were among the entries. Of course, none of them ran very fast, or very far, but each was given a prize for their efforts. Fleet-footed Mary Clark, oldest daughter of Brazilla Clark, who, with his family had driven up to Stanley from Sunbeam Dam where they were living at the time, won all the girls races. There were barrel races, sack races, tug-o-war contests, and horse-shoe pitching contests . . . the latter enjoyed by the men. Also there was much visiting and relaxing by everyone.

Late in the afternoon, when the races and contests were over, everyone congregated at the table to partake of a hearty lunch. Then the table was cleared and taken down to make room for the dancing. By that time dusk had settled over the little community. Trapper Fisher tuned up his fiddle and the dancing began. Surely anyone who was there could never forget that fun-filled night. The smell of pine boughs overhead, the soft glow of the kerosene lanterns, red, white, and blue bunting stirred now and then by a slight breeze, stars winking from the outside darkness, and the voice of Lancelot (Slivers) Hawkins calling out, "Everybody grab your partner for the Over the Waves Waltz."

On into the night, the dancing went on . . . . Two-steps, Polkas, Waltzs, Quadrillas or Square Dances, and Virginia Reels. A few who were there even knew how to dance the French Minuet, a very graceful and beautiful dance. A break was taken at midnight for more refreshment and to rest, and allow the mothers time to bed down their children in the Leslie Niece bunkhouse. Then the dancing was resumed. Periodically, when Trapper would crack down on "Little Brown Jug" or some other foot-stomping ditty, Slivers Hawkins would break in with, "Come on folks . . . . EVERYBODY! Grab your partners!" and around and around the dancers would go while tall, slim Slivers mingled among the dancers singing out the call:
"Oh . . . chase the possum
Chase the squirrel,
Chase that pretty girl
'Round the world' ".

Occasionally, Abe Womack, there in Stanley from Hailey, would relieve Trapper Fisher on the fiddle. Until the sun touched the tops of the mountains, the dancing went on. This was the signal for the last dance. Trapper drew his bow, stood up, and with blue eyes twinkling, played "Home Sweet Home." When the last strains had died away, someone yelled, "HOW ABOUT SOME BREAKFAST?"

At that, off the ladies went to the Niece home kitchen where they made hot cakes with plenty of fresh butter and syrup, and bacon and eggs for those who wanted to stay and eat. Several families, with chores waiting for them back at their ranches, gathered up their children, loaded them into wagons and buggies and headed for home, declaring as they did so, "This has been the best Fourth of July celebration in the whole darned U.S.A."

Back at their respective ranches and properties after the midsummer celebration, the rest of the summer and fall were busy times for the Basin and Valley people. Thanksgiving was usually more of a family affair with invitations extended to different ones of the old bachelors and single men living there. By then snow had begun to choke the roads. But by the time Christmas arrived, those who were well and could make it at all, attended the school plays put on by the students, and the Christmas party at the little schoolhouse in Stanley. This made an excellent excuse for neighbors and friends to get together again for an exchange of news and to visit. Yet while grown-ups enjoyed the get-togethers to the fullest, the children enjoyed them even more. Today, these events are treasured memories of various oldtimers who had a part in one or more of the plays. In fact, the way they tell it, such an affair stands out as a favorite Christmas in 1916 there:

Mrs. Josephine Thompson was the teacher that year. When she began making plans for a Christmas party, her students were overjoyed since this would be the first event of its kind ever held in the little one-room schoolhouse at Stanley. An order for gifts was made out and mailed, a program planned, invitations sent out to parents and friends of the students, and arrangements made for having a large Christmas tree ready to set up at the designated time. Cold weather had come early to the Sawtooth region that year. When the Salmon River formed an ice gorge at "Shotgun Rapids," about eight miles below Lower Stanley, preventing the stage from coming through with the mail, Mrs. Thompson began to fear the children would

Road up Salmon River in winter. Taken just below Shotgun Rapids. About 1916.

be without gifts from Santa Claus on Christmas Eve. Even so, she went ahead with her plans and practice sessions for the play and the Christmas program.

As the day drew near and still no mail arrived at Stanley, it was learned that many packages had gotten as far as Robinson Bar and were stockpiled there until the stage could get on up to Stanley. But the ice gorge held. Mrs. Thompson's concern was shared by parents and children alike. A few days before Christmas, several of the menfolks decided to try to do something about it. Making arrangements by telephone for the stage driver on the Challis to Robinson Bar end of the run to pick up the mail and packages piled high at Robinson Bar and come on up the Salmon River as far as he could below the ice gorge, on the morning of December 22nd, the men hitched a team to a sled and started out, hoping to be able to meet him. By making their way carefully over the narrow, icy road, and by shoveling a runway through the snowslides, and working their way above the gorge, they did make it.

Back at Stanley, Mrs. Thompson and the children watched and waited anxiously, and when the sled was sighted coming up the road, their joy knew no bounds. Now they would all have a glorious Christmas. Excitement ran high the next day when the Christmas tree, so tall it touched the ceiling, was brought in and set up in the middle of the little schoolroom. For weeks the children had been gathering and saving tinfoil with which to cover cardboard cutouts to hang on the tree. *(Note: Aluminum foil as we know it today was unheard of in those days.)* The youngsters made their cutouts and strung popcorn for the decorations. Mrs. Thompson placed candles in old-fashioned holders on the tree. Then with the children's help, she piled the desks to one side of the room leaving space to get around the tree and making seating room for the grownups who would be there for the "big party." At one end of the room a small platform was erected for a stage, and a curtain hung nearby behind which the children would stand until his or her turn to recite.

On Christmas Eve all was in readiness. When everyone had gathered and the adults were seated, the program began. As each child emerged from behind the curtain and gave his or her reading, recited a poem, or sang a song, parents were proud indeed.

Rosemary Paul Hoskins remembers five of the little girls

Christmas Program at Stanley School.... Left to right... Myrta Merritt, Virginia Cothern, Lulu Kregor, Rosemary Paul, Sadie Merritt.

(she was one of the group) were dressed in Japanese kimonos and sat on the floor around a tiny table with small teacups on it while they sang a song about the Japanese children in a far away land. "I thought the kimonos were so pretty with all the bright colors and the large sleeves," she said on recalling the event. "We also held little fans in our hands as we posed and sang our song."

After each child had done his part, the candles on the tree were lighted, and Santa Claus, who was thought to be played by Doc Cothern, made his entrance, passing out a little bag of candy to them and a gift for everyone there ... both children and adults. These were mostly fun things and actually inexpensive, but the pleasure derived by the recipients gave the party a delightful holiday spirit, to say the least. Rupert Niece and Edna Niece McGown remember that there was a bottle with a nipple on it filled with tea water for their uncle, Frank Niece. One man received a funny little frog that, when wound, would hop about, and another got a monkey on a string. So it went. When all the gifts were passed out, Santa Claus kissed each of the little girls and took his leave. After much merriment while the gifts were unwrapped and enjoyed, the folks departed for their homes.

As winter wore on, people in the Stanley-Sawtooth country again longed for a bit of recreation away from their homes and ranches. Many residents in the immediate Stanley area oftentimes used Washington's birthday or St. Patrick's day as a good time to have a dance and party. Sometimes these were held in someone's home, but in 1918 a George Washington's birthday party was held in the large upstairs dance hall of the Benner Hotel. It was a masquerade dance, was planned well in advance, and everyone invited who could come. Mrs. Ellen Niece was especially talented at making costumes, and that year, without revealing her own mode of dress to anyone, she persuaded Jennie Buchanan (Mrs. Bert Buchanan) to mask as Martha Washington, even helping her to make the costume.

On the night of the dance, Trapper Fisher was unable to be there to play his fiddle. The Buchanans arrived, and on learning that Trapper would not be there, Bert offered to pump the pedals of the player piano for the music, "Since I don't dance anyway," he said. Everything was just getting underway when in stepped George Washington straight out of a picture from an American history book . . . complete in his tight, knee-length, black pants, ruffled shirt, frock-tailed coat, white powdered wig, and Quaker buckled shoes. "Who is he?" the crowd whispered. But no one could guess, and the dancing began. Shortly George sought Martha's hand for a dance. Then another dance. Soon, Bert, at the piano, began to notice all the attention George was paying to Martha, (his wife Jennie), and with every turn the couple made around the floor he followed them with his eyes. Finally, reluctant to incite her husband's jealousy farther, Martha went over and sat beside him on the piano bench. After that, when George asked her to dance, she declined, saying she was tired.

Midnight came and it was time for everyone to unmask. When George Washington ripped off his mask, there stood Ellen Niece, who walked over and did a low curtsy in front of Martha Washington and her husband, Bert. A cheer went up from the crowd and everyone laughed and applauded as she turned and curtsied toward them . . . all that is, except Bert Buchanan. He became so angry that he grabbed Jennie by the arm and insisted they go home then and there. No one paid much attention, however, since all knew how Bert was about Jennie, and they went on to finish out the evening with refreshments and having fun. It seems every costumed person there made a great effort to act out the character he had chosen to represent. For instance, Affie Cothern and her brother, Eddie Martin, were dressed as Maggie and Jiggs (funny paper characters), and Maggie had spent a great part of the evening chasing Jiggs around the hall with a rolling pin as he tried to get up a poker game "with the boys" and some of the other things he did in the comic strip. Thus, Ellen Niece was merely acting the role of the costume she wore.

At the dances and parties, sometimes taffy was made and set to cool for the children to pull. A few of the women always made coffee and fixed a lunch to be set out at midnight. While the taffy was cooling the youngsters would play games around in the kitchen, and when it was ready, each child would be given a small piece of the candy to pull. "We didn't always do a good job," one oldtimer, who was a child at that time said, "But we sure had a good time doing it."

Usually the St. Patrick's Day parties were held in someone's home. The music would be Irish tunes, some would give Irish readings or recite Irish poems, games would be played and many Irish jokes told. But regardless of whether it happened to be a George Washington dance or a St. Patrick's day party, those in attendance were always reluctant to leave when it was time to go home. And that is how it was there during the early days . . . a simple way of life with simple, clean entertainment provided for and enjoyed by one and all, no matter what age.

Birthday party at the old Cooper place in Stanley Basin. (1912). Left to right . . . Mr. Cady (Dredge watchman), Matt Womack, Herbert Marshall, Paul Strieder, Joe Boggs, Henry Duffy, and Mrs. Paul Strieder in the foreground.

339

BOOTLEGGING FOR AN
"HONEST BUCK"

BOOTLEGGING!! Yes ... Stanley Country had its bootleggers during the depression years. Two men who started making "moonshine," first as a pastime, and later as a profitable enterprise, were Arch Savage and Ward "Slim" Hendricks, and it was said by those who sampled their "brew" that they made "the best damned moonshine that ever hit the country." Both men had arrived in the area in 1927, and both had spent the winter of 1927 and '28 working at the Seafoam Mine. They were fun-loving, adventurous young fellows, and soon formed a lasting friendship. It was through this friendship, a few years later, that they decided to try a little bootlegging.

Ward "Slim" Hendricks was known as "Slim" Fulton when he first came to the Stanley Country. While living in Washington he had been involved in a bit of illegal "horse-trading," as well as a bootlegging venture, and consequently had landed in jail. After being bailed out by a girl friend, he decided that he had better look for a new location and make a new start. This was when "Slim" came to Idaho, and eventually to the Seafoam Mine.

"Slim" was a handsome young man, tall and broad-shouldered, quite striking in his western style clothes and fancy western boots. He was the rugged outdoor type, and was never happier than when out in the mountains on some camping or hunting expedition. He was an expert horseman, and rode in the Stanley rodeos.

It was not until he met Mildred Cothern, oldest daughter of "Doc" and Affie Cothern in 1929 that he revealed his real name... Ward Hendricks. Even then the name of "Slim" stuck, and this was what he was called by all who knew him. "Slim" and Mildred were married in 1930, and went to live on

340

the George Cumine ranch during the winter of 1930 and '31. With time on his hands, Slim decided to set a "batch" of "moonshine" ... "just to pass the time away."

The next summer, leaving the still and moonshine making equipment at the ranch, Slim and Mildred moved to Stanley. It was that fall that Slim and his friend, Arch Savage, talked the stiuation over and decided that Arch should take over the equipment and "run off a little moonshine" that winter. Their "outfit" could be set up in the blacksmith shop which was located behind the George Cumine ranch home.

Arch Savage, along with his half-sister, Geraldine Peters, and his mother, Cozette Peters, had moved from Montana to the Stanley Basin in 1927. Cozette, being a niece of Matt Womack, one of the Basin's early pioneers, had inherited his property when Matt had died earlier that year, so the family settled on the Womack and Duffy ranch. After working at the Seafoam Mine during that first winter, Arch did the ranch work, worked at various other jobs, and did some trapping in the wintertime, always managing to earn a livelihood. Since the Womack ranch was not far from the George Cumine ranch, the bootlegging sounded like a good way to make an extra "buck" or two.

In 1932, Arch was married to Pauline Walker, who, at the time, was living with her sister, Kathleen Markle, at the Stanley Ranger Station. Arch and Pauline, like Slim and Mildred Hendricks, spent the first winter of their married life at the

Archie Savage with dog team used to haul supplies during winter of 1932 and 1933.

George Cumine ranch. By now the "bootlegging" had developed into a profitable enterprise. Large quantities of sugar, barley, corn, and rye were bought through the Gillispie Store in Upper Stanley and hauled to the ranch before the snow came. The roads were not kept open at that time, so if they ran out of any necessary items they would have to be hauled in by dog-sled.

To quote Arch, "For each batch, or barrel, we would put in about twenty pounds of grain, fifty pounds of sugar, thirty gallons of water, and a little yeast to start the fermentation. We would set about six, fifty gallon barrels at a time. If it was real cold, we would set lighted kerosene lanterns between the barrels for warmth. We had a sawed off broom handle that was just right for stirring the mash. It took about seven days to ferment off all the sugar, then we would strain the liquid into the still, or "the can" as we called it. Each batch would make about twenty-five gallons of liquid. The remainder of the mash would be returned to the barrels, more grain, sugar, and water added, and the fermenting process started all over again."

In further describing the operation he told of the "still" itself being made of a copper boiler with a long piece of copper tubing coming out of a hole in the lid. This tubing curved down into a tub which held about thirty gallons of cold water. It coiled around, then extended out over a container into which the finished whiskey dripped. They could "drip off" about ten gallons in a days time. A furnace built of flat rocks, in which a wood fire was burning, was used to heat the liquid in the copper boiler. It was never to boil, but had to be heated to the point where it would steam freely. The lid was sealed so the steam was forced through the tube and condensed as it passed through the cold water. They had quite a unique way to seal the lid. They would make a stiff flour and water dough which they would spread around the edge of the lid. Then a long strip of cheesecloth was wrapped tightly around and tied to hold the dough in place and force it into the crack, thus sealing the lid onto the boiler. Occasionally through the distilling process, a lighted match would be passed under the drip, and if it failed to keep burning, they knew that the alcohol was all dripped off.

When they finished with a batch of grain it would be dumped into the creek near the house. After the snow melted in the spring, Pauline, Arch's wife, would be amused by watching the antics of the blackbirds that gathered to eat the grain that had been spilled along the creek bank. She said, "They sure did look silly hopping and flopping, trying to fly and landing flat with wings outspread, spinning around in circles, and doing everything but what a bird should do. They were probably the only birds in the country that were too "high" to fly, or that had a hangover after eating." There was a muskrat that feasted on the fermented grain a few times too, but they wouldn't see him after he dived back into the water.

During the winter the snows were deep, but the Savages kept a watchful eye out for the approach of strangers. One day Arch, to quote him, "saw the damnedest looking contraption" about two miles up through the field. He hooked up his dog-team and headed out to meet it, thinking it might be revenue men. It turned out to be two young men who had been trapping in Bear Valley, and who were on their way out with their furs, traps, and all their equipment loaded onto a hand sled. One was pulling and the other was pushing. Arch helped them down to his place and Pauline cooked dinner for them. After dinner Arch traded them whiskey for some of their fur, then he took them on to Stanley with his dog-team.

Storing the finished whiskey was quite a problem, since wooden kegs were in short supply. The whiskey would be "double run," which would make it about 150 proof, then before it was sold it would be diluted to 80 or 90 proof. The kegs of 150 proof would be buried in the snow, and as the snow thawed and settled in the spring the kegs would begin to show. More snow would be shoveled and piled on top of them, but as that too disappeared, the kegs would be hauled to various caches in the timber, or taken to town to be sold.

On one occasion before the road opened in early spring, Arch was taking a keg of whiskey to Stanley with his dog-team, and his wife was to accompany him. He tied the keg firmly to the sled and Pauline sat astraddle of it. As they traveled along a sidling place near Valley Creek the sled tipped over sending both Pauline and the keg of whiskey rolling down toward the water. As they told of this experience, Arch said with his hearty chuckle, "The dogs got away from me." Pauline, laughing merrily said, "I was pregnant at the time, and we wondered what the baby might turn out to be." Upon being asked which Arch rescued first, the whiskey or her, Pauline answered, "Oh, the whiskey, of course. He left me to pick myself up."

Another time when Slim was hauling a load of whiskey to town, he decided to drive his truck across the field rather than chance being seen on the main road. This was soon after the winter snow had melted leaving the field wet and soggy in places, and Slim ended up mired down in the mud. He had to go across the Basin to the Thompson ranch and get John Thompson to come with a team to pull him out. The Thompsons knew of the bootleg operation, for on several occasions as Mrs. Thompson visited with friends on the telephone she would say, "Well, it must be paying off over at Savages today. I see a big smoke coming out of the blacksmith shop."

About two hundred gallons of "moonshine" would be "run off" during a winter's time. This would be divided between the partners, and each would attend to the sale of his share. They usually sold it for $10 a gallon, and it cost approximately $2 a gallon to make it, so by spring the Hendricks and Savages would realize quite a sum of money. As Arch put it, "It was a good way to make an honest dollar. We would go in in the fall with nothing, and come out in the spring with a pretty good little stake."

There were other local people who made "moonshine" on a small scale, and at one time some people from Mackay, Idaho set up a large still in the vicinity of Anderson Gulch and the old Womack and Duffy ranch. This operation was shortlived, however, for one day in their absence their camp and "outfit" burned to the ground, causing them to leave the country. Then, in December of 1933, the 21st Amendment was passed repealing the Prohibition Act, and all bootlegging ceased. Arch Savage and Slim Hendricks turned to other fields. In later years, when Arch was asked if he would object to having the story of his bootlegging days in the Stanley Basin printed in a book, he said, "Hell no, we did anything we could in those days to make an honest dollar."

For the next several years Arch and Pauline made their home in Lower Stanley. Three sons, Robert, William, and Jerry were born to them, and a large comfortable log home was built. Then in 1946, Arch, along with his sister, Geraldine, purchased the Stanley Store from Floyd Markle. They ran this business for two years before selling to Dan and Norma O'Conner of Challis, Idaho. The Savage family then moved to Challis where a daughter, Katherine, was born, and where Arch worked for the Forest Service until his retirement in 1970.

Going back to Slim and Mildred Hendricks: In 1931 and '32

344

they had built what is now known as The Gateway, about a mile North of Lower Stanley on Highway 93. They had a dance hall, lunch counter, and cabins, and, if you knew the ropes, a drink of "moonshine" could be purchased "out back." They named their place "The Red Rooster." One of the first dances held in the hall there in 1932, was Arch and Pauline Savage's wedding dance. While living there two sons, Mike and Dale, were welcomed into the Hendricks family.

In the early 1940s Slim took Herman Schutt in as a partner, and it was then that the name "The Red Rooster" was changed to "The Gateway." Not long after this, Slim sold his interest to his partner, and the family moved to a ranch about three miles West of Challis, Idaho. After a few years there, they moved on to Montana, then, because of Slim's health, they moved to Palmdale, California where Slim passed away in 1975. Through the years the Savage and the Hendricks families kept in touch, and the friendship formed in those early days in the Stanley Basin has endured to this day.

CATCHING UP WITH THE TIMES

Roads and Highways:

Dates appear a bit confused as to the exact year the wagon road was built and completed over Galena Mountain connecting the Wood River country and the Sawtooth Valley. Idaho Historical records indicate it was completed in 1880, but a sign at the Lookout on the side of the mountain overlooking the Valley states 1881. In any case, it was a toll road constructed by the Columbia & Beaver Company of New York who were engaged in mining near Sawtooth City at that time. Alturas County, later changed to Blaine County, granted a franchise in August, 1881 for the road, listing the following rates of toll:

1 wagon and a single span of horses, mules,
or yoke of cattle $1.50
Each additional span of horses, mules, or cattle 50
Each additional trail or other wagon 75
Each horse and carriage 1.50
Each horse and rider 50
Each loaded pack animal 12½
Each unloaded pack animal 06½
Each loose animal or stock 10
Hogs and sheep, each 05

At first the road was extremely hazardous, and although the grades were lessened from time to time until 1918 when it was rebuilt, a trip with a freighting outfit took two days to make . . . one day to reach the top of the mountain and another to make the descent. The coming of the automobile changed the picture some, but even after the road was rebuilt it was still narrow, still perilous, and still very steep-graded in places. Motor cars often backed up the mountain in reverse gear. Esther Foley, a Valley resident in the Twenties, said that in those early days she and her husband called the Galena Summit "Hell's Own Pass." To slow descent when going downgrade, logs were tied

346

*Esther and Carroll Foley with their Model-T on the road over Galena Summit.
(1922) "Hell's Own Pass."*

on the rear of the cars in the same way they were used to help hold down the speed of wagons. For many years a pile of these logs could be seen near the base of the mountain on both the Valley and the Wood River sides. For the most part, the road was closed during the winter months ... especially after the snow became too deep to shovel out by hand. On this note, a group of men would get together and work as a team, making their way up the side of the mountain and down again. During the closures mail and supplies were brought in by dogsled or by carriers on snowshoes.

Back in 1890, when the Arthur McGown, Sr. family moved into the yet unsettled Stanley Basin from the Yankee Fork mining district, the only road into the area was over the Galena Summit. From Stanley down the Salmon River there was only a horse trail. In her diary, telling of the move, Mrs. McGown wrote: "Frank Cook had to bring our wagon in by going over Trail Creek Summit to Ketchum, then over Galena Summit down into the Sawtooth Valley and on to Stanley."

The State Wagon Road, built in 1894-95, from the mouth of Yankee Fork coming up alongside the Salmon River was a great boon to the Basin. Charley Tassel, with the help of twelve or fourteen men from the Yankee Fork, did the job. However, this road too, was very narrow with numerous sharp, dangerous curves. Records state that in April 1900, Custer County Commissioners authorized expenditures of $300 for repairs on this road ... a small sum indeed by today's standards. Although falling rocks and slides are still a hazard along the route, they were more so in those days, due mostly to the narrow, twisting terrain. Arthur McGown, Sr., in Challis from Stanley on April 9, 1895, told the Challis *Silver Messenger Newspaper,* "The State Wagon Road from the mouth of the Yankee Fork to Stanley is in horrible condition and is being made almost impassable by rolling rocks and land slides."

Through the years many Stanley residents sent protests to the Custer County Commissioners concerning the lack of funds spent on the county roads in the area. In May 1922, the following amusing item appeared in the Stanley News Column: "Stanley country has for the past few days been enveloped in a mysterious haze, or smoke. This seems unusual at this time of year. There being no "wise men" among us, we cannot be sure of the reason, but the most feasible reason, we conclude, is the terrible condition of our county road between Stanley and Robinson Bar. The stage driver is a man of few words, BUT!!!"

First road up Salmon River. Taken at Shotgun Rapids about 1916.

Nevertheless, residents and tourists were happy to have the road because of the driving distance saved when going to or from Challis to Stanley and on to Bear Valley and the Boise Basin. It was said that travelers over the route numbered from one to two hundred per week in the summer of 1900. At any rate, in ensuing years the road was well traveled. As the Stanley-Sawtooth country became more populated, finally in the spring of 1922, the Central Idaho Industrial Association was formed. Meeting with the Forestry officials on May 1st that year, they were encouraged to learn of appropriations for road development traversing the area. This was the beginning of U.S. Highway 93. Engineering for the road from over Galena Summit down through the Valley, into Stanley and on to Clayton, was done during that summer and fall. Actual construction began in the spring of 1923. Resolution for the new highway read: "With completion of a through highway, touching Stanley from both ways, and connecting easterly and westerly points of interest to the tourists who come our way, our section of Idaho will be put on the map."

Also in 1922, the Forest Department allotted $100,000 for the start of the Boise-Lowman road (State Highway 21) beginning along the Payette River and near enough to be reached by trail from Stanley. Eventually, this road was extended into the

349

Stanley Basin where it connects with Highway 93, first as a gravel road and later widened and blacktopped as we know it today.

Highway 93 too, began as a gravel road and was constructed in sections with different construction companies doing the work. Items appearing in the *Challis Messenger,* formerly the *Silver Messenger Newspaper,* noted: *December 21, 1927 . . .* Sawtooth roads get $214,500 Forest money. Highway from Galena Summit to Stanley, and from Salmon (town of) to Montana line will benefit.

June 4, 1930 . . . A contract has been let to Utah Construction Company for 12 miles of highway from the foot of Galena Summit down through the Sawtooth Valley to the second bridge across the Salmon River.

April 8, 1931. . . . The last right-of-way necessary for the construction of the "Sawtooth Park Highway" (Highway 93) in the Stanley area, was purchased from Ward Hendrick of Stanley for the sum of $600. This road is paid for entirely by the Bureau of Public Roads, but Custer County pays for the right-of-ways through private property.

May 25, 1931 . . . Work on Highway 93, down the Salmon River from Stanley to Basin Creek will begin today.

April 13, 1932 . . . Opening of the Stanley road was completed this week, and it is now possible for cars to travel Highway 93 to Stanley. Stanley stage made its first trip of the year by car all the way from Challis to Stanley. (This item is in reference to snow and slides being cleared on the route.)

August 10, 1932 . . . $214,000 has been allocated to the Bureau of Public Roads for the "Sawtooth Park Highway" (Highway 93) from Basin Creek to a point near Robinson Bar.

October 5, 1932. . . . Max J. Kuney Company of Spokane, Washington was awarded the contract for seven miles of highway from Basin Creek to the steele bridge above Robinson Bar. Local labor is being hired. The bid was $139,758.

Another contract was let for the building of Highway 93 on the stretch of road from Robinson Bar to below the Sullivan Hot Springs in the summer of 1934, and then again in 1935 to extend it on down to below Clayton. In April of 1935 when the snow was cleared from the Galena Summit section of the highway, drifts were said to have been some fifteen feet deep in places. If snowfall was extra heavy, as it was in 1936, drifts often measured even deeper. Snowslides in the narrow, steep-sided defiles along the route were also a threat and a hazard

350

when a warming trend happened to occur as it did in February of 1936. That month over sixty slides came down in the Sunbeam area alone. Thus, as can be concluded, several stretches of the highway had to be closed for weeks at a time in the winter months of the Thirties and Forties. Even in the Fifties, after the road was blacktopped, when severe storms piled numerous and deep drifts on the section going over Galena Summit, highway crews were unable to clear the road in a matter of hours as they do today. Then, with equipment not as efficient as today, it often required many days to make the road passable.

When cars first came on the scene in the Stanley-Sawtooth country, about 1910-11, horses frightened by the motor's noise could turn a meeting between the two on a mountain road into one of disaster. To lessen such danger, auto drivers usually took the precaution of tooting the horn when rounding curves and on mountain grades and switchbacks ... a practice that is still used sometimes by drivers on back country, one-lane roads as a way of warning other drivers coming their way. Tourists began arriving in autos as early as 1911 in the Salmon River area. Model T Fords were the most common car, followed by the Stanley Steamers and other makes. By 1924, most makes of the time were in prominence along Highway 93 ... owned by tourists and local residents alike. One of the latter tells of driving the route between Challis and Stanley and meeting tourists along the way, saying, "One day my husband and I came upon a lady waving her arms frantically as she walked toward us in the middle of the road. Thinking something terrible must have happened, we stopped to ask her what the trouble was ... and just then a car came into view driving slowly around the sharp curve ahead. The woman told us, "That's my husband coming, and I didn't want you to run into him." After that we wondered if she had walked ahead of him around all the curves on the river road. If she did, she certainly had a long walk."

Walking done by early residents in the region was very commonplace however, and it was never unusual to meet a man on foot. For that matter, if there was no hurry, a great many people preferred walking to riding when they wanted to go someplace. One oldtimer, enroute from Challis to Stanley took four days to make the trek on foot, and one rainy evening in camp sat down and wrote:

"I gathered up some willows
That had grown along the river,
Built a parody on fire
And had a good eight hour shiver,
Then, as the morning sun
Kissed the top of the mountain peaks,
And the early bird shook hands with the
worm,
I continued to journey on."

Telephones:

The telephone played a major role in the changes that took place in the Stanley-Sawtooth country shortly after the turn of the century. The United States Forest Service built and maintained the first lines. Starting at Challis, Idaho in 1911, a line was built first to Parker Mountain, then on to Loon Creek, to the Cape Horn Ranger Station, and down through the Stanley Basin to the Stanley Ranger Station. Any resident or traveler was welcome to stop by a ranger station and make necessary calls, but it wasn't until the late Teens that telephones were installed in some of the business places in the area. These were Forest Service phones.

Forest Service telephone at Redfish Lake Creek for public use during the 1920's.

By 1919 when the Niece Brothers Store was opened for business at Upper Stanley both the Challis Forest and the Sawtooth Forest installed telephones in a booth at one corner of the store. Mr. Niece, or anyone who was working at the store, could relay messages from one area to the other. Later a switch was installed, so that parties on the Challis line could call Mr. Niece, have him ring a party on the Sawtooth line, then push in the switch enabling them to talk directly to their party ... or vice versa. It was at this time, too, that a telephone for public use was installed by the Sawtooth National Forest under a shelter on a tree beside the road, near Redfish Lake Creek.

These early day telephones were the box type that were hung on a wall. Each phone installed had a designated number of rings to which they answered; such as two short and two long rings would perhaps call the Niece Brothers Store, or one long and three short rings would get Mrs. Law's Store in Lower Stanley. The party calling did the ringing by turning a little crank on the right side of the telephone box. All area rings could be heard at each place a phone was installed. This led to people "listening in" or "eavesdropping," if you will.

One instance of this that is well remembered was while Mrs. Law was running the store in Lower Stanley. Mrs. Law was Irish ... had a firy Irish temper and was always ready with a sharp retort to the jokes some of the area residents liked to play on her. One day Ed Huffman, the ranger at the Stanley Ranger Station was talking to Brazilla Clark, then the watchman at the Sunbeam Dam. Hearing a heavy breathing on the line, he guessed that Mrs. Law was "listening in," so he said, "Say, Brazilla, have you heard the latest news?" "No," answered Brazilla, "What is it?" "Well," said Ed, "Mrs. Law shaved today." "Why did she shave?" asked Brazilla, and Ed replied, "Her boy friend, Lew Clawson, is coming up to see her." At that Mrs. Law, very indignant, yelled, "HE IS NOT!" and banged down the receiver.

A later amusing incident of "eavesdropping" occurred after telephones were installed in many of the homes in the Clayton vicinity. It was generally known that a certain lady whom we shall call "Lillie," often succumbed to the desire to "listen in" when she would hear the phone ring. On this day Tillie Ennis was visiting over the phone with a friend in Clayton when they heard the click of a receiver being lifted off the hook. The friend, surmising that it was Lillie, went on talking for a few seconds, then suddenly said, "Hey, Lillie, I smell your beans

353

burning!!" Without thinking Lillie exclaimed, "Oh, DAMN!!" and hastily hung up the receiver.

By the Thirties many area residents had telephones in their homes. These were still on the Forest Service line, and still the box type that hung on the wall, but were connected with the switchboard in Challis, thus enabling the Stanley residents to call through the operator, or "Central" as the operator was called, to make long distance calls. The same was true on the Sawtooth Forest line, with "Central" located at Hailey, Idaho.

In 1938 a branch of the Mountain States Telephone line was built from Hailey into the Sawtooth Valley and on to Stanley, and in 1955, the Custer Telephone Co-Operative signed an agreement with the Salmon River Electric Company whereby they could string telephone lines on the power poles from Challis to the Sunbeam Dam.

The telephones with the little ringing crank on the side are now classed as valued antiques. Today nearly all of the homes in the Stanley-Sawtooth area have the modern dial phones, making communication with the outside world a simple matter of picking up the receiver. Telephone service in the area is accepted as just another of our modern conveniences. Only the few oldtimers who remember the way it was in the early 1900s can truly appreciate the great benefit brought about by the telephone.

Electrical Power

Electrical power did not become available to the Stanley-Sawtooth country until 1954. Up until then, the only electric power in the area was furnished by a few privately owned Delco plants, leaving the main source of night lighting to the kerosene or gasoline lamps, and wood-burning stoves or fireplaces as the source of heating and cooking. Accordingly, a group of citizens from the area and from the town of Challis started a move in 1948 to bring electricity into Custer County by organizing the Salmon River Electric Co-operative. At the time F.R. (Preston) Shaw was elected as one of the directors, continuing to serve on the board until his death in April 1965. This group, by working through the Rural Electrification Administration, was finally able to get the line completed to Challis and energized in 1952. They then began working toward extending the power line on to Stanley and beyond, by obtaining a grant for a fifty year franchise from the village of Stanley. This gave the "Co-op" all rights, privileges and easements for the placement of poles, transformers, et cetra in connection with the distribution of electrical energy to Stanley.

On February 6th, 1953, a contract was let to B.A. Yerian for $373,281 for the installation of a power line from Challis to Clayton, Stanley, and on to Redfish Lake. However, due to the exceptionally mountainous terrain, construction of the line presented extreme difficulties, so in May that year, the Co-op agreed to raise the amount of the contract with Yerain by another $61,000 and grant him a sixty day extension of time, making the completion date December, 1953. In cooperation with the Co-op and Yerian, the U.S. Forest Service granted a Free Temporary Permit for the clearing of trees from the right of way, allowing a sub-contract to be let to Charles W. Winter by the Co-op Board to do the work. The line was completed more or less on schedule and subsequently energized to Clayton in 1953 and to Stanley in early 1954.

Meanwhile, in July, 1953, the summer residents of Pettit and Alturas Lake locality met with the Co-operative Board to ask that the power line be extended to include their area. Lack of funds at the time prevented their request from being granted, resulting in an application made to Washington D.C. for monies to extend said line on to the Pettit and Alturas Lake locale. Thus, when the request was again made by the summer residents there in 1954, it was granted, and the line was forthwith extended on to the Sawtooth Valley.

A street lighting contract for the village of Stanley was accepted in 1955. Also, that year, the Salmon River Electric Co-operative executed an agreement with the Custer County Telephone Co-operative for joint use of the power poles on a rental basis, setting the rate of 90 cents per pole for the first year, and $1.25 per pole for each succeeding year.

Originally, money for the Salmon River Electric Co-operative was borrowed through the Government from the Rural Electrification Administration. Later the Salmon River Electric Co-operative joined the Rural Electric Co-operative Association, thus providing cheaper power. This was noted in 1972 when electric rates in the area were the same as in 1953 when they were first established. The motto of the Salmon River Electric Co-operative is, "Owned by those we serve."

Although repair and maintenance crews are kept busy working on the lines the year round, winter months keep them going constantly. During bad storms, or in case of high winds, the power is sometimes off for hours at a time. Nevertheless, repair men are out braving the elements and restoring service as soon as possible. Since the event of snow-mobiles, crews now use the machines, enabling them to trace the lines and make repairs in less time than ever before in the mountainous region. For those dependent on electricity for heating and cooking facilities, such service is a help indeed.

The Salmon River Electric Co-operative is proud of their organization, and rightfully so. At its 23rd annual meeting in April 1974, Service Award Plaques were given to Dr. V.A. McGowan, president, Garth Chivers, fourteen years of service, and Frank Marrafio for ten years of service. Safe driving plaques were also presented to other Co-op employees . . . Art Edge and Eugene Whalen for thirteen years of safe driving, Ken Miller, nine years, Norma Funkhouser, eight years, Norma LaMunyan and Nick Piva, seven years, and Bob Cunningham, Milton Harkness and Clayton Hurless for one year each.

The subject of the possibility of laying underground lines was discussed to some extent, the conclusion being that the job would not only be an exorbitant expense for the initial installation, but maintenance in the winter when snow is deep would be next to impossible. The possible event of power rates being raised in the near future also came up for discussion, but members and officers alike remain hopeful that the action would not become necessary for some time to come.

Other Changes

As far back as 1917 various people in the Sawtooth area were predicting and advocating the changes in store for the rugged Salmon River country. One George W. Perkins wrote in the *Challis Messenger* that July 11th, "The changes of the last twenty-five years, socially, industrially, and economically, have been great. Yet I believe that they are infinitesimal compared to the changes that are coming. Precedent makes cowards of us all; but the educator, the scientist and the inventor have left us no choice. We must adjust our thoughts and actions to the new conditions."

Many such items appeared in the papers from time to time, and while some of the writers are no longer living, it seems that more than one of these people had the foresight to see what an influx of legions into the area would bring about. While slow in coming to the isolated Stanley-Sawtooth country as compared to other parts of Idaho, changes did come and were surely inevitable ... some welcomed and some not so welcome by its residents.

True to some of the predictions by oldtimers, once roads were built into the area tourists began to arrive by the thousands. Even in 1932, the *Hailey Times Newspaper* reported: An approximate 13,000 people visited the Sawtooth Valley and Stanley Basin, with 7,592 being campers and 1,144 being summer home owners and their guests. More than one out of every twelve cars checked bore out of state license plates."

Dude ranches and resorts began to come on the scene as early as the Twenties. One dude ranch, thought to be the Clark Miller Guest Ranch, was opened in the summer of 1926 under the management of Mr. and Mrs. R.S. Stringfellow with the rates set at $5 per day per person. This was in the Sawtooth Valley, and if it was the Clark Miller Ranch, it went on to expand, and is still in business at this date. The Rocky Mountain Dude Ranch was built in 1929, also in the Sawtooth Valley. Fred and Ellie Iselin are said to have operated it for awhile. Through the years any number of motels, first called tourist cabins, and eating places were established in both Upper and Lower Stanley and all along the Salmon River within the boundaries of The Sawtooth National Recreation Area. One is the Redwood Motel operated for years by Marvin Shaw.

Clyde Torrey

Another is Torrey's Cabins and Cafe, started by Clyde Torrey and now owned by Phil and Val Johnson, located thirteen miles west of Clayton, Idaho. There are many other such establishments, most of which have gone into business in more recent years.

In 1932 an airstrip with two runways . . . one 1900 feet long, and the other 2200 feet, was built about sixteen miles northwest of Stanley, not far from Cape Horn. More recently an airport has been made on a bench to the south and overlooking the town of Upper Stanley. Many private planes fly in and out of here in the summer months . . . business people, landowners, sportsmen, and those who just come to see and vacation in the locality. Now, since Highway 93 is kept open in the wintertime, many sightseers and snowmobilers come to visit Central Idaho's "Winter Wonderland." They like the snow and chilling tempertures, and say seeing the landscape all woven in white, and breathing the sharp, clean air gives them a feeling of exhilaration. Be that as it may, at long last it can finally be said that the Stanley-Sawtooth country has caught up with the times.

Winter Wonderland.

THE WILD STAGECOACH RIDE

The wild stagecoach ride over Galena Mountain.

In the summer of 1904, the road over Galena Summit, now U.S. Highway 93, was still an extremely rough, steep-graded, narrow wagon trail with very few places wide enough for one vehicle to pass another. Yet being the shortest route connecting the Wood River Valley to the Sawtooth-Stanley country, the road was well traveled even in those days. Whether one went by wagon, buggy, or stage, at best the trip could be a trying experience for anyone who journeyed that way . . . or so John T. Breckon was to discover when he began commuting between Ketchum and the Stanley Basin mines that year.

Breckon, a mining engineer, was generally considered a likeable chap by the miners in the Basin. At the Stanley Dredge camp a number of hands overheard him remark that the Sawtooth region did not seem as rugged as he had thought it would be. This led Otto Bassert, John McChrystal, and Austin Tierman to inquire if he enjoyed his ride over Galena Summit.

"Not exactly," he told them. "While the scenery was spectacular, the ride was tiresome and a bit dull."

The three men looked at one another, and later, between themselves, decided here was a greenhorn and it would be a good joke if his return trip to Ketchum could be made more exciting for their new friend. Unknown to Breckon they confided their idea to the stage driver. He listened, chuckled at the thought, and agreed to see what he could do about it.

The next morning, upon departure from the dredge camp, after awhile, the driver handed the reins to Breckon on the seat beside him saying, "Here, you handle the horses, I need a nap."

Glancing at the four horses (two span) stretched before him pulling the stagecoach, Breckon, with some misgivings, took the lines. He soon had the feel of the reins, however, and gaining confidence enjoyed the driving. That is until he reached the top of Galena Summit where he brought the stage to a screeching halt. Looking down before him the road seemed almost a sheer drop of five or six miles.

The driver, slightly unhappy at being jolted awake by the abrupt stop, mumbled, "What'sa matter?" got no answer, so grabbed the lines from his silent companion, cracked the whip over the backs of the horses, and away they went . . . rocks and gravel flying from the coach wheels, as it lurched, rolled, skidded, and slid down the mountain around hairpin curves and switchbacks, one after another, first on the two right wheels, then on the two left, all the way to the bottom of the grade. The entire descent, according to Breckon, took exactly fifteen minutes.

Back at the dredge camp in Stanley Basin a month or so later, Breckon, good sport that he was, was quick to acknowledge his wild ride had been "most exciting," giving his friends a hearty laugh as he told the story in detail. "That wasn't the worst though boys," he said. "True it scared the daylights outta me alright, but it was on the way over this time I thought I was a real goner."

Asking what happened, the sobered men waited with bated breath as Breckon told the following story:

"As we left Ketchum, there were seven of us on the stage, all drinking except another man and myself. Then here comes a rig driven by a saloonkeeper. On the level ground he soon passed us, his rig being the lighter. Evidently this injured our driver's professional pride because he yelled like a banshee,

360

snapped his whip, and we were off like a shot. The saloonkeeper whipped up his team too, keeping well ahead of us until we came to the foot of Mount Galena. We passed him there, but by now the saloonkeeper rose to the challenge, and the race was on. As he passed us on the first wide place available, our driver went wild, yelling and swearing "I'll get ya! I'll get ya!!"

"Such a din you never heard, stage rattling, rocks bouncing off of the wheels, our drunken passengers shouting and screaming, "PASS 'EM! PASS 'EM!," and me fearing we would go over the mountainside any minute."

"From there on it was a tug of war all the way to the summit, the saloonkeeper ahead and us hot on his tail while our driver kept a sharp eye out for a place wide enough to pass him. Both rigs were going lickity split, and with wheels careening almost on the edge of the cliffs, I tell you, I was one scared man. Too, all this time we were being thrown about like a bunch of rag dolls, first on one side of the coach then the other. I was beginning to wish I could have the benefit of a few drinks myself."

"Why didn't you take a nip from one of your fellow passengers?" Otto Bassert interrupted to ask.

"Because there wasn't time," Breckon answered. "Why man, the way we were flying around that mountain, all I could do was pray our driver would be able to bring us through without killing us all. You see, as we neared the point where the road narrows around a canyon, it had become plain that if we both got there at the same time one of us would either have to go over the side or up the mountainside. We got there all right, but the stage being the heavier of the two rigs, our driver got the better of the argument."

"Of course, the saloonkeeper took up the mountainside in preference to going over the cliff, and his buggy was smashed to pieces. Then, as soon as our driver could pull to a stop, everybody jumped out and ran back to see how badly he was hurt. They say the the good Lord takes care of drunks and fools so that must have been the case, since his only apparent injury was a cut on his mouth that left about a square inch of raw flesh hanging loose from his upper lip. Someone cut that off with a pocket knife, helped the old boy onto the stage, we all took a drink, then came on to Stanley without further incident."

Stopping to look at his friends, Breckon noted one or two of them shaking their heads. All was silent for a moment. Then

Breckon commented, "Well, boys, in my occupation I have traveled some mean roads getting to and from the mining camps in this intermountain country, but I will say Galena Mountain furnished me with the most exciting, wildest ride of them all."

Needless to say, John Breckon was never looked on as a greenhorn by anyone in the Stanley Basin after that. In later years, sometimes he told the story of his experiences, usually referring to that summer of 1904 as "one of the most enjoyable and frightening of his life."

NOTE: The above story was first written by Calvin Clawson and published in the *Challis Silver Messenger* in the fall of 1904.

"Scrapbook"
STANLEY-SAWTOOTH COUNTRY

Note: Because of numerous items and bits of information left over, and not directly related to other chapters in this book, we have put them here in what we choose to call our "Scrapbook."

"Yesterday's Fences"

Remains of the first fences ever to be built in the Stanley Basin and the Sawtooth Valley can be seen in places today. There were three types, mainly the "crib" fence, the 'worm,' fence, and the "buck" fence. Although the primary purpose of these fences was to keep livestock within bounds, they also acted as boundary lines and came under the heading of homestead improvements. The "crib" type took more time to build, but required no nails and would last for years with a minimum of maintenance. The "worm" fence did not need nails or wire, but did not hold up as well and required more repairs. The "buck" fence was seldom used in the very early years because nails or wire were hard to come by until the Teens and early Twenties when the needed items became regular stock at the stores in Stanley.

Early settlers began building the crib fence in the Basin about 1906-08. In this land where summers have always been short, fence building was done after the settler had erected his cabin, outbuildings, and corrals. In those days when everything had to be done with a few simple hand tools, and a man had to travel many miles for supplies, every hour counted, from the time the snow melted in the spring until it grew deep again in the fall. Accordingly, after all the essential chores were finished, the settler then turned his attention to fence building. Much of this work would be done after the first snow fell, and carried on until it became too deep for his team to pull a sled through.

363

The old and the new in Stanley Basin. Old fence is the "crib" or "box" type, and the new is the "worm" fence.

To build a crib fence, trees, usually pines that were uniform in size, were cut, limbs stripped off, and the tree cut into short and long lengths. After the logs were hauled to the fence site, all were notched at both ends and the long lengths laid one way with the short lengths another, resulting in a kind of box being formed by the short lengths. Generally, the open box was filled with rocks, if the same were handy, to make the fence more solid. The worm fence was put together much like the old fashioned rail fence, notching the logs and fitting them together in a kind of zig-zag pattern. The buck fence, much easier to build than the crib or worm fences, was made by anchoring crossed poles in the form of an x, then laying long poles in the top cross and nailing or wiring two or three other poles down

364

the side of the cross, depending on the height of the fence. On all three styles, sometimes the bark was peeled off and sometimes not... again depending on the rancher's time. The peeled poles lasted longer, so this was done whenever possible.

In later years these old fences gave way to the more common wire fencing, and for awhile it appeared as if log fences in the Basin and the Valley would go the way of galvanized washtubs and kerosene lamps. Then with shortages and spiraling prices in recent years, ranchers have been motivated back to using pole and log fencing again. Also, since the area is now included within the boundaries of the Sawtooth National Recreation Area, officials declare them more rustic and in keeping with the region's environment. In fact, now in compliance with S.N.R.A. regulations, new homes and business houses use peeled logs in construction... all in keeping with the more picturesque "rustic" look. This, coupled with the revival of the buck and pole fencing, is reassuring to those who, for awhile, mourned the old rail and pole fences passing from the scene. Today one might even say a kind of "Old West" atmosphere again prevails in the Stanley-Sawtooth country where a real cowboy can sometimes be seem riding the range, herding cattle, and mending fences.

Wild Hay Press

In the Stanley Basin, a large sagebrush flat, spread below Nip-N-Tuck Mountain and about five hundred yards eastward above Stanley Creek, conceals the ruins of an old hay press. This unique contraption, reposing in a shallow gully at the base of a natural ramp, or drop-off, in its time worked efficiently and served its purpose well. Although the old press is now all but hidden from view by thick stands of sagebrush, it once set amid waving, lucious grasses valued in the early days as wild hay, and the prime reason the press came to be here.

During the first mining boom in the Yankee Fork district, over the ridge to the east, and before there were roads of any kind into the Stanley Basin, people in the Bonanza and Custer area knew about the wild hay in the Basin. For those needing hay for their stock it was a "God Send." No one had a real claim on it even though some mining had started in the Basin and a handful of settlers had come in, none were actually permament as yet. Therefore, the wild hay was there for the taking by anyone who could cut and pack it out to the Yankee Fork district on pack animals via pack trails.

The author, Esther Yarber, in the foreground with Edna Niece McGown, and her brother, Rupert Niece in background. Picture taken at old hay-press in Stanley Basin in 1973.

While it is not known who built the press, or exactly when, it was made of hand-hewn timbers and put together in a large oblong box-like fashion. When the hay was cut, it was loaded into the press from the natural ramp. Then, after it was pressed, it was fastened with wire and slid from the press on a slant to level ground where it was loaded onto pack animals. To be sure, the person, or persons who built and used the hay press always found a ready market for the hay in the Yankee Fork Mining district for several years.

Today the rotting timbers of the old hay press continue to be ravaged by weather and time. Here in a sea of sagebrush it is passed by, and unseen by, hundreds of travelers every summer along the gravel road across and siding Stanley Creek.

The Lost Prospect

When "Trapper" Fisher, beloved old fiddler in the Stanley Basin back in the early days, first came into the country he sometimes herded sheep in the summer months on the surrounding mountain ranges, doing a bit of prospecting in the process. One summer in the early 1900s, Martha Benner, who

366

operated the store and hotel at Upper Stanley, grubstaked him for such a trip. Camped near Hindman Lake with his flocks, he found a piece of high-grade ore and knew he had a good prospect. However, for some reason or other, he became angry with Mrs. Brenner and did not stake a claim on it. When he went back later intending to locate the ground, he was unable to find his prospect again. Is this another *lost mine?*

Lost Townsite

Legend has it that a Chinese townsite existed over the divide from Sawtooth Valley on the back slopes of the Sawtooth Mountains. The general area, called "China Basin," is where the Middle Fork of the Boise River gathers its headwaters in the Yuba mining district. No records seem to be available of the town, and if it ever had a name no one seems to know what it was. Nevertheless, various people swear there is such a hidden site in a high recess or valley, accessible only by foot trail, in the vicinity of Greylock Mountain some distance from the mining town of Atlanta. Several even claim to have found it and collected different artifacts in the locale. As a result, any number of stories have evolved about the lost townsite . . . lost because no one can seem to find it again after chancing upon it once. Perhaps the most reliable of these stories is one told to Ron Curio of Pocatello by Alfred P. Shultz, who, for many years, was district forest ranger in the Boise River area. The story is as follows:

"Longtime residents have told of hearing of a Chinese settlement of two or three hundred population located somewhere in the rough terrain near the mountain termed "Greylock" by the Chinese because they were unable to pronounce "Greyrock," the name first given to the mountain by early prospectors. Atlanta being the closest town where the Chinese could get supplies, they made frequent visits to buy food, mining tools, and other things they needed, often paying for their purchases with chunk gold. This indicated that the Orientals were doing rather well in their mining efforts."

"After awhile, however, merchants and other people in Atlanta became aware that the Chinese were no longer coming into town. They wondered why, and several of the residents attempted to find out what had become of them. No traces of the Chinese, or of their community, could be found. They even looked for a cemetery without finding a single grave. This appeared significant, since Chinese in America put great store

367

in having their graves well marked so that eventually their bones would be transported back to their homeland."

"A ranger friend, while out hiking in the region one day, stumbled onto the site of this Chinese settlement. He found many housing structures and mine diggings there, and looking for and finding the trash dumps, he collected a large number of dishes, bottles, and opium pipes, all intact. Then knowing he could not possibly carry the articles out on foot, he piled them in an open place with plans to return on horseback for them. Later, when he did try to return, he could not find the site a second time. He tried again and again to no avail. Now, it has become a kind of obsession with him, and every summer he goes out to search for the lost townsite. Will he ever find it? Who knows? We wonder, since time and weather does take its toll. But my friend continues to hope that someday he will again stumble onto this legendary town, collect his momentos, and then bask in the memory of it all."

George Blackman

After the post office was established in Sawtooth Valley, a Negro named George Blackman, would come to Osidian every now and then to pick up his mail. He came by way of Fourth of July Creek trail from his cabin near its headwaters in Washington Basin of the White Cloud Mountain Range. Valley people who knew George said he had lived there for many years, earning his living by mining and guiding hunters in the area. One of these hunters, John H. Thatcher of Okmulgee, Oklahoma, told the following story about George Blackman, as printed in the March 1930 issue of *Scribner's Magazine.*

"It was the summer of 1897. Five young men just out of Princeton University went to Ketchum, Idaho to visit Knox Taylor, a former college mate. At the time Knox was in charge of a mining enterprise in the region, spending all of his spare time fishing the streams and lakes and hunting for bear and mountain goat and sheep in the high country. He told his friends of having heard of an animal resembling the European Ibex said to have been spotted by a black miner in Washington Basin, and asked them if they would like to take a pack trip to the area. Three of the men did. I was one of them. Traveling over a steep trail to an elevation of 10,000 feet, we found George Blackman at his small, sod-roof cabin."

"The black man was congenial and, inviting us in, he promised to guide us to the place where he had seen the animals he thought to be ibex. The next day he took us there, and through our binoculars, we saw the animals, but the terrain was so rugged we could never get a shot at them. While we were there George told us a little about himself. Said he had been raised and educated by a white family in Iowa and had come West with gold seekers in the Eighties. Then, finding a good prospect in his present mining claim, he had built the cabin and settled down to live in the Washington Basin. He told us he worked his claim mostly in the wintertime, and in the early summer packed a few tons of ore out for shipment. This, he said, paid for his winters provisions and other supplies, and that he always packed everything in during the month of August. Impressed by his resourceful ways, I asked him what he would do if he broke a leg. He only grinned and answered, "Well, we mostly don't break legs."

"When we were ready to leave for our return to Ketchum, we asked George what we owed him. Refusing money for pay, he said all he wanted was a subscription to *Scribner's Magazine*. Thirty years later I took my son and revisited Washington Basin in Idaho's rough back country, where I found George Blackman still living, with his memory still sharp and clear of my first visit with him and our hunt for the ibex. On a shelf in his cabin I saw several old copies of *Scribner's Magazines* which, I am sure, had been read and reread many times throughout the years."

The Miner's Darling

People in the Salmon River country knew her only as "Cowboy Jo." Tall, redhaired, beautiful and charming, even in a drunken state, Jo appeared in Stanley-Sawtooth country sometime in the late Seventies at the beginning of the first mining booms there. It was a man's world at first, and the lonely miners and prospectors valued and enjoyed her companionship. Some called her their "Angel of Mercy" since no trail was too steep or long for her to take medicine and supplies by horseback up some out-of-way mountainside to nurse a sick miner or prospector back to health. Her one weakness was drink. Yet she was loved and accepted, even by womenfolk when they came on the scene in the Eighties and Ninties. Her sunny disposition and child-like manner won her friends wherever she roamed.

And roam she did, first from one mining camp to another and then back again. When she married Pete Albert and went to live with him on his ranch in the Loon Creek area, everyone thought she would surely mend her nomadic ways and settle down. But not Jo . . . restless as always, she would take off on a drinking bout with some of her old friends, usually staying and living it up until Pete either came after her, or sent for her. Back on the ranch again she would be content for awhile, then go again.

One such incident occured in 1894. Pete had located Jo at Sawtooth City. Fearing she would move on before he could go after her, he sent word to Arthur McGown Sr., who at that time was operating the store at Upper Stanley, to pick Jo up and keep her with his family until he could make the trip over Loon Creek Summit after her. Mrs. McGown (Della), telling the story later, said, "Poor old Jo was so unkept and still half drunk when Arthur brought her to our home. But she never argued when we poured hot coffee down her, and I insisted she take a bath and wash and iron her clothes. I combed her hair, and it was a matted mess. It took me hours, but when it was done and braided up around her head the way she liked to wear it, she looked real nice."

"After that, while she waited for Pete, she helped around the place and played with the children. They loved her. When Jo was sober she had many good qualities. You see, we had met her on the Yankee Fork at Custer, and knew her traits quite well, because no bigger-hearted woman ever lived than Cowboy Jo."

While living at Upper Stanley, Mrs. McGown saw Jo a couple of other times on jaunts away from her home with Pete on Loon Creek. "On one occasion I was going to Bonanza on horseback and met her slumped in her saddle and a man leading her horse," she recalied. "Jo was so drunk she didn't recognize me. I had to turn my horse uphill out of the trail to let them pass. On another occasion I found her at Tony Martena's cabin cooking and caring for him when I went to deliver some meat up to the Sturkey and Challis Mine above Kelly Gulch. I stopped to drop off some meat for Tony and see how he was doing, so seeing Jo there was a nice surprise. She acted real glad to see me, and, of course, we had a good visit."

In later years, when Pete died, Jo moved to Bonanza and maintained a cabin there for several years, continuing her way of life until she became old and ill. She died at the Custer County Poorhouse at Challis, Idaho and was buried in the Challis Cemetery.

Frank, Tom, and Joe

Frank Brockway, Tom Horton, and Joe McGown, all living in the Salmon River country in the early days, had many things in common . . . all three had been married at one time, all were in their forties, "footloose and fancy free," and all were "good drinking buddies." Each of them would work on occasion in the local mines for a stake to go on a drunken spree. Starting out, they would drink until all three were broke, having a glorious time in the doing. All three men had a great sense of humor and usually they did no harm. Nevertheless, every now and then, their pranks and misadventures landed them in jail, often providing people who knew them with a hearty laugh.

After doing one of these "hitches" in jail, Tom Horton took possession of the old jail house at Custer, on the Yankee Fork of the main Salmon River. When he had it all fixed up for his bachelor quarters, he wrote a note to the sheriff of Custer County reading, "I just wanted you to know that I have my own jail now, so all I need is some of your old bread and water."

One fall the trio gathered at Stanley for one of their drinking bouts, and after a few days celebrating, decided to go to Mackay in Idaho's Lost River area. Loading into Tom's old Model-T Ford, they started out. This was before Highway 93 was built, and the gravel road trailed alongside the Salmon River, on the right from a short distance below Sunbeam on past the Robinson Bar Dude Ranch, then owned by Chase Clark. Just north of the Bar, a place called "Five Points" was particularily narrow with several very dangerous curves and hazardous for even a sober driver, much less a drunken one. As they went bumping along at a good clip, around one of these curves they ran head on into a new car driven by Chase Clark himself. The three landed in jail at Challis and a hearing was arranged to be heard before Judge Henry Nichols. On the day of the hearing, the first question the Judge asked was, "Who was driving the car?"Neither Tom, Frank, or Joe answered. Thinking they did not hear him, the Judge asked again, "Which one of you was driving the car?" Still the trio remained silent. Raising his voice in obvious exasperation, he said again, "I asked you which one of you was driving that car!" Aroused at last by the Judge's tone of voice, Frank Brockway spoke up, his face as straight and sober as the judge in front of him. "Well, Judge," he said, "Come to think of it, we were all three in the back seat." Frank, Tom, and Joe were sentenced to ten days in jail, but were straightway bailed out by friends.

On another occasion, Frank was driving stage between Obsidian and Stanley for Clyde Gillispie who had the mail contract at that time. One day Dave Williams and his daughter-in-law, Phyllis Williams, came upon the stage stopped beside the road with Frank lolling on the seat, a bottle beside him, and singing at the top of his voice. Stopping to see what the matter might be, Dave asked him if there was anything he could do for him. "No not now," Frank answered. "You should have thought of that last night." Then, sizing Frank up, Dave asked, "Are you going to be alright?" Frank laughed and replied, "Oh, yes . . . sure, I'm just resting a little." Dave, still worried, said, "Do you have any left?" And Frank, thinking Dave wanted a drink, handed him the bottle. "Thanks, Frank," Dave said, and much to Frank's surprise drove off down the road. Needless to say, Frank brought the mail through on that run without any more stops on the way.

On another day, Frank drove his team up to the Stanley Store. As he pulled to a stop, one horse was lagging a little behind the other. A man there, after watching him drive up, walked over and said, "Sure looks like that one horse is slower than the other." "Oh, I don't know," Frank told him as he climbed down from the seat, "I've come about twenty miles and that's as far as he's gotten behind."

Frank Brockway

Claude Gillispie the Guide

As noted under "Other Settlers in the Sawtooth Valley," Claude Gillispie established a dude ranch in the Valley during the Thirties, and for several years acted as a guide for tourists in the area. Excerpts from an article about him in a 1942 issue of the *Saturday Evening Post* appears below:

"In 1942 Claude Gillispie guided the Trail Riders sent into the Sawtooth Mountains by the American Forestry Association. The U.S. Forest Service and the National Park Service cooperated by sending foresters, rangers, and naturalists with the expedition. They explored parts of the rugged Sawtooth country that had not previously had trails blazed."

"Claude's advice on particularily steep and rugged mountain sides was: "Keep the horses climbing, give them their heads, and hang on.""

Mrs. Josephine Thompson (first schoolteacher in the Stanley Basin), age sixty-six, was a member of this party of thirty-three people. They had sixty-nine horses for riding and packing. The trip took them as far as fifty miles from any road. An average day's ride would be about fifteen miles, and the trip took from ten days to two weeks. Two thousand pounds of food and provisions were packed along, and more supplied by packers who met them at predesignated places along the route."

"They saw, and were able to take pictures of deer, elk, eagles, mountain goats, and mountain lion, but seldom saw bear. The bear are cagey animals. Tracks were plentiful . . . proof that they were there."

Who, Who, Who-oo

A funny story is told about Jennie Gleason who came with her husband, Jack Gleason, to the Stanley Basin where he was interested in a mining claim with Bill Soule in the Twenties. Jennie, a young, pretty girl from Salt Lake City, Utah, was a real city girl unused to country living. One evening, when Jack failed to return to camp before it began to get dark, she started along the trail to meet him. Walking along near timberline, she kept watching the shadows beneath the trees.

Suddenly an owl sounded a loud mournful "Whoo-whoo." Jennie had never heard an owl before. "I am Jennie Gleason," she answered, and kept walking. Soon the owl called again,

Who, Who, Whooo.

"Whooo-whooo." Jennie answered again, louder this time, "I'm Jennie Gleason." By the time the owl called "Whoo . . . whoo" the third time, Jennie was beginning to wish she was safely back in camp. Now thoroughly frightened, she raised her voice and yelled back, "I told you I'm Jennie Gleason, you darned fool! Now what do you want?" At that moment Jack appeared around a bend in the trail. Naturally he had heard her yelling back at the owl, and later had to tell it as a joke on her.

Governor in the Limelight

While visiting in the Stanley Basin in the summer of 1921, Governor David W. Davis (Idaho's 12th governor) and his two sons went with J.N. Apgar, deputy game warden in the Basin, and O.T. Jones, State Game Warden, to plant a truckload of fish in Redfish Lake. It was early August, and started out as a beautiful day. Then, while the group was in the boat out on the lake, a sudden storm came up. The water became choppy and rough, but wanting to finish the job, and thinking to lighten the load, the wardens put in to shore and dropped the Governor and the two young boys off.

Swinging back into the choppy waters, Jones and Apgar hoped to reach an inlet where they wanted to plant the rest of the fish. The storm raged on, and before they could get the boat motor functioning properly, the craft was caught and overturned by a huge wave about fifty feet off shore. Both men were swimmers, but Jones was only fair. He started for shore while Apgar clung to the overturned boat. A short distance away Jones found that his heavy boots and clothing were dragging him down. "I can't make it!" he yelled, "My clothes are pulling me under!" Apgar quickly grabbed an oar and pushed it out to Jones, dragging him back to the boat. When Apgar saw that the boat would not hold the weight of both of them, he struck out for shore, calling out to Jones, "Hang on. I'll get help."

Meanwhile, on shore, Governor Davis saw the boat settling deeper into the churning water with Jones barely able to keep his head clear. First, rushing to the aid of an exhausted Apgar at the waters edge, he pulled him in and stripped off his heavy clothing then began to strip off his own. With the help of his boys and Apgar, he wrenched at a dead log caught in a pile of driftwood at the edge of the lake. When the log was free, pushing it in front of him, the Governor started towards Jones whose head was almost under water. By the time he could get near enough to push the log to Jones for him to grab onto, he was going down for the second time. Coming up, Jones called out, "I'm all in."

Davis shouted back, "For God's sake man! Hang on!" In another second the log was within Jones' reach, and hanging on weakly, Davis started towing him to shore. Having by now regained his strength, Apgar swam out, dived down and pulled Jones more to the surface, and between himself and the Governor, the drowning man was brought safely to shore where a fire was built and all the wet clothing dried. Later, walking the two miles back to camp, Jones recounted his experience of going under water that second time. "My eyes were open," he said, "and I could see a limb on that log. Somehow, I got to it and held on with all I had left." Governor Davis had only one remark to make . . . "Thank God you did!" Apgar's comment was, "Amen."

Hunting Accident

Edward Cummings lived in the Stanley Basin. His parents and younger brother, Amos, also lived there. On October 10th, 1921, Cummings went on a hunting trip in the Loon Creek area. Jim Barlogi, a deputy sheriff in Gooding County, Idaho, went hunting in the Loon Creek area at the same time. On seeing something white, which he thought was the rump of a moving deer, Barlogi raised his gun and fired. Going to see

375

what he had shot, the deputy sheriff was horrified to learn that he had killed another hunter instead of a deer. His victim was Edward Cummings. The shot had entered the body just under the right shoulder blade and passed completely through the body.

On Tuesday, the following day, Dr. C.L. Kirtley of Challis went with the Custer County Sheriff to the scene, and upon investigation, decided an inquest was not necessary. The body was brought out by Edward Cummings, Sr. and Arthur "Tuff" McGown, and burial made in the Stanley Cemetery. Besides his parents and brother, Edward Cummings, Jr. left a wife and daughter.

Human Interest Story

When A.F. Kavanaugh parted company with his two young sons in 1890, he had no way of knowing it would be thirty-five long years before he would see them again. Yet it happened exactly that way. Prospecting and moving from one mining area to another for some thirteen years, he came to Custer County and on to Stanley Basin in 1903. When the country began to be settled, he became one of its boosters and a prominent citizen there. In about 1922 or 23 he bought the Stanley Garage from George Aldredge.

Two years later, in early summer of 1925, Mr. Kavanaugh was in Hailey, Idaho, on business when, through sheer accident, he found one of his nephews working in a local drugstore. This nephew knew the whereabouts of one of Kavanaugh's sons, B.B. Kavanaugh. He was living at Seattle, Washington, and was district manager of the W.O.W. Lodge there. Telegrams were exchanged between father and son and as it turned out, the other son also lived on the West Coast. To be sure, it was a time of rejoicing for the aging Mr. Kavanaugh. That fall he sold his garage to Frank Niece, boarded a train, and went to pay his two sons a visit. All was well with them, but unused to city life, after visiting awhile, the old gentleman returned to Custer County where, on October 29th, 1927, he passed away at the Challis Hot Springs and was buried in the Challis Cemetery.

Sunday School and Church

The entire Sawtooth region has always seemed to be God's House, in that no church of any denomination has ever been built there to this date. This is not to say the residents have never been good, God-loving people all through the years. On the contrary, many of the settlers were very religious, and any time a circuit (traveling) minister came to the small Stanley community, everyone who could turned out for the services. In fact, when a Presbyterian minister came there in April, 1914, the first Sunday School was organized with Mrs. H.D. Gerrish as Superintendent, L.S. Niece as Treasurer, and Con Doty as Secretary and teacher.

First Sunday School class in Lower Stanley (1914). Front row, left to right . . . Rebecca Sewell, Edna Niece, Irene Micheal. Back row . . . Rupert Niece and George Sewell

As it turned out, however, the class was held only one Sunday because Con Doty, the teacher, went to Challis, got drunk, returned to Stanley and resigned his position saying, "I'm not fit to teach the word of the Lord." In repeating Con Doty's words, the oldtimer recalling the incident went on to remark, "You know, back then, and unlike the way things are today, a circuit riding man of the cloth really preached the gospel and the word of God without an eye on the dollar sign. So old Con was right in resigning if he couldn't set a good example for the kids in his Sunday School class."

In recent years a movement promoted by Reverend James J. Fleming of Jerome, Idaho, to construct a Meditation Chapel began. The building would be rustic in design, non-denominational, and would face the majestic Sawtooth Peaks, similar to the Church of Transfiguration at Moose, Wyoming

377

Taken at Lower Stanley (1914) Left to right ... Leslie Niece, Unknown, Baptist Minister (name unknown), Ellen Niece, Carlton Gerrish, Conrad Doty, Mrs. Gerrish, Mr. Gerrish. Girls in front, Edna Niece and Irene Michael

in Grand Teton Park. If this plan does materialize, Jack Niece and his wife, Ruth, who operate the State Liquor Store at Upper Stanley, say the Chapel will stand on a knoll to the south of town. Surely no site is more fitting where tourists and residents may stop and offer a prayer, if they so choose, to the Creator of this rugged, scenic beauty surrounding them. Truly, this is God's domain.

Snowslides

Snow slides and avalanches, always a danger in the Stanley-Sawtooth country, were even more so during the early days. When warming trends start the heavy snow packs to moving down the mountain sides after a series of bad winter storms, the best policy is, and was then, to stay away from slide areas. However, this was not always possible when people were compelled to travel on snowshoes or skiis as a means of getting from one place to another back then. As a result many persons lost their lives. Notations from the *Silver Messenger Newspaper* on the various tragedies are listed as follows:

From the February 9, 1909 "20 Year Ago" column. . . .

William Evert, better known as "Teko Bill," was killed in a slide on January 3, 1889, about one-half mile from the Greyhound Mine. Duncan Cameron, Custer County Coroner,

378

was notified that the deceased was buried at Greyhound and that death was accidental. The letter was signed by:

T.J. Preno	Roy Myres	Frank May
Alfred Neyberg	Andrew Phelps	John Duggan
M. Mathison	John Strikes	Frank McDonald

Snowslide near Mormon Bend with crew shoveling road so mail sleigh could get through.

February 1, 1910

Harry Friend, a placer miner living alone on Rough Gulch on the Salmon River, was buried in a snowslide. His tracks were traced to the edge of the slide, and none showed on the other side.

This item was followed by another on February 25, 1910, reading....

The body of Harry Friend has been found about sixty feet from where his tracks entered the slide area. A brother has arrived from Nebraska. The body was found near a large tree, and there was evidence that he had taken shelter there and had not been killed instantly, but had tried to dig his way out.

January 13, 1914

David Williams, Stanley mail carrier, was fifty hours late arriving at the Pierson post office because of snowslides. About three miles from Galena, where the canyon is narrow, there were five slides in less than twenty minutes. Mr. Williams and his sleigh and horses were covered up with just the horses ears visible. He managed to extricate himself, the horses, and the mail, leaving the sleigh. He then loaded the mail on one horse and rode the other to Galena.

March 22, 1916

J. H. Mahoney was killed March 7th in a snowslide near the Greyhound Mine in the Stanley Basin. The slide was a small one, and Mr. Whipple, who was a short distance behind Mr. Mahoney, said that he was thrown headfirst into a tree, and when Whipple got to him and pulled him out, he was dead. Mr. Whipple, assisted by Pat Rasche, dragged the body down to the wagon road near the Greyhound on poles and buried him.

Rustlers

Although some cattle rustling has gone on in the Stanley Basin in late years, very little rustling of any kind went on there in the early days. The two incidents mentioned here, although of no great consequence, involved a horse rustler and a woman cattle rustler. The first occurred in August 1902, when a man who said his name was Daley, stole two horses from a man at the Valley Creek Mine and sold them for $40. The owner recovered his horses, but the rustler got away. The woman rustler dressed poorly and pretended poverty. Caught the first time, she won the owner's sympathy and was let off with a warning. But when dead animals were found with only a quarter of the meat taken, the game warden was called, and she was caught in the act. The woman was promptly taken to Stanley and given a choice of paying a heavy fine, serving a long jail term, ... or leaving the country and never coming back. She departed without argument, and as far as is known, was never heard from again.

Stanley Basin Rodeos

The first rodeo ever to be held in the Stanley Basin is thought to have been in August, 1919, on ground which was a part of the William Rose homestead. This rodeo was advertised as such, and was put on by the Chivers Brothers and Theodore "Dad" Cameron. It was small, as were other rodeos until August, 1928, featuring horse racing with race horses brought in from Jackson Hole, Wyoming by John Cherry, plus bucking horses and a few other events.

The 1928 rodeo was advertised in the *Challis Messenger* as

Theodore "Dad" Cameron with his pack horses in Stanley Basin.

featuring calf roping, bronc riding, bareback contests, wild horse races, relay race, and best bucking horse with an entry fee of $2.50 for each event. Lasting two days, the rodeo was a huge success "from the first 'Whoopee' on opening day to the riding of the last horse on the second day." In 1930 the time for this popular sport was extended to three days instead of two, and was held August 15, 16, and 17, on grounds up Cape Horn way, about six miles from Upper Stanley with Al Ellis as manager, Theodore Cameron, president, and Roy Chivers the secretary.

Slim Hendrick, who later became a partner in a bootlegging venture with Arch Savage, was noted for his bronc busting ability in connection with his ranch work. A good horseman and rider, he perfected quite an act he called his "Drunken Buckaroo Ride" for the rodeos. To accomplish this, Slim would emerge from the chute astride a spirited horse, hanging tightly to the bridle reins with one hand and a bottle of whiskey in the other, held high for all to see. Then, as his snorting mount would leap high, bucking and twisting this way and that, Slim would slip and sway in the saddle, pretending to be falling. This generally caused the spectators in the grandstand to rise to their feet, chorusing fearful "Ohoo...oos and Ahh...hhs." While they held their breath Slim would right himself and even manage a swig from the bottle now and then as he made two or three turns around the arena putting on his act until rescued from the bucking horse by hazers. On the ground, still clutching the bottle, Slim would bow to the crowd, wave his bottle high amid a loud round of applause, turn and walk back to the corrals, perfectly sober, of course.

Drunken Buckaroo Ride.

A tragedy occurred at the August, 1931 rodeo when a plane crashed and burned near the site of the rodeo grounds in the field of the old William Paul ranch. All three men aboard, the pilot, Paul Workman, and two passengers, Jim Roarck, age 24, and Fred VanOver, age 20, were killed instantly. The plane had been carrying sightseers over the rodeo grounds and surrounding areas all afternoon, and just before the crash, Mr. and Mrs. Wallace Lightfoot alighted to be replaced by the two young men killed in the accident.

Mrs. Lightfoot (Laura) and Kathleen Markle operated a rather crudely constructed lunch stand in competition with a brightly striped awning tent stand on the grounds during the 1931 rodeo. Awed by the impressive competition, the Stanley ladies proceeded to serve breakfasts, hamburgers, hot dogs, pop, and coffee to the crowds, soon noticing that only a few people were patronizing the other stand. Whether it was the difference in the way Mrs. Markle and Mrs. Lightfoot prepared the food, or the fact that both were local ladies, certainly the appearance of their stand mattered not at all. When the rodeo was over Laura and Kathleen were delighted with their profits while surmising that their competition did well if they met expenses during the three days there.

Small Items of Interest From Old Newspapers

Wood River Times ... relayed to *The Silver Messenger,* dated August 25, 1896 ... "Hordes of flies moved into the Sawtooth Valley and the Stanley Basin during July and early August. Prospectors there are calling it "The Fly Plague." They say the flies have grey bodies and green heads. These flies descend on the area in great hordes, eating man and beast alike, driving stock crazy and wild game out of the country."

Wood River Times ... T.E. Picottee, the paper's proprietor and publisher, commented in one of his editorials ... spring issue, 1886, "Writing a friendly epitaph is like watering last years garden."

Silver Messenger....
July, 1899 ... "Proposed 'Idaho Midland' Railroad to be built from Boise through the mountains, down through the Stanley Basin, and on down Salmon River to Salmon City."
May 3, 1922.... "Rancher, George Cumine, and prospector William Lutz, two of Stanley's ancient pioneers, can be seen daily along Salmon River these spring days fishing for white fish. Leave it to them to bring home the fish."
May 3, 1922.... "Mrs. Will Paul was brought from her ranch to Stanley on a hand sled in a serious condition. Mrs. Paul was suffering from a kidney and bladder disorder, and needed medical attention. She is able to be around again now."
June 15, 1927.... "Idaho Falls people will erect 50 cabins in the Stanley Basin and put boats on Stanley Lake. W.S. Walters and J.E. Feischman are the officers of this company." *Note: Nothing ever came of this.*
January 22, 1929.... "Mercury dropped to 46 degrees below zero in the Stanley Basin."
January 29, 1929.... "Mercury has now dropped to 52 degrees below zero in the Stanley Basin."
March 12, 1930.... "Stage from Stanley to Robinson Bar changed from sleighs to wheels this week."
November 4, 1936.... "The C.C.C. boys from the Bonanza camp, under the direction of the Forest Service, have completed the Sunbeam Springs bath house project. There are four

showers and dressing room units, two each for men and ladies, one bath tub, and laundry equipment, all furnished with hot water from nature's hot water supply." *Note. This facility was destroyed by vandals later.*

June 5, 1943 . . . "Clyde Torrey is installing a service station and tourist cabins on his property on the Salmon River."

As might be observed, weather was always a factor in the Stanley-Sawtooth country before roads could be kept open during the winter months. Without any medical facilities to speak of at Stanley, and the area isolated by the deep snows, a severe case of illness was often a dangerous situation. One example was when Clyde Gillispie fell critically ill in February of 1943. It had been an especially hard winter. Snow was three feet deep in Stanley. Hearing of Clyde's plight, Ranger Charley Langer went to his aid. With the help of Highway equipment, he managed to take Clyde to Hailey, Idaho, requiring all night to make the trip over Galena Summit. About this same time Pauline Savage also fell ill. Her family made the long, torturous trip to Hailey by way of Challis and Arco in order to reach a doctor. Needless to say, people in need of medical attention sometimes died during those early days in the Stanley-Sawtooth country before a doctor could be reached. Naturally, it was easier to transport a patient to where medical aid was available in summer when roads were clear. But even then, with time being of essence, the long, grueling trip to the nearest doctor might have proven fatal had it not been for the true neighborliness of the kind-hearted residents who never hesitated to go to the aid of someone in need, be he or she a friend or a stranger in their midst. As a result it became apparent that some sort of medical facility was sorely needed in the little town of Stanley. Yet it took many years before one could be established.

A clinic and ambulance service was founded in the early Seventies, headed by a specially trained nurse practitioner, Mrs. Marie Osborn from Boise, Idaho. To begin with, almost everything was acquired through donations, including certain equipment from a retired doctor (name unknown) and housing in the former C.A. Gregory home that had been purchased and its use offered by Marvin and Fern Larson. Even the ambulance, an old 1958 model, was donated, and finally replaced in 1975 by a new one, thereby fulfilling an almost impossible dream for the tiny community. In 1974 a new building, 28 by 40 feet, with an attached garage for the ambulance was built.

Today, equipped with modern furnishings, medical machines and supplies, the clinic is designed with two treatment rooms, a combination pharmacy and laboratory, an examination and x-ray room, a reception room, and a furnace room. Nearly everything included in the clinic ... labor, time, effort, and even most of the monies required came through donations.

To the people of Stanley-Sawtooth country, the clinic represents a hard-won victory. One of the movements leaders, Jerry Funderburg of Lower Stanley, said, "We had anywhere from two to twenty people working on the building about every day in the spring and summer of 1974. Specialized labor, including ducting on the heating system by the Van Gas Company, and all the electrical work was done by Doyle Perkins, an electrician from Boise ... why, we even had doctors along with many other people who were just passing through who stopped to work on it." To be sure the Stanley people are proud, for now they no longer have to fear needless suffering or death for the lack of medical aid.

Yesterday's Advertising

During the early days, wages of $3.00 to $3.50 per day with room and board, as paid in the mines in the State of Idaho, seems to have averaged in accordance with prices of goods kept in the general merchandise stores throughout the Salmon and Wood River areas. Following are a few items listed in the local newpapers, reflecting trends and going prices of the times.

In 1904, for example, a man could buy a pocket knife for as little as 30 cents, or as much as $1.85, depending on the kind of knife he wanted and could afford. He could get a pair of pants for $1.50, a suit for $8.00, a waterproof coat for $2.50, a suit of long underwear for 80 cents, and a pair of shoes for $1.75. For 85 cents he could get a good straight razor, and pay 35 cents each for a shaving brush and a razor strop. A gold pan cost 20 cents, and a fairly good pocket watch could be bought for $1.00.

Lion Coffee was the most popular brand of real coffee, while Kneipp Malt Coffee was advertised as a substitute and a health drink. Climax and Star seemed to be the main brands of chewing tobacco. The Star Company even listed different premiums one could get by saving a certain number of the little tin stars on each cut purchased ... 25 would get you a French Wood Briar pipe, or 75 a real nickel alarm clock. A gold watch could be had for 200 stars, a set of Roger's silver plated knives and

385

forks for 500, an automatic hand gun of 32 or 38 caliber for 600, and if a man could accumulate as many as 2,000 he could get a fine shotgun.

The lady of the house could purchase yard goods for as little as 10 cents a yard, or a ready made dress for $1.98. For her kitchen an ordinary coffee grinder priced at 25 cents, a bread pan at 29 cents, an iron skillet (sometimes called a spider) for 35 cents, and a cast iron teakettle or stove pot for $1.00 each. A nice round solid oak, 6-foot table could be bought for $8.70, a rocking chair for $3.20, and a whole bedroom suite for $14.90. A little boy's wagon, advertised as one of the best made, sold for $1.50, and a doll for a little girl cost from 80 cents to $1.00 if it had a china head and a kid-skin body.

The R.N. Hull and Frank Nickerson Grocery and Dry Goods Stores at Challis advertised and carried many of the items listed above. Charles Harris operated a furniture store and Leon Fuld ran a general merchandise store at Hailey. Both Harris and Fuld, along with Tom Taig, who owned a store at Ketchum, inserted ads in the *Wood River Times*. Bakery bread was called "Lite bread," and advertised as such in all the towns. In 1913, after cars came on the scene, this paper also ran an item noting "The Bush" Automobile, priced at $1,045 and claimed to be the lightest weight touring car ever built. Although little advertising was done by L.S. Niece, manager of the Herbert Marshall store at Lower Stanley in 1914-18, he stocked almost all of the merchandise carried by the Challis and Hailey stores, with prices approximately the same.

The Challis Silver Messenger, aside from local advertising, carried ads from various companies across the nation. For instance, the John M. Smyth Company stated, "Elegant guitar for only $2.95. A fine upright piano was available from the Alder Music Company for $150.00. The fur companies of H.A. Schenen and Silbirwan Brothers of Chicago were advertising for mink, bobcats, fox, marten, beaver, wolf, and racoon pelts, specifying high prices being paid for prime pelts in 1911. Hewlett's products were such items as cocoa, spices, extracts, baking powder, tea, coffee, and so forth ... all included valuable coupons to save for genuine Roger's Silverplate.

And of course, there were always the numerous ads for patent medicines in all the papers, some claiming to cure everything from rheumatism to "consumption" (tuberculosis). For the latter, there were Pisco's Cure and Duffy's Pure Malt

Medicines relied on by oldtimers in the early days.

Whiskey Remedy, and while you may doubt the claims of either of these remedies, it is expected the alcohol content did make the person who took them feel better. The same thought has been voiced by oldtimers in connection with Lydia E. Pinkham's Vegetable Compound and Wine of Cardui relied on by the womenfolk to help them through their childbearing years back in the early days. In fact, both tonics were said to be so good, when a woman taking either of them became "in the family way," it was a standard joke to remark, "Well, sure, there's a baby in every bottle."

For liver and stomach ailments, Black Draught ads declared it would purge the bowels of impurities and give you better health. Ballard's Snow Liniment was for aches and pains, Chamberlain's Cough Remedy was for coughs, colds, and croup, and Fletcher's Castoria was something babies cried for. St. Jacob's Oil and Sloan's Liniment was for soreness and stiffness, while Bromo-Quinine Tablets for 25 cents a box were a sure cure for "LaGrippe," which we now call influenza, or flu virus. Hall's Canker and Diptheria Remedy ads stated their product never failed to help the throat, mouth, stomach and bowels. For those who did not believe in patent medicines, he could take a warm bath with "Cuticura Soap" at bedtime to relieve itching and burning. Or he could obtain relief from catarrh of the head, a fever, or any bronchial infection by drinking "Microtine Tea."

The list of medical companies who advertised in *The Silver Messenger* and the *Wood River Times* during the early years were many, and their products varied. The ones mentioned here we have picked at random from issues printed from 1898 to 1914. Today many of these products can still be found on our drug store shelves . . . believed by some to be effective, and still relied on by different people in hopes of saving a trip to the doctor.

••••••

Nature's Touch:

While many of these advertised items concocted by man claimed to perform miracles, certainly none could compete with the miracles wrought by Nature in way of geographical features. For instance, by exercising a bit of imagination, one can see in the rock formations such things as the lady's face in "Lady Face Falls" located in the Stanley Creek Gorge near Stanley Lake, or "The King's Throne" high in the Sawtooth Peaks as seen from Galena Mountain, or "The Sleeping Stage Driver" reclining on a hill overlooking Highway 93 as it winds along the Salmon River below Clayton. As the seasons come and go, these, and other scenic wonders considered landmarks by oldtimers, have not changed since first beheld by human eyes.

And so God said, "To everything there is a season, and a time to every purpose under the sun." And surely all the settlers and homesteaders in Central Idaho's scenic Stanley-Sawtooth country had theirs . . . as did all the early pioneers who came to tame the wildernesses of the West. They came, and they endured, and each in his own way contributed his or her bit to our heritage of which we can be justly proud. And although some legal records were kept here, the region's history was made by people. As Dr. Samuel Johnson once wrote: "History can be formed by permanent monuments and records; but lives can only be written from personal knowledge, which is growing every day less, and in a short time is lost forever."

End

BIBLIOGRAPHY

Early issues of *The Silver Messenger,* later *The Challis Messenger Newspaper* printed at Challis, Idaho.

Early issues of *The Wood River Times Newspaper,* printed at Hailey, Idaho.

The Herald Recorder Newspaper, printed at Salmon, Idaho.

The Outdoorsman, printed at Boise, Idaho . . . 1971 issue.

Idaho Historical Society's *Idaho Yesterdays,* Spring Vol. 1965, Boise, Idaho.

Idaho Historical Society's *Reference Series No. 282,* Boise, Idaho.

Bureau of Mines and Geology, Pamphlets No. 102, 112, & 57, Moscow, Idaho.

Idaho Fish & Game Department, *Wildlife Review,* 1968, 1971-72-73 issues, Boise, Idaho.

U.S. Forest Service, Challis, Idaho Office.

Bureau of Land Management, Department of Interior, Boise, Idaho.

U.S. General Service Administration. National Archives Record Service, Washington D.C.

Salmon River Electric Co-operative, Challis, Idaho.

Blaine County Courthouse Records, Hailey, Idaho.

Custer County Courthouse Records, Challis, Idaho.

Diary of Adele Brouilette McGown, 1890 to 1895.

Diary of Frank Wise Shaw, 1900 to 1905.

Notes from Author, Ferris Weddle, Kamiah, Idaho.

The New Little Giant Cyclopedia, by K.L. Armstrong, copyright 1903 by Francis J. Shulte, Monarch Book Co., Chicago, Ill.

Fur Traders of the Far West, by Alexander Ross, London, England, 1895.

History of Idaho, by C.J. Brosman, University of Idaho, about 1938 or 1939, Moscow, Idaho.

Fifteen Thousand Miles by Stage, by Carrie Adell Strahorn, G.P. Putman's Sons, London, England, 1911.

History of Alturas and Blaine Counties, Idaho, 3rd Edition, by George A. McLeod, published by *The Hailey Times Newspaper,* 1950, Hailey, Idaho.

The State of Idaho 1905, published by The Bureau of Immigration, Labor and Statistics, Boise, Idaho.

Ghost Towns and Live Ones, by Frank R. Schell, Twin Falls, Idaho.

Memories of Old Alturas County, by Lucille Hathaway Hall.

The History of Idaho, by John Hailey, Syms-York Inc., Boise, Idaho.

California Heritage, by John and Laree Caughey, Ward Richie Press.

Middle Fork History, by Joe Midmore.

Stanley Basin and Sawtooth Valley Oldtimer's Recollections.

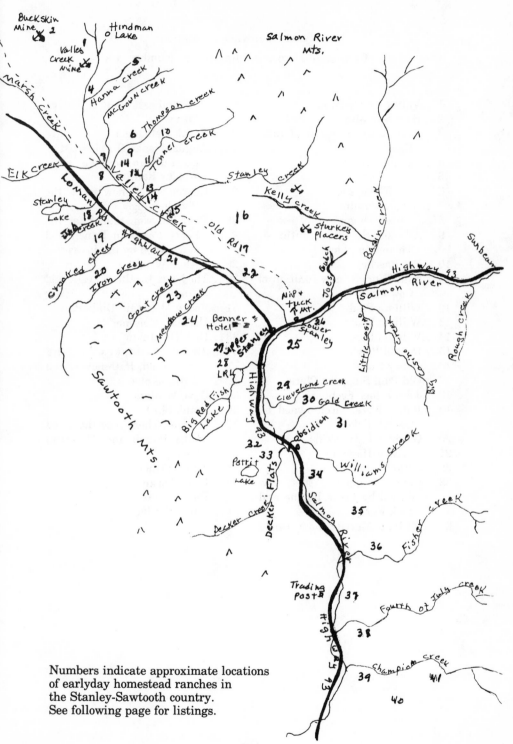

Numbers indicate approximate locations
of earlyday homestead ranches in
the Stanley-Sawtooth country.
See following page for listings.

Identifying Approximate Locations
of Earlyday Homestead Ranches by Number

1...Valley Creek Mine
2...Buckskin Mine
3...Tom Kelly, later the Lanier Ranch
4...Savilla Driskell
5...Alice Olsen
6...John Thompson
7...George Cumine
8...Charley Thompson
9...Ulysus S. Pless, later J. Thompson place
10...Pat Rasche
11...Sam Tennell, now location of Cow Camp
12...William Paul
13...William Soule
14...William Rose
15...Donald Rowles
16...Henry Duffy
17...Old Paul Stopping Place
18...John Elmer Focht
19...Ralph Kyte, later owned by Carroll Foley
20...Gardner P. Hawkins
21...Lancelot Hawkins
22...Oscar Lerow
23...Henry (Trapper) Fisher, now owned by Louis Racine and Jack Furey
24...William Merritt, now owned by Louis Racine and Jack Furey
25...Frank Hellsinger
26...August Fisher, first located by Ed Huffman, now the Dan Wooley Ranch
27...George Sewell, now part of the Piva holdings
28...Paul Imerson, then later the Perry Franklin Ranch and now owned by the Pivas
29...Arthur Wright
30...The Niece Brothers, Leslie and Frank
31...Rocky Mountain Dude Ranch
32...Herman Meissner
33...Dick Horstman
34...Obsidian...takes in the Critchfield, Rathmeyer, and Gillispie places
35...Dave Williams
36...Frank Shaw
37...George Achen, now the Boyd Ellis Ranch and "Trading Post"
38...Frank Fisher
39...Paul Clarke
40...Dave Clarke
41...Harry Stroble

INDEX

Ace of Diamonds dance hall 127
Adair, "Doc" 49,50
Adair, Judge Ralph 143, 144
Aiken (Achen), George 148
Aiken (Achen) place 179, 182
Alamo Club 280
Albert, Pete 369
Aldredge, George 116, 376
Allen, Buck 28
Allen, R.E. 70
Alturas Lake Resort 281
Alturas County 346
American Forestry Association 373
American River 64
American Steel & Wire Co. 54
Anderson Gulch 309, 344
Apgar, J.N. (game warden) 87, 374
Arbuckle, Chas. (Idaho's first game
    warden) 89
Armeson, Walt 28
Arrow A. Ranch 271
Auchenbaugh family 196
Auchenbaugh, Ray 197
B & B Ranch (cow camp) 309
Baker, Jess 268
Banjo Bill 304
Barlogi, Jim 375
Basin Creek 90
Basques 103, 104, 106, 176, 223
Bassert, Otto 359, 361
Baxter, Ralph 32
Bayhorse Creek 90
Bayhorse, Idaho 248, 308
Bear Valley 88, 112, 173, 247, 288,
    343
Beaver Creek 4, 10, 152
Beaver Canyon 10, 12, 14
Beech, Thomas 95
Beldon, George 13
Bell, (State Mine Inspector) 31
Bellevue, Idaho 13, 159
Bennard, Capt. Ruben 17, 18
Benner, H.L. (Henry) 109, 110, 119,
    123, 124, 165, 212
Benner Hotel 116, 142, 143, 145, 199,
    211, 228, 250, 267, 338
Benner, Martha 111, 113, 165, 211,
    241, 366
Benner Place 56, 96, 113, 169, 267,
    320

Benner Store 116, 215, 239, 267, 270
Bevins, Maurice 105
Big Casino Mining Co. 44
Billingsley, Elizabeth Jane 176
Billingsley, family 176
Binkley, Inez 244
Blackhawk Mining Co. stockholders
    20
Blackfoot, Idaho 143, 150, 156, 307,
    315
Blackman, George (Scrapbook) 209,
    368
Blackburn, Benjamin 308
Blaine County 122, 176, 346
Boggs, Joseph 326
Boise Basin 8
Boise National Forest 94
Boise River 8
Boise Statesman Newspaper 151
Bonanza City, Idaho (now ghost
    town) 10, 18, 22, 95, 124, 240, 269,
    304
Borah, Senator Wm. E. 166
Bowen, Billy 41, 51
Boyd, John 32
Bradford, Hughie 115, 281
Bradford, Maggie 115, 281
Bradford, Sam 113
Breckon John T. 359, 361
Brockway, Electa 156
Brockway, Frank 371
Brooks, Sandy 126, (profile 208), 186
Brown, Bennet 76, 81
Buchanan, Bert 123, 191, 197, 338
Buchanan, Berdina 191, 193, 197
Buchanan, Jennie 121, 122, 191,
    197, 295, 338
Buchanan, President 146
Buckley Bar 16, 39, 57
Buckskin Mining Co. 37
"Bull Durham Tobacco" 160
Bureau of Public Roads 291
Cady, Mr. 242
Calkins, Fred 32
Camas Lilly 6, 17, 88
Camas Prairie 17
Cameron, Theodore (Dad) 274, 380
Campbell, Tom 291
Cape Horn Landing Field 37
Cape Horn Licks 20

Cape Horn Lodge 127
Cape Horn Ranger Station 105, 352
Carrigan, family 288
Cassabella Nursing Home 260, 330
Casino Creek 43, 44, 98, 214, 305,
    311
Casto, Carrie 171
Casto, Frank 230
Casto, William (Bill) 12, 39, 171, 264
Caston, Wm. 12
Cearley, James (Jimmy) 230
Central Idaho Industrial Ass'n. 349
Centauras, Otto 105
Centauras, Will 126, 173, 241
Challis, Alvah P. 16, 39, 44, 45, 68,
    300, 308
Challis Cemetery 305, 309, 370, 376
Challis, Idaho 16, 45, 69, 76, 126,
    138, 140, 147, 173, 195, 254, 274,
    301, 344
Challis Hot Springs 205, 306, 376
Challis Silver Messenger Newpaper
    21, 31, 43, 44, 46, 63, 76, 80, 85,
    102, 123, 212, 302, 304, 348
Challis Messenger Newspaper 57, 76,
    98, 151, 280, 294, 324, 356, 380
Challis, W.W. 57, 302
Champion Creek 123, 125, 147, 157,
    181
Cherry, John 238, 380
Chilly, Idaho 255
Chivers, John 96, 100
Chivers, Melvin 96
Chivers, Tom 88, 96, 99, 100
Chivers, Tom, Sr. 95
Chivers, Roy 99, 100, 274, 381
Chivers, William (Bill) 96
China Creek 18
Chinese, placer miners 5, 17
Civil War 308
Clark, Brazilla 105, 333
Clark, Chase 371
Clark, Lee 26, 319
Clark, Mary 105, 333
Clark Miller Guest Ranch 158, 181,
    357
Clarke, David (Dave) Pierson 73,
    120, 154, 156, 164, 221
Clarke, Louise 152, 154, 164, 221
Clarke, Fred 153, 154
Clarke Hot Springs 73, 153, 162

Clarke, Nellie Fisher 88, 121, 123
Clarke, Paul 152, 154, 221
Clarke ranch 123, 154
Claude Gillispie the Guide (Scrap-
    book) 373
Clawson, Calvin 362
Clawson, Lewellyn (Lew) 353
Clayton Cemetery 252, 266
Clayton, Idaho 252, 254, 353
Clyde, Florian 113, 115, 120, 228
Clyde, Jennie 113
Clyde, F.L. 268
Cochern family 264
Cochran, John 141
Cole, Mr. & Mrs. (hotel owners) 118
Cold Springs Creek 68
"Come Back Country", Shaw saying
    186
Connyers, Clifton 70, 288
Connyers, family 288
Connyers, John 144, 288
Cook, Frank 348
Cooper, Bertha 50, 107, 264
Cooper, Daisy 107, 264
Cooper, Francis 365
Cooper, Timothy (Tim) 12, 39, 50,
    107, 264
Cothern, Affie 47, 110, 228, 276, 312,
    338
Cothern, R.B. "Doc" 47, 118, 141,
    142, 228, 276, 312, 337
Cothern, Mildred 47, 228, 276,
    340
Cothern, Virginia 47, 228, 276
Cowboy Jo 50, 369
Critchfield, Andrew, Sr. 190, 197
Critchfield, Andrew, Jr. 23, 92, 126,
    190, 244
Critchfield, Bonda 190, 229, 272,
    295, 315
Critchfield, Leafy Ann Kimpton 190,
    315
Crooked Creek 68
Crow, Mr. 302
Cumine, George 43, 136, 215, 261,
    277, 305, 310, 341
Cumine, Reverend and Rosalie 310
Cummins, F.W. 144
Cummings, Amos 375
Cummings, Edward, Jr. 375
Cummings, Edward, Sr. 376

Curio, Ron 367

Custer County 80, 89, 120, 255, 291, 370, 376

Custer County Commissioners 125, 139, 146, 236, 348

Custer County Courthouse (Records) 54, 114, 143, 145

Custer, Idaho (now a ghost town) 10, 69, 95, 173, 195, 371

Custer County Bd. of Health 142, 145

Custer County School Boards 131

Custer Mill 14, 30

Custer Telephone Coop. 354

Czolosz, Leon 273

Danners 70

Davis, Altha 58, 60

Davis, R.W. (Slim) 58

Davis, Gov. David W. (1921) 374

Davis, Miss Grace (Teacher) 149

Davis, Cy 47

Day, Ernest 168

Day, Ivan W. (Doc) 60, 315

Dead Man's Cabin 50

Death Valley Scotty's Castle 321

Decker Creek 73

Decker Flat 73, 85, 122, 125, 191, 193, 195, 197

Decker, James M. (Jim) 121, 123, 159

Decker Mountain 73

Decker, Ray 73, 195

Dellen Hotel 269

Denny, Lucille F. 120

Dickson, George 319

Dipp, family 209

Dodge, Leslie 69

Dodd, Mr. (mining man from Boise) 160

Dodd, (U.S. Postal Inspector) 115, 123, 281

Dogtown 107, 114, 143

Doran Gulch 49

Doty, Cornelius (Con or Conrad) 41, 327, 377

Dougherty, Henry 244

Dougherty, Judge 235

Drake, M.L. 82

Driskell, David 267

"Drunken Buckaroo Ride" (Scrapbook) 381

Duffy, Henry 51, 308, 327

Duffy, family 209

Dunn, Miss Mary (teacher) 144

Dupont, David 327

Eldredge, (mining engineer) 26

Elk Creek 50, 90, 261, 311

Elk Meadows 50 136

Ellis, Al 381

Ellis, Alta Horton 103, 179, 184

Ellis, Boyd 179, 184

English, John 159 (profile 208)

Ennis, Tillie 353

Ernst, Charley 266

Evans, Mrs. Viola 49, 330

Falls, Bartlett 111, 113, 143, 147, 219, 228

Falls, Eva 111

Farmer, Robert A. (Codestral Engineer) 113

Federal Homestead Act 149, 150, 328

Feltham Peak 23

Finlay, Robert 270

Finlay, Mrs. Robert (Lucy) 216, 333

Fisher, August 110, 119, 227, 287, 325

Fisher Creek 4, 73, 161, 162, 163

Fisher, Charles 276, 287, 325

Fisher, Henry C. (Tapper) 89, 92, 106, 136, 271, 292, 318, 334, 338, 366

Fisher, Frank G. 73, 121, 123, 148, 156, 197

Fisher, Electa Brockway 155, 156, 197

Fisher Mines 161, 162, 201

Fisher ranch 125

Fisher, Uncle Stant 156

Fisher, Vardis 82

Fishhook Creek 4

Fitch, Catherine 162

"Five Point" 371

Fleischmann Whiskey Co. 273

Fleming, Ed. 200

Fleming, Fred 200

Fleming, Harry 125, 126, 199

Fleming, Mattie 200

Fleming, Marine Pierce 125, 126, 199

Fleming Sawmill 191

Fleming, Reverend James J. 377

Float Creek 20
Focht, Elmer 328
Foley, Carroll 71, 180, 197, 328
Foley, Esther Missman 148, 157, 180, 228, 346
Fontes Creek 27
Forest Service Visitor's Center 286
Fort Pitt Mining Co. 32
Founders Trust Corp. 58
Fourth of July Creek 71, 146, 148
Fox, Dr. 127, 244, 278, 312
Fox, J.C. 123
Frank, Tom, and Joe (Scrapbook) 371
Franklin, Charles 52, 264, 325
Franklin, family 269
Franklin, Mattie Mott 269, 315
Franklin, Perry 268, 287
Frakes, Lee and Agnes 118
Freeport Sulpher Co. 34
French Creek 4
Friedman General Store 243
Friend, Harry 44
Friend, John W. 44
Funderburg, Jerry 119
Furey, Jack 168, 246
Furey, Sherman 168
Galena Mountain 4, 6, 158, 220, 346
Galena (Stopping Place) 56, 179
Galena Summit 56, 97, 125, 155, 176, 182, 187, 190, 200, 269, 328, 359
Garadina, Joe 43
Gardner, L.H. 77
General Land Office (Hailey, Idaho) 113
Gateway 345
Gerrish, Carlton 69
Gerrish, Mr. and Mrs. Henry D. 69, 377
George Blackman (Scrapbook) 368
Germania Basin 95, 161
Gillispie Bros. Store 118, 318, 342
Gillispie, Claude 116, 166, 198, 229, 260, 373
Gillispie, Clyde 116, 118, 119, 120, 125, 146, 198, 229, 283, 372
Gillispie, Gertrude, Doris, and Jack 199
Gillispie, James 198
Gillispie, Mary Snyder 166, 198
Gillispie, May and Evelyn 198

Gillispie, Reva Moore 198, 283
Gini, Andrew 82
Gini, Andrew 82
Gini (cattlemen) 95
Gleason, Jack and Jennie 44, 318, 373
Goat Creek 5, 294
Goaz, Annie 121, 122, 123
Goaz, Fred (family) 209
Gold Creek 4, 294
Governor in the Limelight (Scrapbook) 374
Grandjean, Emil (Charley) 71, 94, 173, 264
Grandjean, Nathalia 201, 202, 264
Greeley, Horace 149
Green, James 20
Green, T.R. (Trapper) 89, 330
Gregory, Charles A. 120
Greyhound Lookout 28
Greyhound Mining Community 20
Greyhound Mining & Milling Co. 19, 23, 29
Grossenback, Paul 70
Grow, Galusha (Congressman 1860) 149
Grubb, Johnny 28
Gunnell, Frank H. 33, 34
"Gumshoe Sal" 139
Gwinn, Judge James G. 144
H.H.H. Ranch 274
Hailey, Idaho 13, 30, 112, 123, 125, 127, 258, 269, 278, 321, 354
Hall, E.O. 12
Hall, Mrs. Marie 303
"Ham Fat" Claim 49
Hansen, Selby 245
Hailey Times Newspaper 357
Hansen, Charles (Chuck) 111, 200
Hansen, Miss Grace 262
Hardman, I.S. 126
Harlan, Dr. Harry 166
Harrah, Bill 275
Hawkins, Gardner P. 139, 271
Hawkins, Hallie 272
Hawkins, Lancelot E. (Slivers) 91, 145, 271, 334
Haywood, family 147, 196
Haywood, Pearl 147, 196
"Hell's Own Pass" 346
Hell Roaring Creek 195

Hellsinger, Frank (ranch) 192, 271
Henderson,(Custer Co.Recorder)214
Hendrick, family 345
Hendrick, Mildred Cothern 344
Hendrick, Ward (Slim) 125, 277, 312, 340, 344, 381
Henry's Fork 6
Hershey, Dave 43, 241, 305
Hill, Walter Hovey 29
Hoff, Herman 126
Hoffman, George 124, 212
Hohman, J.J. 47
Horn, Bob 321
Horstman, B.B. (Dick) 73, 159, 193, 198 (profile 203)
Horstman Peak 73
Horton, Judge 213
Horton, Alta 176, 177
Horton, Elizabeth Billingsley 177
Horton, John 176
Horton, Peak 73
Horton, Tom 371
Horton, Wm. (Bill) 71, 73, 102, 176
Hoskins, Rosemary Paul 53, 249, 336
Howard, General 17
Hudson Bay Trappers 89
Huffman, Edger P. 69, 143, 227, 267, 353
Humphreys, Fred 168
Human Interest Story (Scrapbook) 376
Hyde, George 213
Hyde, Pat 39, 50
Hunting Accident (Scrapbook) 375
Hutchings, James M. (writer) 64, 65
Idaho, Central 4, 94, 102, 293, 308, 324, 388
Idaho City 9
Idaho County 9, 17
Idaho Fish & Game Dept. 77, 78, 89, 118, 286
Idaho Farmer Magazine 258
Idaho Guide Book 82
Idaho Historical Society 123
Idaho Legislature 77
Idaho Primitive Area 23
Idaho State A.A.A. (Triple A. Club) 81
Idaho State Bd. of Education 133, 142, 257
Idaho State Bd. of Welfare 142

Idaho State Dist. Court No. 6 — 143
Idaho State Dist. Court No. 9 —
Idaho State Highway 21 (Lowman Rd.) 8, 23, 83, 107, 181, 186, 271, 349
Idaho State Liquor Store (Stanley) 378
Idaho, Southern 102
Idaho Supreme Court 144, 145
Idaho State School Board 131
Idaho Territory 8, 44, 77
Idaho Wildlife Federation 81
Idaho's "Winter Wonderland" 358
Indians 5, 10, 16, 17, 18, 40, (Reservations 17, 156, 174)
Imeson, Paul 238, 267
Imeson, ranch 240
Iron Creek 294
Iselin, Fred and Ellie 357
James Bros. (outlaws) 308
James, William (Bill) 291
Jenks, Will and Frank 164
Jensen, Jim 118
Jerry's Country Store 117, 235, 275
Job Creek 69, 74, 181
Job, Wallen 69, 74
Joe's Gulch 39, 41, 43, 313, 327
"John" or "Two-Holer" 134
Johnson, Phillip and Valerie 358
Johnson, Dr. Samuel 388
Jones, O.T. (State Game Warden, 1921) 374
Jones, Ora 41
Jordan Creek 62
Josephus Creek 62
Kavanaugh, B.B. 376
Kavanaugh, Arthur F. 85, 118, 120, 321, 376
Kavanaugh, Dan 96, 270, 291
Kelly, A.D. (game warden) 78, 82
Kelly Creek 16, 49, 74, 327
Kelly Gulch 39, 50, 264
Kelly, Thomas (Tom) 43, 74, 89, 90, 160, 215, 233, 305, 311
Kelleher, Miss Jennie (Co. School Supt.) 141
Kerr, Lee 280
Ketchum, Idaho 22, 56, 97, 102, 125, 159, 174, 182, 275, 348, 359
Ketchum Keystone Newspaper 12

Kimpton, Clarence 27, 28
Kimpton, Dave 71
King, Lizzie 325
Kingston, Miss Mary (teacher) 141
Kirtley, Dr. C.L. 23, 142, 309, 376
Kovalicky, Tom 70, 71, 89
Krom, George S. 205
Kruse, Wm. 12
Kruz & Allison 65
Kyte, Ralph 328
Lakes 5, 21, 29, 51, 69, 71, 73, 74, 75,
    77, 78, 81, 158, 238, 254, 286, 324,
    355, 367, 374
Lake Canyon 10
Lake Creek 10
Laidlow Creek 74
Langer, Charley 70, 74, 231
Langer Peak 70, 74
Lanning, family 209
Lanier, Barney 92, 244, 284, 319, 321
Lanier, Luna May 284
Lanier, Nellie Merritt 285, 319
Lanier, Webb 92, 284
Larson, Fern 28, 172
Larson, Marvin 27, 172
Larter, A.V. 82
Law, Elizabeth 110, 113, 115, 117,
    275, 281
Law Store 353
LeFevere, H., Jr. 12
Leuzinger, Fred and Catherine 253
Lerow, Oscar 267, 325
Lightfoot, family 275
Lightfoot, Dick 5, 17, 173, 326, 370,
    375
Lightfoot, Laura Sullivan 275, 291,
    382
Lightfoot, Wallace 275
Lime Creek 28
Lincoln, Pres. Abraham 149, 150
Library of Congress 65
Lloyd, Chester 244
Loon Creek 5, 17, 173, 326
Loon Creek Summit 18
"Lonely Hearts Column" 272
Long Island, N.Y. 56
Lord, C.H. 58, 59
Lost River 6, 255, 371
Lost River Valley 255, 371
"Lost Townsite" (Scrapbook) 367
Love, Frank (Slim) 26
Lowman Road 8, 107
Lutz, Wm. 32, 49, 50, 327

Lyman, L.B. 33
Lyman, M.A. 33
Lynch Creek 313
Lynch, family 313
Lynch, Jessie 315
Lynch, Pat 241, 313
Lynch, Walter K. (Walt) 57, 313
Lynn, Henry 52
Maag, family 291
Mackay, Idaho 169, 255, 309, 331,
    371
Mahoney, Ray 31
Malm, Emma 69
Marshall, Herbert H. 52, 74, 109,
    110, 118, 119, 125, 131, 139, 214,
    226, 231, 264, 307
Marshall, Mary (Mother) 41, 232,
    270, 312, 333
Markle, Floyd 119, 275, 344
Markle, Helen 70
Markle, Kathleen 70, 341, 382
Markle, Merle 70, 77, 82
Martin, Bros. (Will and Charley) 222
Martin, Edward, Jr. (Eddie) 279, 222
Martin, Edward, Jr. (Eddie) 279, 338
Martin, Edward, Sr. 279
Martin, Mary or Mamie 329
Martin, R.F. (State School Supt.) 141
Martena, Tony 50, 370
Mathis, David 70
Matuse (Chinese) 17
Masonic Lodge members, Hailey
    (Clarke funeral) 155
Mass & Steffan Fur Co. 92
May, family 147, 195
Mayfield Creek 18
McChrystal, John 359
McDougall, Rev. George 212
McDonald, James 73, 158
McDonald, Peak 73
McGowan, family 276
McGowan, Lena 116
McGowan, George, Sr. 23, 95, 101,
    108, 309
McGowan, Wells 108, 116, 126
McGown, Della 37, 41, 83, 86, 107,
    108, 119, 121, 173, 302, 304, 348,
    370
McGown, Arthur, Jr. (Tuff) 230, 296,
    376
McGown, Arthur, Sr. 22, 41, 73, 86,
    101, 107, 108, 121, 233, 264, 288,
    348, 370

398

McGown, Joseph (Joe) 107, 307, 371
McGown, Lulu 107, 307
McGown, Edna Niece 41, 87, 295, 337
McGown Store 108, 169
McGown Creek 73
McGown Peak 73
McKee, E.E. (Forest Supervisor) 82, 97
McKee, Mac 96
McKinley, President Wm. 273
Meachum, H. 124
Megeown, Lewis E. 205
Meissner, Herman 159, 199 (profile 205)
Merritt, J.D. (Bill) 32, 124, 134, 150, 238, 267
Merritt, Sadie 110, 132, 142, 143, 146, 150, 238, 267, 269, 333
Merritt, Sadie (daughter) 110, 132, 238
Merritt, Myrta 110, 238
Merritt, Nellie 242, 285
Merritt, William (Stub) 237, 244
Merritt, Stella 193, 244
Merritt, Peggy (Baby) 240
Merritt, Vella Williams 244
Merritt, family 215, 250, 297
"Mesa Del Monte" (Foley ranch) 181, 187
Micheal, Earl J. 30, 69, 82
Micheal, Irene 69
Michael, Mamie 69
Mill Creek 308, 327
Middleton, Henry 49, 58, 59, 106, 159, 195, 329
"Miner's Consumption" 270
Miner's Ten Commandments 64, 65, 66, 67
Mines, 10, 19, 20, 21, 23, 30, 37, 39, 41, 43, 44, 45, 52, 58, 222, 242, 308, 311, 313, 324, 340
Miners 8, 10, 11, 16, 19, 20, 21, 30, 32, 37, 39, 41, 43, 44, 45, 52, 54, 57, 59, 147, 162, 220
Mining Camps (early) 7, 8, 99, 116
Montazuma Gulch 50, 52
Moore, George 283
Moore, Alta 120, 283
Moore, Reva 198, 283
Morris, Isador 12
Mormon Bend 44
Mother Lode Country 64

Mott, Mattie 268, 269
Mt. Heyburn 75
"Mountain Meadows Ranch, Foley's 181, 186
"Mountain Folk Never Live in Haste", Shaw saying 166
Mountain States Telephone 354
Muskeg Creek 28
National Park 81, 373
Nature's Touch (end of Scrapbook) 388
Newcomer, Robert 70
Nichols, Judge Henry 371
Niece, Bonda Critchfield 125
Niece, Edna 105, 132, 222, 232, 243, 305, 321
Niece, Ellen Martin 110, 132, 136, 139, 220, 231, 242, 270, 312, 321, 333, 338
Niece, family 250
Niece, Frank (Juggy) 114, 118, 222, 320, 337, 376
Niece, Jack 378
Niece, Leslie S. (Tink) 32, 87, 104, 110, 113, 115, 120, 123, 132, 136, 140, 198, 220, 320, 377
Niece, Leslie (son of Rupert) 239
Niece, Mary Peterson 222, 242, 320
Niece Twins, Margaret and Francis 320, 322
Niece, Rupert 23, 47, 92, 104, 125, 126, 132, 147, 193, 221, 321, 337
Niece, Ruth 151, 378
Niece Store 113, 115, 116, 118, 191, 198, 199, 222, 232, 277, 318, 353
Nip-N-Tuck Gulch 109, 233
Nip-N-Tuck Mountain (hill) 44, 50, 56, 151, 221, 233, 240, 309, 318
Nip-N-Tuck road 54, 250
Notre Dame College 324
Obsidian, Idaho 73, 88, 121, 122, 372
Obsidian Post Office 122, 123, 125, 153, 158, 198
Obsidian Mountain 122
O'Conner, Dan and Norma 119, 344
O'Day, Josephine 254
Odd Fellows Home, Caldwell, Idaho 303
O'Dell, Cyrus (Cy) 41, 307
Olds, Henry S. 109, 119
Olsen, Alice (Red Olly) 110, 267
Olsen (Custer County Assessor) 102
Orfino Creek 8

399

"Operation, Gold Bowls" 58
Osborn, Mrs. Alice 236
Oster, Wm. 273, 327
Owens, Capt. 14
Pacific Iron Works 11
Pahsimeroi Valley 96, 213, 254
Palmer, Judge, 209
Papworth, James 266
Park, Frank 108
Paul, Goerge 54, 221, 247
Paul, Johnnie B. 140, 250
Paul, Lillian Webb 131, 136
Paul, Mary Mannix (Molly) 54, 221, 240
Paul ranch 138
Paul, Rosemary 131, 243
Paul Stopping Place 54, 221, 240, 247
Paul, William B. (Bill) 44, 53, 125, 131, 136, 143, 242, 248, 318
Paul, Wilmot 250, 253
"Pearl L", (dredge boat name) 52
Perk's Saloon, Mackay, Idaho 173
Perry, Frank 51
Peters, Louise 152
Peters, Cozette 309, 341
Peters, Geraldine 341
Perkins, George 356
Peyton, Larry 127
Pfeiffer, Charles 69
Phemspace Mining Co. 43
Philadelphia Smelter 11
"Phinalihopper" 60
Pierce, Dick 43
Pierce, Martine 199
Pierce, Mrs. (ran boarding house) 110
Pierce, Ricky 49, 50
Pierson Post Office 112, 120, 153
Pierre's Hole 6
Pinchot, Gifford (Conservationist, 1905) 71
Pioneer Mercantile Co. 53
Pittsburg Mining & Milling Co. 31
Piva, family 96
Piva, Mabel McGowan 100
Piva, Piero 96, 99
Piva, Pete (father) 96, 101, 270
Piva, Robert (Bob) 100
Pole Creek 4, 71
Pole Creek Flats 72, 105
Pole Creek Ranger Station 71, 73,

176, 178
Pollock, Martin 162
Potato Mountain 313
"Post Office on Wheels" 115
Powell, Len and Fred 165
Prospectors, Early 8
Prohibition Act, 1933 . . . 240, 344
Prowety Fur Co. 92
Pyrennes Mountains (Spain) 103
Qunatrill's Raiders (Clark) 308
Racine, Louis 168, 246
Ramey, John S. 18
Rapid River 18, 22, 28
Rapp, Benjamin Frank 51, 109, 119, 304
Rasche, Patrick (Pat) 51, 124, 217, 324, 333
Rathmeyer, Mrs. 197
Rathmeyer place 122
Rathmeyer, family 197
Ray, Walter and Marie 291
Reberk, Jake 266
Red Mountain 230, 318
Redfish Lake Resort 193, 286
"Red Rooster"345
Reid, Mrs. Tom 152
Rest Haven Motel 295
Reynolds, Dale 167
Reynolds, Florence 271
Rideout, William 20
Riggins, Idaho 4
Roarck, Jim 382
"Robber's Clay" 54
Roberts, Eva and Sid (daughter and father) 52
Robinson Bar 87, 99, 116, 123, 169, 170, 276, 336, 371
Rocky Mountain Dude Ranch 172, 198
Roosevelt, Pres. Franklin D. 58
Roosevelt, Pres. Theodore (Teddy) 273
Roschling, Charley (Dutch) 92
Rose, Mae Thomas 110, 117, 119, 136, 235, 273, 333
Rose, William (Bill) 92, 117, 119, 120, 136, 235, 273, 282
Rowland, Dean C. 70
Rowles, Donald 282, 309
Rowles, Florence 141, 142, 145, 183, 282, 309
Rowles, Gridley 282

Rough Creek 44
Ruffneck Peak 70, 74
"Running Springs Ranch" 179
Rural Electrification Administration 354
Rustlers (Scrapbook) 380
Salmon, Idaho 16, 53, 199, 253, 293
Salmon River 4, 8, 17, 28, 43, 58, 59, 62, 76, 88, 112, 126, 138, 156, 191, 287, 311
Salmon River Country 138, 156
Salmon River Electric Coop, Officers and Employees 354, 355
Salmon River, East Fork 95, 170, 248, 266, 268
Salmon River, Middle Fork 260, 386
Salmon River Mountains 4, 8, 16, 132, 221, 256
Salmon River Wilderness 292
Sawtooth City (now a ghost town site) 12, 15, 85, 108, 122, 147, 152, 239, 346, 370
Sawtooth Hotel 118
"Sawtooth Jack" (bear's name) 86
Sawtooth Mining District 10, 11, 40, 107
Sawtooth Mountains 4, 5, 56, 75, 80, 132, 147, 153, 156, 163, 171, 238, 252, 373
Sawtooth National Forest 68, 112, 353
Sawtooth National Recreation Area 62, 71, 82, 168, 357, 365
"Sawtooth Park Highway" 350
Sawtooth Placer Mining Co. 52, 53, 308
Sawtooth Placer Mining Co. Boarding House 53, 57
Sawtooth Valley 4, 30, 56, 70, 73, 100, 108, 122, 126, 147, 149, 151, 157, 161, 165, 178, 198, 200, 239, 348, 357
Sawtooth Valley Ranger Station 71
Saturday Evening Post Magazine 373
Savage, Arch 340
Savage, family 344
Savage, Pauline Walker 342
Savage & Peters (partners) 119
Scharff, Fern 291
Scribners Magazine 368, 369
Schindler, Fred 33, 35, 252, 319

Schindler, Wm. (Bill) 35, 253
Schadey, Miss Ida (teacher) 146
School District No. 5 . . . 148, 181, 182
School District No. 6 . . . 113, 116, 139, 143, 257
School District No. 6 Bd. of Trustees 141, 142, 143, 145
School District No. 56 . . . 146
School District No. 181 . . . 147
Schutt, Herman 345
Seafoam Area 18, 107, 247
Seafoam Creek 29
Seaform Community 20
Seafoam Mine Corp. 23, 126
Seafoam Mining District 21, 27, 108, 308
Seafoam Ranger Station 27, 28, 70, 73
Seagraves, Jack 44, 106
Seattle, Wash. Fur Exchange Co. 93
Sewell, family 215, 270
Sewell, George Jr. 140
Sewell, George Sr. 32, 267, 270
Sewell Lucy Bowman 270
Sewell, Rebecca 140
Session's Lodge 122, 123, 190
Shaw, Alden 145, 165, 167
Shaw, Catherine (Kitty) Fitch 162, 167
Shaw, E.B. 12
Shaw, Frank W. (Dad) 56, 148, 153, 156, 162, 167, 181, 186, 268
Shaw, Marvin (Redwood Motel) 357
Shaw, Majorie 147, 165, 167
Shaw, Preston 127, 162, 167, 180, 199, 242, 354
Shaw ranch 122, 168, 169, 180
Shaw, Sylvia 167
"Shaky" (Trapper Fisher's dog) 295
Sheek, Jack 293
Shepard, Mel 26
Sheepeater Indians 5, 326, (War 40)
Sheepeater Indian Springs 28
Sheepmen 103, 105, 167, 196, 329
Sheep Mountain 27
"Shotgun Rapids" 335
Shortline Railroad 102
Shultz, Alfred P. 367
Silver King Mining & Milling Co. 11
Silva, Arthur 296
Silbaugh Nursing Home 298

Slouthower, Aaron 22, 32
Slouthower, family 220
Small Bros. Ranch 212
Small Items of Interest (Scrapbook) 383
Smiley Creek 4, 10, 103, 151, 171
Smiley Canyon 10, 14
Smiley Creek Lodge 105
Smiley Levi 10
Smith, George 41, 165, 217
Smith, Judge Arthur R. 51, 173, 269, 328
Smith, Mrs. Merle 285
Smith S.M. 19
Snake River 4
Snedecor, Palmer G. 207
"Snowshoe Thompson" 126
Snowslides (Scrapbook) 378
Snowslide Victims 378, 379, 380
Snyder, George 122, 193, 198, 199
Snyder, Lizzie 193, 198, 199
Snyder Mary 198, 199
Soldier Creek 28
Soule, Claude 317, 319
Soule, Howard 319
Soule, Wm. (Bill) 33, 35, 44, 116, 242, 252, 294, 315, 317, 373
Spar Canyon 170
Speed, Sarah (Sadie) 212
Spud Creek 250
Squatter's Rights Law 80, 112, 150, 268
"Squawtown" 107, 114
Stanley Basin 4, 9, 40, 62, 70, 73, 80, 92, 100, 107, 149, 151, 181, 186, 247, 263, 313, 345, 359
Stanley Basin Co. (Boarding House) 53
Stanley Basin Ranger District 50, 51
Stanley Basin Rodeos (Scrapbook) 380
Stanley, Capt. John 75, 151
Stanley Cemetery 74, 172, 263, 312, 315, 319, 323, 376
Stanley Creek 45, 49, 52, 54, 57, 73, 90, 107, 151, 279, 313, 365
Stanley Dance Hall 127, 315
Stanley Dredge Co. (Lord's) 59
Stanley Dredge Camps 359
Stanley Garage 321, 376
Stanley Gold Mining Co. 30
Stanley Hotel 285
Stanley Mercantile Co. 111, 233

Stanley Party 10, 16
Stanley Post Office 108, 124, 294
Stanley Rodeo Grounds 274
Stanley Store 275, 344
Stanley, town of (Lower) 4, 43, 56, 73, 87, 107, 109, 112, 116, 126, 139, 226, 252, 274, 332, 353
Stanley, town of (Upper) 19, 37, 51, 56, 73, 87, 107, 109, 112, 116, 126, 138, 142, 151, 234, 252, 276, 314, 342, 353, 372
Strider, Mrs. Paul 110
Stringfellow, R.S. 357
Stroble, Harry 160, 195 (profile) 207
Storher, Mose 21, 108, 109, 169, 212
Stout, Harve 126, 213, 240
Sturkey, Henry 16, 39, 44, 45, 110, 165, 233, 300
Sturkey Placers 45, 276, 303, 329, 370
Sullivan Hot Springs 291, 350
Sullivan, Marie Williams 70
Sulphur Creek 19
Sunbeam Consolidated Mining Co. 273
Sunbeam Dam and Store 8, 62, 99, 138, 170, 199, 273, 333, 353
Sunday School and Church (Scrapbook) 376
Sweet's Candy Co. 33
Sweet, M.M. 302
Tassel, Charley 348
Taylor, John 50
Taylor, Knox 368
Tennel Creek 74
Tennel, Samuel 46, 74, 250
Terrell, Dr. and Mrs. (Dora) 295
Thatcher, John H. 368
Thompson Creek 74, 256
Thompson, Charley 116, 136, 142, 254, 261, 282, 332
Thompson, Dee 70
Thompson, Dorothy 261
Thompson, George 95
Thompson, John 32, 69, 74, 113, 131, 143, 242, 254
Thompson, Josephine O'Day 131, 139, 229, 242, 254, 279, 312, 333, 373
Thompson, Lottie Way 136, 261
Thompson ranch 131, 138, 227, 253, 344
The Alamo Club 280

"The Great Depression" 58
"The Gateway" 345
The Hunting and Fishing Guide
(publication) 85
The Lost Prospect (Scrapbook) 366
The Miner's Darling (Scrapbook) 369
The National Prohibition Act 280
The Pine Knot Service Station 275
"The Red Rooster" 345
"The River of No Return" 260
The Trading Post 179
The Womacks (gold dredge) 53
Thunder Mountain 54, 169, 218
Tierman, Austin 359
Torrey's Cabins & Cafe 358 (Clyde
357)
Trent E. & M. Co. 41
Twin Falls Times Newspaper 151
U.S. Agricultural Experiment Sta-
tion 166
U.S. Congress 149
U.S. Dep't. of Agriculture 112
U.S. Dep't. of Interior 112
U.S. Forest Service 22, 35, 68, 97,
176, 349, 352, 373
U.S. Highway 93 . . . 7, 71, 98, 107,
119, 126, 179, 180, 275, 345, 358
U.S. Gen. Service Administration
119, 120
U.S. Land Office (Hailey) 145, 149,
150, 162
U.S. Postal Dep't. 115, 120, 281
Union Iron Works 58
Vader Creek 74
Valley Creek 4, 30, 68, 81, 109, 271,
311, 343
Valley Creek Camps 31, 34
Valley Creek Mine 30, 31
Van, Alice 147
Vance, Clay and Priscilla 311
Vanity Mountain 21, 24, 29
Vanity Summit 22, 24, 29
VanOver, Fred 382
Vaughn, Russell and Susie 323
Vaught, Jason 110, 118, 275
Vienna Consolidated 11, 14
Vienna Mine 198
Vienna Reporter Newspaper 12
Vienna, town of (now ghost town
site) 11, 15, 30, 40, 122, 147, 171,
239, 264
Vipont Mine 192
Wadley, Harold 70

Wagon road over Galena Mountain
11
Wagon road over Vanity Mountain
22
Wagontown 21, 24, 108
Wall, Wm. (Bill) 127
Walker, Pauline 341
Warm Springs Creek 161, 170
Warner, Garner 244
Washington Basin 369
Way, Charley E. 91, 145, 262
Way, Earl 145, 263
Way, Grace Hansen 262
Way, Willis (Bill) 262
Webb, Mrs. Jason 250
Webb, Lillian Sullivan 250
Weddle, Ferris (Idaho Writer) 188,
203
Weeks, Atwood 43, 113
Weeks Gulch 43, 47
Weidman Camp 47, 330
Weidman, John 47, 60, 106, 329
Wells, Otis 185
Wells, Mrs. and sons, Hod and Will
264
"Welcome to a Stranger" 106
Western Gold Exploration Co. 33, 35
Western Mineral Magazine 33, 35
Wheeler, Mrs. Fred 235
White Cloud Mountains 4, 162, 173
White's Hot Springs 73, 152
White, Mr. (Initials unknown) 152
White Knob Mountains 255
Who, Who, Whooo, (Scrapbook) 373
Wild Hay Press (Scrapbook) 365
Wilcox, family, 209
Willis Co. Inc. 54, 240
Willis Dredge 242
Willis, Henry 54, 162, 279, 326
Willis, Jessie M. 54
Willis, Marian 56
Willis, family 54
Williams, Carrie Casto 171, 172
Williams Creek 4, 73
Williams, David M. (Dave) 70, 76,
88, 122, 126, 146, 148, 154, 156,
169, 171, 172, 197, 199, 269, 372
Williams, Elliott (Ted) 76, 88, 122,
126, 322
Williams, Johnny (Indian) 174
Williams, Marie 171
Williams, Morgan 171
Williams, Mitzi 322

Williams, Norma 171
Williams, Phyllis 171, 322, 372
Williams ranch 187, 198, 290
Williams, Thomas (Tom) 73, 76, 89,
    113, 116, 143, 164, 169, (Profile
    202) 211, 275
Williams, Vella 170, 297
Wilson, James (Sec. of Agr. 1905) 71
Wilson, Loren 96
Winter, Charles W. 355
Winters, family 290
Womacks, Abe 24, 334
Womack, Madison (Matt) 12, 52,
    308, 327, 341
Woods, Joe 280
Wood River 10, 103, 112, 125, 174,
    187, 359
Wood River country 13, 158, 200
Wood River Times Newspaper 13,
    155, 219, 383
Wooley, Daniel (Dan) 110, 287
Wooley, Juana 286
Wooley, Lela Mae Harbaugh 286

Wooley, William (Bill) 110, 227, 286
World War I . . . 180, 198, 332
World War II . . . 27, 62, 231, 259,
    275, 315
Workman, Paul 382
Wright, Arthur 113, 116, 211
Yacomello, Tony 203
Yankee Fork of the Salmon River 5,
    10, 16, 22, 30, 44, 62, 107, 240, 304
Yankee Ford Gold dredge 290
Yankee Fork Mining District 22, 44,
    95, 366
Yellowbelly Lake 77
Yellow Pine Basin 51
Yerian, B.A. 355
Yesterday's Advertising (Scrapbook)
    385
Yesterday's Fences (Scrapbook) 363
Young, Bruce 159, 197
Young, Calvin 197
Young, families 197
Young, George 197
Yuba River 64

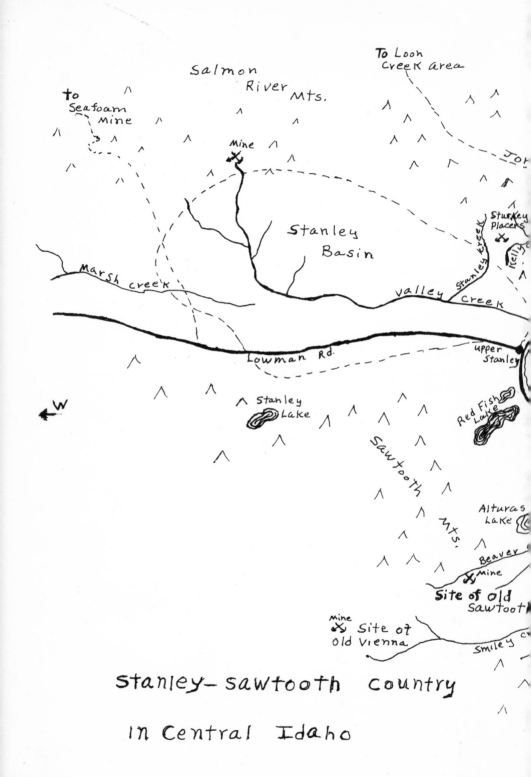

Stanley—Sawtooth country

In Central Idaho